KU-607-158

Educating and Understanding Autistic Children

Robert L. Koegel
University of California, Santa Barbara

Arnold Rincover
University of North Carolina, Greensboro

Andrew L. Egel
University of Maryland, College Park

ch
COLLEGE-HILL

San Diego, California

THE CITY OF LIVERPOOL COLLEGE
OF HIGHER EDUCATION

LIBRARY

185781 (371.92)

College-Hill Press, Inc.
4580-E Alvarado Canyon Road
San Diego, California 92120

(c) 1982 by College-Hill Press

All rights, including that of translation, reserved. No part of this publication may be reproduced, stored in a retrieval system, or transmitted in any form or by any means, electronic, mechanical, recording, or otherwise, without the prior written permission of the publisher.

Library of Congress Cataloging in Publication Data

Educating and understanding autistic children.
  Bibliography: p.
  Includes indexes.
  1. Autism.   2. Autistic children — Education.

I. Koegel, Robert L.,
II. Rincover, Arnold,
III. Egel, Andrew L.,
RJ506.A9E38   371.94   81-12204

ISBN 0-933014-68-6   AACR2

Printed in the United States of America.

Preface

The purpose of this book is to provide a useful guide for teachers and therapists of autistic children. The scope of the book is limited primarily to behavior modification interventions, because those are the ones we feel we know best. However, within this framework, we have attempted to be rather thorough. Material is provided to guide in the assessment of autistic handicaps; to guide the development of special teaching techniques for individual children's learning characteristics; and to guide the teaching of autistic children both within classroom groups and home situations. Each of these areas is dealt with from the perspective of years of direct, "hands-on" experience. In addition, primary emphasis is devoted to techniques which have been empirically verified through extensive research. In general, this book presents relatively little opinion, but rather a considerable amount of factual material which has proven itself to be useful. We anticipate that the reader should develop a number of useful strategies for teaching autistic and autistic-like children, and in so doing will come to develop a better understanding of the children and their disorder in general.

It is also worth commenting on the characteristics of the contributors to this text. Each of the contributors have numerous years of successful experience in teaching autistic children and in conducting research which has helped to further our understanding and ability to teach such children. Their combined experience represents expertise in many areas of the health and social sciences. They work in medical schools, psychology departments, speech and hearing centers, research institutes, and departments of special education. The composite number of years that went into the development of the material presented here is extremely large, and every attempt has been made to present only the most thoroughly documented teachniques and findings which have taken place during this time.

In essence, we are quite certain that the techniques described in this book will work. We are also certain that those properly trained can teach autistic children many new behaviors. However, we also know that the children are capable of learning a great deal more than we are capable of teaching them at this time. It is our hope that this book will do more than describe existing techniques for teaching autistic children. It should also stimulate an understanding of the disorder, which will permit the continued development of techniques that will eventually eliminate the horrendous problems autism has produced. The start that is available at this time is considerable, and at the very least, we cannot help but be optimistic.

Robert Koegel

Santa Barbara, California

Acknowledgements

P reparation of this volume was aided by U.S. Public Health Service Research Grants MH28210 and MH28231 (Robert L. Koegel and Laura Schreibman, principal investigators) from the National Institute of Mental Health; U.S. Office of Education Research Grant #G007802084 (Robert L. Koegel and Arnold Rincover, principal investigators) from the Bureau of Education for the Handicapped; and by U.S. Office of Education Model Demonstration Grant G008001720 (Andrew L. Egel, principal investigator) from the Bureau of Education for the Handicapped. We are especially grateful to the families whose children participated in the research; to Lynn Kern for her provision of the photographs used throughout the volume; to Ginny Kostigen for typing the large number of preliminary drafts of the manuscript; and to Jean Johnson, who coordinated the extremely complex editorial process throughout the years of preparation of the book.

Contents

Preface
Acknowledgements
Contributors

Educating & Understanding Autistic Children

Contributors

Norman Anderson
University of North Carolina, Greensboro
Karen R. Britten
University of Kansas, Lawrence
John C. Burke
University of California, Santa Barbara
Christopher Button
University of Maryland
Edward Carr
State University of New York, Stony Brook
A. Richard Cook
University of North Carolina, Greensboro
Jeanne Devany
University of North Carolina, Greensboro
Glen Dunlap
University of California, Santa Barbara
Jean Johnson
University of California, Santa Barbara
Jack Mills
Claremont Graduate School
Crighton D. Newsom
State University of New York, Stony Brook
Robert E. O'Neill
University of California, Santa Barbara
Gina S. Richman
Florida State University
Mark Runco
Claremont Graduate School
Dennis C. Russo
Harvard Medical School
Laura Schreibman
Claremont Men's College
Karen Simon
University of Pennsylvania
Jan Traphagen
Santa Barbara County Schools
Amy Wetherby
University of California, San Francisco

Section

Assessment, Diagnosis and Curriculum

1

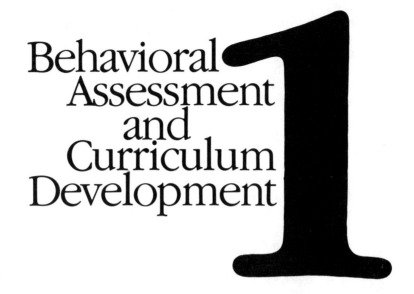

Behavioral Assessment and Curriculum Development

Introduction

Although autism is among the most severe and disruptive childhood disorders, its isolation as a unitary syndrome has been extremely difficult and complex. The current multiplicity of diagnostic criteria arises from a population of children whose characteristics and needs are very heterogeneous, presenting many difficulties in assessment and design of therapeutic programs. In an effort to develop a more functional evaluation of autistic children, researchers and clinicians are currently applying methods of behavioral assessment for diagnosis of the disorder and evaluation of treatment intervention. This approach allows systematic identification and definition of specific behaviors and learning difficulties, and suggests empirical methods for treatment design. Treatment methods can then be evaluated for effectiveness, generalization, and validity in social contexts. Further, the behavioral assessment of autistic children suggests empirical directions for the development of more meaningful and functional curricula for autistic children.

Traditional Assessment

Diagnostic Development and Review of Symptomatology

Kanner (1943) first described *infantile autism* as a psychological disorder characterized by "an extreme autistic aloneness from birth," along with language and perceptual abnormalities and ritualistic, obsessive behaviors. Over the years, his

*This chapter was authored by **Jean Johnson** and **Robert L. Koegel**, University of California, Santa Barbara.*

definition has been interpreted and elaborated upon by many researchers and clinicians (cf., Ritvo and Freeman 1978; Rutter 1978; Schopler 1978). While current definitions differ somewhat in content and emphasis (Newsom and Rincover 1979; Schopler 1978), the autistic disturbance is generally considered to include some combination of the following symptoms:

1. Autistic children exhibit a profound failure to relate to other people, which is often apparent from birth. They may show an absent or delayed social smile, and may not reach upwards in anticipation of being picked up. Some children fail to form emotional attachments to significant people in their environment, for example, not showing distress when their mother leaves the room. Similarly, a child might play in the vicinity of other children without interacting or participating with them.

2. Autistic children commonly show various levels of impaired or delayed language acquisition and comprehension. Many autistic children are mute and others may show *echolalia*. For example, a child may repeat numerous phrases or conversations previously heard without indication that the words convey meaning. Immature grammar, pronoun reversals, and/or the inability to use abstract terms may also be apparent.

3. Many children show apparent sensory dysfunction, as if they do not see or hear some environmental events. They may exhibit under- or overresponsiveness to touch, light, sound, or pain. For instance, the child may not exhibit a startle to a loud disturbance, but may respond to the sound of a candy wrapper, or may tantrum excessively every time a siren goes by.

4. Many autistic children show inappropriate and/or flat affect. They may not display appropriate facial expressions and may not exhibit fear in dangerous situations, such as crossing the street. They may respond to even simple requests with severe, prolonged tantrums. They may also laugh and giggle uncontrollably in the absence of any apparent eliciting stimuli, or cry inconsolably for hours.

5. Typically, autistic children will occupy themselves for hours in stereotyped, repetitive *self-stimulatory behaviors,* which serve no apparent purpose other than providing the child with sensory input. Commonly, self-stimulatory behaviors take the form of manipulation of hands or fingers in front of the eyes, eye crossing, repetitive, meaningless vocalizations (e.g., "aeh, aeh, aeh,. . ."), suspending or spinning objects in front of the eyes, mouthing objects, hand tapping, body rocking, and other stereotyped behavior. Such behaviors have been found to significantly impair learning in autistic children (Koegel and Covert 1972).

6. Autistic children often fail to develop normal, appropriate play. They may forsake toys altogether, preferring instead to spin a lampshade or flick a light switch on and off. If they do interact with toys, they may do so in an abnormal manner. For instance, the child may arrange, stack, or sort stimuli repetitively, over and over in the same pattern, and may show extreme disruption if the pattern is altered. Or they may turn a truck over and spin the wheels rather than roll it on the ground. Social play with

peers may develop spontaneously, but usually does not.

7. Finally, autistic children commonly show obsessive, ritualistic behaviors which have been characterized as a profound resistance to change in the environment or normal routines. Familiar bedtime routines, insistence on one type of food, one type of furniture arrangement, and particular routes to familiar places are examples of routines which, when altered even in minor fashion, can create extreme disruptions in a child's behavior.

Neurological disorders   Traditionally, autism has only been diagnosed in the absence of evidence of known neurological dysfunction (see Rutter 1978). However, the preponderance of evidence now strongly suggests that autism may involve a neurological disorder (Hier, LeMay and Rosenberger 1979; Blackstock 1978; Damasio and Maurer 1978; Student and Sohmer 1978; Tanguay 1976; Hauser, DeLong and Rosman 1975). For example, follow-up studies show that autistic individuals who do not show evidence of neurological abnormalities as children may develop epileptic seizures in adolescence (Rutter 1970). In addition, recent evidence suggests that there may exist some impairment of auditory processing in the language-dominant hemisphere of autistic children (Wetherby, Koegel and Mendel, in press; also see Wetherby and Koegel, Chapter 2 in this volume). Ritvo and Freeman (1978) suggest that the symptoms of autism are expressive of some physical dysfunction within the central nervous system which remains to be characterized. Whatever the exact cause is, however, neurological improvement does appear possible with behavioral intervention (cf., Chapter 2).

Differentiation From Other Disorders

Autism has many characteristics in common with several other disorders, however, differential diagnoses can usually be made according to certain specific criteria. For example, the major differentiating factor between the autistic disorder and mental retardation relates to evidence of the *uneven* development delays discussed above (Ritvo and Freeman 1978). While retarded children show relatively even deficits in all functioning areas, autistic children may evidence isolated, "splinter" aptitudes for high level functioning in areas such as mechanical, mathematical, or musical abilities (Applebaum, *et al.,* 1979; Rimland 1978).

Autism is typically differentiated from childhood schizophrenia on two bases: 1) Childhood schizophrenia usually has an older age of onset (5–12 years), while the autistic syndrome appears to be present from birth and is readily apparent prior to 30 months of age; and, 2) schizophrenic individuals commonly show higher levels of language ability characterized by thought disorder or word salad, while autistic individuals exhibit a very limited use of language (typically mutism or echolalia, as noted previously).

Because autistic children commonly show "disturbances" or irregularities in their responses to sensory stimuli, they have often been mistakenly diagnosed as deaf or blind. The distinction from actual deafness or blindness is best noted in the *variable* nature of the presumed sensory deficit. For instance, the child's apparent threshold level for an auditory stimulus may differ dramatically when the stimulus is neutral as compared to when the auditory stimulus has been associated with reinforcement (Koegel and Schreibman 1976).

In differentiating autism from central disorders of language processing *(aphasia)*, we look for language delays which are accompanied by disturbances in responses to sensory stimuli and/or inappropriate relations to people and objects (Ritvo and Freeman 1978).

The autistic disorder has been reported in virtually all parts of the world. Due to the difficulty of obtaining accurate diagnoses, statistics on the exact incidence of the disorder are unknown at this time. However, the most reliable estimates to date suggest that autism occurs once in approximately 2,500 births, and that it occurs approximately four times as often in males as in females (Ritvo and Freeman 1978).

Review of Problems Associated with Traditional Diagnoses

Although the disorder is believed to be present at birth, it may not be formally diagnosed until the child is from two to five years old, as the deficiencies in social relations and language become increasingly evident and problematic. At this time, most clinics do not have professionals trained in the diagnosis of autism, and when the disorder is brought to the appropriate professional attention, securing a diagnosis still may not be a straightforward task. The multiple definitions of the syndrome lead to disparity in the way the diagnosis is applied. This may be further compounded because an autistic child may exhibit a majority of but not all of the symptoms. These factors may contribute to the relatively low reliability among professionals in diagnosing the same child as autistic (Newsom and Rincover 1979; Rimland 1971). The difficulties in diagnosis reflect an extremely heterogeneous population of children characterized as autistic, showing large differences in specific characteristics and needs. For example, two autistic children might both exhibit the general characteristics relating to the language disorders discussed earlier, yet they may differ greatly in specific behaviors, such that one might exhibit mutism and the other, echolalic speech.

The wide heterogeneity of the autistic population has led many investigators to question the utility of traditional diagnostic criteria. Involvement with many autistic children will readily illustrate that the label "autism" does little to communicate the specific characteristics or abilities of any individual child. Similarly, "autism" does not suggest the direction of treatment intervention, in that different children often require very different treatment interventions. Consider the example relating to mutism vs. echolalia or the fact that some autistic children may exhibit severe self-destructive behavior, while others do not evidence this behavior at all. Clearly, such great differences in symptomatology result in large differences in treatment prescription. Finally, it is important to note that the general label of "autism" does not suggest a prognosis for individual children. Knowing only that a child has been diagnosed autistic, we cannot say exactly which children will improve or exactly how the amount of improvement may vary between children (Schreibman and Koegel 1981).

Behavioral Assessment_____

Purpose

In an attempt to develop a more functional definition of autism, many researchers in the field have begun to apply behavioral assessment techniques for assessment and treatment evaluation. Behavioral assessment seeks to "identify meaningful response units and their controlling variables for the purposes of understanding and altering human behavior" (Nelson and Hayes 1979, pg. 491). The behavioral approach to the assessment of autism is directed towards observing, defining, quantifying, and altering problematic behaviors. Its concern lies with the maintaining causes of the child's current behaviors, rather than defining the underlying nature or etiology of the autistic disorder (Newsom and Rincover 1979).

Behavioral assessment differs from traditional assessment in three important ways. First, each child receives an individual assessment based on the specific behaviors that child exhibits, rather than being grouped (classified) with many children exhibiting the highly variable characteristics of the syndrome of autism. Second, the assessment of specific behaviors and their controlling variables suggests specific and empirical directions in treatment and allows continuous evaluation of treatment effectiveness. Finally, the behavioral assessment allows prognostic inferences based on the empirically determined treatment methods; that is, when the variables controlling a behavior are known, the prognosis is good. For behaviors for which controlling variables are undefined, the prognosis is more guarded (Schreibman and Koegel 1981). The detailed procedures used in behavioral assessment are explained below.

Five Phases of Behavioral Assessment

The application of such an evaluation to autistic children follows five phases of assessment (cf., Cone and Hawkins 1977). These divisions are not exclusive and independent. They interact throughout the treatment program, promoting maximal therapeutic progress through ongoing evaluation and adaptation.

1. The initial phase involves *screening and evaluating general disposition.* This process may employ methods including interviews, direct observation, and behavior checklists to identify general problems (such as social unresponsiveness) and general areas of difficulty (e.g., severe tantruming).
2. These areas are more finely assessed during the second phase, *definition of the problem.* This phase requires that specific problems be defined in a manner which allows reliable independent measurement. For example, social responsiveness might be measured, in part, by the number of times the child displays a return glance to a therapist (or parent) when the adult calls the child's name.

Another aspect in the second phase of assessment is *hypothesis formation.* The therapist should be generating hypotheses regarding environmental factors which might be manipulated to influence particular behaviors.

3. The third phase in assessment proceeds to *pinpoint and design the intervention programs.* The clinician selects target behaviors and attempts to test the hypotheses generated in phase two regarding environmental factors which can be made to influence the children's responses. Following target behavior selection and outline of treatment intervention, the therapist establishes a baseline level of responding before the treatment intervention is introduced.

4. The fourth step in assessment requires the *monitoring of treatment progress* against the child's pre-intervention baseline. As each target behavior exceeds its predetermined performance criterion, new target behaviors may be introduced into the treatment program. If a behavior is not improving, the therapist may have to re-evaluate the hypotheses regarding the environmental variables controlling that behavior and re-design a new treatment intervention.

5. The final assessment phase provides for an *evaluation of treatment intervention.* The behaviors manipulated in the treatment setting are measured in other environments, with other people, and over periods of time. The effects of the treatment on other's (e.g., parents, teachers, neighbors) perceptions of the child may also be measured to establish the validity of improvements in a social context.

Such a systematic assessment provides multiple advantages in describing the autistic child and in designing and evaluating treatment procedures. Empirical considerations in treatment effectiveness will, in turn, stimulate new understanding and efficiency in design or curriculum programs for autistic individuals.

Defining and Measuring Existing Behaviors

During the child's initial screening, the parents are interviewed while the child is observed in interactions with his parents, staff personnel, and play objects. General questions are directed toward identifying the child's prominent behavior patterns, including level of language function, amount of social and environmental responsiveness, and level of tantrumous or self-stimulatory behaviors. The parents may also be asked to complete a behavior checklist, sampling the current or previous occurrence in their child's behavior of many typical behaviors exhibited by autistic children.

Identifying target behaviors   The therapist uses the information thus compiled to help identify target goals for the child. The specific goals selected should consider the demands placed on the child by his natural environment. The discussion of curriculum planning presented later in this chapter outlines a logical procedure which might be employed to ensure meaningful curricular programs for autistic students. The selection of target tasks should attempt to balance the control of maladaptive behaviors with the teaching of appropriate ones. In this manner, a therapist seeking to reduce tantrumous behavior may concurrently try to establish and lengthen periods of eye contact and compliance to verbal instructions to replace the tantrumous behavior with appropriate behaviors which will receive positive reinforcement.

Defining target behaviors   Every response identified for treatment must be operationally defined. The definition should specify all aspects of the behavior which will be used in its measurement. Such areas would include the exact shape or form (topography) of the response, its frequency of occurrence, its duration, and its occasion of occurrence. It is important to stress that, according to the behavioral approach, definitions must specify observable behaviors and avoid hypothetical constructs. While we cannot measure "frustration" or "hostility", we can observe and quantify "hitting," "biting," etc. In this manner we seek to objectively measure behaviors and minimize attempts to interpret them (Sulzer and Mayer 1972).

Measurement   The test of an adequate definition is its ability to adequately measure the behavior in question, so the proper behavioral treatment can be initiated. Accurate measurement serves to quantify the initial severity of the target behavior and allows daily evaluation of teaching procedures and effectiveness.

The approach to measurement procedures is determined by the type of response being measured and the type of information (i.e., frequency, duration, etc.) which is desired (Sulzer and Mayer 1972; Hall 1971). Discrete events, such as isolated vocalizations or instances of eye contact can be tallied to provide a frequency count. If it is desirable to measure the length or duration of a response, such as tantruming or social interaction, a stopwatch or second-hand of a watch or clock can easily be employed. Interval and time-sampling methods are used to sample the rate of a behavior over longer periods of time. Behaviors such as self-stimulation or appropriate play, which occur intermittently, can be quantified on an interval or time-sampling basis (Sulzer and Mayer 1972; Hall 1971). Other measurement procedures, including trial-by-trial recordings and measurement of permanent products (e.g., Rincover and Koegel 1977a), can also be used to quantify child improvement during treatment programs.

The integrity of the behavioral definition and the measure chosen for the behavior is established by assessing the "reliability" of the recording procedures (Sulzer and Mayer 1972; Hall 1971). If two observers using the same behavioral definition can independently measure the same behavior at the same time with a high degree of agreement, the measure is said to be reliable. If agreement cannot be achieved at 80 percent or above, the definition of the target behavior or the measurement procedures may require re-evaluation and modification until the reliability measure reflects that the behavior is, in fact, adequately defined and measurable.

Designing a Treatment Intervention

Following the reliable definition and measurement of the child's responding, the therapist is left with a relatively specific and detailed inventory of the child's behavioral repertoire. This inventory describes the child in terms of a conglomeration of the individual behaviors he/she exhibits, and allows for a very individualized approach to treatment development and evaluation. The heterogeneity of the autistic population presents a lesser problem because every child has an individual assessment of problem areas and needs. In this manner, behavioral assessment leads directly into individualized treatment development.

Use of previous research   Once target behaviors are selected, defined, and measured, the therapist may need to examine the environmental conditions supporting the behavior and then manipulate the environment to alter the behavior in the desired direction (Schreibman and Koegel 1981). The first step in this procedure often involves a literary search. Many difficult behaviors have already been extensively studied, for example, self-destructive behavior, and much is known about the variables that control it (Carr 1977). In such cases, treatment programs may already be established.

Isolating controlling variables   If, however, the literature has not isolated the variables, or if more than one variable may influence the child's responses, the therapist may want to attempt to isolate specific controlling variables. This typically involves a systematic examination of the events immediately preceding and following each occurrence of the target behavior(s). With behavior problems, for example, it might be found that the child is being reinforced by attention to inappropriate behavior. Or, it might be suspected that one type of instruction is more effective than other instructions for a particular child (cf., Koegel, Dunlap, Richman and Dyer, 1981). To test this hypothesis, the therapist might want to teach the child using one type of instruction first and then the other. At this point, it would be important to keep all other aspects of the teaching situation (such as stimulus materials and reinforcement contingencies) the same across the two conditions to clarify the influence of the two types of instruction. By measuring aspects of the child's behavior presumed to be influenced by the different types of instructions (e.g., percent appropriate child responses), a pre-intervention baseline can be established using one type of instruction. The therapist can then manipulate the instructional condition believed to influence the behavior within the framework of a multiple baseline or reversal design (Hersen and Barlow 1976). These designs establish that it is the instruction — and not some other variable — that has generated an improvement in the child's responding. As environmental influences on an increasing variety of behaviors are understood, those behaviors which have similar controlling variables may be grouped into functional units for which similar treatments can be readily applied to all the behaviors of that group.

Ensuring Program Effectiveness

Behavioral assessment includes a built-in component to measure and improve treatment effectiveness. Similarly, the effectiveness of the treatment can be assessed in extra-therapy settings, and over a period of time following discontinuation of treatment. Finally, the assessment seeks to evaluate the actual validity of the treatment through the view of significant others in the child's environment.

Treatment evaluation   The process of treatment evaluation begins with assessment of the effectiveness of the intervention on the desired target behavior. The therapist begins by measuring the occurrence of the behavior before treatment is begun. After a stable baseline is obtained, (perhaps varying steadily, but not increasing or decreasing), the therapist may introduce treatment. Data on the dependent variable are collected and plotted (daily or weekly, or trial-by-trial, etc.) and progress is measured. If treatment has no effect or an undesirable effect, some aspect of the treatment may require modification. For instance, in attempting to control tantruming during teaching tasks by removal of attention, the therapist may be providing negative reinforcement by the coincidental contingent removal of task demands, and tantruming may increase. In the above situation, the therapist may be better off ignoring the tantruming behavior by "working through" the tantrums without providing any more or less attention than previously given to the child (Carr, Newsom, and Binkoff 1980; Plummer, Baer, and LeBlanc 1977), and without reinforcing the tantrums by removal of task demands.

Generalization   If the treatment indicates progress against a baseline, the therapist should consider how to best promote the performance of the behavior in other, unmanipulated settings, and the maintenance of the behavior over time (see Chapter 15). Several approaches to programming generalization over people, settings, and tasks have been investigated. For instance, the use of similar (more consistent) reinforcement schedules between treatment and non-treatment settings (Koegel, Egel and Williams 1980; Koegel and Rincover 1977b) and teaching in multiple (preferably natural) settings (Brown, Branston, Hamre — Nietupski, Pumpian, Certo and Gruenwald 1979) may help promote increased generalization across settings (Stokes and Baer 1977). Other considerations are discussed in more detail in the *Curriculum* section of this chapter.

Along a similar vein is the problem in generalization across people. Researchers have been able to affect some limited improvement by incorporating multiple therapists, but a more immediately practical contribution to generalization across both people and settings is to incorporate the child's parents as the primary therapists (see Chapter 14). The behavioral teaching techniques can be easily taught to parents (Koegel, Glahn and Nieminen 1978) — who have the distinct advantage of being with the child in almost every setting — allowing daily routines to be laced with various teaching tasks. It has been found that from a practical point of view, parent training is a very powerful aid in generalization (Lovaas, Koegel, Simmons and Long 1973). It may also have the added advantage of providing the parents with methods of interacting more productively and positively with their children.

Maintenance   Parent training also provides an effective program to encourage the maintenance of treatment gains through intermittent reinforcement of target behaviors, preventing their extinction. Similarly, approaches toward developing reinforcers and reinforcement schemes which occur naturally in everyday environments should promote maintenance of acquired behaviors (cf., Williams, Koegel, and Egel 1981; Koegel and Williams 1980; Egel, Chapter 15 this volume). In these ways, maintenance of treatment gains may be built into the child's program to ensure long-lasting effects and continued progress.

Social validity   The crux of behavioral assessment and treatment evaluation can only be measured through its influence on the social significance of the changes in the child's behavior (cf., Wolf 1978, and Chapter 5 in this volume). The teaching of selected behaviors such as academic tasks, social speech, and behavior control, should demonstrate an effect on the child's well being as a whole. To this end, researchers in the field of behavior modification with autistic children have attempted to sample and document the attitude of observers (naive with respect to autism) to autistic children's behaviors randomly sampled before and after behavior therapy (Schreibman, Koegel, Mills and Burke, in press). In order to obtain information about the exact behaviors community members felt were important for a child's acceptance into the community, the observers were presented with videotapes recorded in a play setting. They were then given questionnaires sampling aspects of their emotional reactions to the child (e.g., "Do you like this child?"; "Would you babysit this child?"; "Would you adopt this child?"), and reactions to the child's behavior (e.g., "Does this child seem hyperactive, lethargic," etc.). Attitudes toward specific individual behaviors were also sampled to determine whether certain target behaviors were more important to community members than others. From these samplings, researchers determined that attitudes toward the children showed a distinct improvement due to the therapeutic intervention, in that the children's treatment gains were perceptible to naive observers, resulting in more favorable attitudes and behavior intentions toward the children.

Behavioral Assessment and Curriculum Development_____

Because autistic children present such heterogeneous and profound handicaps it has been very difficult to design curricular programs which are flexible and comprehensive enough to provide an autistic child with the skills he/she will require as a relatively independent adult. Literature suggests, however, that new approaches to curricular design may yield programs which are more functional for the students in the long run, and which may hold significant advantages for autistic children in facilitating the performance of learned skills in the natural environment. A major component of these novel approaches entails the application of the behavioral assessment procedures to the children's natural environments; in effect, to inventory the demands on the child resulting from present and future natural environments, and the skills which the child will need to deal adaptively with those demands. The primary goal is to mainstream the autistic individual into the least restrictive environments in which he can ultimately function in a productive manner, including the home or group home, school, community, and vocational environments.

Sequence Issues in Curriculum Design

Autistic children are usually so severely delayed that a logical starting point in curricular design in the past has been to determine the child's developmental level as compared to the normal development of non-handicapped children. The autistic student's curriculum is then structured on the basis of the sequence in which non-handicapped children learn the same tasks. This approach has been described as "horizontal" (Guess, *et al.,* 1978), because it assumes that all curricular domains are at equal levels of maturation or capability, and that previous steps in a sequence must be mastered before subsequent abilities can be taught. There are indications that developmental levels may be useful in determining some activities and materials which help to heighten students' interest and motivation during teaching sessions. However, there may also be some additional considerations when using this approach for programming curricula for autistic children. First, autistic children are characterized by *uneven* abilities across normal developmental areas (Ritvo and Freeman 1978), and there is no evidence to indicate that a deficiency in one area would predict similar deficient functioning in another area (Wetherby and Gaines in press; Applebaum, *et al.,* 1979; Rimland 1971). Also, since autistic children of all ages are seriously deficient in most skill areas (prior to treatment), they may be placed at curricular levels involving tasks typically mastered by normal children of a much younger age. Further, depending on the specific child, as the autistic child grows older, the discrepancy between his chronological age and developmental level may increase and the curriculum for the child may become increasingly non-functional, artificial, and inappropriate for his age (cf., Brown, Branston, Hamre-Nietupski, Pumpian, Certo and Gruenwald 1979). (For example, autistic men who were over 20 years old have been observed playing on childrens "horsie" swings — with a basketball court not 30 feet away).

In response to these concerns, curricular programming has also been approached from a remedial framework. This approach seeks to teach those skills which will improve the individuals' ability to function productively, regardless of the developmental order in which normal children learn the same tasks. The goal is to minimize the differences between the autistic individual and his non-handicapped peers. Guess, *et al.* (1978) describe the remedial approach as a "vertical" approach in which functioning in any one curricular domain is not assumed to parallel other domains. In this manner, progress in a domain in which the student is particularly proficient (for example, academic skills) should not necessarily be affected by deficiencies in other domains (such as self-help skills). Still, within any one domain, the remedial framework instructs the student in a bottom-up" skill sequence (Brown, Branston, Hamre-Nietupski, Pumpian, Certo and Gruenwald 1979) in which behaviors must be built upon previously existing ones, and the question remains whether a student can progress far enough and fast enough to approach normal adult functioning.

Generation of Age Appropriate and Functional Curricula

When curricula are designed for autistic children from either a developmental or remedial framework, it often happens that the children are instructed in (1) tasks or skills which are inappropriate for their chronological age; (2) skills which are not functional in their natural environments; or (3) skills taught in highly artificial settings. To a large extent these current limitations may contribute to the inadequate generalization and maintenance of learned skills to the natural environment, and may significantly hinder the social validity of the treatment. Ultimately, subsequent to years of special education, autistic children may still be unable to manage their own living space and activities, to work productively and independently, and to direct themselves in appropriate leisure and recreational activities, i.e., they cannot live relatively independent and productive lives (cf., Brown, Branston, Hamre-Nietupski, Pumpian, Certo and Gruenwald 1979). These problems indicate a growing necessity for more efficient design of curricula for autistic individuals in terms of what they will be taught, i.e., the content of their educational programming.

The generation of chronologically age appropriate and functional curricula for autistic children is best approached by a systematic consideration of environments and activities in which the student might ultimately participate (cf., Brown, Branston, Baumgart, Vincent, Falvey and Schroeder 1979). Curricular domains can be defined in terms of the "life spaces" in which all severely handicapped adults will need to function, including domestic living, vocational, leisure/recreational, and community functioning. These curricular domains are chosen by reference against the "requirements of relatively independent adult functioning," and differ in this important way from traditional curricular concentrations organized around such basic skill areas as language, social and self-help skills, gross and fine motor development, and academic skills. In this manner, an effective curriculum should consider where and how the autistic student will need to function in those areas, and how activities should be chosen and presented to promote success.

Procedures for Curriculum Development   Brown and his colleagues have suggested specific procedures for the delineation of age appropriate and functional curricular tasks. They suggest that within each of the four curricular domains mentioned previously, the teacher should 1) Delineate the variety of natural environments in which the severely handicapped students function or might function; 2) delineate and inventory the subenvironments in which severely handicapped students function or might function; 3) delineate and inventory the activities that occur in the sub-environments; 4) delineate the skills needed in order to engage in the activities; and 5) design and implement the instructional programs necessary to ensure performance of the delineated skills in the natural environments (Brown, Branston, Hamre-Nietupski, Pumpian, Certo and Gruenwald 1979).

This approach has numerous strengths. In the first place, every skill delineated by such a curriculum would be directly *relevant* to increased independent functioning. Only those behaviors which have a purpose and an opportunity to be performed in the students' natural environment are included in the teaching programs. In addition, the requirements for functioning in *future,* progressively less restrictive environments are incorporated into the curriculum due to its reference against relatively independent adult functioning. This assures that all behaviors being taught are related to a specific, functional, long-term goal for the autistic adult in the natural environment. Delineating future skills also prevents a student from being held too long at a "stepping stone" skill that serves only as a step to a larger, more complicated, functional skill (Dunlap and Koegel 1980a). The consideration of the variety of environments in which a skill might be performed (and, thus, taught in) deals with the problem of generalization of a learned skill to outside environments. Finally, the derivation of the curriculum from the natural environments and activities in which the student now functions or might ultimately function assures that the activities will be chronologically age appropriate, thereby helping to teach activities, skills and behaviors that will help reduce the stigmatizing behavioral discrepancies between handicapped individuals and their non-handicapped peers.

By choosing tasks which emphasize chronological age-appropriateness and functionality in natural environments, we can greatly increase the chance that what the child learns in school can be used appropriately, even if only partially, in natural environments. Thus, the approach encourages opportunities to enhance "partial participation" by autistic individuals in all their pertinent daily functioning activities, such that, for example, even if an autistic student cannot fully dress himself, he may be able to help pull the pants on. Increased participation on the student's part can be initiated as instructor participation is rapidly reduced to simple prompting and then faded out altogether. The greater the partial participation, the less dependent the student may become upon the constant attention of an aide when it is not truly necessary (cf., Brown, Branston, Baumgart, Vincent, Falvey, and Schroeder 1979). Sensory deprivation literature (see Koegel and Felsenfeld 1977) shows that an impoverished environment, as opposed to an enriched environment, can adversely affect learning abilities and performance levels. In addition, Baldwin and Baldwin (1976) hypothesize that through a process of gradual habituation to complex stimuli, organisms will further seek out stimuli of increasing complexity. If the cognitive, behavioral, and social deficiencies of an autistic child's life can be considered to result in a functionally impoverished environment, partial participation can be analogized to result in *gradually* increasing the complexity of stimuli influencing the child's behaviors. These types of considerations relate to the (presumed) benefits of community and vocational integration of autistic individuals, and the detrimental effect on learning that segregation into institutions or isolated schools may entail.

Inter-relationships between behavioral assessment and curriculum development   Through the processes of parental interview and direct observation of the child in his/her home, school, classroom, future classroom, or any other location, a teacher will be able to assess the environmental demands placed on the child currently and those which will be present in the future. The student's parents can also provide valuable information about the skills the child does and does not exhibit, and the skills which the child will need to learn to deal efficiently with the environment. The teacher's direct observations will be useful in defining the activities and precise tasks and goals which will effectively teach the student those important skills. At this point the behavioral assessment systematically assesses the behaviors the child does and does not exhibit, and in doing so, establishes the beginning of the pre-treatment baseline that will later be used to measure the child's progress.

A functional, chronological age-appropriate type of skill delineation can be facilitated by placing the handicapped individual in the future environment and defining and measuring the exact behaviors needed to facilitate independent functioning. For example, an important aspect of independent community function is the ability to secure appropriate transportation. For many severely handicapped individuals, adequate public transportation systems can provide accessible and effective means of transportation. By accompanying the student for a ride on a bus, an analysis such as that just described can be operationalized (see Sample Curricular Program #10). The variety of natural environments in which the activity will occur might include trips to the grocery store, the record store, the library, a job, the school, the roller arcade, the theater, a friend's house, and many other locations. The subenvironments in which the student will be required to function will include the bus stop, the entrance door, the fare box, the aisles, the seated or standing position on the bus, and the rear or front exit door. The activities required in each subenvironment can now be easily delineated. For instance, at the bus stop, the student should be able to locate the bus stop, sit or stand quietly awaiting the bus, and should choose the bus which will take him/her to his/her destination. At the fare box, the student should greet the bus driver, ask how much the fare is, if necessary, and count out the correct amount and deposit it. At each step in the process, the component, requisite activities will become clear. Each of these activities will require specific skills, some more advanced than others. The exact skills which the student will need to learn will be evident by his/her baseline or untreated responding in each subenvironment. For instance, at the fare box, the student will ultimately require the communicative skills to greet the driver and to ask the fare. He/she will then need some arithmetic skills to count the appropriate fare, and motor coordination to deposit the correct amount. The design and implementation of instructional programs to teach these skills follow the principles of teaching simple discriminations, expressive language, mathematical principles, etc., and behaviors can be built on each other through shaping and chaining.

An example of the use of current functioning abilities and deficits in the determination of treatment programs has been provided by Russo and Koegel (1977). In this study, an autistic child's normal public school educational placement was in jeopardy because of her maladaptive and inappropriate behaviors. The experimenters assessed the target behaviors in terms of which behaviors were necessary for that child to function productively and remain in that classroom. The three behaviors targeted for the performance of appropriate activities in the classroom were increased social interaction, decreased self-stimulation, and increased verbal response to the teacher's questions and instructions. The activities, including group and individual working, story time, and peer playtime, were similar to those in any kindergarten class. The design and implementation of treatment programs utilized token reinforcement to influence the target behaviors in the desired direction. The important consideration is that the evaluation of the child took place in the actual environment and situation in which she needed to develop appropriate functioning. This assured a selection of target tasks that were functional, age appropriate, and pertinent in the scope of the ultimate goal of retaining her position in the normal classroom.

Parent input   Another avenue for generating functional age-appropriate curricula to fulfill the "criteria of ultimate functioning" is the incorporation of parental input and parent training into curriculum development. That is, the parents of the student will be able to provide significant input into the delineation of currently functional tasks and in the specification of long-range "ultimate functioning" goals which they desire the student to develop. In addition, parent training allows a practical means of introducing and directing functional tasks in the child's varied natural environments, helping to promote generalization of skills.

In summary, curricula can be generated by direct observation and behavioral assessment of the child in his/her present and future natural environments, and by involved parental input in the identification of ultimately functional programs.

Applications to the Classroom or Clinic Setting

The foregoing discussion is best applied to the classroom in considering and prioritizing target behaviors for individual children in a class. Basically, we can consider the curricular behaviors outlined for our students by asking:

1. Will this student have the opportunity to use this behavior in his/her daily functioning?
   a. How many opportunities will arise for application of the behavior in natural settings, relative to other possible target behaviors?
   b. Can learning situations be tailored to increase the chances of the behavior or concept being applied by the student to the natural environment?
2. Does the student look natural performing this behavior or skill, or, conversely, does the student look unnatural because he/she cannot perform this behavior or skill?
   a. Will this target behavior help the student fit in with age-appropriate peers?
   b. Will this behavior, skill, or concept promote successive approximations of age-appropriate, independent functioning?

Let us consider some specific target behaviors to illustrate this type of analysis.

Toilet training   It is relatively straightforward to see that many natural opportunities will arise to use this behavior in natural environments. Learning situations can be enhanced by using natural environments as opposed to artificial ones, and by teaching a signal which can be interpreted in all the student's natural environments (i.e., a word or phrase for verbal autistic individuals, such as "potti" or "I'm going to the toilet," or, for nonverbal students, a symbol which can be widely interpreted, such as a manual pat on the lower abdominal area). These signals would increase the chance of the student being understood in the natural environment and thus, presumably, the tendency for the student to use the signal appropriately. This is certainly an important behavior to teach with regard to normalization of the age appropriateness and independence of any autistic person over the age of 2-1/2 to 3-1/2 years. Above that age it is stigmatizing for the individual to be diapered and changed, or to toilet themselves inappropriately.

Leisure/recreation   According to the above considerations, leisure, or play, activities are important target behaviors in several respects. These behaviors may have several applications to the child or older autistic individual's normal environment as a play, leisure, or transportational activity. They are appropriate at any age, facilitating participation with age-appropriate peers, and can be seen to enhance the autistic individual's ability to entertain themselves or get around town independently. An important consideration with these behaviors could arise from the contexts and materials used for teaching. For example, it might be desirable to increase an autistic child's coordination and play repertoire by teaching him to ride a tricycle. Obviously, while the same targets of increasing coordination and play might be beneficial for an adolescent autistic individual, a tricycle becomes inappropriate for his/her age. A teacher can teach the same task, choosing for apparatus an adult's tricycle or a two-wheeled bike. While both are appropriate, teaching the autistic individual to ride an adult's tricycle merely emphasizes his/her discrepant abilities and serves as a deterrent to effective mainstreaming. Even if the student cannot be expected to manipulate a two-wheeled bike, he/she can be aided with training wheels that can be effectively faded out as the student becomes more familiar with the bike riding activity.

Similarly, as music has been noted to be strongly reinforcing for many autistic individuals, it would be beneficial for a teacher to capitalize on this fact by teaching an autistic student to operate a musical mechanism. Again, the age appropriateness of the task should be emphasized. While a younger autistic child might enjoy a toy music box or a toy flute, an older student should receive instruction in manipulating a radio or stereo, or entertaining themselves with a full-sized piano or drum set. Equally important as the materials used is the concept of self-recreation. It is important in the effective mainstreaming of autistic individuals that they learn to keep themselves entertained in an appropriate manner, as opposed to engaging in continuous, inappropriate self-stimulation.

In the long run, besides de-emphasizing the behavioral discrepancies between handicapped and non-handicapped persons, the concept of age-appropriate skills will facilitate the integration of these groups of individuals. If autistic adolescents are taught behaviors exhibited by 8-year-old normal children, they will fit in with neither the normal 8-year-olds nor the normal adolescents. By instructing the autistic person in skills and activities commonly joined in by his/her normal chronological age peers, he/she will have increased opportunity to generalize skills to appropriate environments and groups, and further learn appropriate behaviors through peer modeling (cf., Egel, Richman, and Koegel 1980, and Chapter 13 this volume).

Seeking assistance   It is easy to imagine that autistic individuals will have recurrent opportunities (needs) to seek assistance from others. Similarly, it seems apparent that it is not considered appropriate behavior for any but the youngest of normal children to sit, confused and distracted from an activity without seeking help. It is also a skill which will greatly facilitate independent functioning, freeing the student from constant supervision by teaching him to recognize the need and seek out assistance only when necessary (see Sample Curricular Program #6).

Some behaviors or skills may not readily appear to fulfill the types of considerations noted above. In some situations, though, they might be modified to serve a functional, age-appropriate purpose. For instance, a gross motor imitation task (i.e., "arms up") would rarely occur naturally in a student's environment, and does little to increase the student's behavioral similarities with chronologically aged peers, or the student's own independence. However, teaching this imitation in the context of putting on a T-shirt makes the exact same target behavior more likely to be applied to the student's natural activities, and makes the child more age appropriate and independent in the initiative taken for self-dressing.

Using these types of considerations, we can imagine that individual curricula will reflect individual levels and needs, and may entail a variety of target skills being taught within any one classroom of children. Once the teacher isolates the behaviors that will promote a child's abilities to deal with his/her natural environments, these behaviors or tasks can be examined in terms of the exact skills needed to enable the student to perform them adaptively, age appropriately and independently.

Delineation of Target Skills

While it is true that autistic students are extremely individual in their abilities and needs, it is also true that, as a group, some behaviors can be suggested which occur or are lacking in many of the children. In addition, the demands placed on individuals by the environment in general may show many commonalities (cf., White 1980). Different students may show the same skill at different levels, or may show different levels of sophistication in acquiring the same skill. The following detailed examples illustrate a progression of steps or skills suggested to teach particular behaviors. These behaviors are only examples of skills which are age appropriate and can be applied by the students in their environments, and that might be used in most classrooms. This list is only a sampling of the pool of suitable target behaviors for autistic children.

In isolating the steps or component skills necessary for teaching such behaviors as a general class, every step in learning a certain activity is listed, no matter how minute. Such steps are often included as a result of trial and error, or "probing" the student. For instance, in the examples for teaching an autistic individual to answer the phone, the therapist included the step "holding receiver to ear" as a result of the students' attempting to answer the phone with the receiver held at the hip level. However, it is probable that different students will need less prompting and fewer steps. When activities requisite for learning certain skills or behaviors are defined, it is expected that some students will skip certain steps and that the steps they do skip will vary across students. Similarly, a student may learn latter parts of the chain more rapidly or more efficiently than earlier steps (via partial participation throughout an activity). Thus, the examples suggest a likely progression of skills students will need to perform the behavior in question, but they do not imply a strict progression or sequence to be used in teaching such behaviors. It is also important to note that there are many ways to achieve the same end result or function of a behavior. The doctrine of critical function (White 1980) and the criteria of ultimate functioning (Brown, Nietupski and Hamre-Nietupski 1976) encourage us to concentrate on the *purpose* of a behavior rather than its exact form or progression of motor acts.

Many concepts can be taught in the context of functional activities. For instance, this child is learning expressive and receptive use of concepts "pour" and "in" during partial participation in recreational activities.

Child requests the ball "fast" or "slow" during a game of bat and ball.

In general, the following examples, as a group, share the important common feature of promoting increased independence for students in their natural environments. In addition, each task relates to a specific skill leading ultimately to independent adult functioning, so that as adults, autistic individuals will learn to rely more and more upon themselves for their daily functioning. Some of the examples relate to independent function in one specific skill, such as brushing hair or getting a drink. However, in teaching a student a skill such as seeking assistance when necessary, we are helping him/her learn a general skill which can be applied to many situations to promote independent functioning. Similarly, behaviors such as crossing the street and taking the bus increase the individual's mobility, promoting independence in a larger variety of (social) experiences.

Also illustrated by these examples are the principles of interspersing many instructional tasks within larger target behaviors. For instance, in the example discussing table setting, one skill which will be embedded in that behavior is discrimination of the left versus the right side of the plate (for silverware placement). Similarly, to learn to ride the bus efficiently, the individual may also need to learn how to tell time so he/she will know when to meet the bus. At this point, note how the principle of partial participation applies to this example. There would be no reason to withhold training in bus riding until telling time is learned. There are many bus-riding skills which could be trained concurrently with the skill of telling time. By working through the total behavior cluster, prompting when necessary, the individual can gain experience with the entire skill cluster, gradually taking increasing responsibility for more complex steps.

The types of behaviors we often find ourselves working on as adjuncts to more comprehensive or complicated living tasks (curricular programs) are listed in Table 1. Within any treatment program, the disruptive behavioral excesses often engaged in by autistic children (including self-abusive behaviors, aggression, tantrums, and self-stimulatory behaviors) must be controlled first. In addition, various abilities which are incidental within the overall curricular programs must often be taught. The most common example occurs in the incidental teaching of language concepts in almost every program presented to autistic students (cf., Hart and Risley 1980). Language concepts, which are often taught incidental to other programs, include relationships such as same/different, first/last, before/after, the use of pronouns and possessives, responses to questions relating to the

TABLE 1 –	**Examples of Incidental Target Behaviors**
CATEGORIES	**EXAMPLES**
Behavioral excesses	
Self-abusive behaviors	Eliminate hitting, biting, scratching oneself, and so forth.
Aggression towards others	Eliminate kicking, hitting, biting, pinching, and so forth.
Tantrums	Eliminate yelling, crying, jumping up, and down, and so forth.
Gets into or messes up things	Eliminate getting into cabinets, scattering books and toys, playing in water, and so forth.
Self-stimulatory behaviors	Eliminate staring at fingers, rocking, handflapping, and so forth.

Behavioral deficits

Learning readiness	Eye contact on request; follows simple commands such as "Close the door," "Sit down," and so forth.
Gross motor skills	Plays ball; rides tricycle; and so forth.
Fine motor skills	Copies lines; colors; uses scissors; prints; and so forth.
Nonverbal imitation	Claps hands; points to body parts; imitates mouth movements or positions; and so forth.
Verbal imitation	Emits speech sounds spontaneously; imitates vowels and consonants; imitates syllables; imitates stress or inflection in phrase; and so forth.
Simple functional speech	Answers questions with at least one word; asks for things with one or more words; answers "I don't know" to question he does not know; is able to request and transfer information; and so forth.
Identifying, labeling, and describing (receptive and expressive)	Follows commands; identifies familiar people; labels body parts; labels colors; labels common objects; labels alphabet; labels numbers 1 to 20; labels different money values; labels big and little; describes shape of object; describes objects by size and color; identifies emotions; and so forth.
Using general concepts and relationships	Matches alike (similar) versus dissimilar; identifies many action verbs; uses prepositions; uses genetive pronouns; uses nominal case pronouns; uses pronouns to describe personal characteristics; uses "and"; understands "don't"; understands the order command of "then"; understands relationship of "first" and "last"; understands relationship of "before" and "after"; answers "yes" or "no" to questions involving desires; recalls what's missing when an object is removed from a group; recalls what he did in the immediate past; recalls a few things from the remote past; discriminates right and left; discriminates singular and plural; counts up to 10 objects; relates a written number to a number of objects; understands simple money exchange; tells time; knows days of week in order; and so forth.
Using functional concepts	Identifies function of many personal objects; describes function of many personal objects; identifies function of different body parts; identifies function of many common objects; describes function of common objects; identifies pairs of objects that belong together; understands concepts cold, tired, hungry; answers "why" questions with "because"; and so forth.
Story telling	Comprehends sentences; describes picture of an activity; makes up story with beginning, middle, and end; makes up story about a topic or subject; and so forth.
Socialization	Follows commands of other children in a group; answers questions asked by other children; initiates nonverbal interaction with other children; initiates verbal interaction with other children; and so forth.
School readiness	Works independently on a task for at least 5 minutes without being distracted; participates in small group activities; seeks help when can't solve problem; and so forth.
Self-help skills	Dresses self; drinks from cup or glass unassisted; uses eating utensils properly; washes hands unaided; washes face unaided; bathes self unassisted; is toilet-trained; and so forth.

student's desires ("Are you cold, hungry, tired?" "Why are you happy, sad, angry, frustrated?"), and language concepts extending beyond the here and now ("What's missing?", "What did you do last week?", "Make up a story."). Finally, many opportunities are presented for learning socialization skills, especially those concerning the student's response to his natural peers, such as initiating and responding to peer interactions.

These examples also illustrate the "long term" planning of curricular goals and how programs relate to each other. For example, in teaching an individual to print, a basic skill is being worked on which opens many doors to adult functioning. The use of printing skills should be encouraged in leisure activities such as writing a letter to a friend, or writing down a phone message.

Sample Curricular Program #1
Domain: Domestic living
Environment: Home
Subenvironment: Bathroom
Activity: Brushing hair

SKILL CLUSTER #1 — *Finding the brush*
Skills Required:
     a)   locate appropriate drawer or cabinet
     b)   open drawer or cabinet
     c)   locate brush from among other items
     d)   remove brush and place on counter

SKILL CLUSTER #2 — *Holding the brush*
Skills Required:
     a)   pick brush up off counter
     b)   orient bristles toward scalp

SKILL CLUSTER #3 — *Brushing hair*
Skills Required:
     a)   apply bristles to top of head
     b)   pull brush downward through hair
     c)   repeat systematically until all hair has been brushed

SKILL CLUSTER #4 — *Parting hair*
Skills Required:
     a)   lean head forward and down
     b)   brush hair forward and down
     c)   locate comb in drawer
     d)   remove comb from drawer
     e)   hold comb so that one end is applied perpendicularly to the top of the head (or part)
     f)   pull comb forward and down
     g)   orient head upwards
     h)   separate portions of hair defining the part
     i)   brush hair downward again on both sides

SKILL CLUSTER #5 — *Replacing brush and comb*
Skills Required:
     a)   locate and open appropriate drawer or cabinet shelf
     b)   replace brush and comb
     c)   close drawer or cabinet

[1] The authors would like to acknowledge the following clinicians for their very creative curricular programs: Glen Dunlap, Gary Graves, Lynn Kern, Mary O'Dell, Ilene Schwartz, Heather Sutherland.

Sample Curricular Program #2
Domain: Domestic living
Environment: Home
Subenvironment: Kitchen
Activity: Pouring milk (or other liquid)

SKILL CLUSTER #1 — *Locate milk*
Skills Required:
- a)   locate and open refrigerator
- b)   locate shelf milk is on
- c)   locate milk from among other items
- d)   pull milk from shelf and from among other items
- e)   set milk on counter
- f)   close door

SKILL CLUSTER #2 — *Locate glass*
Skills Required:
- a)   open appropriate cupboard
- b)   select glass of appropriate size
- c)   place glass on counter
- d)   close cupboard

SKILL CLUSTER #3 — *Pouring the liquid*
Skills Required:
- a)   raise container over glass (with both hands, if necessary)
- b)   tip container slowly so liquid falls into glass
- c)   tip container backward when glass is full or desired limit is reached
- d)   place container back on counter

SKILL CLUSTER #4 — *Cleaning up a mess*
Skills Required:
- a)   locate clean, damp cloth
- b)   wipe around spill towards center
- c)   transport wet cloth to sink, rinse and wring
- d)   go over spot again
- e)   rinse cloth again

SKILL CLUSTER #5 — *Putting milk back*
Skills Required:
- a)   open refrigerator
- b)   locate appropriate shelf and make room if necessary
- c)   pick up milk from counter and place in refrigerator
- d)   close refrigerator door

Sample Curricular Program #3
Domain: Domestic living
Environment: Home
Subenvironment: Kitchen or dining room
Activity: Setting table

SKILL CLUSTER #1 — *Identifying the objects*
Skills Required:
- a)   receptive language ability to identify
  - – plate   – spoon
  - – fork   – napkin
  - – knife   – glass

SKILL CLUSTER #2 — *Location of appropriate objects (see above) and placement on table*
Skills Required: Plate(s)
- a)   location of plate(s)
- b)   removing plate(s) from cupboard
- c)   approaching table with plate(s)
- d)   placement of plate in front of each chair at table

Skills Required: Napkin(s)
- a)   location of napkin(s)
- b)   removing napkin(s) from drawer
- c)   approaching table with napkin(s)
- d)   placement of (one) napkin on left side of each plate

Skills required: Silverware
- a)   location of silverware
- b)   remove knife(ves), fork(s), spoon(s) from drawer
- c)   approaching table with silverware
- d)   placement of knife on right side of plate
- e)   placement of spoon on right side of plate, on right side of knife
- f)   placement of fork on left side of plate, on napkin

Skills Required: Glasses
- a)   location of glass(es)
- b)   removing glass(es) from cupboard
- c)   approaching table with glass(es)
- d)   placement of one glass above each knife & spoon.

Sample Curricular Program #4
Domain: Domestic living
Environment: Home
Subenvironment: All rooms
Activity: Watering plants

SKILL CLUSTER #1 — *Find water container*
Skills Required:
- a)   find water container
- b)   remove from cupboard

SKILL CLUSTER #2 — *Fill container with water*
Skills Required:
- a)   approach sink.
- b)   turn water on
- c)   fill container
- d)   turn water off

SKILL CLUSTER #3 — *Water plants*
Skills Required:
- a)   approach plant
- b)   pour water proportionate to each plant in pot

SKILL CLUSTER #4 — *Putting water container away*
Skills Required:
- a)   approach sink
- b)   empty out any remaining water
- c)   approach cupboard and open
- d)   put container away
- e)   close cupboard

Sample Curricular Program #5
Domain: Community
Environment: Outdoors
Subenvironment: Street
Activity: Crossing the street

SKILL CLUSTER #1 — *Approaching side of street*
Skills Required:
    a)   locate crosswalk or corner
    b)   walk unassisted to side of street (stop at corner)
    c)   push signal activator, if present, and wait for "WALK" signal

SKILL CLUSTER #2 — *Determining "safeness" to cross*
Skills Required:
    a)   look left to check for cars approaching at close range
    b)   look right to check for cars approaching at close range
    c)   wait for approaching cars to pass
    d)   look left and right again before initiating crossing

SKILL CLUSTER #3 — *Crossing the Street*
Skills Required:
    a)   after "WALK" signal or assurance of no approaching cars,
        step into street at crosswalk or corner
    b)   walk across shortest distance
    c)   walk across without delay

Sample Curricular Program #6
Domain: All (e.g., Vocational)
Environment: All (e.g., Training workshop)
Subenvironment: All (e.g., Assembly shop)
Activity: Seeking assistance

SKILL CLUSTER #1 — *Discriminating a situation (problem) in which assistance is required*
Skills Required:
    a)   identifies goal response (e.g., putting batteries in flashlight)
    b)   attempts solution (e.g., attempts to take apart flashlight)

c) attempts to solve problem for *X* (e.g., three) minutes
d) leaves problem stimulus (e.g., puts flashlight down)

SKILL CLUSTER #2 — *Identifying helper and soliciting assistance*
Skills Required:
a) locates a potential helper (e.g., another person)
b) requests assistance (e.g., says, "Help me, please")
c) discriminates affirmative versus negative response ("yes," "sure," or "OK," versus "no," "too busy," "not now,")
d) if negative, repeats steps a–c
e) if affirmative, leads helper to problem stimulus
f) nonverbally or verbally indicates problem stimulus
g) specifies goal to helper (e.g., points to batteries and then flashlight; says "Batteries in. . .")
h) waits and observes while assistance is provided
i) says "Thank you" to assistant

Sample Curricular Program #7
Domain: Communication
Environment: Home/School
Subenvironment: Any
Activity: Printing

SKILL CLUSTER #1 — *Holding writing tool (pen or crayon)*
Skills Required:
a) grasping pen or crayon in one hand
b) holding pen or crayon at the correct angle to page

SKILL CLUSTER #2 — *Applying pen or crayon to paper*
Skills Required:
a) moving pen or crayon in an undirected fashion over the page

SKILL CLUSTER #3 — *Progressively finer use of pen or crayon and paper*
Skills Required:
a) keeping markings within gross borders on the page
b) keeping markings within finer borders on a page
c) tracing lines printed on page
d) tracing curves printed on page
e) tracing lines and curves from progressively faded models

SKILL CLUSTER #4 — *Imitating a printed model*
Skills Required:
a) copying a line from printed model on clean space of paper [| :]
b) copying a curve from a printed model on clean space of paper [ ) :]
c) printing line independently without printed model when asked to "Draw a line"

SKILL CLUSTER #5 — *Putting lines together to make letters*
Skills Required:
a) tracing three lines to make a letter [A; H; N]
b) tracing three line patterns from progressively faded model
[$\bigwedge$ $\overset{\wedge}{/\text{-}\backslash}$ $\overset{\wedge}{/\text{:}\backslash}$]
c) copying letter made of three lines from a printed model
d) printing letter made of three lines spontaneously when asked to "Print *A*"

SKILL CLUSTER #6 — *Putting lines and curves together to make letters*
Skills Required:
- a)   tracing lines and circles to make a letter [D, B, P]
- b)   tracing straight and curved patterns from progressively faded model
  []
- c)   copying lines and curves to make letter from a printed model
- d)   printing letter spontaneously when asked to "Print *D*"

SKILL CLUSTER #7 — *Correspondence of letter to its name*
Skills Required:
- a)   recognition of pattern as unique from other letters by matching (stimuli = A + B; student given A and told to match A)
- b)   symbol names ("What letter is this?")
- c)   response to letter name without model present ("Give me 'A')
- d)   written response to letter name without model present

SKILL CLUSTER #8 — *Printing strings of letters*
Skills Required:
- a)   sequentially modeling the individual letters (for example, in the child's name)
- b)   spontaneously printing letters (of child's name) in sequence
- c)   modeling and printing letter sequences of other common objects or words (food, dog, cat)

SKILL CLUSTER #9 — *Supplement writing program with beginning reading program, associating letters with sounds*

SKILL CLUSTER #10 — *Printing strings of letters on appropriate classroom oriented (or otherwise appropriate) writing pages (e.g., normalizing size, shape and spacing of letters)*

Many skills may be shaped into new, more elaborate skills. In this photograph, an adolescent uses his previously taught typing skills to write a letter to his friend.

Sample Curricular Program #8
Domain: Leisure/Recreational
Environment: Home
Subenvironment: Living room
Activity: Writing a letter to a friend

SKILL CLUSTER #1 — *Locating materials*
Skills Required:
- a) locate paper
- b) locate pencil, pen or typewriter
- c) clear off workspace

SKILL CLUSTER #2 — *Writing the letter*
Skills Required:
- a) salutation and date
- b) description of recent activities
- c) inquiries regarding recipient's activities
- d) description of attitudes, thoughts, or feelings
- e) conclusion and salutation

SKILL CLUSTER #3 — *Preparing the envelope*
Skills Required:
- a) writing friend's address
- b) writing return address
- c) stamp

SKILL CLUSTER #4 — *Mailing the letter*
Skills Required:
- a) locate nearest mailbox
- b) insert letter

Sample Curricular Program #9
Domain: Leisure/Recreational
Environment: Home
Subenvironment: Living room
Activity: Leisure reading

SKILL CLUSTER #1 — *Obtaining reading material*
Skills Required:
- a) locate newspaper or book of interest
- b) locate comfortable spot with good lighting
- c) open reading material to appropriate starting place

SKILL CLUSTER #2 — *Reading*
Skills Required:
- a) ability to read and comprehend written material (from a previous basic reading program)
- b) directed attention to reading material for an adequate amount of time (e.g., 10 to 30 minutes)
- c) discriminate end of page and turn page
- d) direct attention to top of next page

SKILL CLUSTER #3 — *Replacing reading material*
Skills Required:

- a)   discriminate the end of "free time" or the desire to stop reading
- b)   place bookmark in book to mark place or fold newspaper appropriately
- c)   replace material to its original location
- d)   restore location to original state
- e)   turn off light

Sample Curricular Program #10

Domain: Leisure
Environment: Home
Subenvironment: Living room
Activity: Telephone conversation

SKILL CLUSTER #1 — *Answering the phone*
Skills Required:

- a)   approach phone when ringing
- b)   pick up receiver
- c)   put receiver up to ear
- d)   signal acknowledgement (e.g., "Hello")
- e)   identification (e.g., "This is John")
- f)   pause, awaiting response from caller
- g)   discriminate if call is for self or another person (see SKILL CLUSTER #2 or #4)

SKILL CLUSTER #2 — *Identify and notify the person in the room the call is for*
Skills Required:

- a)   response to caller (e.g., "Hold on please; I'll get him/her")
- b)   lay phone receiver on table
- c)   look for person in immediate vicinity
- d)   notification of person, "It's for you"
- e)   hand person phone

SKILL CLUSTER #3 — *Discriminations required when person is not in immediate vicinity*
Skills Required:

- a)   respond to caller (e.g., "Hold please; I'll see if he/she's around")
- b)   lay phone receiver on table
- c)   discriminate proximity and availability of person
- d)   request whereabouts from others in environment
- e)   if person available, notification (e.g., "The phone is for you")
- f)   if not available, notify caller (e.g., "He/she's not here; please call back")

SKILL CLUSTER #4 — *Conversation on phone initiated by another*
Skills Required:

- a)   answer questions within his repertoire
- b)   if question is not in repertoire, child must answer with generalized response (e.g., "I don't understand; please call back later")

Sample Curricular Program #11

Domain: Community/Vocational
Environment: Community
Subenvironment: Bus
Activity: Travel alone by bus to school or work

SKILL CLUSTER #1 — *Determining time of departure*
Skills Required:
  a)   able to tell present time
  b)   knowledge regarding required arrival time at school or work
  c)   able to determine time of bus departure
  d)   travel between home and bus stop prior to time of bus departure

SKILL CLUSTER #2 — *Boarding the bus*
Skills Required:
  a)   able to wait calmly in immediate vicinity of bus stop
  b)   able to discriminate the appropriate bus to take to work
  c)   boarding bus quickly when it stops
  d)   depositing the fare
  e)   communication with driver when necessary
  f)   proper conduct between fare box and seated or standing position on bus

SKILL CLUSTER #3 — *Departing from the bus*
Skills Required:
  a)   recognition of landmarks preceding desired bus stop
  b)   signaling driver to stop
  c)   preparation to depart (gathering books, umbrella, etc.)
  d)   standing and walking quickly to exit door
  e)   deboard bus and wait until it pulls away

SKILL CLUSTER #4 — *Walking to work*
Skills Required:
  a)   walk to work and enter
  b)   greet fellow employees

Generalization Issues and Curricular Programming

Generalization to outside environments   Although significant improvements can be made in teaching autistic individuals, a persistent problem occurs in the generalization of treatment gains across environments (see Chapter 15). One possible reason for the lack of generalization may be a lack of adequate stimulus control (Rincover and Koegel 1975). When the discriminative stimuli encountered in the environment are not sufficiently similar to the discriminative stimuli which exercise control in the treatment setting, transfer of the skill to the untreated setting cannot be ensured. By developing curricula which have, as a criterion for task inclusion, a consideration of the applicability of the skill to the student's daily environments, the stimulus situations guiding the task in treatment and untreated settings can be made more similar than when the same concept is taught using non-functional contexts or materials. For instance, the stimulus dimensions of a real wall clock or a watch remain relatively similar across most wall clocks or watches. The student who learns to tell time using these appropriate functional materials may not have the extreme difficulties in generalizing his/her skill to natural settings that a student who learned to tell time on a makeshift or toy clock with extra-large numbers or moveable hands might encounter.

Similarly, increasing the functionality of curricular tasks may encourage the development of more natural reinforcement schemes. Ferster (1967) describes a natural reinforcer as a stimulus that exists in the environment and motivates the child to exhibit some behavior to acquire it. The motive for the natural reinforcer comes from the individual and the natural stimulus situations, as opposed to an arbitrarily defined relationship between response and reinforcement which has been arranged by a therapist. For example, teaching object labeling using household and personal items as stimuli can be directly and reliably reinforced in the natural environment when the child requests an object using the label and is reinforced by acquiring that object. Appropriate purchasing behaviors can be naturally reinforced when the individual buys a desired item. Use of appropriate language to purchase a theatre ticket can be naturally reinforced by getting in to the movies. The advantage is that whether or not treatment personnel are present in the natural environment, the student's ability to apply skills learned in treatment to natural settings will have a greater chance of being reinforced. In other words, access to reinforcement in the natural environment should increase, as should the child's motivation to use his/her behaviors to acquire those reinforcers.

As one behavior is naturally reinforced, it may open up possibilities of many other reinforcing consequences for other behaviors (Ferster 1967). For example, teaching a child to walk by mother's side without straying may initially be reinforced by being allowed to go on neighborhood walks with mother. This behavior can be expanded to walking to stores, parks, or theatres; the reinforcers the environment can offer become multiplied, as the parent "brings the child into better contact" with the wide variety of natural reinforcers available in the child's natural environments. As a final note, the variation in reinforcing consequences offered by the environment should prove very effective in motivating autistic children, as evidence shows that the children respond at a higher level with shorter latencies when reinforcing consequences are varied than when a singular reinforcer is available on a continuous basis (Egel 1980).

Age appropriateness and generalization It is also possible that increasing the chronological age appropriateness of skills taught to autistic students will encourage entry into more "natural communities of reinforcement." For example, Baer and Wolf (1970) describe the peer group as an "effective community of fellow behavior modifiers, their programs practiced, effective and running, waiting only for an introduction to the subject" (p. 320). The point is that if a child can be taught a pivotal response (or a "trapping" response, as Baer and Wolf describe) so that the autistic student can be successfully introduced to his or her peer group, the peer group may effectively "take over the teacher's project" by naturally reinforcing their autistic peer for appropriate social behaviors and punishing or ignoring inappropriate behaviors. The "trapping" response, or the response which will gain the child exposure to this natural community of reinforcement, can be whatever example of social behavior is currently in the autistic child's repertoire (cf., Ferster 1967) which the child shows or can be prompted to show. At that point, the child may become "trapped" into the natural community of his peers, due to the contingent rewards offered for appropriate social behavior. Entry into natural communities of reinforcement such as the peer group may then expose the autistic child to the possible positive effects of peer modeling (Egel, Richman and Koegel 1980; Egel, Richman, and Button, Chapter 13 this volume), and to an increased number and variety of available natural reinforcers.

Maintenance It is similarly possible that use of functional age-appropriate tasks and the effectiveness of natural reinforcement schemes which may result from a possible increase in generalization may help in the maintenance of generalized skills in natural environments. With autistic children, it is often found that when reinforcement is no longer available for a certain behavior, the behavior may "extinguish." Research has shown that problems often interpreted as a lack of generalization may reflect a behavior that did, in fact, generalize to new settings, but was not maintained due to the lack of reinforcement in that setting. Further, when the reinforcement schedules were altered, such that non-contingent reinforcement was subsequently available in the generalization environment, more durable responding in this environment was observed (Koegel and Rincover 1977). It seems likely (although still a question that must be resolved by research) that since functional curricular tasks may capitalize on the great variety of natural reinforcers available, behaviors should not extinguish in natural environments over time; that is, natural reinforcers are available in all environments and do not depend on the presence of the therapist (cf., Ferster 1967). The reinforcing consequences for appropriate behaviors will persist in all environments, maintaining the performance of learned behaviors outside the treatment environment.

Social validity A major thrust of attempts to establish the efficacy of behavioral treatment with autistic children is to empirically establish the perceptions of community members regarding the child (Schreibman, *et al,* in press). Increasing the functionality of the curriculum suggests (by definition) that the autistic child will have many natural opportunities to engage in or display his/her learned skills. In addition, the age appropriateness of learned tasks should help to reduce the stigmatizing discrepancies between autistic children and their non-handicapped peers. The more the autistic child can approximate the behaviors of his/her peers, the greater the opportunities for mainstreaming in school and community. Mainstreaming will result in greater opportunities for peer modeling and entrance into effective communities of reinforcement, which, in turn, should help to improve community members' perceptions of the improvements in autistic children.

Conclusion

Although the education and treatment of children with autistic characteristics has effected dramatic improvements in many children, their significant deficiencies in so many skill areas suggest that the effectiveness of therapy will be maximized when it emphasizes both the present and future environmental demands confronting an autistic individual. By referencing curricula against the requirements of normal adult functioning, we can ensure that autistic individuals' experiences with their environments can be most beneficial when partial participation and natural reinforcement schemes are emphasized as parts of the teaching program. Future research will clarify the parameters of the potential benefits which orientations toward functionality, age appropriateness, partial participation, and natural reinforcement schemes may convey on the generalization, maintenance, and social validity of behavioral treatment programs for autistic individuals.

Notes

Preparation of this chapter was supported by USPHS Research Grant No. MH28210 from the National Institute of Mental Health, and by the U.S. Office of Education Research Grant No. G007802084 from the Bureau of Education for the Handicapped. The authors would like to extend special appreciation to Glen Dunlap for his careful readings and helpful suggestions.

Audiological Testing

T he assessment of auditory function is instrumental to the diagnosis and management of autism. Inconsistent and inappropriate responses to auditory stimuli and delayed language development often lead to an early suspicion of hearing loss prior to a diagnosis of autism (Ornitz 1973; Kanner 1943). It is important to rule out the existence of a hearing loss or identify a hearing loss coincident with autism before devising an educational program for the autistic child. While autistic children generally do not show primary perceptual deficits (Damasio and Maurer 1978), central auditory dysfunction may be associated with some autistic behaviors (Wetherby, Koegel, and Mendel, in press) and should be considered in educational management.

An assessment of the integrity of the auditory system in autistic children seems necessary to aid in delineating a possible cause of their inconsistent responses to auditory stimuli and their delayed language development. The amount of information obtained from the audiological assessment will vary for each autistic child, depending upon the child's ability to respond. The responses required for tests available to the audiologist include no behavioral response (as with the auditory electroencephalic response), a behavioral orienting response, nonverbal responses (such as dropping a block in a box when a sound is presented), and verbal responses (such as repeating what was heard). Audiological procedures developed for use with young children and difficult-to-test children are often well suited for the autistic child (see Brooks 1978; Hodgson 1978; Martin 1978).

This chapter will be concerned with the use of the *Staggered Spondaic Word* test battery with autistic children. This test battery requires verbal responses and therefore is only appropriate for use with verbal autistic children. (For a review of

*This chapter was authored by **Amy Wetherby,** University of California, San Francisco and **Robert L. Koegel,** University of California, Santa Barbara.*

techniques available to assess auditory function in nonverbal autistic children see Lowell 1976.) Adaptations of these techniques are generally suitable for most nonverbal autistic children. In some cases pretraining procedures (using shaping and stimulus fading procedures as exemplified later in this chapter) may be necessary to assess auditory function in autistic children.

Anatomy and Physiology of the Auditory System

A basic knowledge of the anatomy and physiology of the auditory system will facilitate understanding the assessment of auditory function. A brief overview of the structure and function of the auditory system follows (also see Noback and Demarest 1977; Yost and Nielsen 1977; Glattke 1973; Zemlin 1968).

Airborne sound energy travels through the external auditory canal, is amplified by the mechanical action of the tympanic membrane and ossicular chain, and is conducted to the inner ear. This is referred to as *air conduction*. Sound energy may also reach the inner ear by *bone conduction,* i.e., the cochlea can be stimulated by vibrations of the bones of the skull. While hearing by bone conduction does not serve an important purpose in normal auditory function (Yost and Nielsen 1977), it is useful in audiological testing to differentiate types of hearing losses. Any interference in the transmission of sound through the outer and middle ear will cause a conductive hearing loss. Usually conductive hearing losses can be treated medically or surgically. A sensori-neural hearing loss results from damage to the cochlea or cochlear nerve (VIII cranial nerve). Recent testing techniques can distinguish between a sensory (i.e., cochlear) hearing loss and a neural (i.e., retrocochlear – VIII nerve and brainstem) hearing loss (Katz 1978).

Neural impulses are transmitted from the cochlea to the primary auditory cortex along a highly complex pathway. The cochlear portion of the VIII cranial nerve leaves the cochlea and synapses within the ipsilateral (i.e., same side of the) cochlear nuclei in the brainstem. Most of the fibers from the cochlear nuclei cross and ascend the contralateral (i.e., opposite side of the) brainstem, while some fibers ascend ipsilaterally (Carpenter 1976; Glattke 1973). Many nuclei are inter-posed in the course of the ascending auditory pathways, including the superior olive in the pons, the inferior colliculus in the midbrain, and the medial genicu-late body in the thalamus. From the thalamus, fibers project to Heschl's gyrus, the primary auditory reception area located in the temporal lobe.

Bilateral representation first occurs at the level of the superior olive. That is, the major tracts and nuclei from the level of the superior olive and above receive fibers from both ears. The crossed pathway from the ear to the contralateral temporal lobe is stronger or dominant. The two primary auditory cortices (Heschl's gyri) in the temporal lobes are interconnected via fibers projecting through the corpus callosum and anterior commissure.

Auditory information relayed to Heschl's gyrus is first processed within the temporal lobe. Wernicke's area, located in the posterior aspect of the temporal lobe adjacent to Heschl's gyrus, is presumed to be involved in the recognition and decoding of spoken language (see Hollien 1975). Wernicke's area is anatomically connected with other areas of the brain, and one pathway links Wernicke's area to

FIGURE 2–1.   The highly complex pathway through which neural impulses must travel between the cochlea and the primary auditory cortex of the brain. (From Mendel, M.I. and Gilchrist, D. *Autotutorial in Neuroanatomy and Neurophysiology for Speech and Hearing.* Copyright 1978, by the University of California at Santa Barbara. Reprinted by permission.)

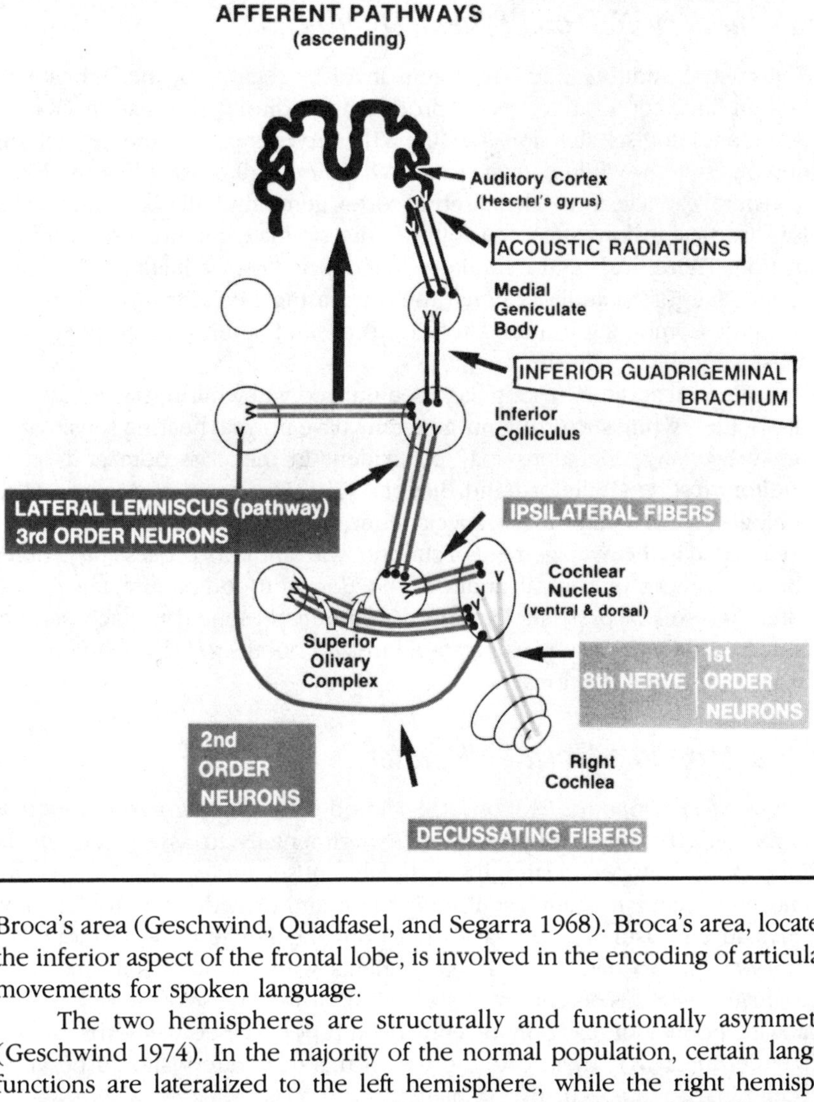

AFFERENT PATHWAYS
(ascending)

Auditory Cortex
(Heschel's gyrus)

ACOUSTIC RADIATIONS

Medial
Geniculate
Body

INFERIOR GUADRIGEMINAL
BRACHIUM

Inferior
Colliculus

LATERAL LEMNISCUS (pathway)
3rd ORDER NEURONS

IPSILATERAL FIBERS

Cochlear
Nucleus
(ventral & dorsal)

Superior
Olivary
Complex

8th NERVE   1st
ORDER
NEURONS

2nd
ORDER
NEURONS

Right
Cochlea

DECUSSATING FIBERS

Broca's area (Geschwind, Quadfasel, and Segarra 1968). Broca's area, located in the inferior aspect of the frontal lobe, is involved in the encoding of articulatory movements for spoken language.

The two hemispheres are structurally and functionally asymmetrical (Geschwind 1974). In the majority of the normal population, certain language functions are lateralized to the left hemisphere, while the right hemisphere appears to be specialized for visuospatial and musical functions (Searleman 1977; Krashen 1976; Kimura 1973; Bogen 1969; Penfield and Roberts 1966). Thus, Broca's and Wernicke's areas are generally located in the left hemisphere. However, there is variability in the direction and degree of cerebral lateralization in the normal population. Furthermore, cerebral lateralization is not clearly related to handedness. The left hemisphere is dominant for language in 90–99 percent of right-handed individuals and in 50–70 percent of left-handed individuals (Searleman 1977). While almost all right-handed people are left dominant for language, left-handed individuals tend to be less lateralized for language functions.

Central Auditory Nervous System Dysfunction

The central auditory nervous system involves regions of the brainstem, cerebellum, and cerebral cortex in processing auditory information (Katz 1978). Some audiologists also consider the VIII nerve as part of the central auditory nervous system. While damage to the VIII nerve will cause a hearing loss in the ipsilateral ear, a lesion in the cerebral cortex generally will not produce a hearing loss. Cortical lesions affect the ability to discriminate and process auditory information. Therefore, central auditory function is best evaluated by reducing the redundancy of the auditory signal, thus increasing the difficulty of the discrimination task. Competing stimuli, filtered speech, and other difficult speech tasks are sensitive to lesions in the brain.

Central auditory testing has been utilized with children who have learning disabilities. While such students generally have normal hearing sensitivity, auditory processing difficulties may be evident in the classroom and on central auditory testing (Willeford and Billger 1978). The combined efforts of the audiologist, speech pathologist, special education teacher, and other professionals are needed in the management of children with auditory processing problems. In the assessment of central auditory function, the audiologist can control the intensity level of presentation and the stimuli presented to each ear, and can reduce ambient noise by using sound-treated booths to achieve the most standardized testing conditions.

Staggered Spondaic Word Test Battery

The *Staggered Spondaid Word* (SSW) and *Competing Environmental Sound* (CES) test battery have been used experimentally to assess central auditory function for competing stimuli in echolalic autistic individuals. The SSW test was chosen because it is an easy listening task and provides both quantitative and qualitative measures of central dysfunction. The SSW test was developed by Katz in 1960, and to date, over 10,000 patients with various disorders have been evaluated with this procedure (Katz 1977b). However, use of the SSW test with the autistic population has only recently been reported (see Wetherby, Koegel, and Mendel in press). Therefore, the use of this test battery should be viewed as preliminary and speculative in nature.

The SSW test has been shown to be an effective standardized test in examining central auditory nervous system disorders for individuals 11 to 60 years of age (Brunt 1972). Normal limits have been strictly defined and there is little variability among normal listeners within this age group. Normative results for children are poorer and more variable than for adults. SSW norms have, however, been obtained on children from 11 to 5 years (White 1977; Katz and Illmer 1972). The typical error pattern for normal children is a poorer score in the left ear and response bias, suggesting incomplete maturation in anterior auditory processing areas of the brain, and possibly that cerebral lateralization is not yet complete (Brunt 1978; White 1977). Adjusting the SSW scores in a standard manner helps to eliminate processing errors and provides a purer measure of the integrity of the auditory reception area. White (1977) found that, at all ages, the SSW adjusted scores were normal or close to normal by adult standards. She suggested that "the SSW test may be used in the future to evaluate not only the auditory reception center in children, but related cortical auditory processing areas as well" (White 1977, p. 332).

Analysis of SSW results may indicate the location of a lesion (i.e., either anatomical damage or physiological dysfunction) within auditory pathways of the brainstem and cerebral hemispheres. Confidence in predicting the location of lesions has developed from data on patients with medically and surgically confirmed sites of lesion (Brunt 1978; 1972). Specific criteria for categorizing the SSW scores have been devised and established by Katz (1977a; 1968), based on normal subjects and patients with peripheral and/or central problems. Each SSW score falls into a category of normal, mild, moderate, or severe, which facilitates the differential diagnosis of auditory dysfunction.

Performance difficulty is partly determined by onset-time differences of each test item (Katz, Harder, and Lohnes 1977). Severe or moderate SSW scores in the poorer ear suggest a central distortion arising from an auditory reception involvement in the contralateral hemisphere, involvement of the interhemispheric pathway (corpus callosum/anterior commissure), or an ipsilateral brainstem involvement. Patients with cortical dysfunction sparing the auditory reception area show normal or mild SSW scores. Since test items are counterbalanced for each ear to receive the first spondee, response biases should not normally contaminate the SSW scores. When evident, response biases have diagnostic significance in localizing brain dysfunction in specific auditory processing areas of the brain, ie., fronto-temporal, fronto-parietal, temporo-parietal, and temporo-occipital regions (Brunt 1978).

The Competing Environmental Sound test, also devised by Katz (1976), is based on the SSW and serves as a companion procedure to it. It may be effective in supplementing the SSW results in the differential diagnosis of auditory reception versus corpus callosum/anterior commissure dysfunction. It may also be effective in identifying the impaired hemisphere when compared to the SSW test (Katz 1976). Although the CES test is still in the preliminary stages of clinical application, it does provide supplementary information to the SSW test.

The specific purpose of using the SSW test battery was to determine whether empirical measures of central auditory processing for dichotic stimuli might be indicative of problems underlying deviant auditory responses and deviant linguistic systems of echolalic autistic children. While the use of this test battery with autistic children is still in the experimental stages, preliminary findings indicate that the SSW test battery is a potentially useful measure of central auditory dysfunction in autistic individuals. Reliance on any one measure is not recommended; therefore, the SSW test battery should be used in conjunction with available neurological and behavioral measures related to auditory processing, as well as a complete case history.

Test Procedures

The SSW/CES test battery is comprised of two monaural hearing tests and two dichotic tests designed to assess central auditory function. A description of the test battery and the pre-training procedures devised to facilitate administering the tests to autistic subjects are provided here.

Monaural hearing tests   Hearing for speech presented monaurally was assessed separately for each ear with *speech reception threshold* (SRT) tests and *word discrimination scores* (WDS). SRT provides a direct measure of hearing sensitivity for speech, and was established with the recorded CID W–1 spondaic word test using a descending method and 5 dB increments. WDS measures the degree of clarity with which the child hears speech. WDS was obtained with the recorded CID W–22 monosyllabic word test (Lists 1D and 2D) presented at 40 dB above SRT. SRT and WDS are part of the routine audiometric test battery used to indicate the presence or absence of a hearing loss, and the degree of loss, if present.

Dichotic tests   Central auditory function for competing stimuli was assessed with the Staggered Spondaic Word (SSW) test (List EC) and the Competing Environmental Sound (CES) test (List E1) presented at 50 dB above SRT. (For a complete description of the SSW test see Brunt (1978) and Katz (1977a).) The raw SSW (R-SSW) scores were summed and converted to percent error scores in competing (C) and noncompeting (NC) conditions for the right and left ear. The corrected SSW (C-SSW) scores and adjusted SSW (A-SSW) scores were calculated. Additionally, the results were analyzed for ear effect, order effect, reversals, and Type A pattern response biases (see Katz 1977a). The CES scores (see Katz 1976) were summed and converted to percent error scores for the right and left ear. The eight equations based on the SSW and CES test comparisons were calculated to suggest the hemisphere involved (Katz 1976). The SSW and CES tests should be administered and interpreted by an audiologist trained in these procedures.

Audiological testing procedures   The SRT, WDS, SSW, and CES test stimuli were prerecorded on commercially available tapes from Auditec of St. Louis. The tapes were presented by earphones (Telephonics TDH–39) to each child via a high-quality tape player (Viking 433) and diagnostic audiometer (Maico MA–24) and were administered in a sound-treated booth (General Acoustics) meeting ANSI standards. Each testing session lasted between one and two hours, depending on the subject's cooperation. The training procedures and audiological test battery were completed in one to four sessions, depending on the subject's level of functioning.

SRT and WDS pretraining procedures   The SRT and WDS require verbal repetition of bisyllabic and monosyllabic words, respectively. Verbal repetition tasks are well suited for the echolalic autistic child with intelligible speech.

To ensure reliable responses to the prerecorded test words, the following pre-training procedures were used.

Words not contained on the test lists were used for training items. The subject was taken to the sound-treated booth, and an assistant remained with the subject throughout pretraining and testing. The training items were first presented at a comfortable volume with the experimenter's monitored live voice in sound field. Next, the training items were presented with prerecorded voice in sound field, and finally, with prerecorded voice binaurally over earphones. The subject was praised for repeating each training item. As few trials as possible were used to prevent the child from becoming tired or bored. Testing began when the child would repeat five consecutive prerecorded words presented over earphones. (Note: If a child has difficulty transferring from live to prerecorded voice, an additional step may be needed in which the prerecorded word is presented in sound field, and the experimenter immediately presents the same word with live voice in sound field to prompt the child's response. A fading procedure can also be used to transfer responding from live voice to the prerecorded training items). (See Chapter ten for an overview of behavior modification principles.) After pretraining with bisyllabic words and obtaining SRT for each ear, pretraining with monosyllabic words was completed and WDS was obtained for each ear.

SSW pretraining procedures   Because the severely autistic subjects were unable to follow the relatively lengthy prerecorded instructions given to normal subjects, it was necessary to provide the following pretraining procedures in place of the instructions. These procedures were designed to accomplish the same result as the prerecorded instructions (i.e., to instruct the children to repeat groups of words). The procedures were based upon principles of shaping and stimulus fading as outlined by Lovaas, Schreibman, and Koegel (1974), Schreibman and Koegel (1981), Rincover and Koegel (1977), and Risley and Wolf (1967).

Taking advantage of the subjects' echolalic speech, each subject was first asked (live voice) to repeat a one spondee training item from the CID W−1 Spondaic Word list (i.e., spondees not contained on the SSW test). Each item was preceded by the carrier phrase, "Are you ready?" The subject was praised for repeating the training item, and was told no for repeating the carrier phrase, or for failing to repeat all of the training item. After the subject would reliably repeat any one, or two spondee training items, a fading procedure was implemented in order to transfer responding from live voice to the regular prerecorded SSW training stimuli. The procedure began with the female experimenter's live voice, followed by her tape recorded voice, presented first in sound field and then binaurally over earphones. This was followed by a male experimenter's tape recorded voice presented binaurally over earphones, and then the male prerecorded voice on the regular SSW training items presented binaurally over headphones. This training procedure was terminated when the subject would repeat five consecutive two spondee training items presented binaurally over headphones. At this point, the subjects would respond to the standard prerecorded SSW practice items in the same manner as a person who followed the prerecorded instructions. Therefore, it was possible to administer all 40 of the SSW test items under standard conditions.

CES pretraining procedures   The following pretraining procedure was used instead of the more complicated instructions on the prerecorded CES tape. The subject was first shown pictures representing each sound from the CES tape, and asked to "point to (name of a sound)." Next, each test sound was presented (in sound field) and the subject was asked again to point out the sound. The sounds from the CES training items were then presented binaurally over headphones, first one sound at a time and then two sounds sequentially before the subject was asked to point to the pictures. Finally, the CES test itself was presented in the normal manner, with two competing sounds and the subject pointing to two pictures.

Case Studies

To demonstrate the use of the SSW/CES test battery with echolalic autistic individuals, six case studies are presented here. All six subjects were diagnosed autistic according to criteria of the U.S. National Society for Autistic Children (Ritvo and Freeman 1978), by Wetherby and Koegel, and at least one independent source. For purposes of administering the SSW test, all subjects were able to repeat intelligibly at least four syllables and all were eight years of age or older, because of the clearer normative data on the SSW test for these age groups. Subjects were selected to exemplify a range of language abilities and severity of echolalic behavior as often exhibited by autistic children.

Descriptions of each subject are provided, along with the results of two standardized receptive language tests as a comparative measure of each subject's language development. Total raw scores, followed by age-equivalency scores in parentheses (years– months), are presented for the *Peabody Picture Vocabulary Test* (PPVT) (Dunn 1959), and the *Carrow Test for Auditory Comprehension of Language* (TACL) (Carrow 1973). In addition, degree of hand preference, as measured by recording the hand used with 10 common objects (Oldfield 1971), is included for each subject.

Quantitative and qualitative results of the SSW/CES test battery are reported for each subject. The SSW and CES test results were analyzed and interpreted independently by Amy Wetherby and by Jack Katz. In all instances, the two scorers were in agreement as to the interpretation, however, Dr. Katz (the second scorer) suggested a more detailed interpretation for Subject 3.

Because of the variability in autistic children's behavior, it is recommended that the SSW test be administered two or more times, with an interval of at least one month, to ensure reliability of results. For all of the subjects, (except Subject 4, who received five tests) the SSW test was readministered after an interval of three to four months to check test-retest reliability. The test-retest results of the SSW test were fairly consistent and stable for these subjects. The reported response biases were the same from test to retest, although the percent error scores varied slightly. The CES test was administered only once at about the time of the second SSW test.

Longitudinal data collected on the SSW test may be useful to chart change in performance on the central auditory test, particularly in younger autistic children prior to cerebral maturation (before puberty). In the case of Subject 4 (who received a year of intensive language treatment), the SSW test was administered a total of five times at two to three month intervals; twice within the first six months of treatment (Early Treatment), and three times within the last six months of treatment (Late Treatment) as a progress measure of central auditory function. Additionally, Subject 3 was retested a third time after an interval of one year.

Subject 1, a 24-year-old male, lived in a foster home and attended a training center for disabled adults. His expressive language was limited to extensive and frequent immediate and delayed echolalia, short one and two-word labeling, and one-word responses to questions. He had a tendency to perseverate on a few particular delayed echolalic utterances (e.g., "want some coffee," "that's disgusting"). Although he had very little comprehension of written material, he could read and write most words. Given a pencil, he would incessantly write words until the pencil was removed from his hand; this was analogous to his verbal behavior, which consisted of incessant delayed echolalia. His intonation patterns were bizarre, giving his voice a high pitched, shrill quality. He exhibited self-stimulatory behavior (i.e., finger manipulation, strange vocalizations), toe walking, disruptive behavior (i.e., slapping), was excessively active, and easily distracted.

Subject 1 showed severe language comprehension problems; on the PPVT his raw score was 46 (4– 7), and on the TACL his score was 52 (3– 0). He showed a lack of hand preference, i.e., 5 of the 10 objects were used with each hand.

On the monaural hearing tests, SRT was zero dB and WDS was 96 percent in each ear. As seems to be the case with most autistic children, these results indicate normal hearing for speech.

The test-retest results on the SSW and the CES scores for Subject 1 are shown at the top of Figure 2– 2. On the SSW test, Subject 1 demonstrated depressed scores (elevated percent errors) bilaterally, with a greater number of errors in the competing than in the noncompeting conditions. The C– SSW scores for test and retest were in the moderately depressed range, and the A– SSW scores were in the mild range. Additional calculations (not shown in Figure 2– 2) showed significant Ear High/Low (more errors on the items beginning in the right ear) and Order Low/High (more errors on the second spondee) response biases. CES scores were depressed in the right ear. These results are suggestive of a central auditory dysfunction in the posterior temporal region. The involvement may be in the auditory reception area of the left hemisphere, possibly extending deeply to the corpus callosum/anterior commissure. The diagnosis is consistent with the subject's severe language comprehension problem and incessant echolalia.

Subject 2, an 18-year-old male, lived at home and attended a class for autistic children. He did not initiate speech, and his language consisted of one-word

FIGURE 2–2.   Measures of central auditory function: SSW test results for the echolalic subjects who did not receive treatment during the test/retest period (Subjects 1, 2, & 3). Corrected SSW percent error scores for the right and left ear competing (C) and noncompeting (NC) conditions for test and retest. CES percent error scores are shown for the right ear (RE) and left ear (LE). (Wetherby, A., Koegel, R.L., and Mendel, M. In press. "Central Auditory Nervous System Dysfunction in Echolalic Autistic Individuals," *Journal of Speech and Hearing Research*. Copyright by American Speech, Language and Hearing Association. Reprinted by permission.)

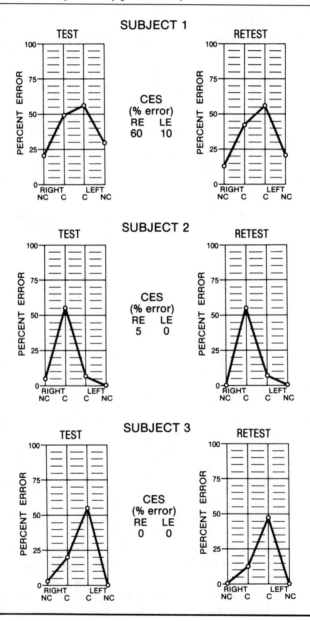

utterances and moderately frequent (approximately 15–20 percent of total utterances) immediate echolalic responses. His receptive abilities were better than his expressive abilities in that he could follow commands and respond appropriately to questions, but he had a tendency to give the minimum possible response. He could read and write with some elementary comprehension. His voice was monotonic and he tended to whisper. His self-stimulatory behavior was extensive and included rocking, hand flapping, and swishing saliva.

On the receptive language tests, Subject 2 scored 60 (6–10) on the PPVT and 61 (3–8) on the TACL, showing better understanding of vocabulary than syntax. He showed a slight right-hand preference (23 percent).

Subject 2 displayed normal hearing for speech on the monaural tests. SRT was 5 dB and WDS was 100 percent in each ear.

The results of the SSW and CES tests for Subject 2 are shown in the middle of Figure 2–2. On the SSW test, Subject 2 demonstrated depressed scores in the right-competing condition. The C-SSW scores were in the moderately depressed range, and the A-SSW scores were in the mild range. He showed significant Ear High/Low, Order High/Low (more errors on the first spondee), reversals (change in word order), and Type A pattern (more errors in the right-competing condition for items beginning in the right ear) response biases. Performance on the CES test was good in both ears. These results suggest a dysfunction in the posterior temporal lobe of the left hemisphere (not involving the auditory reception area) and extending anteriorly to the fronto-temporal region. This diagnosis is consistent with both the subject's level of language comprehension and his extreme lack of spontaneous speech.

Subject 3, a 14-year-old male, lived at home and attended a special education class in a junior high school. His language was characterized by a lack of spontaneity (he did not initiate speech) and by the presence of occasional (less than 10 percent of total utterances) immediate and delayed echolalia. He could follow commands requiring nonverbal responses, but generally responded inappropriately to questions requiring verbal responses (i.e., inappropriate use of yes/no; echoed phrases; pronoun reversals; confused word orders). He could read and write at the third grade level. His voice quality was characterized by a monotonous inflection. He often covered his ears with his hands in the absence of any loud external sound. He exhibited some self-stimulatory behavior (i.e., finger flicking and hand flapping), and disruptive behavior (i.e., wrist grabbing and slapping).

On the receptive language tests, Subject 3 scored 59 (6-8) on the PPVT and 67 (4–1) on the TACL. Subject 3 showed a strong right-hand preference (80 percent), however, his parent reported that as a young child, the subject preferred his left hand. (The degree of right-handedness may be influenced by early teaching in manual skills.)

Subject 3 displayed normal hearing for speech on the monaural hearing tests. SRT was 5 dB and WDS was 100 percent in each ear. Because this subject was able to respond reliably to pure tone testing without additional pretraining procedures, air and bone conduction pure tone thresholds were also obtained. His pure tone air conduction thresholds were -10 dB at 250 and 2,000 Hz, and 0 dB at 500, 1,000, 4,000 and 8,000 Hz in the right ear, and 0 dB at all frequencies (250– 8,000 Hz) in the left ear. His pure tone bone conduction thresholds were -10 dB at 250, 1,000 and 2,000 Hz, and 0 dB at 500, 4,000 and 8,000 Hz in the better ear without masking. These pure tone thresholds were consistent with Subject 3's SRT and WDS, and indicate normal peripheral hearing. It is suspected that the other subjects also had normal peripheral hearing.

The results of the SSW and CES tests for Subject 3 are shown at the bottom of Figure 2– 2. On the SSW test, Subject 3 demonstrated depressed scores in the left-competing condition. The C– SSW scores were in the moderately depressed range, and the A– SSW scores were in the mild range. He showed significant Order High/Low, reversals, and Type A pattern (more errors in the left-competing condition for items beginning in the left ear) response biases. He achieved perfect scores for both ears on the CES test. These results may suggest a dysfunction in the temporal lobe of the right hemisphere (not involving the auditory reception area) and extending anteriorly to the fronto-temporal region; or, because of the interconnections of the temporal lobe with deeper structures of the brain, these results may suggest involvement of the corpus callosum/ anterior commissure. Again, this diagnosis is consistent with both the subject's level of language comprehension and his extreme lack of spontaneous speech.

It seems reasonable to assume from his SSW and CES test results that Subject 3 is right dominant for language. His depressed scores in the left ear on the SSW test suggest involvement of the right hemisphere. The SSW test (a verbal task) was moderately depressed in performance, while the CES test (a nonverbal task) was performed without error. It therefore seems likely that the right hemisphere was impaired, and that it was the language-dominant hemisphere for this subject. Additionally, comparing the results of Subjects 2 and 3 reveals that they are very similar, except the depressed scores are in opposite ears. This supports the contention that Subject 3's cerebral lateralization is the reverse of that of Subject 2 and of the more common left lateralization of language.

Subject 3 was retested a third time on the SSW test one year later at the age of 15. The results were essentially the same as the first two tests shown in Figure 2– 2. Corrected SSW percent error scores were 2.5 percent in the right noncompeting condition, 12.5 percent in the right competing condition, 60 percent in the left competing condition, and 0 percent in the left noncompeting condition. He displayed the same response biases and severity of error scores as on the first two tests. The stable performance on the central auditory test over a period of one year may reflect the relatively complete maturation of the brain due to the subject's older age. This stable performance is in contrast to the next subject, who was tested five times over the course of one year at a younger age.

Subject 4, an eight-year-old male, lived at home and attended a special education class while being mainstreamed into a normal first-grade classroom. At the time of this study, he was participating in a one-year clinic treatment program. At the beginning of treatment (Early Treatment), his expressive language consisted of moderately frequent (approximately 15– 20 percent of total utterances) immediate and delayed echolalia, perseverative question asking, and responses inappropriate to context. His academic skills were minimal and he did not interact with other children. He occasionally exhibited self-stimulatory be-havior (i.e., hand flapping). His score was 25 (2–9) on the PPVT at the beginning of treatment.

Over the course of a year, this subject learned to read and write at the first grade level and learned basic first grade math concepts. By the end of treatment (Late Treatment) he played appropriately at a kindergarten/first grade level with children he knew at home and school. He initiated elementary conversations and asked appropriate questions, but often perseverated on particular phrases or topics and talked excessively. He rarely exhibited immediate echolalia, al-though he still evidenced some delayed echolalia. He displayed hand flapping only when he was particularly excited. His language comprehension improved over the year; by the end of treatment his score was 48 (4–11) on the PPVT and 59 (3–6) on the TACL. He showed a moderate righthand preference (50 percent).

On the monaural tests, Subject 4 displayed normal hearing for speech. His SRT was 10 and WDS was 96 percent in each ear.

The results of the SSW and CES tests for Subject 4, who received treatment during this investigation, are shown in Figure 2–3.

The first two tests administered during Early Treatment (Tests 1 and 2 shown at the top of Figure 2–3) showed depressed scores in the right-competing condi-tion, with some improvement from Test 1 to Test 2. (These depressed scores were far poorer than the normal children tested by White (1977), who showed errors up to 35 percent in the competing condition). A depressed right ear score is atypical in children and may be suggestive of a problem in the posterior tem-poral region of the left hemisphere. He showed an Order High/Low response bias on the first two tests, which is commonly found even in children at this age, and may suggest that the anterior part of the brain is not yet fully mature in han-dling SSW material. During Late Treatment (when he showed considerable im-provement in his functional language ability) he was tested three additional times (Tests 3, 4, and 5 shown at the bottom of Figure 2–3). These tests showed improved central auditory function compared to the Early Treatment period. The right-ear scores (the mean of the right competing and noncompeting scores) were well below the Early Treatment level (from a right-ear score of 48 on Test 1 to 18 on Test 5), and there was no response bias on any of these three tests. The Late Treatment SSW results suggest a persisting but milder problem in the posterior left hemisphere and an improvement in anterior cerebral function. The results of the CES comparison with the SSW were consistent with a left hemisphere problem. The suggested improvement in posterior and anterior functioning might be seen as relating to Subject 4's improved verbal com-prehension score (PPVT results) and improved spontaneous speech. That is, he improved in only certain areas of language functioning, and is still functioning overall at a severely impaired level.

Subject 5, an eight-year-old male, lived at home and had been mainstreamed into a normal second-grade classroom. He was *previously* diag-nosed as autistic by the same diagnosticians using the same criteria employed for the other subjects. However, his parents had participated in an extensive

FIGURE 2–3.   Measures of central auditory function: SSW test results for Subject 4, who was assessed over a year of intensive treatment. Corrected SSW percent error scores for the right and left ear competing (C) and noncompeting (NC) conditions for Tests 1 and 2 during Early Treatment and Tests 3, 4, and 5 during Late Treatment. CES percent error scores are shown for the right ear (RE) and left ear (LE). (Wetherby, A., Koegel, R.L., and Mendel, M. In press. "Central Auditory Nervous System Dysfunction in Echolalic Autistic Individuals" *Journal of Speech and Hearing Research.* Copyright by American Speech, Language and Hearing Association. Reprinted by permission.)

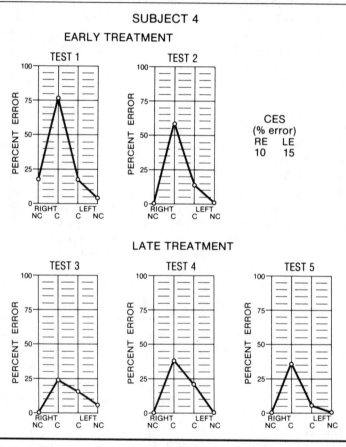

parent-training treatment program when he was three years of age. Prior to treatment, his language consisted of moderately frequent immediate echolalia. At the time of the present tests, his receptive/expressive language abilities and his academic skills were adequate for the second grade. His conversational speech, other than containing some confabulations, was normal. His receptive language abilities were normal for his age as measured by his score of 79 (10– 5) on the PPVT and 96 (6– 11+) on the TACL. (The TACL is standardized for ages 3– 0 to 6– 11; a child older than 6– 11 would be expected to achieve a score close to 101, as did Subject 5). He showed some preference for right-handedness (38 percent).

Subject 5 displayed normal hearing for speech on the monaural tests. His

FIGURE 2–4.   Measures of central auditory function: SSW test results for Subjects 5 and 6 who were previously echolalic, but had received early treatment and had normal language at the time of these tests. Corrected SSW percent error scores for the right and left ear competing (C) and noncompeting (NC) conditions for test and retest. CES percent error scores are shown for the right ear (RE) and left ear (LE). (Wetherby, A., Koegel, R.L., and Mendel, M. In press. "Central Auditory Nervous System Dysfunction in Echolalic Autistic Individuals," *Journal of Speech and Hearing Research.* Copyright by the American Speech, Language and Hearing Association. Reprinted by permission.)

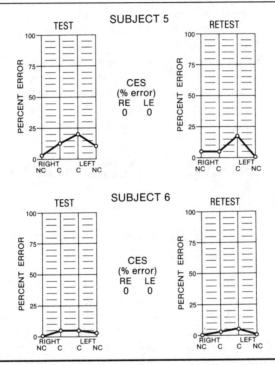

SRT was 10 dB in the right ear and 5 dB in the left ear, and WDS was 100 percent in each ear.

The results of the SSW and CES tests for Subject 5, who had completed extensive treatment in the laboratory (and who no longer evidenced language abnormality) are shown at the top of Figure 2–4.

Subject 5 demonstrated a typical error pattern for an eight-year-old child, with slightly depressed scores in the left-competing condition. The A – SSW scores were within the normal range by adult standards. He showed Order High/Low, reversals, and Type A pattern response biases, which are commonly shown in children and suggest that the fronto-temporal region has not yet fully matured. He achieved perfect scores on the CES test, in addition to the normal SSW results. Thus, his central auditory diagnosis is consistent with his normal language behavior.

Subject 6, a 13-year-old female, lived at home and attended regular seventh-grade classes in junior high school. Similar to Subject 5, she was *previously* diagnosed as autistic by the same diagnosticians using the same criteria employed for the other subjects. Her parents had also participated in an extensive parent-training treatment program beginning when she was five years of age. Prior to treatment, her language consisted of frequent immediate echolalia and perseveration of phrases and questions. At the time of the present tests, she carried on normal (but excessive) conversational speech, talking on and on about topics of special interest to her (i.e., art and history). On the receptive language tests, she performed normal or above normal for her age. On the PPVT her score was 118 (18–0), and on the TACL it was 97 (6 – 11+). She showed a complete preference for right-handedness (100 percent).

Subject 6 showed normal hearing for speech. On the monaural tests her SRT was 5 dB and WDS was 100 percent in each ear.

The results of the SSW and CES tests for Subject 6, who also received extensive treatment in the laboratory and who evidenced normal language function, are shown at the bottom of Figure 2–4. Like Subject 5, she demonstrated normal central auditory function by adult standards on the SSW test, indicated no response bias, and scored perfectly on the CES test.

Implications of Central Auditory Test Results

The major results of the use of the SSW/CES test battery may be summarized as follows:

1. Although all of the subjects had normal hearing on the monaural speech tests, there was reliable indication (from test to retest on the SSW test battery) of central auditory nervous system dysfunction in the language-dominant hemisphere inferred from the dichotic tests for those subjects displaying echolalia, and essentially normal dichotic test results for those subjects who were previously diagnosed autistic but were no longer echolalic.
2. The subject who received a year of intensive language treatment showed improvement in the dichotic test of central auditory function, which appeared to be consistent with the language improvement.
3. The locus of central auditory dysfunction inferred from the assessment measures was consistent with the language deficits for each subject.

Language Abilities and SSW Performance

These results show that performance on the SSW test appears to be related to language ability. This is consistent with the fact that the performance of normal children on the SSW test improves with age and, thus, with language development, reflecting maturation of the anterior auditory processing area (White 1977).

The errors made by our subjects were probably not a result of a general inability to take a test of this nature, because all of the subjects repeated two spondees in a binaural mode. For similar reasons, the poor test results probably do not reflect a short-term memory deficit. Rather, poor test performance seems more likely to have been due to cerebral immaturity (probably impaired development), or cerebral dysfunction of the auditory processing areas. These interpretations seem particularly likely in the subjects over 11 years of age (Subjects 1, 2, 3, and 6). Improvement in Subject 4's test performance may reflect cerebral maturation, or the effects of treatment on abnormal brain functioning, suggesting the possibility of an interaction of neural plasticity and treatment. Further support for such an interaction comes from the results of the two subjects (Subjects 5 and 6) evidencing normal central auditory function. These subjects were previously diagnosed as autistic by the same criteria as the other four subjects, but they had received early treatment and had essentially normal results.

Hemispheric Locus of Dysfunction

Of the other four subjects who evidenced central auditory dysfunction on the dichotic tests, their results were associated with a disturbance at a locus involving one hemisphere or the corpus callosum/anterior commissure. Analysis of the SSW and CES test results indicates a left or language-dominant hemisphere dysfunction in Subjects 1, 2, 3 and 4. Speculation of an underlying neuropathology of the left hemisphere (see Tanguay 1976) has been formulated to explain receptive and expressive language deficiency in autistic children in marked contrast to proficiency in various nonverbal and musical abilities (Applebaum, *et al.* 1979; Lockyer and Rutter 1970). Autistic children tend to show strengths in abilities presumed to be lateralized to the right hemisphere, and weaknesses in left hemisphere functions.

These results support recent evidence of a structural (Hier, LeMay, and Rosenberger 1979; Hauser, DeLong, and Rosman 1975) and functional (Blackstock 1978) abnormality of the left hemisphere in autistic children. A disruption in or a deviation from the normal process of cerebral lateralization (Moscovitch 1977) may account for some autistic features such as abnormal language development and inconsistent responses to sensory stimuli. Furthermore, incomplete right-handedness was evident in most of the subjects. This may be a clinical indicator of early brain pathology. The lack of hand preference is consistent with large-scale studies of handedness in autistic children showing a higher frequency of nonright-handedness in autistics as compared to normals (Boucher 1977; Colby and Parkinson 1977).

Intrahemispheric Locus of Dysfunction

Analysis of the SSW test results indicates that the cortical dysfunction is primarily in or near the region of the anterior motor speech area (Broca's area) in Subjects 2 and 3, and in or near the region of the posterior auditory association area (Wernicke's area) in Subjects 1 and 4. This is particularly interesting because the predominant characteristic of both Subject 2 and Subject 3's language behavior is paucity of spontaneous speech, which is consistent with disturbances of expressive speech associated with anterior lesions acquired in adulthood (Luria 1980; Brown 1972). In contrast, Subjects 1 and 4 showed a more severe language comprehension problem, which is consistent with receptive language problems associated with posterior lesions as their SSW results might imply (Luria 1980; Brown 1972). Furthermore, the lower frequency of echolalia in Subjects 2 and 3 is similar to the nonfluent character of an aphasic with an anterior lesion, while the higher frequency of echolalia in Subjects 1 and 4 resembles the fluent nature of an aphasic with a posterior lesion.

The neurological substrata underlying echolalia in acquired brain damage in adults have previously been discussed as an isolation of the speech area in which Broca's and Wernicke's area and the connecting pathways are at least partially intact and disconnected from higher cortical functions (Geschwind, *et al.,* 1968; Goldstein 1948). Similarly, the underlying mechanism of echolalia in autism may be partial damage in the region of Broca's or Wernicke's area, leading to impaired development of higher cortical association areas.

In contrast to damage incurred in an adult with a fully developed use of language, damage in early infancy prior to language acquisition has a disruptive effect upon the formation of neural systems underlying language (i.e., Luria 1973). In children, complete development of higher cortical function is dependent upon the integrity of the lower areas. It is possible that dysfunction in brainstem nuclei, thalamic nuclei, and/or subcortical structures disrupts the development of higher cortical association areas. Therefore, the results are consistent with speculations that lower areas may be involved (Coleman 1979; Damasio and Maurer 1978; Ornitz 1974). A further implication of this line of thought is that the concommitant effect of treatment and neurological maturation may be instrumental in the recovery process of autism, indicating that treatment intervention is most effective before completion of postnatal development of the brain (i.e., early treatment such as that given to Subjects 5 and 6 in this investigation).

Clinical Application

The SSW test battery appears to be sensitive to cerebral dysfunction in these echolalic autistic children. Preliminary findings support the accumulating evidence of a neurogenic etiology of autism. Future research should be directed at validating the use of this test battery on a larger population of autistic subjects. Use of the SSW test battery was intended for research purposes, and interpretations of the test results presented in this chapter are speculative in nature. It is hoped that this chapter will serve as a stimulus for the systematic study of this area. Continued research in this direction, in conjunction with direct neurological measures, may ultimately lead to the clinical application of these tests with autistic individuals.

A hearing loss in childhood can be detrimental to language development, and the effects of a hearing loss can be particularly dramatic for the autistic child. As with normal children, an autistic child may acquire a conductive hearing loss from infection or trauma to the outer or middle ear, and the identification and treatment is important for learning. The incidence of hearing loss is higher in children with prenatal and perinatal complications (Martin 1978), and should not be overlooked in the autistic child.

However, the results of this research and that conducted in other laboratories suggests that peripheral hearing problems in autistic children may be atypical in contrast to what may be a characteristic central auditory dysfunction. Central auditory dysfunction may be present in spite of normal hearing sensitivity, and will influence the ability to process auditory information. It has been demonstrated how some autistic children have difficulty handling competing messages in the sound-treated booth. The child with central auditory dysfunction will have difficulty attending to and sorting out the relevant auditory stimuli in the classroom with extraneous noise and auditory and visual distractions (Willeford and Billger 1978). Such difficulties may also relate to work in the area of stimulus overselectivity (see Chapter 6). The use of operant teaching techniques described in other chapters may facilitate the remediation of auditory processing difficulties of autistic children. Techniques such as gaining the child's attention before presenting stimuli, using clear, simple auditory stimuli, and systematic teaching and data collection to assure that the child is learning the relevant auditory stimulus may be especially important.

Application of the SSW test to differentiating subgroups of echolalic autistic children (i.e., anterior versus posterior dysfunction) may also lead to more effective language intervention programs. While autistic children show problems in both receptive and expressive language, a systematic assessment from auditory input to verbal output may help to elucidate the nature of the language breakdown. The SSW test battery is a useful diagnostic tool in differentiating two patterns of language breakdown. Expressive language problems of autistic children may be primarily associated with an anterior dysfunction leading to a lack of initiation of speech, or a posterior dysfunction disrupting language comprehension and leaving speech fluent but not necessarily meaningful. Language intervention should be based on the nature of the language breakdown.

Koegel and Schreibman (1976) suggested that the lack of speech development in nonverbal autistic children may be a function of their inconsistent response to auditory stimuli. If the failure to develop verbal language is due to difficulties in auditory processing of speech, it may be beneficial to capitalize on the child's optimal modality for language intervention. For example, sign language may be used to facilitate speech, as an alternative system of communication (see Chapter 9), or to attempt to remediate the processing problem (especially in younger children). Before devising a language intervention program for the autistic child, it is recommended that a complete audiological assessment is obtained to help identify the precise nature of the language breakdown.

Note_____

This research was supported by U.S. Public Health Research Grant No. MH 28210 from the National Institute of Mental Health and by U.S. Office of Education Research Grant No. G007802084 from the Bureau of Education for the Handicapped. The authors would like to extend special thanks to Dr. Jack Katz for interpretation of the SSW test results and for his comments and review of the manuscript, and to Dr. Maurice Mendel for his valuable assistance. Special thanks to Glen Dunlap, Andrew Egel, Julie Lozow, and Mary Ann Van Voorhis for assisting with the pretraining.

Vision Testing

T he large majority of severely retarded and psychotic children never receive adequate vision screening. When such children are suspected of having a loss in visual acuity (the ability to discriminate small spatial separations), they are generally referred for evaluation by "objective" methods. In an objective evaluation, each eye is examined with a retinoscope and a gross estimate of acuity is made, based on the apparent refractive properties of the eye. More accurate measurements of acuity can be obtained only in a "subjective" evaluation, in which the child looks at a standard set of stimuli and indicates their discriminability by naming them (e.g., the letters on the Snellen chart or the pictures on the Kindergarten chart) or by indicating their orientations (e.g., the Snellen Es on the Illiterate E chart). However, commonly used subjective acuity tests for children (reviewed by Macht 1971; Hirsch 1963) require the comprehension of verbal instructions and the reliable reporting of perceptions. These are skills that severely developmentally disabled children do not have as a result of their minimal or nonexistent proficiency in language. In addition, it is often difficult to motivate such children to participate in test procedures long enough to obtain conclusive results.

One successful approach to the measurement of visual acuity in nonverbal children is based on operant conditioning. Noting that researchers in animal psychophysics (see Stebbins 1970) have been measuring vision in nonverbal organisms for some years, Macht (1971; 1970) devised a successive discrimination

*This chapter was authored by **Crighton D. Newsom**, The May Institute for Autistic Children, and **Karen M. Simon**, University of Pennsylvania.*

This chapter appeared originally as "A Simultaneous Discrimination Procedure for the Measurement of Vision in Nonverbal Children," *Journal of Applied Behavior Analysis*, 1977, 10, 633–644. Copyright by Society for the Experimental Analysis of Behavior. Reprinted with permission.

procedure for use with nonverbal retarded and brain-damaged children. The children were taught to discriminate left- and right-facing Snellen Es through the reinforcement of bar-press responses when one orientation was presented and the extinction of responses when the other orientation was shown. By systematically varying the sizes of the stimuli and the distance between the child and the stimuli, Macht was able to obtain accurate, reliable thresholds from four previously untestable children in 6.8 to 106 hours of training and testing.

The present study describes a different operant procedure for measuring subjective visual acuity thresholds in nonverbal children, suggested by Blough's (1971) method for measuring distance acuity in pigeons. First, a simultaneous (choice) discrimination paradigm was used in training and testing because basic research with normal and retarded children indicates that simultaneous discriminations are learned more rapidly than successive discriminations when the stimuli are similar (Horowitz 1965; Lipsett 1961; Loess and Duncan 1952). Second, a graduated stimulus change, or fading, procedure was used to teach a discrimination between Snellen Es differing in vertical-horizontal orientation, since fading procedures have successfully taught other orientation discriminations to retarded and psychotic children (Schreibman 1975; Macht 1971; Touchette 1971). Third, a limit of 4 hours was imposed on the total time devoted to training and testing, since the ultimate goal of this research program was to develop a vision test for low-functioning children that would approach maximum efficiency. Fourth, equipment was kept to a minimum in an effort to make the procedure usable in virtually any setting. Only the stimulus cards were specially made; the additional equipment (tables, chairs, and a blackboard) is readily available in institutions and schools. Finally, only children with primary diagnoses of autism or childhood schizophrenia were studied. Such children are often suspected at some time in their lives to suffer from sensory deficits, yet there are apparently no previous reports describing the successful measurement of their subjective visual acuity.

Method

Subjects

Nine autistic and schizophrenic children were selected on the basis of their availability for testing from the nonverbal residents of the Children's Treatment Center of Camarillo State Hospital. Two additional autistic children were referred from the Santa Barbara County Autism Project. The children's chronological ages ranged from 5 years seven months to 16 years; their mental ages, as recorded in their records, ranged from untestable to 5 years nine months. Seven of the children were mute or made only unintelligible vocalizations; four (Dana, Debbie, Ruth, Melissa) used a few one- or two-word requests. All of the children responded appropriately to very simple instructions (e.g., "sit down," "hands quiet"), but none reliably responded to more complex commands. All but Harry were toilet trained. None played appropriately with toys or engaged in age-

TABLE 3–1 Subject Characteristics

Name[a]	Sex	CA	MA[b]	Diagnosis
Ben	M	10-6	5-9	Autism
Dana	F	5-7	3-5	Autism
Debbie	F	13-1	4-5	Schizophrenia
Mickey	M	11-3	4-2	Autism
Denny	M	16-0	2-10	Schizophrenia
Ruth	F	11-2	2-3	Schizophrenia
Mac	M	10-10	4-3	Autism
Melissa	F	8-9	2-5	Schizophrenia
Harry	M	14-5	U[c]	Autism
Jack	M	10-0	U	Schizophrenia
Brandon	M	9-1	1-9	Schizophrenia

[a]Fictitious
[b]Peabody Picture Vocabulary Test
[c]Untestable, i.e., unable to achieve a basal MA of 1-9.

appropriate social interactions with peers or adults. All but Dana and Mickey exhibited considerable repetitive, stereotyped, self-stimulatory behavior in unstructured situations. One boy, Denny, engaged in severe head-banging episodes three to six times a week on his home unit, where they were being treated with some success with contingent timeout. Mac had been found by EEG audiometry to have a severe binaural hearing loss. There were no reports of either objective or subjective visual acuity examinations in any of the children's records. All the hospitalized children were given brief peripheral ocular examinations during their yearly medical evaluations, but no ocular pathologies were noted in the records and none of the children wore glasses. The children serving as experimental subjects are listed and characterized in Table 3-1.

To determine the validity of the experimental procedure, four additional children from the Center were tested with both the experimental stimuli and an American Optical Company Illiterate E Chart. These children were diagnosed with one of the behavior disorders of childhood (e.g., unsocialized aggressive reaction, overanxious reaction), and their chronological ages ranged from 10 years eight months to 15 years. All had IQs in the dull normal to normal range and were normal language users. None had been prescribed glasses and all had passed vision screenings at a level of 20/20 during annual medical examinations.

Equipment

Two sets of stimulus cards were constructed with white poster board and ink. One set (the training cards) was used for training a discrimination between a Snellen E whose prongs pointed down (S+) and one whose prongs pointed left (S−) from the child's viewpoint. The other set (the test cards) was used for measuring the acuity threshold. All cards were 16 cm square and were covered with transparent Contact Paper. Figure 3–1 illustrates selected pairs of training and test cards.

Two S+ cards were used in training the E discrimination. The first had three 159.6- by 31.9-mm vertical black stripes and served as S+ in all training steps

FIGURE 3–1. Representative stimulus cards showing the sequence of steps (from left to right) used in training and testing.

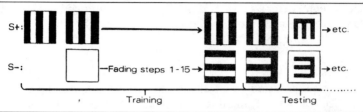

except the last. The other S+ card bore a downward-pointing Snellen E with 159.6- by 31.9-mm segments. It was used in the last training step and also served as the first S+ test card. Eighteen S− cards were used in training. They included (a) one blank card; (b) 16 cards with three 159.6- by 31.9-mm stripes, which decreased in brightness across cards from very light gray to fully black; and (c) one card bearing a leftward-pointing black Snellen E with 159.6- by 31.9-mm segments, which also served as the first S− test card.

There were 16 pairs of test cards, each pair bearing black Snellen Es of the same size but different in orientation. On the 16 S+ cards, the Es pointed down; on the 16 S− cards, the Es pointed to the left. The widths of the segments and spaces of each E in a given pair were equal and subtended 1 minute of visual angle in the "normal" eye at a distance in feet specified in the denominator of the Snellen acuity ratio corresponding to the test letter. The following formula, derived from one given by Riggs (1971), was used to calculate these widths: segment width (in mm) = distance from stimulus to subject as specified in the Snellen ratio denominator (in mm) × 0.0002908 (the tangent of 1 minute of visual angle). For example, the widths of the segments and spaces in the 20/30 E were found by multiplying 9144 mm (= 30 ft) by 0.0002908, which equals 2.7 mm after rounding off. The overall size of a Snellen test letter is found by constructing an imaginary square whose sides are five times the width of each segment. Thus, the size of the 20/30 E was 13.5 mm² (= 2.7 × 5), and the sizes of the Es on each pair of test cards may be similarly calculated with reference to one of the right-hand ordinates in Figure 3-2. The numerator in the Snellen ratio specifies the stimulus-to-subject distance in the test situation. This distance was always 6.1 m in the present study, as is standard in clinical acuity evaluations. Acuity ratios will be referred to in English rather than metric notation throughout this chapter, since that convention is still current and familiar.

The room used for training and testing was 7.3 by 3.4 m in size. Against the wall at one end stood a large easel-type blackboard, 1.2 m wide and 1.9 m high. Its chalk tray, used to display the stimulus cards, was 0.93 m from the floor. Four tables, each 1.5 by 0.74 m, were arranged in the form of a T: three tables placed end to end joined one table placed crosswise at the stimulus display end of the room, 0.83 m from the front of the blackboard. Thus, the tables formed a barrier down the middle of the room, creating a passageway on either side for the child to approach the blackboard. An adult experimenter sat at the middle of the table at the top of the T to conduct the procedure and record data. The child sat at the opposite end of the tables (the bottom of the T), 6.1 m from the blackboard. The room was illuminated by fluorescent lamps mounted in the ceiling. The illumination of the stimulus cards was 107.6 1× (as measured with a Sekonic L–28c incident light meter), a level within the range recommended for vision screening (National Society for the Prevention of Blindness 1971).

Procedure

Trials were conducted identically in the training and test phases as follows. The adult placed a pair of stimulus cards on the chalk tray of the blackboard, one at each end, then looked at the seated child and said, "*(name),* look at the cards." When satisfied that the child had looked at both of the cards, the adult commanded: "Come touch the correct card," or simply, "Come get it." The child stood up and began walking down one of the passageways toward a card. If the side chosen was correct, the adult praised the child as he/she approached and delivered an edible reinforcer (an M&M, a sip of soda, or a bite of ice cream) when he/she arrived and touched the card. If the wrong side was chosen the adult said: "No — wrong one; go sit down," as soon as the child had clearly entered the wrong passageway. While the child returned to the seat, the adult removed the cards. The cards for the next trial were not displayed until the child was seated again at the full test distance. The left-right position of the correct card was determined by a Fellows (1968) order.

Training phase.   Initially, the experimenter placed only the first, vertically striped S+ card on the chalk tray on each trial until the child readily came to the correct side on two successive unprompted trials (During the first two or three trials with some children, an assistant manually prompted the child to stand up and start walking toward the correct card when the experimenter commanded an approach.) The S+ card was then paired with the blank S− card until the child chose the S+ card on two successive trials, once on each side. At this point, the program for fading in the horizontal stripes on the S− cards began. The S− card with the lightest horizontal stripes was presented with the S+ card; if the child made the correct choice, the S− card with the next-darkest horizontal stripes was presented with the S+ card, and so on. As long as correct choices were made, S− cards with successively darker stripes continued to be presented at the rate of one brightness step after each correct response. When the child made an incorrect choice, the fading program stopped and remained at the brightness step at which the error occurred until the child made five correct choices in a row. Superimposed on this "program stop" procedure was a correction procedure: after each error, the left-right arrangement of the cards was repeated on the following trial and succeeding trials until a correct response was made, whereupon the Fellows order resumed. The purpose of the correction procedure was to eliminate the possibility that the child would adopt a strategy of always going to one side and thus obtain at least 50 percent of the reinforcements without learning the discrimination. If the child could not make five correct choices in a row within 15 trials, he/she was returned to the beginning of the training program. Three such restarts were allowed before the training procedure was considered inadequate for a given child and training efforts ended. After the child made five correct responses in a row within 15 trials, the regular fading program resumed at the rate of one step per correct response. When the child reached the next-to-last fading step (16: fully black S− stripes), five successive correct responses were again required to ensure that the terminal vertical-horizontal discrimination was well learned.

The last manipulation in the training phase was the conversion of the vertical and horizontal stripes to a downward-pointing Snellen E and a leftward-pointing Snellen E, respectively. This was done in Step 17 by substituting the 20/360 S+ test card for the first S+ training card and the 20/360 S− test card for the last S− training card. Once again the child was required to make five successive correct choices in 15 trails before continuing into the test phase.

Test phase. Testing began immediately after the child met criterion on Step 17 of training. Starting with the 20/360 cards, pairs of test cards with progressively smaller Es were presented until an error was made. When an error occurred, the child was given seven additional trials at that size to make five consecutive correct choices (a "criterion run"). If he/she did so, the next smaller pair of Es was presented, and the child was again required to make five consecutive correct choices. If the child failed to make a criterion run, the experimenter presented the next larger Es and again required a criterion run before continuing. Thus, the commission of the first error in the test phase changed the rate at which the size of the Es could be changed. After the first error, all movements — either forward to smaller Es or backward to larger Es — required that the child pass or fail the criterion of five successive correct choices in eight trials. It was not necessary that all eight trials be completed; as soon as the five consecutive correct trials were completed, or as soon as it became impossible to satisfy the criterion by making an error on the fourth or any later trial, the change to the next smaller or larger size was made. The test phase continued until the child's trial-by-trial record showed a regular oscillation between sizes only one step apart, achieved by alternating three criterion runs at a given size with failures to meet criterion at the next smaller size. The acuity ratio corresponding to the size at which the three successful criterion runs occurred was considered to be the child's subjective binocular distance acuity.

Each session lasted a variable number of trials (26 to 96) and a correspondingly variable length of time (30 to 90 minutes). The basis for terminating a session was the experimenter's judgement that the child's motivation was waning, as indicated by increasing delays in approaching the stimulus display and slowness in consuming reinforcers. Sessions were conducted one to seven days apart, late in the afternoon just before the child's dinner. No reliability checks were made, since the choice of one passageway or the other was unmistakable.

Validity assessment. Each of the four nonpsychotic children was tested with the experimental procedure in the same manner as the other children, with two major exceptions. The E discrimination was established by instruction, using the 20/360 cards, and the indicator response was an exaggerated pointing movement of the arm and hand. Following threshold determination with the experimental procedure, the children were tested with the Illiterate E chart. For two children, testing with the chart was conducted by the experimenter, who instructed each child to point in the directions of the Es in each line of figures, until one or more errors occurred. The line on which the first error occurred and the lines immediately above and below it were each presented at least two more times. The acuity ratio corresponding to the line at which no errors occurred over three presentations was considered the child's threshold for validity purposes. The two remaining children were referred for a binocular acuity assessment by the Center's pediatrician, who was not informed of the experimental reason for the referral. She routinely used the Illiterate E chart in conducting vision screenings.

Results

Every child learned to approach the S+ card when it was presented alone and when it was paired with the blank S− card within seven trials at the start of training. Of the 11 children observed, eight were successfully trained and tested, four within a single session. Three children failed to learn the vertical-horizontal stripe discrimination during four training attempts and consequently were not tested.

Figures 3-2 and 3-3 show each tested child's progress through the fading program and the vision test. Figure 3-2 shows that Ben, Dana, Debbie, and Mickey learned the vertical-horizontal E discrimination and were successfully tested in one session. Ben's progress through the training phase was errorless, and Dana, Debbie, and Mickey made only one to three errors in learning the orientation discrimination. During the vision test phase, these children correctly discriminated progressively smaller Es until they made errors at a size that was one or two sizes smaller than their eventual thresholds. Each child failed to advance beyond the point of his/her first error because an additional error was made on the fourth trial (Ben, Debbie, Mickey) or on the sixth trial (Dana). When Debbie was backed up to the next larger E size, she immediately began a series of three criterion runs separated by failures to satisfy the criterion at the next smaller size. The acuity ratio corresponding to the size at which she made the criterion runs was 20/15. Ben, Dana, and Mickey each backed up two sizes before beginning the criterion runs that would establish their acuity ratios. Ben and Mickey, like Debbie, had excellent vision, i.e., 20/15. Dana's acuity ratio was 20/50, which is significantly worse than the mean acuity of children her age (20/30), according to Weymouth (1963).

The bottom panel of Figure 3-2 shows the results for Denny, who was trained and tested in two sessions. Denny learned the E discrimination with three errors, and during initial testing progressed down to the E size that would later be established as his threshold. At this point, however, a temporary breakdown in stimulus control occurred; Denny was unable to make a criterion run until he was returned all the way back to the largest Es. When the test phase was repeated the following day, Denny produced a threshold curve indicating a seri-

FIGURE 3–2.   Performance during training and test phases of Ben, Dana, Debbie, Mickey, and Denny. (The left ordinate indicates fading steps; the right ordinate indicates the sizes of the test Es in terms of the denominations of their acutiy ratios. The horizontal segments of each curve represent correct choices and dots represent incorrect choices. A single vertical line separates phases conducted within a session; double vertical lines separate sessions.)

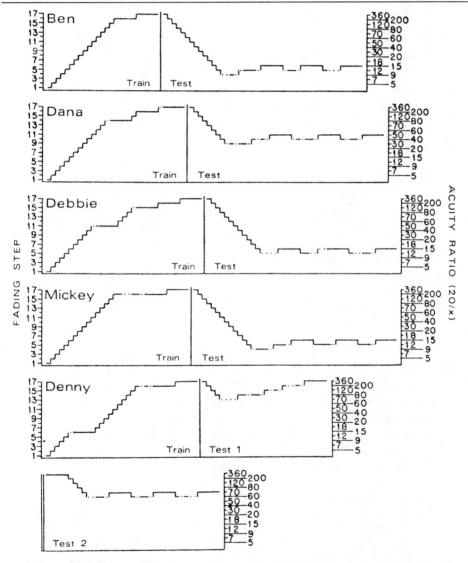

ous vision impairment; his acuity ratio was 20/70. (Mean acuity of children 12 years and older is 20/20 [Weymouth 1963]).

Figure 3-3 shows that Ruth, like Ben, learned the E discrimination errorlessly. During the test phase, she worked down to an E size near her threshold before making an error. She immediately satisfied the criterion for continuing to

FIGURE 3–3.   Performance during training and test phases of Ruth, Mac, and Melissa.

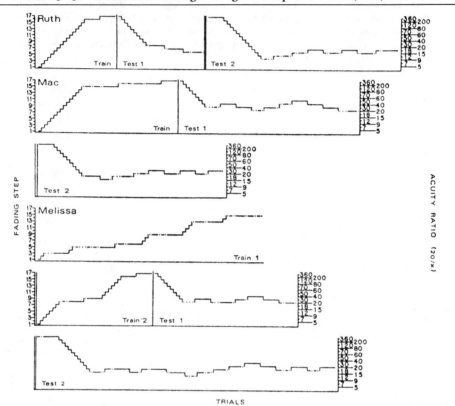

TRIALS

the next smaller size, where she again made one error followed by five correct choices. At the 20/15 size, she failed to make a criterion run, and testing was terminated because she appeared satiated. In the following session (Test 2), she made consecutive correct choices until she overshot her threshold, then backed up and produced the curve that established her visual acuity as 20/18.

Mac and Melissa (Figure 3-3) were more difficult to train and to test than the other successful children. Mac progressed easily through the fading program until he reached Step 15, the darkest gray S– stripes; he had considerable difficulty making a criterion run at this step and at Step 16, the fully black S– stripes. In his first vision test, Mac moved down to the E size of his eventual threshold (20/30) before making an error, and subsequently moved back and forth around this size, but failed to satisfy requirements for establishing an acuity threshold. During the next session, Mac's test performance was once again erratic at the beginning, but stabilized during the second half of the session and resulted in the curve establishing his acuity at 20/30.

The entire first session with Melissa was devoted to training (Figure 3-3). Numerous errors resulted in program stops at six steps, ending at Step 15. In the second session, Melissa was started at the beginning of the training procedure once more. This time she succeeded in mastering the orientation discrimination after making mistakes at only two steps. Vision testing began during the same session, but because she failed to satisfy the threshold-determination requirement she was tested again during a third session. This time, she eventually made a series of choices that resulted in a satisfactory threshold curve, with a corresponding acuity ratio of 20/20.

FIGURE 3–4. Performance during training phases of Harry, Jack, and Brandon.

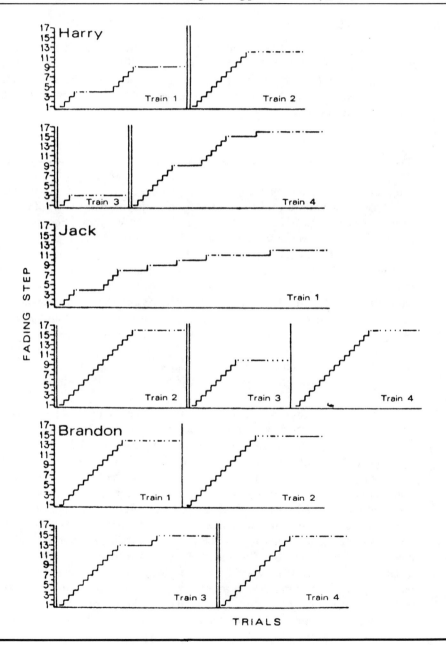

TRIALS

Figure 3-4 shows that we failed to teach the orientation discrimination to Harry, Jack, and Brandon using the fading program in four attempts with each boy. Harry and Jack both advanced to the penultimate step (16), but neither was able to make five correct choices in a row in the allotted 15 trials. Brandon progressed to Step 15 in each of his three final attempts, but was never able to move beyond that step to the terminal discrimination.

Validity Measures

Each of the four nonpsychotic children tested with the Illiterate E chart achieved an acuity ratio of 20/15 in the experimental procedure. Two of these children were tested with the chart by the experimenter and achieved ratios of 20/15 and 20/20. The two who were examined by the pediatrician were reported to have ratios of 20/20 and 20/30.

Discussion

Subjective visual acuity thresholds can be obtained from many nonverbal, severely psychotic children relatively rapidly and inexpensively. Each of the autistic and schizophrenic children who were successfully examined required a total of 1 to 3 hours to be trained and tested. The present experimental procedure made possible the measurement of significant acuity impairments in two children whose subnormal vision was previously unsuspected. These two children were referred for opthalmic evaluations. Denny, the self-destructive boy, was found to have a lesion 1 by 3 mm in size in the central posterior lens capsule of each eye. Corrective lenses of −3.00 diopters were prescribed and worn successfully in situations where he could be closely supervised. The opthalmologist who examined Dana, the 5-year-old-girl, found no structural abnormalities, but suggested that she be given preferential seating in school and be examined regularly so that glasses can be prescribed if her vision fails to improve as she matures.

The three children who failed to learn the vertical-horizontal discrimination were apparently victims of our fading procedure, which required a shift in stimulus control from stimulus intensity to stimulus orientation. By the fourth training attempt, each child's stimulus control breakdown occurred very late in the fading progression, either at the step constituting the final stripe discrimination (Harry, Jack) or at the step just before it (Brandon). The locations of these disruptions coincided with the elimination of the difference in intensity between the S+ and S− stripes, suggesting that the boys' choices were controlled by the intensity dimension to such an extent that they never came under the additional control of the orientation dimension. Several investigators (Sutherland and Mackintosh 1971; Touchette 1971; Ray and Sidman 1970; Schusterman 1967) have suggested that stimulus control of a response by two stimuli must exist simultaneously at some point during fading if control is to shift from one stimulus to another. Fields, Bruno, and Keller (1976) demonstrated such simultaneous control before successful shifts in stimulus control in pigeons. It may be significant that the three children whose choices failed to transfer from intensity to orientation were the lowest-functioning children in the study (see Table 3-1). Schover and Newsom (1976) found that the tendency of both psychotic and normal children to attend to one dimension of a stimulus overselectively, or to the exclusion of other relevant dimensions, increases as developmental level decreases. Other failures in transferring stimulus control with developmentally disabled children have been reported by Koegel and Rincover (1976), Schreibman (1975), Sidman and Stoddard (1966), and Touchette (1971). These failures highlight the continuing need for the development of more effective discrimination training procedures for this population.

The validity assessment showed that acuity ratios obtained with the present procedure are acceptably close to those obtained with the Illiterate E chart. In three of the four cases, the experimental procedure yielded slightly lower thresholds, and these discrepancies may have occurred for one or more of the following reasons. First, it is known that measurement with stimuli differing in only two orientations results in somewhat lower acuity thresholds than does measurement with letters in four orientations like those on the Illiterate E chart (Emsley 1948). Second, the contrasts between the letters and backgrounds of the experimental stimuli (as measured with a Macbeth illuminometer) ranged from 94 to 97 percent, slightly yet discriminably greater than those of the stimuli on the Illiterate E chart (90 to 94 percent). Third, it is known that visual acuity can be improved through training (e.g., Province and Enoch 1975; Cornsweet and Crane 1973), and Rosenberger (1970) noted that tracking procedures can function like fading programs to shape progressively finer discriminations. The present study does not allow a conclusion regarding the extent to which these factors may have been responsible for the lowered thresholds of three of the four nonpsychotic subjects in the experimental procedure. However, the tendency of the present procedure slightly to overestimate a child's acuity seems a negligible risk when the alternative may be no estimate at all.

The present study, along with Macht's (1971), represents the beginning of a technology for the measurement of subjective vision in nonverbal retarded and psychotic children. The present findings are particularly significant with regard to autistic children, a population whose "apparent sensory deficits" often raise the first suspicions of abnormality by parents (Lovaas and Newsom 1976). Clearly, it is important to develop rapid, accurate procedures that will separate actual deficits from such "apparent" deficits (i.e., those due to orienting and attentional abnormalities) so that appropriate diagnostic and treatment decisions can be made.

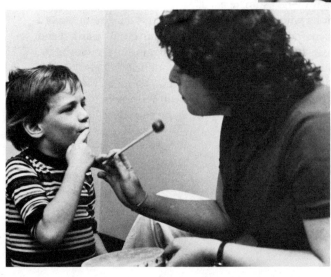

Selection of Initial Words for Speech Training with Nonverbal Children

K anner (1943) reported that a distinctive characteristic of autistic children was their failure to use language for the purpose of communication. In fact, many autistic children fail to develop speech altogether. In a follow-up study of 63 autistic children of nine years or older, seen at Johns Hopkins Hospital for at least four years, Eisenberg (1956) concluded that the degree of disturbance in language function clearly emerged as an important indicator of prognosis. He reported, "In the absence of speech, the probability of emergence is vanishingly small, apparently without regard to which of the currently available treatment methods are employed."

Somewhat later, Hewett (1965) and Lovaas, *et al.* (1966) systematically applied operant conditioning procedures to teach imitative speech to mute autistic children. Since then, a *moderate* number of studies have utilized operant conditioning procedures to teach speech to nonverbal children (e.g., Marshall and Hegrenes 1970; Schell, Stark, and Giddan 1969; Fineman 1968; Lovaas 1968; MacAulay 1968; Nelson and Evans 1968; Sloane, Johnston, and Harris 1968; Kerr, Meyerson, and Michael 1965).

Such studies provided the first systematic and empirically measurable speech improvements, and, therefore, some hope regarding establishment of speech in nonverbal autistic children. Nevertheless, these procedures frequently produce very gradual improvement, particularly in the beginning. For example, Lovaas, *et al.* (1966) reported sessions conducted six days per week, seven hours per day, for two weeks in order to teach the first two words. It is quite likely that such difficulties play a major role in the overall pessimism regarding the prognosis for teaching nonverbal children to talk (cf., Rincover and Koegel 1977;

This chapter was authored by **Robert L. Koegel,** *University of California, Santa Barbara and* **Jan Traphagen,** *Santa Barbara County Schools.*

Lovaas, *et al.* 1973). It is interesting to note, however, that the major slowness appears restricted to teaching the production of the first few words. Rapidly thereafter most studies report being able to teach both speech production and word meaning at rates as high as 15 or more words per day (e.g., Lovaas 1977).

It is possible, however, that a systematic selection of the first words taught might provide some help in overcoming the initial slowness. Those studies which provided systematic procedural steps utilized a variety of different criteria for the selection of words used in initial speech training. Hewett's (1965) rationale for selecting the word "go" as the initial word to teach an autistic child was that, "It denoted action and would lend itself to meaningful transfer." Other studies (Schell, *et al.* 1969; MacAulay 1968; Sloane, *et al.* 1968) did not emphasize selection criteria for initial words, but suggested that some type of criterion might be useful. Lovaas, *et al.* (1966) suggested three useful criteria for selecting vocal sounds that the child may readily learn: (1) that vocal sounds be selected that can be prompted by manually moving the child through the sound; (2) that selection of words or sounds be centered on their concomitant visual components; and (3) that those words or sounds that the child already can use (those most frequently used) be selected for training. However, no method for systematically selecting words for initial speech training was suggested.

The intent of the present study was to explore the value of systematically evaluating the autistic child's pretreatment vocalization repertoire for the presence of phonemes (or close approximations), and to utilize the information obtained in the selection of words used in initial remediation. It is hoped that systematic selection criteria might increase the rate at which the production of the important first few words might be taught, and further, that such an improvement might favorably affect therapist morale. The experiment described below describes a method for significantly improving both of these aspects.

Subjects

Two children were selected for participation in the study on the basis of the following criteria: (1) they had a primary diagnosis of childhood autism; (2) they appeared to produce vocalizations primarily for the intent of auditory self-stimulation and not to communicate a desire or need; and (3) they had never been reported to exhibit any recognizable speech. Child I was a 7–1/2-year-old boy who was enrolled in an autism classroom in a southern California elementary school. He attended school four hours per day, five days per week, along with three other autisticlike children. His classroom functioning was at the "preacademic" level and tasks included simple classification of clothing, food and toys, tracing of shapes and completion of eight piece puzzles. His receptive language level was 2–1/2 years, as measured by the Peabody Picture Vocabulary Test (PPVT). Receptive language skills included comprehension of nouns commonly found in the classroom and home environment, simple commands, and body parts. His autisticlike mannerisms were characterized by hand flapping, twirling of pencils or string in front of his eyes, visual preoccupation with inanimate objects, and tantrums.

Child II was a 9-years-11-month-old boy who was continuously institutionalized in a California state hospital for the past four years. He attended the hospital school four hours per day, five days per week. He was scored "untestable" on standardized IQ tests and was placed in the school's "prekindergarten" classroom with five other autisticlike children. His classroom activities included matching and sorting tasks. Receptive language skills were limited to approximately 30 nouns, and the following of simple commands such as "come here," "sit down," "give me." His autisticlike mannerisms were characterized by stereotyped rocking, humming, hand flapping, twirling string or pieces of paper in front of his eyes, visual preoccupation with inanimate objects, toe walking, and tantrums.

Therapists

Therapist I was Child I's autism classroom teacher, and Therapist II (for Child II) was employed by the state hospital as a speech and language specialist. The therapists' aides acted as recorders for this study. Neither the therapists nor the recorders were informed of the experimental conditions of the study; they were merely asked to teach certain specified words to the children.

In addition to their formal academic training, all of the therapists and recorders attended a five-day workshop conducted by the Santa Barbara Autism Classroom Dissemination Project. The workshop was based upon the procedures outlined by Koegel, Russo and Rincover (1977) and Schreibman and Koegel (1981), and focused on (1) contingency management, (2) "discrete trial" teaching techniques, which included behavior modification procedures of reinforcement, punishment, prompting, shaping, chaining, etc., and (3) methods of data collection and data-based teaching evaluation. The therapists and recorders observed live demonstrations (with other children) of appropriate teaching procedures, supplemented by actual supervised practice with those children. (Chapter 11 presents a detailed description of this procedure.)

Child I received treatment in a 15' × 15' partitioned area in his classroom at the elementary school. Three elementary-size chairs, a table, an adult desk and chair, and an enclosed cabinet to hold instructional material were present. During treatment sessions, Child I sat with his back to the partition and Therapist I sat opposite the child. The reliability recorder sat slightly behind and to the left, with a clear view of the child's face. Child II received treatment in a small (approximately 10' × 20') room designated at the hospital for clinical speech and language remediation. The room was equipped with three chairs, a desk, and an enclosed portable cabinet and shelves for instructional materials. During the treatment session, Child II sat opposite the therapist. The recorder sat slightly behind and to the left, with the child's face easily visible.

A modified within-subject reversal design was employed. In one condition, the therapists attempted to teach words constructed from those phonemes that were *within the child's pretreatment vocalization repertoire;* in the other condition, the words were composed of phonemes *not* in the child's pretreatment repertoire. The independent variable was the source of the phonemes utilized to construct the target words.

The major dependent variables in this study were: (a) the number of trials required to establish each phoneme and phoneme combination under imitative control, (b) the highest step reached in the treatment program within a maximum of six weeks, and (c) the therapists' attitudes toward teaching the children.

Assessment Procedures

Pretreatment Phoneme Repertoire Assessment

Previous to any selection of phonemes for the construction of the words to be taught in the treatment program, the following assessment procedures were conducted.

1. A recorded spontaneous vocalization sample consisting of thirty minutes of the child's vocalizations was obtained. Preceding the collection of the sample, the child's parents and teachers were asked to record on a sheet of paper, for a week, the occasions and situations where the child vocalized most often. If the child did not produce vocalizations for any period exceeding three minutes, an object or a replaying of previous vocalizations was provided to stimulate vocalizations. Fifteen one-minute random segments of the spontaneous speech sound sample were transcribed using the International Phonetic Alphabet (IPA). Each English phoneme or approximation to a phoneme recorded was analyzed by phonetic position, releasing or arresting position, and the frequency of occurrence of each phoneme was calculated (see Table 4–1).

2. The experimenter originated a consonant imitation test consisting of the following phonemes: /p, b, t, d, k, g, m, n, f, v, s, z, r, l, ʃ, tʃ/. It tested each consonant in the releasing (initiating a syllable) and arresting (ending a syllable) positions, with a closed front vowel /i/ (e), and an opened back vowel /a/ (a). Each phoneme was presented three times consecutively for the subject to imitate and was recorded as either being imitated correctly (X) or incorrectly (O). During assessment, the experimenter reinforced behaviors other than the phonemes, such as appropriate sitting or eye contact on a variable ratio schedule (on the average, one reinforced behavior for every three presentations of the testing stimulus.)

3. The experimenter also originated a vowel imitation test. The test consisted of the following vowels and dipthongs: /i, I, E, e, ə, æ, u, ʊ, o, ɔ, a, aI, aʊ, ɔI, ɝ/, which were tested in isolation. The same procedures were followed as in the consonant imitation test.

Construction of the Target Words

Three target words were constructed for Child I, and four target words were constructed for Child II from the types defined below.

TABLE 4-1	Pretreatment Phoneme Repertoire

CHILD 1

	SPONTANEOUS SAMPLE (FREQUENCY OF OCCURRENCE)		IMITATIVE SAMPLE (% OCCURRENCE)			
			w/ /i/		w/ /a/	
Consonants	Releasing	Arresting	Releasing	Arresting	Releasing	Arresting
p	7	0	33	0	0	0
b	159	1	33	0	66	0
t	2	0	33	0	0	0
d	1	0	33	33	66	0
k	21	0	0	0	33	0
g	211	1	100	0	66	33
f	0	0	0	0	0	0
v	0	0	0	0	33	0
s	0	0	0	0	0	0
z	0	0	0	0	0	0
m	125	0	66	0	66	0
n	5	0	0	0	33	0
l	25	0	66	0	100	0
r	0	0	0	0	0	0
ʃ	0	0	0	0	0	0
tʃ	0	0	0	0	0	0
w	4	0	33	0	33	33
j	9	0				

CHILD 1

	SPONTANEOUS SAMPLE (FREQUENCY OF OCCURRENCE)		IMITATIVE SAMPLE (% OCCURRENCE)
Vowels	Pre-Consonant	Post-Consonant	In Isolation
i	3	144	100
I	0	0	66
e		1	0
ɛ	0	0	33
æ	0	0	66
u	4	38	100
ʊ	2	79	0
o	5	53	33
ɔ	0	0	33
a	7	126	33
ə	28	111	66
aɪ	1	4	0
aʊ	1	1	0
ɔɪ	0	1	0
ɚ	0	1	0

CHILD 2

| | SPONTANEOUS SAMPLE (FREQUENCY OF OCCURRENCE) | | IMITATIVE SAMPLE (% OCCURRENCE) | | | |
| | | | w/ /i/ | | w/ /a/ | |
Consonants	Releasing	Arresting	Releasing	Arresting	Releasing	Arresting
p	3	0	66	0	66	0
b	84	0	66	0	66	0
t	1	0	66	0	0	0
d	14	0	100	0	100	0
k	16	3	33	33	66	0
g	26	0	66	0	66	0
f	0	0	0	0	0	0
v	0	0	0	0	0	0
s	0	0	0	33	0	0
z	0	0	0	0	0	0
m	34	0	0	0	33	0
n	53	2	0	0	33	0
l	52	0	0	0	0	66
r	0	0	0	33	0	0
ʃ	0	0	0	0	0	0
tʃ	0	0	0	0	0	0
w	3	1	0	0	0	0
h	11	0				
j	7	1				
ŋ	2	0				

CHILD 2

| | SPONTANEOUS SAMPLE (FREQUENCY OF OCCURRENCE) | | IMITATIVE SAMPLE (% OCCURRENCE) |
Vowels	Pre-Consonant	Post-Consonant	In Isolation
i	9	26	66
I	0	2	33
e	0	1	0
ɛ	0	0	0
æ	1	7	66
u	7	62	0
ʊ	0	1	100
o	0	25	0
ɔ	27	0	100
a	1	66	100
ə	11	55	33
aɪ	2	4	0
aʊ	0	0	0
ɔɪ	0	0	66
ɝ	0	0	

Within Sample Target Words These target words were constructed from phonemes whose frequency of occurrence was high in the child's pre-treatment vocalization sample. The steps in constructing the words were as follows.

1. A list of words was obtained for each child, which parents and teachers felt the child might have occasion to use in his school and/or home environment.
2. Words were selected from the list which could be constructed from phonemes in the child's pretreatment vocalization sample. For each child, one word (Child I, *bug;* Child II, *ball)* was composed entirely of phonemes strongest in the spontaneous sample, and one word (Child I, *lamb;* Child II, *dog*) was composed of phonemes strongest in the imitative sample.

Not-within Sample Target Words The target work *cheese* was also selected from the children's functional word list (obtained from parents and teachers), but was composed of some phonemes which were and some which were not in the children's pretreatment vocalization sample. Two phonemes in each word were of non-occurrence in the children's pretreatment sample. Also, one phoneme in each word was of high occurrence in the children's spontaneous sample. For Child II, an additional target word *(face)* was constructed entirely from phonemes of non-occurrence in the child's pretreatment sample.

Presentation of the Target Word A random order table was used to randomize the order of presentation of the target words within each session for each child. Each target word was trained for an equal number of trials within each session. Each child participated in three or four, twenty- to forty-five minute treatment sessions per week for a period of six weeks.

Program Each clinician followed a program that generally utilized the behavior modification procedure of forward chaining to establish each target word. The program was designed to establish: (1) the initial phoneme, a consonant (C), of a target word in isolation; (2) the initial and second phoneme, consonant-vowel (C-V), in combination; and (3) the initial, second, and final phoneme (C-V-C) of the target word in combination, so that the complete monosyllabic target word was imitated by the child. When the child had met the performance criterion for imitation of the initial phoneme in isolation, a probe of five trials was given to determine if the first and second phoneme (C-V) combination could be established without teaching the second phoneme in isolation. The same probing procedure was implemented to determine if the final phoneme required teaching in isolation before combining it with the first and second phoneme combination.

The criterion for moving from Step 1 (phoneme in isolation) to Step 2 (two-phoneme combination), or from Step 2 to Step 3 (whole words) was five consecutive perfect articulation responses or 9 out of 10 correct responses. Criterion for completion of Step 3 (whole word) was that the child imitate the whole word with perfect articulation on 50 percent of the trials, and that the child was understandable on at least 90 percent of the other trials. Typically, in our clinical program we do not require perfect articulation on every trial until after the child has mastered a large number of words. However, for comparison with the other steps of the program (individual phonemes and two-phoneme combinations), the therapists continued to work on whole words in an attempt to determine the number of trials it would take to achieve a 90 percent perfect articulation criterion.

Each therapist utilized prompting and shaping procedures to establish a phoneme or phoneme combination under imitative control. A prompt was provided when the child did not respond correctly or make approximations to the therapist's auditory stimulus. The clinicians utilized *Corrections of Defective Consonant Sounds* (Nemoy and Davis 1972) as a source for possible prompts to use for eliciting phonemes. A shaping procedure was used when the subject made some degree of approximation to the phoneme or when prompting procedures were not possible.

The specific consequences delivered for each subject were determined by the clinician. Contingent upon a correct response, the child received (1) a food reinforcer, such as orange juice, raisins, cereal, or an apple, and (2) a social reinforcer, typically, "good boy," "nice going," and so forth. Contingent upon an incorrect response, the therapist said no.

Inter-observer Reliability for Judging Articulation Responses

Reliability recorders were assigned to record articulation responses for the child's treatment sessions on the average of once every three sessions. Reliability measures were obtained for correct and incorrect responses. The therapist and recorder recorded the child's response as correct or incorrect on precoded data sheets. If both the therapist and recorder recorded a particular response as correct or incorrect on a given trial, they were said to be in agreement. If on any trial, either recorded a response as correct and the other recorded it as incorrect, they were said to be in disagreement. Reliability was calculated according to the following formula:

$$\text{Reliability} = \frac{\text{Number of agreements per session}}{\text{Agreements and disagreements per session}} \times 100$$

A reliability recorder was present during seven of Child I's 25 sessions. The mean percentage of agreement for correct responses was 94.8 (range: 86 – 100 percent), and the mean percentage agreement for incorrect responses was 92.5 (range: 75 – 100 percent). A reliability recorder was present during six of Child II's 20 sessions. The mean percentage of agreement for correct responses was 90.4 (range: 79 – 100 percent), and the mean percentage agreement for incorrect responses was 96.5 (range: 93 – 100 percent).

Results _____

Within versus Not-within Pretreatment Vocalization Sample

Figure 4–1 shows the final results for all of the words taught to both children. Steps of the treatment program are plotted on the abscissa for each phoneme and phoneme combination (in every word). Whether or not the child met criterion is plotted on the ordinate.

As can be seen, only the phonemes, phoneme combinations, and whole words constructed from the child's pretreatment sample met criterion within the six week period. None of the phonemes or phoneme combinations met criterion for the words composed of phonemes not in the pretreatment vocalization sample. It is interesting to note that whether a phoneme came from the spontaneous sample or imitative sample was not a variable. That is, all phonemes and combinations from the pretreatment sample met criterion.

The details of these results are shown in Figure 4–2, which shows the number of trials a therapist spent at each step of the program (for every word) before criterion was met.

FIGURE 4—1 Whether or not criterion was reached for each level (individual phonemes, two-phoneme combinations, and whole words) in the therapy program. The words for the Child I were *bug, cheese,* and *lamb,* respectively. The words for Child II were *ball, cheese, dog,* and *face,* respectively.

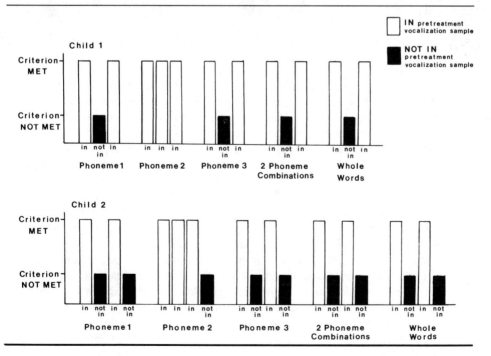

FIGURE 4—2 The number of trials a therapist spent at each level (individual phonemes, two-phoneme combinations, and whole words). Asterisks indicate that the 90 percent perfect articulation criterion was not met within the six week time period. The words for Child I were *bug*, *cheese*, and *lamb*, respectively. The words for Child II were *ball*, *cheese*, *dog*, and *face*, respectively.

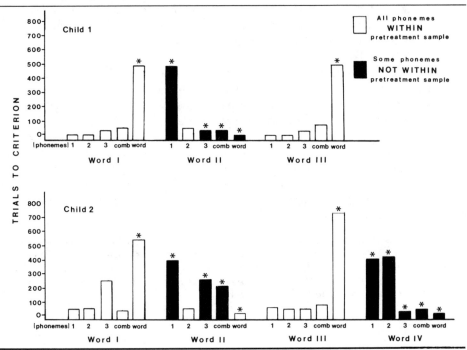

Figure 4– 2 shows that words constructed from phonemes within the pretreatment vocalization sample rapidly met criterion at the level of individual phonemes and two-phoneme combinations (usually in less than 50 trials.) At the level of imitating the whole (C-V-C) word, the 50 percent articulation criterion also was rapidly met in about the same number of trials. However, the therapists were unable to reach a 90 percent perfect articulation criterion within the six week period. This was true for every word, for every child, even though they typically presented about 500 or more trials at that level.

The words constructed from phonemes not present in the pretreatment vocalization sample show a much different pattern. Typically, the therapists presented 500 or more trials at the level of teaching individual phonemes without ever reaching criterion (on those phonemes that were not present in the pretreatment sample). For both children the therapists also made a number of attempts to teach the two phoneme combinations (in spite of failure to teach all of the phonemes in isolation). In one case (Child II, word 2), 200 trials were presented; however, in no instance was criterion ever reached.

In summary, the results show that when the target words were constructed of phonemes within the pretreatment vocalization sample, the therapists were rapidly able to proceed to the point of establishing imitation of two phoneme combinations, and with slightly more effort, to achieve some degree of success with whole words composed of three (C-V-C) phonemes. In marked contrast, after six weeks (and almost 3,000 total trials) criterion was never reached at any step of the program for words constructed (even in part) of phonemes not present in the pretreatment vocalization sample.

Therapist Morale

At the termination of the experimental program, each therapist was asked to rate each target word with respect to whether or not the amount of effort to teach the word was worth it, and their personal assessment of the child's prognosis to learn.

The rating scale for both questions was based on a 9-point scale, with points 1 through 3 representing that the word was "not worth the effort" to teach (Question 1), and that the prognosis to learn was "unlikely" (Question 2); points 4 through 6 represented that the word "may be worth the effort," and similarly, that the prognosis to learn was "probable;" and points 7 through 9 indicated that the word was "worth the effort" to teach, and that the child's prognosis to continue learning was "likely."

For Question 1 (see Table 4–2) both therapists rated the within sample phoneme constructed words as "worth the effort" to teach. Out of a maximum of 9, these words were rated 8 and 7 for Child I, 9 and 6 for Child II.

The not-within sample and combination of within and not-within sample phoneme constructed words were rated by both clinicians as "not worth the effort." Both words for Child I were rated at 3, and for Child II at 2.

Question 2 (see Table 4–2) was directed toward evaluating the therapist's prediction of the child's prognosis to learn. Both therapists rated the children as "likely" to learn after teaching the within sample phoneme constructed words (8 for Child I; 9 and 8 for Child II). In marked contrast, after teaching the not-within sample and combination of within and not-within sample phoneme constructed

		THERAPIST 1		THERAPIST 2		
Condition		Question 1	Question 2	Question 1	Question 2	Condition Average
Within Pretreatment Vocalization Sample	Word I	9	9	8	8	7.9
	Word III	7	8	6	8	
Not-within Pretreatment Vocalization Sample	Word II	2	1	3	3	2.5
	Word IV			3	3	

TABLE 4– 2 Therapist Questionnaire Results*

* For Question 1, numbers 1-3= "not worth the effort" to teach; 4-6= "may be worth the effort;" 7-9= "worth the effort." For Question 2, numbers 1-3= "unlikely" to learn; 4-6= prognosis to learn is "probable," 7-9= "likely."

words, the children were rated as "unlikely" to learn (3 for Child I, and 1 for Child II.)

In summary, the within sample words generally were rated as "worth the effort," and the prognosis was "likely" to learn. All of the not-within sample words were rated as "not worth the effort" and "unlikely" to be learned. The overall average score for both questions was 7.9 out of a maximum of 9 for the within sample words, suggesting considerable optimism. Conversely, the overall score for the not-within sample was 2.5, suggesting considerable pessimism.

Discussion _____

Within PreTreatment Sample versus Not-within PreTreatment Sample as a Selection Criterion

The target words constructed from phonemes within the pretreatment sample were learned more rapidly. This was true both for the phonemes in isolation and in C-V combination. As the termination of the study, the within sample target words were at higher steps in the program than the not-within sample target words. Both children could easily be understood, although their articulation was not consistent. In contrast, the not-within sample target words were still at the level of establishing individual phonemes and two-phoneme combinations, and criterion was never reached at any step within the six weeks time period.

C-V-C versus C-V as a Selection Criterion

The final step of the program was designed to establish the C-V-C monosyllabic target word. In spite of the presentation of a great number of teaching trials, ranging from 480 to 490 for Child I and 535 to 708 for Child II, the within repertoire target words were never considered to be under consistent imitative control. The children appeared to have occasional difficulty in combining the final consonant with the previously learned C-V phoneme combination. The reason for this is not clear. One feasible explanation might be that C-V-C combinations may require a much higher level of oral musculature and motor development, or a higher level of perceptual development or both, than does C-V combinations. This seems supported by research in child language acquisition (Smith 1973; Jakobson 1968), which reported on the use of C-V or V-C word combinations by normal children before more elaborate phoneme combinations were used. Further, this is consistent with the results reported by Hewett (1965), who taugh5 more complex words only after a small repertoire of C-V or V-C combination words had been established.

The issue of efficiency in speech teaching is extremely important, because speech is often not viewed by teachers or speech and language clinicians as a viable system of communication for nonverbal autistic children. The major argument is that the effort in teaching speech is too great in spite of the advantage of the universal applicability of speech. Some have speculated that sign, plastic chip communication (Carrier 1974; McLean and McLean 1974; Premack 1970), or other simplified systems of communication may be more rapidly taught than conventional speech (see Chapter 9 for a detailed discussion of this point). However, teaching speech with initial target words *carefully selected* from C-V combinations of phonemes within the child's pretreatment repertoire may be even more readily taught than by selecting nonverbal targets. This is an empirical question, and only further research can answer it. However, the results of this study suggest considerable optimism.

Simple C-V combinations might supply a basis for further expansion of the child's vocabulary (i.e., new phonemes may appear in the child's repertoire). Almost all of the studies reporting speech training with mute autistic children have reported rapid success after the first few words were established. Nevertheless, although the children were then talking, the articulation has typically been reported as imperfect even after years of work (cf., Lovaas *et al.* 1973). Long term phoneme analyses conducted throughout a child's treatment program may provide additional understanding of both language development and training for mute children in general.

Summary ⸺⸺⸺⸺⸺⸺⸺⸺⸺⸺⸺⸺

The purpose of this study was to assess the efficiency of utilizing a nonverbal autistic child's pretreatment vocalization sample as a selection criterion for words to be used in initial speech training. In a modified reversal design, two nonverbal autistic children were taught monosyllabic words constructed of phonemes that occurred within their pretreatment vocalization sample as compared to equivalent words constructed of phonemes not-within the sample.

The results are discussed in relation to the issues of (a) efficiency of speech training, and (b) therapist morale. Results indicated the following:

1. Words based on phonemes within the pretreatment vocalization sample required very few trials to establish imitative control. This was true for words with phonemes from either the spontaneous or imitative samples.
2. In marked contrast, words constructed from phonemes not in the pretreatment vocalization sample never reached criterion within six weeks.
3. In addition, questionnaire results showed that the clinicians judged the "within repertoire" words to be "worth the effort" to teach, and judged the children's prognosis as "likely to learn" whereas the "not-within repertoire" words were considered to be "not worth the effort" to teach and "unlikely" to be learned.

Note ⸺⸺⸺⸺⸺⸺⸺⸺⸺⸺⸺⸺⸺⸺⸺⸺

The authors are grateful to Julie Williams, Roberta Elman, Jan Costello, and Carol Prutting for their comments on an earlier draft of this manuscript.

Teachers' Judgments of Improvements in Autistic Children in Behavior Therapy: A Social Validation

Recent literature contains numerous descriptions of improvements in autistic children that have resulted from a behavioral approach to treatment (cf., Egel, Koegel, and Schreibman, 1980; Schreibman, Koegel, Charlop and Egel, in press). Yet the treatment process is complex and the progress of the children may be slow. This is certainly not surprising when one considers the extent and severity of the disabilities characteristic of these children (cf., Schreibman and Mills, in press). What therapists and researchers hope to achieve is a substantial improvement in the quality of life for persons afflicted with autism. One key to this goal is keeping autistic children in their natural settings, such as home and school, and out of caretaker institutions. Thus, it is important that skills taught to autistic children be those which will allow them to function in community settings and win the approval of significant others in the natural environment (i.e., parents, siblings, teachers, and peers).

It is current practice for therapists to set treatment goals and implement treatment programs in the clinic setting. The success of a treatment program is assessed by systematic observations of easily defined behaviors, such as correctly responding to the command "put the ball in the cup" (in the case of teaching the preposition *in*). The systematic observation-assessment procedure has the advantage of being easily and reliably scored, and its use has provided a solid empirical basis for a variety of treatment strategies (Schreibman, Koegel, Mills and Burke, in press).

As in all types of experimental activities, however, the question of validity is of central importance. For example, psychometricians are concerned that the

*This chapter was authored by **Laura Schreibman,** Claremont Men's College, **Mark A. Runco** and **Jack I. Mills,** Claremont Graduate School, **Robert L. Koegel,** University of California, Santa Barbara.*

tests they create will accurately predict behavior which is functional to a given setting (i.e., predictive validity). Likewise, social theorists are concerned that the measures they use reflect behavior which is theoretically relevant and not behavior which is created by the measurement technique itself (i.e., construct validity). As stated previously, a validity issue of importance to behavior therapy is that behavior change occurring in the clinic should be meaningful and relevant to significant persons in the community. Children may well learn prepositions and other important behaviors in the clinic, but it should also be demonstrated that these changes are observable and relevant to persons outside the treatment setting. Recognizing this need, it has become increasingly more common for clinicians to submit the goals, procedures, and outcomes of behavior therapy to its potential consumers for evaluation. This has been labeled *social validation,* and thorough presentations of the technique are available in Kazdin (1977) and Wolf (1978).

The social validation technique has proved useful to several areas of behavior therapy research. For example, Minkin, *et al.,* (1976) employed members of a community as judges in a study of the conversational behavior of female junior-high students. They found that the apparent poor social skills of the teenagers could be attributed to their failure to ask questions, provide positive feedback, or spend very much time talking. On that basis, the investigators were able to improve the conversational ability of the teenagers to a level substantially better than their untrained peers, as rated by a panel of judges from the community. Many other examples of social validation can also be found in Wolf (1978).

Social validation in regard to the treatment of autism is perhaps most useful as a means to assess the global improvement of children. This is because behaviors important in the real world are likely to be multifarious (Minkin, *et al.,* 1976). For example, observers may focus on one aspect of the social behavior of autistic children — the lack of eye contact, the failure to initiate interactions — and ignore the fact that a child complies with every adult request. Similarly, the speech of an autistic child may appear to be highly abnormal because of pronoun reversals and its dull, emotionless quality. Each individual who observes an autistic child — and especially those who actually rate the child's behavior — will use their own personal, implicit definition of the *behavioral components* relevant to appropriate or inappropriate conduct. Meaningful behavior is, to a large extent, observed and noted in a subjective manner. What is relevant for settings outside the clinic cannot be completely ascertained by objective measures, such as tests of cognitive and social maturity or observational assessments. This requires the judgment of those individuals who will habitually interact with the child in the child's natural environment.

With this in mind, Schreibman, Koegel, Mills and Burke, (in press) decided to evaluate the effects of behavior therapy of autistic children by comparing the subjective impressions of naive judges with the systematic ratings of trained observers. The trained observers scored eight operationally defined categories of behavior (e.g., self-stimulation, appropriate verbal) from the pretreatment and posttreatment video tapes of 13 autistic children. Table 5–1 presents brief descriptions of these objective behavior categories. College undergraduates rated the same children with a scale of 25 subjective Likert item descriptors (e.g., "engages

---

TABLE 5–1 Operational Definitions of the Objective Categories

---

1. *Self-Stimulation:* A stereotyped, repetitive behavior which has no apparent purpose other than sensory input. It must last three seconds or occur several times throughout the 10-minute session. Examples include rolling eyes, staring at the lights, sticking out tongue, putting objects in mouth, body rocking, arm flapping, repeated jumping, or shaking a toy.
2. *Exploratory Play:* Using a toy but not for its primary purpose — tracing the edges of it, for instance — or mechanical, repetitive play. The child must actively interact with the toy rather than just hold it.
3. *Appropriate Play:* Using a toy in an appropriate manner.
4. *Psychotic Verbal:* Speech out of context, e.g. "word salad," or immediate and delayed echoing. This does *not* include unintelligible speech or crying and yelling.
5. *Appropriate Verbal:* Appropriate speech.
6. *Social Nonverbal:* Behavior that demonstrates that the child is responsive to the presence of the adult. This includes compliance, cooperation, and initiating interaction.
7. *Noncooperation:* Not responding to the adult's commands to do a verbal or nonverbal action.
8. *Tantrum:* Tantruming used in order to manipulate the adult's actions.

---

in repetitious behavior," "answers questions"). These 25 items were generated by a panel of naive observers, who were asked to write essays describing the important characteristics of the children. The Likert rating scale was constructed such that for every systematically observed behavior there was a corresponding subjective rating. In this way, positive correlations were expected between the judges' ratings of descriptors like "tantrum," and the systematically observed category "Tantrum." Other item pairs were expected to have negative correlations, such as the subjective descriptor "cooperates with mother" and the objectively recorded "noncooperation." In addition, the naive judges' assessments of pre- and posttreatment differences could be analyzed for each item. Finally, a social distance scale asked the undergraduates about the apprehension or lack of apprehension they would feel about spending time with the children they observed in the tape segments. Specifically, the judges were asked if they would be willing to have the child in the same neighborhood, have the child in the same room, take the child for a walk, babysit the child, or even adopt the child. This scale was another means for comparing differences between the pretreatment and posttreatment tape segments for each child. The undergraduates were not informed of the children's diagnoses, and viewed the pre- and posttreatment segments in a randomized order.

The results showed that the undergraduates agreed with the trained observers as to which children improved markedly, and which children improved only slightly. Further, many of the individual subjective-objective item correlations were in the expected direction. Apparently, naive observers perceived particular behavior components that are similar to the particular behavioral components scored by trained observers.

One could argue, however, that college undergraduates are not the potential consumers of this type of treatment activity. In addition, when community members are called upon to make subjective evaluations of this nature, a familiarity with normal developmental patterns may be crucial (Furman 1980). Presumably, elementary school teachers have just this type of acumen and experience. Therefore, replication of the study was conducted with teachers making the subjective judgments.

TABLE 5–2 The Questionnaire

To what extent is the child:	very little					very much	
	1	2	3	4	5	6	7
restless	—	—	—	—	—	✓	—
coordinated	—	—	—	—	—	—	—

To what extent does the child:

name objects	—	—	—	—	—	—	—
speak clearly	—	—	—	—	—	—	—
echo words	—	—	—	—	—	—	—
talk to himself/herself	—	—	—	—	—	—	—
answer questions	—	—	—	—	—	—	—
start conversations with mother	—	—	—	—	—	—	—
speak with the mother	—	—	—	—	—	—	—
show an interest in toys	—	—	—	—	—	—	—
play with toys appropriately	—	—	—	—	—	—	—
show wandering attention	—	—	—	—	—	—	—
engage in repetitive behavior	—	—	—	—	—	—	—
tantrum	—	—	—	—	—	—	—
show an interest in mother	—	—	—	—	—	—	—
cooperate with the mother	—	—	—	—	—	—	—
appear to be abnormal	—	—	—	—	—	—	—
concentrate on tasks	—	—	—	—	—	—	—
concentrate on one activity for too long	—	—	—	—	—	—	—
cooperate only if he/she is interested	—	—	—	—	—	—	—
appear to be normal	—	—	—	—	—	—	—
show awareness of surroundings	—	—	—	—	—	—	—

In a classroom would the child:

need extra attention from teacher	—	—	—	—	—	—	—
disrupt the setting	—	—	—	—	—	—	—
attract undue attention from classmates	—	—	—	—	—	—	—
be able to work on tasks without supervision	—	—	—	—	—	—	—
be ready to learn fine motor skills	—	—	—	—	—	—	—
be ready to learn gross motor skills	—	—	—	—	—	—	—

I would enjoy working with this child — — — — — — —

What is the appropriate placement for this child?
special education classroom __(1)__ normal classroom with aide __(2)__
kindergarten __(3)__ normal classroom __(4)__ what grade _____

TABLE 5–3 The Social Distance Scale

Would you be willing to teach this child if he/she was in a classroom completely separated from the other children? ___(1)___ yes ___(2)___ no

Would you be willing to have this child in your class two days per week? ___(1)___ yes ___(2)___ no

Would you be willing to have this child share recess and lunch with your class? ___(1)___ yes ___(2)___ no

Would you be willing to have this child in your class for one-half of every day? ___(1)___ yes ___(2)___ no

Would you be willing to have this child in your class at all times? ___(1)___ yes ___(2)___ no

---

Pre- and posttreatment videotapes of four autistic children were objectively scored by trained observers and compared to the subjective ratings of 24 elementary school teachers. Most of the teachers were in their early 30s. They had an average of eight years of teaching experience. About half of the teachers had experience with handicapped children (although not with autistic children). The same checklist of descriptors was used, but additional items asked the teachers about their anticipated enjoyment derived from working with these children, and about the appropriate school placement for the children. A new social distance scale was created to focus on classroom situations, i.e., "willingness to work with this child twice a week," "half of every day," "all day, every day," and "willingness to work alone with this child", or to have this child "share recesses and lunch with your class." The subjective rating scale and social distance scale are presented in Tables 5–2 and 5–3, respectively.

Results

The enjoyment item, the placement item, and four of the five social distance items all showed extremely significant differences between pre- and posttreatment (see Table 5–4). Table 5–5 presents the pre- and posttreatment statistical comparisons for the other descriptors. Out of the entire 28-item subjective scale, only one pre-/posttreatment comparison ("shows an interest in toys")

TABLE 5–4 A Comparison of Before and After Treatment for Judgments of Enjoyment, Placement, and Willingness to Interact with the Child

	Mean Before	Mean After	*t*	Probability
Enjoyment	3.84	5.38	7.9	.000
Placement	1.41	2.24	4.28	.000
Willingness to				
work separately?	1.2	1.14	1.35	.179
in class twice/week?	1.48	1.13	6.18	.000
share recess & lunch?	1.19	1.02	3.82	.000
one-half of every day?	1.54	1.20	5.66	.000
in class at all times?	1.75	1.42	5.21	.000

TABLE 5–5 Comparison of Pretreatment and Posttreatment Means[1]

Item		Pre	Post	t	Significance
1.	Restless	5.30	3.60	7.28	.000
2.	Coordinated	3.32	4.46	4.51	.000
3.	Name Objects	2.66	4.68	7.93	.000
4.	Speak Clearly	2.06	3.53	5.93	.000
5.	Echo Words	2.07	3.68	6.38	.000
6.	Talk to Self	1.97	2.88	4.10	.000
7.	Answer Questions	2.80	5.26	11.57	.000
8.	Start Conversations	1.47	2.16	4.52	.000
9.	Speak with Mother	2.43	4.69	10.26	.000
10.	Show Interest in Toys	5.46	5.54	0.40	.689
11.	Play with Toys Appropriately	4.21	5.45	5.38	.000
12.	Show Wandering Attention	4.36	3.80	2.16	.033
13.	Engage in Repetitive Behavior	5.09	3.00	8.24	.000
14.	Tantrum	3.93	1.42	8.40	.000
15.	Show an Interest in Mother	2.34	4.34	8.72	.000
16.	Cooperate with Mother	2.78	6.01	14.96	.000
17.	Appear Abnormal	5.35	3.51	7.36	.000
18.	Concentrate on Tasks	3.81	4.93	5.01	.000
19.	Concentrate for Too Long	4.47	2.55	6.41	.000
20.	Cooperate Only if Interested	5.65	2.84	11.26	.000
21.	Appear Normal	2.39	4.20	8.38	.000
22.	Show Awareness of Surroundings	3.70	4.96	5.67	.000
23.	Need Extra Attention from Teacher	6.53	4.85	9.05	.000
24.	Disrupt the Classroom	5.89	3.47	11.79	.000
25.	Attract Undue Attention from Class	5.93	3.81	9.63	.000
26.	Be Able to Work without Supervision	2.22	3.69	6.48	.000
27.	Ready to Learn Fine Motor Skills	3.07	4.54	6.10	.000
28.	Ready to Learn Gross Motor Skills	4.93	6.00	4.81	.000

[1] The comparison was done with a "correlated" t-test for paired observations.

failed to reach statistical significance. All but "echoing" and "talking to self" were in the direction of improvement as perceived by the teachers.

The teachers' subjective ratings were next correlated with the objective scores of the trained observers. These results are shown in Table 5–6. Here, several trends stood out, and these are most easily understood by looking at three general areas of behavior.

Social

A failure to develop normal social relationships is one of the hallmarks of autism. The children do not seek attention from adults, nor do they initiate interactions for purely social reasons. They may, however, use adults to obtain desired objects, such as food or toys. Autistic children tend to avoid other children. Thus, they do not play cooperatively nor imitate peers. Play, then, is solitary and usually consists of repetitive, self-stimulatory use of objects.

TABLE 5–6 Correlations between Objective and Subjective Ratings

Subjective	OBJECTIVE							
	Tantrum	SelfStim	Explay	ApproPlay	ApproVerb	PsyVerb	Social	NonCoop
1. restless	.345	.603	.507	-.385	.139	.396	-.756*	.293
2. coordinated	-.630*	-.335	-.589	.768	.266	-.492	.704	-.644*
3. name objects	-.173	.310	-.779*	.450	.839**	.161	.737*	-.644*
4. speak clearly	-.347	-.239	-.528	.193	.598	-.084	.641*	-.403
5. echo words	-.282	-.171	-.621*	.099	.603*	.158	.629*	-.439
6. talk to self	-.017	.038	-.609	.136	.868**	.186	.372	-.440
7. answer questions	-.236	.251	-.796**	.575	.744*	.013	.813**	-.771*
8. start conversations	.082	.535	-.604	.426	.860**	.245	.282	-.626*
9. speak with mother	-.051	.349	-.831**	.505	.827**	.113	.730*	-.78 *
10. interest in toys	-.281	-.518	.046	.436	-.325	-.830**	.225	-.252
11. play appropriately	-.191	-.267	.880**	.672*	.564	-.497	.859**	-.855**
12. wandering attention	.163	.468	.045	.065	.432	-.006	-.233	-.285
13. repetitive behavior	.186	.010	.816**	-.556	-.572	.286	-.902**	.855**
14. tantrum	.925**	.072	.180	-.519	-.175	.010	.473	.191
15. interest in mother	.135	.135	-.876**	.631*	.650*	-.101	.802**	-.862**
16. cooperate	-.365	.059	-.832**	.695*	.658*	-.136	.839**	-.807**
17. appear abnormal	.624*	.187	.604*	-.646*	-.478	.223	-.795**	.576
18. concentrate	-.212	-.325	-.476	.396	-.047	-.085	.494	-.159
19. concentrate too long	.204	.061	.699*	-.443	-.614	.316	-.735**	.835**
20. cooperate only if interested	.498	.062	.772*	-.632*	-.533	.081	-.872**	.664*
21. appear normal	-.583	-.158	-.651*	.602	.471	-.186	.837*	-.568
22. aware of surroundings	.127	.259	-.826**	.448	.846**	-.098	.655	-.884**
23. need extra attention	.584	.182	.651*	-.652*	-.416	.222	-.836**	.546
24. disrupt setting	.598	.329	.567	-.523	-.158	.302	-.862**	.484
25. attract attention	.592	.308	.546	-.534	-.175	.316	-.854**	.499
26. work without supervision	-.459	-.219	-.749*	.654*	.291	-.254	.919	-.632*
27. fine motor skills	-.241	-.152	-.902	.620	.527	-.259	.960**	-.781*
28. gross motor skills	-.388	-.178	-.844**	.685*	.525	-.321	.905**	-.812**

As you would expect, the teachers consistently noticed the autistic social behaviors. Not only did they agree with the trained observers as to what constituted appropriate play, but they demonstrated a reasonably consistent idea of the trained relationship between play and other behaviors. "Exploratory Play" on the trained observers' list was negatively correlated with "plays appropriately," "interest in mother," "cooperates with mother," "aware of surroundings", and "able to work without supervision." It was positively correlated with "repetitive behavior," "concentrate for too long," and "need extra attention." Fortunately, "Appropriate Play" was positively correlated with "plays appropriately", as well as "shows an interest in mother," "cooperates with mother", and "be able to work without supervision." Moreover, this objective category was negatively correlated with "appears abnormal" and "need extra attention."

"Social Nonverbal" and "Noncooperation" on the trained observers' list also showed the expected trends. Of the 11 items on the teachers' checklist that correlated with these two categories, all were either positive for one and negative for the other, or vice versa. This included items that focused on verbal behavior, like "speaks with the mother," and "answers questions," and also motor items like "plays appropriately" and "engages in repetitious behavior." Clearly, these teachers were aware of the idiosyncratic behaviors that define autistic social behaviors

Speech

Autistic children generally do not use speech for communicative purposes. Instead, their speech is typified by echolalia — the repetition of words and phrases, a failure to use personal pronouns (e.g., "Jimmy wants to go outside"), and a lack of inflection, making their speech sound emotionless. The children also have a limited comprehension of the speech of others, making them appear to be noncooperative.

With this in mind, it is interesting that the teachers did not discriminate between inappropriate and appropriate speech. The objective category "Psychotic Verbal" only correlated with "interest in toys," and, as one would guess, that was negative. Of course, the operational definition of this category only includes out-of-context speech, like echoing, and excludes crying, yelling and unintelligible speech. Furthermore, teachers are probably accustomed to a diversity of language patterns from their young students. Thus, "Appropriate Verbal" positively correlated with "talks to self" and "echos", as well as "name objects," "answers questions," "start conversations", and "speaks with mother."

Bizarre Behavior

Another hallmark of autism is bizarre, inappropriate behavior. Autistic children use nearly every body part for self-stimulatory purposes. This can take the form of repetitive movements, such as twirling objects, flapping their arms and jumping, or it may appear as grotesque whole body movements, grimacing, or staring at objects. Another form of their bizarre behavior is inappropriate affect. The children may engage in hysterical laughter independent of any cause in the environment, or they may suddenly begin a violent tantrum in order to get a cookie or at the sight of a feared object.

Looking again at the correlations between the trained observer's ratings and the teacher's judgments, there were very few significant correlations. "Self-Stimulation" was not associated with any of the checklist items. Since the operational definition of this category is very complex, and the behavior itself is individualized, this paucity of correlates might be expected. "Tantrum" in the objective data was positively correlated with "tantrum" in the teachers' eyes, and also positively correlated with "appears abnormal." It was negatively correlated with "appears coordinated," so it might be stated that the teachers were aware of or influenced by the "bizarre" behavior of autistics only in extreme forms of normal behavior, like tantrumming, but not influenced by atypical forms of behavior, like subtle self-stimulation.

Overall, the correlations suggest that teachers view some behavioral components as more important than others. The correlates of the eight observed categories are such components, and assuredly there are others beyond the scope of this instrument. Those significant correlates were significant both in a statistical and in an applied sense. Clinicians and teachers might rely on the objective categories that had several significant correlates, and view the objective categories that had few or no correlates as dubious. "Self-Stimulation" and "Psychotic Verbal" were poor predictors of those behaviors listed on the teachers' questionnaire, while "Social Nonverbal" and "Noncooperation" were relatively good predictors. Information such as this can be used to modify the objectives for treatment, and even to modify the operational definitions of what types of behaviors are noted by significant others. For example, social behavior and cooperation may be especially important target behaviors if we wish to improve the degree to which these children are accepted within the school system.

The next logical step in this social validation is to replicate the study with special education teachers who are experienced with autistic children. Presumably, they could add even more insight into what types of behavior components are most relevant for the child and the community. Moreover, since such teachers are instrumental in determining the educational placement of autistic children, they may, indeed, be even more "significant" others than normal classroom teachers. Such a social validation study involving special education teachers is being undertaken.

Summary

There are several important results of this research. First and most obvious is the social validation of the treatment. Teachers perceived the efficacy of treatment, as demonstrated by the differences between the pre- and posttreatment ratings. They viewed the specific and global behaviors in a way that was similar to that of the trained observers, who scored objective changes in the precise percent occurrence of each behavior. Thus, it appears that the behavior therapists' objective measures of behavior change are similar to the behavioral components used by others in the child's community to evaluate behavior improvement.

A second major result of this research was that certain behaviors seemed to be especially significant in influencing teachers' judgments about autistic children. Such behaviors might be especially important targets for behavior change if we wish to influence these children's acceptability into the community.

Note

Preparation of this chapter was supported by U.S.P.H.S. Research Grants 28231 and 28210 from the National Institute of Mental Health, and by U.S. Office of Education Research Grant G007802084 from the Bureau of Education for the Handicapped. The authors wish to acknowledge Marjorie H. Charlop and John C. Burke for their helpful comments.

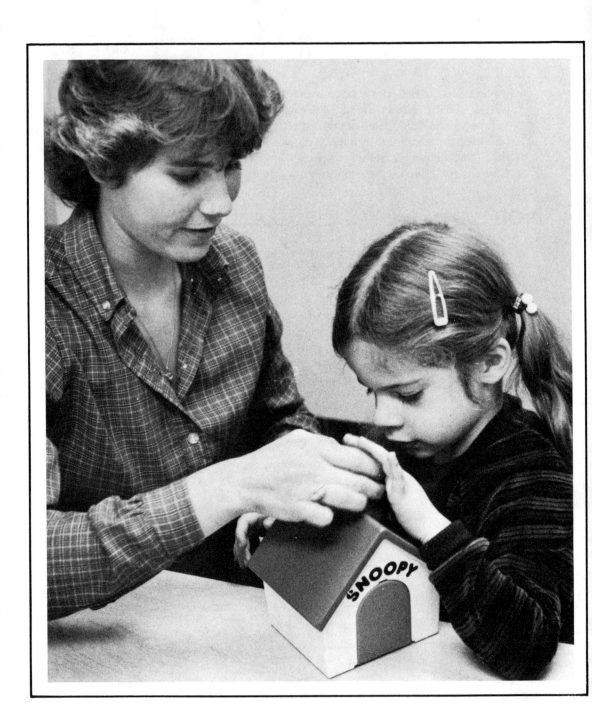

Section

2

Learning
Characteristics

Stimulus Overselectivity and Stimulus Control: Problems and Strategies

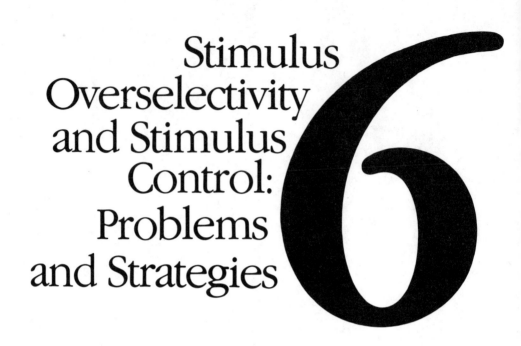

One of the most pervasive characteristics of autistic children is their inconsistent responding to environmental stimuli (Kanner 1944; Rimland 1964). This inconsistent responding is evidenced when a child sometimes fails to respond to his name, seems unaware of people around him, or fails to perform behaviors previously learned. As a consequence of such behavior, observers have often described these children as "living in another world" or "withdrawn into a shell" (Kanner 1944). It is not uncommon for them to be suspected of being blind or deaf, although vision and hearing examinations generally fail to reveal sensory abnormalities.

In an attempt to understand this inconsistent responding, researchers have begun to explore the nature of *attention* in autistic children. Two types of attentional problems have been identified. First, many studies report that autistic children typically respond to a more restricted portion of environmental stimuli than do normal or even retarded children, a phenomenon labeled *stimulus overselectivity* (Lovaas, *et al.* 1971). Second, studies have shown that autistic children often perseverate on certain response strategies, not coming in contact with reinforcers available for other responses or responding to changes in reinforcement schedules.

Each of these deficits have proven to be formidable problems in various teaching situations. For example, autistic children may learn certain tasks only on the basis of incidental hand movements by the teacher (Rincover and Koegel 1975) or respond to a written word on the basis of a single letter (Rincover 1978). Rather than respond to both the S+ and S− stimuli on discrimination tasks, many autistic children respond by *avoiding* the S− stimulus (Cushing and Rincover 1978), or respond to the S+ as a function of a particular S− (Cook and Rincover 1978), or else perseverate on a particular stimulus independent of the reinforcement schedule. These phenomena allow autistic children to respond correctly to

This chapter was authored by **A. Richard Cook, Norman Anderson,** *and* **Arnold Rincover,** *University of North Carolina, Greensboro.*

the S+ stimulus while learning little or nothing about the training stimuli. Since most learning situations require responding to multiple, contiguous cues, it is apparent that children who respond overselectively and/or perseveratively will necessarily fall behind their normal counterparts. In fact, since stimulus control deficits are considered to be so pervasive among autistics, and since they would be expected to interfere with language, social, and affective development (cf., Lovaas, *et al.* 1971), some authors have offered it as a possible contribution to the severity of autism.

This chapter is designed to provide an overview of current research on the nature and treatment of stimulus control deficits in autistic children. A review of research on stimulus overselectivity and its theoretical implication will be presented as well as studies on perseveration in autistic children. Finally, the chapter will address issues relating to the remediation of both overselectivity and perseveration.

Stimulus Overselectivity in Autistic Children

In the first overselectivity study, Lovaas, *et al.* (1971) trained groups of autistic, retarded, and normal children to respond (bar press) in the presence of a stimulus complex involving auditory (a burst of white noise), visual (red floodlight), and tactile (blood pressure cuff) components. Responding to this complex was reinforced with candy until a child responded correctly on at least 90 percent of the trials, and then the schedule of reinforcement was thinned from CRF to FR4. In order to assess the amount of stimulus control achieved by each of the three component cues, probe trials were introduced on nonreinforced trials in the FR4 schedule, that is, each cue was presented alone, and correct responding was recorded. It was found that each of the normal children responded uniformly to all three cues, while the autistic children responded to only one of the three cues presented. The retarded children varied between these extremes (i.e., one child responded to three cues, one child to one cue, and three children to two cues).

A second study was conducted to determine if the overselectivity found in the previous study would be evident if only two cues were presented. Lovaas and Schreibman (1971) trained normal and autistic children to respond to a stimulus complex containing only the auditory and visual cues used in the initial study. The results were compatible with the findings of Lovaas, *et al.* (1971): normal children responded uniformly to both cues, while the autistic children generally responded to only one of the two cues. It is important to note that, in both of these studies, the nonfunctional cue(s) became functional for the autistic children when trained in isolation, suggesting that the deficits in responding were not due to a sensory abnormality.

Overselective responding on the part of autistic children has also been found when both cues were presented in the same sensory modality. Koegel and Wilhelm (1973) trained autistic and normal children to respond to one of two cards, each containing two visual forms. The forms for a particular pair of cards were either geometric (e.g., an S+ containing a circle and a square versus an S− containing a triangle and diamond) or familiar objects (e.g., girl plus house versus bicycle plus tree). To assess the control achieved by each of the S+ forms, a child was presented on probe trials with two stimulus cards, one containing one form from the correct card and the other containing one form from the incorrect card. The authors reported that 12 of the 15 autistic children showed overselectivity, responding on the basis of only one of the two S+ forms, while 12 of 15 normal children responded to both of the S+ forms. Similar results have been attained with multiple auditory cues (Reynolds, Newsom, and Lovaas 1974).

A study by Schreibman and Lovaas (1973) was designed to teach autistic children to discriminate between *social* stimuli. In this study, normal and autistic children were trained to differentiate between male and female dolls. After learning to discriminate between the dolls, extensive assessments of stimulus control were conducted by systematically varying the clothes and body parts of the dolls. The authors found that the normal children were differentially responding to cues having to do with the dolls' heads. In contrast, the autistic children responded to a very specific article of clothing, such as a belt or a shoe. It is interesting to note that a number of uncontrolled observations also confirm this overselectivity to social stimuli. For example, it was found that a child being treated at UCLA displayed a lack of responsivity to his father when that parent's glasses were removed, but readily hugged his father when glasses were worn.

The detrimental effect of this overselectivity in learning situations has also been reported in teaching speech to autistic children (Lovaas, *et al.* 1971). To facilitate acquisition of verbal imitation, the therapist often provides visual as well as auditory cues. When the therapist presents the auditory stimulus to be imitated, he also presents the visual cue(s) of mouth movements, which may be exaggerated or accentuated. Since the different sounds have distinct visual and auditory components, the child is presented with two relevant cues. While a child seemed to be learning verbal imitation, the authors found that when the therapist removed the visual cue by covering her mouth, the child no longer responded. The child was selectively attending to the therapist's mouth movements and learned nothing about the sounds.

Rincover and Koegel (1975) discovered that when taught a new behavior in one setting, autistic children often failed to display that behavior in other settings. Instead, the children often "hooked" on a very small component of the training setting, producing restricted and often bizarre stimulus control. One child, for example, was taught to respond to a verbal command, "touch your chin," in the therapy room. When the child was tested in a novel extra-therapy setting and with a novel experimenter only 1-2 minutes after the criterion for acquisition was met, no correct responding was evident. Probe trials were subsequently designed to determine what had acquired control over responding in the training setting. It was discovered that the child's response was actually controlled by an incidental hand movement (a hand raise by the experimenter) that always preceded the verbal command during training. Similar incidental cues were found to be functional for other children.

The most important implication of this overselective attention is that it is likely to retard or prevent learning. Most learning depends on the contiguous or nearly contiguous presentation of stimuli. In classical conditioning paradigms, the CS (conditioned stimulus) is presented temporally close to the UCS (unconditioned stimulus). In operant conditioning paradigms, contiguous presentation of stimuli occurs when one seeks to achieve a transfer in stimulus control, as when a teacher presents a prompt (an extra stimulus to guide correct responding). Therefore, selective attention to a single cue would result in a failure to learn. The extreme selective attention found in autistic children may therefore account for their retarded social, emotional, and language development. For example, consider some of the implications of overselective attention for certain kinds of learning (cf., Lovaas, *et al.* 1971):

1. Various authors report that the acquisition of conditioned reinforcers (e.g., verbal praise, smiling, etc.) is a necessary prerequisite to the development of most human behavior (e.g., Ferster and DeMyer 1962). If conditioned reinforcers are acquired by association with primary reinforcers, then it is possible that overselective attention would account for the difficulty in training autistic children with conditioned reinforcers (cf., Lovaas, *et al.* 1966) that may lead to the deficits in subsequent language and intellectual development.
2. The lack of appropriate affect in autistic children is also well known. Overselective attention may also be implicated in the deficit in emotional behavior if affect is acquired by the contiguous presentation of two stimuli (an UCS and a CS). Some authors (e.g., Lovaas, *et al.* 1971; Newsom and Rincover 1979) have pointed out the general difficulty of autistic children acquiring new behaviors through classical conditioning.
3. Most autistic children are either mute or echolalic (repeating words or phrases immediately or after a delay). Echolalic speech is contextually impoverished. To the extent that context for speech requires a number of cues, one might expect autistic children to overselect and fail to learn.
4. Stimulus overselectivity might also contribute to failures in the acquisition of new behavioral topographies (e.g., nonverbal imitation) and receptive language. The usual means of teaching new behaviors requires prompting, where a teacher underlines, points to, or otherwise emphasizes the target stimulus. This presentation of extra stimuli may actually increase the difficulty of learning if the child selectively attends to the prompt stimuli.

The growing body of literature studying selective attention in autistic children has found them to be overselective when compared with normal or retarded children. While attentional deficits are extremely severe and have been shown to be detrimental in a variety of learning situations, the nature and generality of overselectivity is not entirely clear. Several studies may shed some light on the parameters determining stimulus overselectivity.

The Nature of Overselectivity

The fact that autistic children learn about their environment in a less efficient manner than normal children is well documented in the discrimination training literature. Although we know from this research that there is a problem, it is extremely difficult to specify exactly what the problem is. Given the data on overselectivity previously reviewed, it would appear possible that autistic children do not attend to more than one cue at a time, i.e., that this is a generalized problem that would be evidenced on a variety of tasks. A recent study by Anderson and Rincover (1980), however, suggests that this might not be the case. In this study, the subjects were eight autistic children, who evidenced overselectivity on a preassessment task, matched for mental age with eight normal children. All children were trained on three tasks to determine if overselectivity was generalized or varied as a function of different stimulus conditions. Each of the three tasks

FIGURE 6–1. Training and test stimuli are illustrated for each of three conditions (Small Dot, Medium Dot, and Large Dot). Across the three conditions, dots varied in size, number, and separation, and the test (probe) stimuli assess whether children learned about the gestalt (circle), or overselected on the component features (dots) under each of these conditions.

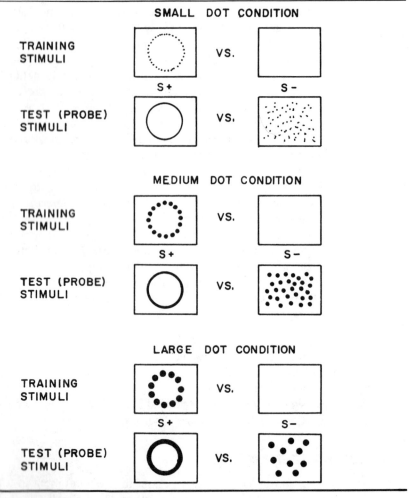

involved training a child to respond to (i.e., touch) a card containing a circle (S+) and to avoid a blank (S−) card. In each case, the circle was comprised of a series of dots, as shown in Figure 6–1. One difference between the three circles (tasks) was the distance between successive dots making up the circle. In addition, in the minimal separation condition, the dots were smaller in size and greater in number than in the larger separation conditions.

Of concern was whether autistic children learned about the *gestalt* (i.e., the circle), which required attention to multiple cues, or whether children would overselect and respond to the dots. The results showed the following. First, stimulus overselectivity was found not to be a generalized deficit in autistic subjects; instead, it varied as a function of the stimulus (task) variables. Second, gestalt responding was dominant when dots were closest together, while overselectivity was dominant when they were furthest apart. Third, the stimulus variables manipulated in this study similarly influenced the responding of both normal and autistic children.

Although the results of Anderson and Rincover suggest that stimulus overselectivity is not a generalized way in which autistic children view the world, but instead is influenced by task parameters, the precise stimulus dimensions that brought about the changes in stimulus control are not clear. It was found that three stimulus variables — size, spacing, and number of dots — could *together* be manipulated in order to bring about variations in the stimulus control over autistic children's responding. It remains possible, however, that gestalt responding was facilitated specifically by an increase in the number of dots making up the circle, a decrease in the size or spacing between dots, or some combination of these three factors.

Eason and Rincover (1980) designed an experiment to determine if stimulus control by multiple cues is influenced primarily by the distance between those cues. During pretraining, discrimination between a circle and a diamond was established, as shown in Figure 6–2. Subsequently, the pretrained stimuli were surrounded with two rows of numbers — 1's and 3s around the S^D (circle) and 2s and 6s around the S^Δ (diamond). Two conditions were planned — in the Small Distance condition, the numbers were closer to the pretrained feature than in the Large Distance condition. Each child was trained in both conditions, in a counterbalanced order. The Stimulus Control Test assessed which of the three individual S^D features acquired control over responding — the circle, the 1s, and/or the 3s — by making all other cues redundant and irrelevant. Stimulus 1 assesses learning about the inner circle, Stimulus 2 assesses learning about the middle row (in this case, 1s), and Stimulus 3 assesses learning about the outer row (3s).

The results are shown in Figure 6–3. The plain bar represents responding from the Large Distance condition; the striped bar represents responding in the Small Distance condition. The results for the first pretrained feature (the circle) are shown in the upper graph, S^D Feature 1. The data reveal that the children responded to the pretrained circle in both the large and small distance conditions. However, the results for S^D Feature 2, the numbers closest to the circle, tell quite a different story. All of the children responded to it when it was close to the

FIGURE 6–2.   Illustration of training and test stimuli to assess the effect of distance between components on learning. Children are first trained on the inner feature, e.g., to touch a circle and avoid a triangle (pretraining). Pretrained features are then surrounded by two rows of additional features, in this case 1s and 3s around the S^D(circle) and 2s and 6s around the S^A (diamond). In the Small Distance condition, the features are minimally reported, and in the Large Distance condition, they are further separated. The stimulus control test then assesses which of the three components of the S^D (Stimulus 1, 2, and 3) the children responded to.

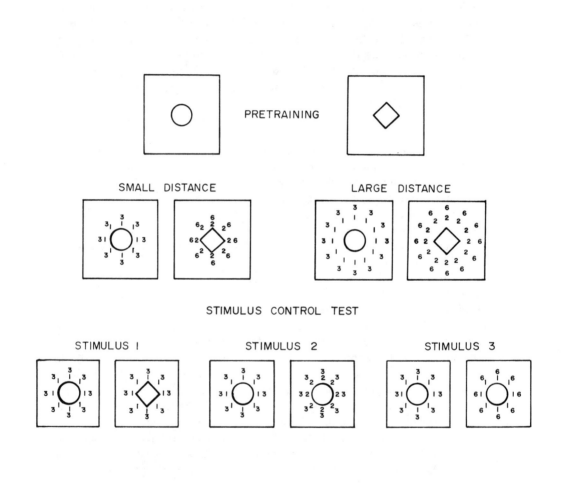

pretrained feature, but none of the children responded to it when it was a few centimeters further from the pretrained feature. The third, or outer stimulus, shown in the bottom graph, did not acquire control over responding in either condition; however, in a subsequent phase, when the outer stimulus was moved even closer to the pretrained feature, the children responded to all three components of the S^D (see Figure 6–4).

FIGURE 6–3.   Autistic children's responding to each of three S^D features when those features are minimally separated (slashed bar) or maximally separated (open bar). S^D Feature 1 represents the inner pretrained feature, S^D Feature 2 represents the middle row of features surrounding the inner feature, and S^D Feature 3 represents the outer row of features.

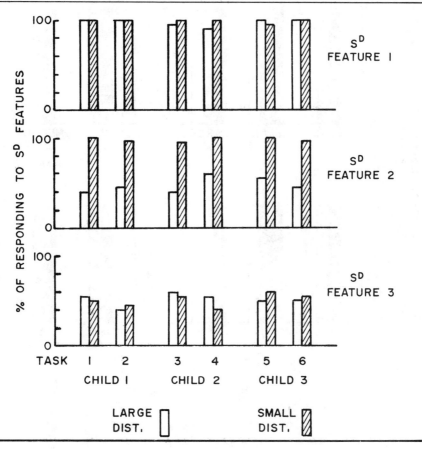

This suggests that multiple-cue responding was determined by the distance between stimuli: autistic children overselected on one cue when it was some distance from another, but responded to both cues when they were brought closer together. It should be noted that normal children tended to respond to all three cues in all of the conditions, regardless of distance.

The above studies suggest that the notion of autistic children responding to only a single cue at a time may not be the most appropriate account of their attentional deficits. A more adequate explanation might be that they exhibit a type of *tunnel vision,* and the only stimuli that would become functional for an autistic child would be those in his/her restricted field or "tunnel" of vision. One way of conceptualizing this is in terms of the relative location or distance between cues. If a child's responding is under the control of one stimulus (S_1) then the probability of that child responding to another stimulus (S_2) simultaneously would be, in part, a function of its distance form S_1. Using this hypothesis, the

FIGURE 6–4.   Percent of correct responding on stimulus control probes for autistic Subject 1.

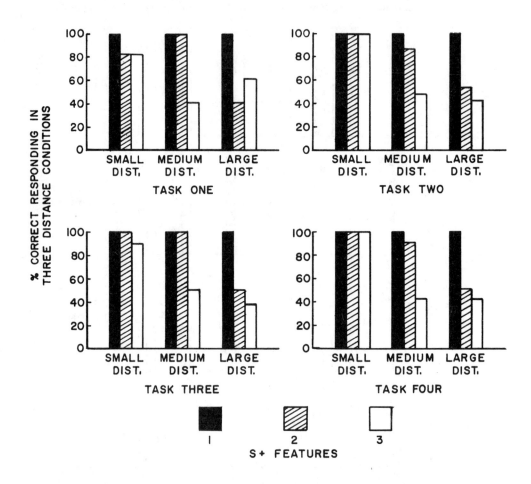

functional element in overselectivity may not be the number of cues involved, but rather the *location of those cues relative to each other*.

The tunnel vision conceptualization could also explain much of the available data on overselectivity. For example, Schreibman (1975) and Rincover (1978) both found that autistic children were better able to learn a discrimination when a prompt was superimposed on the S+ during fading (*within-stimulus* prompt), than when it was spatially separate from the S+ (*extra stimulus* prompt) as in the case of a pointing or underlining prompt. Rincover (1978) also found that children learned to respond to multiple features of the S+ stimulus when within-stimulus prompts were used, but not when extra-stimulus prompts were used.

One important question concerns the possible role of tunnel vision in auditory and cross-modal tasks. At first glance, it would appear that a tunnel vision theory would be of limited utility in explaining research that has demonstrated overselectivity with nonvisual stimuli, such as auditory (Reynolds, *et al.,* 1974) and cross-modality stimuli (Lovaas, *et al.* 1971). For instance, Reynolds, *et al.* (1974) found that when autistics were trained to respond in the presence of two auditory stimuli (a pure tone and a relay click), only one gained control over responding. However, several possibilities exist for applying the notion of tunnel vision to these instances of auditory overselectivity. One possibility is that autistic children do in fact respond to relative location with respect to the *sources* of different auditory stimuli. That is, as the physical distance between two auditory sources (e.g., persons) becomes greater, the probability that both will come to control a child's behavior decreases. This hypothesis, however, was not supported in the Reynolds, *et al.,* study, as only one source (i.e., speaker) was used to produce both auditory stimuli.

Perhaps a more appropriate way of applying tunnel vision to auditory overselectivity is by conceptualizing auditory stimuli as varying along the dimensions of tone, pitch, and frequency (somewhat analogous to size, spacing, and number in the Anderson and Rincover study). It may be that autistic children are responsive to sounds within a certain range of pitch or frequency, but not to sounds outside that range; that is, given responding to one auditory stimulus (S_1), the probability of responding to a second, simultaneous auditory stimulus (S_2) will vary inversely with difference in pitch, tone, and/or frequency. This phenomenon may account for frequent anecdotal observations, such as the oft noted instance of the autistic child who does not respond to a loud noise, but approaches a rustling candy wrapper in the next room. This effect could be attributed to a child's extensive history or pretraining with stimuli similar to rustling candy wrappers, and the great distance of the loud noise from the pretrained auditory cue(s).

The data set forth here refute the notion that autistic children respond only to a single cue when presented with multiple relevant cues. This suggests that single-cue responding is not the generalized, pervasive deficit previously assumed, and that it cannot easily be implicated as a cause of the behavioral deficits in autism. At the same time, however, while stimulus control in autistic children may not be solely a function of the *number* of cues, the present data do support the possibility that stimulus overselectivity is influenced by the *relative location* of cues; consequently, while single-cue responding does not seem to be a generalized problem, it is possible that *tunnel vision* might better characterize the attentional deficits of autistic children, and describe the way in which such children generally attend to their environment.

Perseveration

Perseveration occurs when a child repeatedly emits a single response, or responds only to a single stimulus, instead of sampling other responses (or stimuli) when they are available to him/her. With autistic children, perseveration has not received as much attention as overselective responding; however, it appears to be a response strategy that results in deficits in learning similar to those produced by overselectivity.

In the past 10 years, several studies have been concerned with the problem of perseveration responding with autistic children. In a study by Hermelin and Frith (1971), normal, retarded, and autistic children of the same mental age were each presented with verbal word messages which they had to subsequently recall. Each subject was given two types of six word messages: random messages (e.g., "spoon-horse-spoon-horse-horse-spoon") and highly redundant messages (e.g., "mouse-mouse-mouse-bag-bag-bag"). The authors found that the groups did not differ significantly on the percent of correct recall for words in the random messages. For the highly redundant messages, however, the autistic subjects showed significantly poorer recall than the normal and retarded groups, which did not differ significantly from one another. An analysis of the type of errors made by each group indicated that the normal and retarded children exaggerated the predominant feature of the message, whether it was the repetition of one word or the alternation of two words. The autistic subjects also showed *rule exaggeration,* but they usually applied the repetition rule whether or not it was the predominant feature of the word message, e.g., "spoon-horse-spoon-horse-horse-spoon" was recalled as "horse-horse-horse-spoon". The authors concluded that the autistic subjects' insensitivity to the pattern of the stimuli presented and their repetitive and rigidly structured response patterns might account for some of the stereotyped behavior typical of autistic children. Moreover, this study suggests that autistic and normal children do not utilize the same response strategies.

Boucher (1977) also noted a preference for repetition instead of alternation in autistic children. She used normal and autistic subjects matched for mental age, chronological age, and sex, in a maze-solving task. When two paths were available to solve the maze, significantly fewer sequential alternations between routes were made by the autistic than the normal subjects; the autistics generally followed only one path. In addition, when a third route was opened, significantly fewer autistic than normal children chose to follow it, indicating a lack of responsiveness to novelty. These data indicate that, unlike normals, the autistic children appear to select one response and continue to use it without sampling others.

Prior (1977) compared performances of autistic and normal children on a conditional matching-learning-set task. Groups of eight autistic, retarded and normal children, matched for mental age, were required to both match and avoid matching stimulus cards containing common shapes (e.g., circle, triangle) on the basis of an abstract symbol appearing on the stimulus card. For example, a child was presented a sample card containing a triangle. In addition, either a W or a Y appeared above the triangle. A child was then presented two other cards, one showing an identical triangle and another showing a circle (neither containing a symbol above the stimulus). On the trials where the W appeared on the sample card, the child was reinforced for selecting the match card (i.e., the triangle); when the Y appeared on the sample card, the child was reinforced for selecting the non-match card (i.e., the circle). The results revealed that the normal and retarded subjects showed improvement on the task over trials, while the autistic children did not. The author also noted that the autistic children tended to exhibit repetitive responding to position cues or to impose differential alternation rules.

FIGURE 6–5.   Mean percentages of Stimulus, Position, and Total Perseveration for the Autistic, MA-Matched Normal, and CA-Matched Normal children.

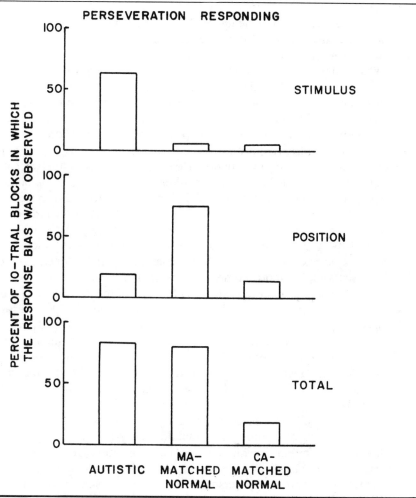

This again suggests that the response strategies used by autistic children are different from those of normals.

In the three studies described above, perseverative responding was found with the autistic children, but not with normal children sharing the same mental age. This might suggest that perseveration may be common to autistic children as a function of their diagnosis and not because of the low mental age at which they are operating. However, others have proposed that perseveration may very well be correlated with mental age.

Cook and Rincover (1979) assessed the patterns of responding displayed by autistic and normal children in order to identify their response strategies and to investigate the role of mental age in the response strategies utilized by both groups. Autistic subjects were matched on mental age with one group of normal children, and on chronological age with a second (older) normal group. The study compared the baseline (unreinforced) responding of children on a two-choice visual discrimination task involving unfamiliar stimuli. The results are presented in Figure 6–5.

On each graph in the figure, the subject groups are shown on the abscissa, and each group's mean percentage showing a response bias (at least 9 of 10 responses are to some position, stimulus or alternation pattern) is plotted on the ordinate. Stimulus perservation is shown in the upper graph, position perseveration in the middle graph, and total perseveration (their sum) in the lower graph. The data reveal that the autistic children engaged primarily in stimulus perseveration, (upper graph) while the mentally age-matched (MA) normal children displayed position perseveration (middle graph). However, the children in both groups showed significantly more perseveration responding than the chronologically age-matched (CA) normal children (lower graph). In addition (not shown in the figure), the CA-matched normal children frequently engaged in alternation responding and were found to switch their response strategies during the task (e.g., from repetition to alternation), while the lower MA autistics and normals rarely changed response patterns. Moreover, the study suggests that mental age is highly correlated with the flexibility of response strategies used, as low MA children (autistic and normal) typically perseverated on a single strategy, while high MA children sampled more of their environment.

If perseveration responding is a function of mental age, this would be consistent with some of the stimulus overselectivity studies in which overselective responding has been found to be common to autistic, retarded, and normal children with low mental ages (Schover and Newsom 1976; Wilhelm and Lovaas 1976; Kovattana and Kraemer 1974). In fact, as perseveration and overselectivity both represent problems of stimulus control, it is of interest to consider the possible relationship between the two. At first glance, perseveration does not appear simply to be an instance of overselectivity, but rather they seem to be two different deficits. Typically, overselectivity has been used to describe responding to a restricted portion of a stimulus, for example, identifying a wagon solely by its wheels instead of by the entire stimulus complex. Perseveration responding, on the other hand, indicates overly repetitious responding. Perseveration responding may include cases of stimulus overselectivity, if the repetitive responding is to a restricted portion of a stimulus, but perseveration is not limited to such responding as it can include position, alternation between stimuli, alternation between position strategies, and so on. Thus, perseveration and overselectivity may represent different problems, and therefore occur independently, though they may be compatible under certain circumstances. Both types of responding indicate a failure to sample alternative stimuli and responses and, as a result, they tend to restrict what a child learns. In this regard, overselective responding and perseveration responding are much alike.

Implications for Treatment _____

The difference in response patterns found between autistic and normal children, be it overselective or perseveration responding, has important implications for the treatment of autistic children. For example, when one wishes to determine whether a child has learned the appropriate label for a particular stimulus, 90-100 percent correct responding on a given discrimination is often used as a criterion; if the child reliably selects the target stimulus from the pair of stimuli presented, it will be assumed that he/she has learned to associate the label with the particular stimulus. On the other hand, 100 percent correct responding may not be a sufficient criterion for the measurement of learning, as a child may perseverate on one stimulus, or overselectively respond to a stimulus without learning anything about the verbal instruction. This indicates that it is essential to carefully assess stimulus control *after* discriminative responding has been established. This can be done in two ways: (1) by presenting the target stimulus with several other stimuli (if the child has been responding to the appropriate cues of the target stimulus, discriminative responding should be maintained); and (2) by changing the instruction and asking the child to identify a different stimulus. This would assess whether a child learned about the instruction, as differential responding to the two verbal instructions would indicate that the child had associated the proper verbal instruction with the proper response.

While such assessments may allow for the identification of inappropriate stimulus control, they do not eliminate the problem. Several studies have investigated procedures for ensuring that stimulus control is established during training as intended. Cushing and Rincover (1978) compared the stimulus control acquired by the reinforced stimulus (S+) and nonreinforced stimulus (S−) after mastery of a two-choice visual discrimination task. When an autistic child had been trained to reliably respond to the S+, probe trials were conducted in which the S+ and the S− were each presented with novel stimuli. The results indicated that some of the children had learned to avoid the S− instead of approach the S+. To remediate this problem, a procedure was implemented in which the S+ was presented with multiple S-s *during* training. This prevented the children from responding solely to the S− and ensured learning about the intended training stimulus (S+).

Cook and Rincover (1978) noted similar unintended stimulus control with autistic children. They found that some children responded consistently to the S+ in the presence of certain S− stimuli, yet did not respond to the same S+ when in the presence of other S− stimuli. To alleviate this inconsistent responding, the authors devised two different S− fading procedures. One fading procedure involved gradually changing the form of the nondisruptive S− (the one which did not interfere with responding to the S+), until it took the form of a previously disruptive S− (one which previously interfered with responding to the S+). In the other fading procedure, the S+ card was initially presented with a blank (S−) card, and then a previously disruptive S− was intermittently introduced in place of the blank S−; the percent of trials in which the disruptive S− was presented was gradually increased until it reached 100 percent (i.e., replaced the blank card). The results of the study showed that both S− fading procedures were effective in establishing responding to the S+, despite the presence of the previously disruptive S−.

Attempts have been made to increase the effectiveness of prompts with autistic children. Schreibman (1975) compared the effectiveness of two different prompting procedures for teaching visual and auditory discriminations. One procedure, extra-stimulus prompting, consisted of adding an extra cue as the prompt (e.g., pointing to the correct stimulus). The other procedure, within-stimulus prompting, first involved the exaggeration of the dimension on which two stimuli differed (e.g., exaggerating the slash line on the Q to teach a child to discriminate between the letters O and Q). Then the exaggerated component was gradually reduced to its original dimension. Schreibman found that the children never learned the discrimination when the extra-stimulus prompting procedure was employed, but usually did master the discrimination when the within-stimulus prompting procedure was used.

Rincover (1978) continued this line of research, training autistic children to respond correctly on a discrimination task by pretraining a distinctive feature of the S+. For example, to discriminate between the printed words *JAR* (S+) and *SON* (S−), he taught the child to respond to the horizontal line atop the *J* in the word *JAR*. After a child mastered a discrimination, probe trials were conducted to determine if the child was responding to only the pretrained feature, or if he had learned about other features of the S+. The results indicated that the children continued to respond correctly when the pretrained feature was eliminated (e.g., *JAR* versus *SON*) or made irrelevant (e.g., *JAR* versus *EON*), but failed to discriminate correctly when the entire letter containing the distinctive feature was made irrelevant (e.g., *JAR* versus *JON*). Thus, the subjects had learned more about the S+ word than just the pretrained feature; however, the features to which they were responding were limited to the first letter of the S+ word.

As an alternative to utilizing procedures that allow the autistic child to use his/her deviant response patterns, other studies have employed treatments designed to eliminate the stimulus control deficits. Schover and Newsom (1976) found that they were able to increase the number of cues the autistic children responded to by overtraining (50 additional trials) them on a discrimination they had already acquired. Similarly, Schreibman, Koegel, and Craig (1977) found that the breadth of stimulus control increased somewhat with exposure to the target stimulus. Extending this line of research, Koegel and Schreibman (1977) taught autistic and normal children a conditional discrimination that required responding to multiple cues. The children were reinforced for making a bar press response when both auditory and visual cues were presented together, but were not reinforced for making the response when either cue was presented alone. The results revealed that the autistic children learned to respond only when both cues were presented, but with greater difficulty than the normal children. In addition, the authors trained an autistic child in a series of successive conditional discriminations to determine if she could learn to respond to *new* discriminations on the basis of both component cues. They found that after training on only two conditional discriminations, the child learned to approach new discriminations by initially responding to both cues, suggesting some generalization of multiple-cue responding.

All of these attempts to eliminate stimulus control deficits have focused on increasing the number of cues to which the child responds. This, of course, assumes that these deficits result from responding to too few cues. If, however,

ADvantage
TICKETING SYSTEMS
P.O. Box 1070, Bristol BS12 1EQ
Tel: 01454-417479 Fax: 01454-419170
The Ticket and Advertising Specialist

stimulus control deficits are a result of tunnel vision, then merely increasing the number of cues a child responds to will not eliminate the problem. To date, no attempts have been made to alleviate tunnel vision.

In light of the perseveration and overselective response strategies utilized by autistic children, some new target behaviors may be useful in their treatment, behaviors that might be prerequisites to most social and intellectual skills. Typically, treatment has involved teaching these children specific social, academic, emotional, and play skills; however, this is a very slow and tedious process. For example, Lovaas, Koegel, Simmons, and Long (1973) report that after a year of intensive daily behavior therapy, the frequency of the autistics' social behavior increased only from about 2–9 percent and, more generally speaking, children's gains were analogous to moving "10 to 20 steps on a 100-step ladder." A more efficient approach would be to identify *key* target behaviors which may result in more widespread behavior change. For example, if perseveration and overselective responding are the cause of many of the deficits of autistic children, then perhaps teaching them how to sample their environment might result in their learning a variety of new (language, social, play) behaviors from the natural environment. This would require further study of the normal development of sampling strategies, so that we would know more precisely what to teach. However, a training program could be devised to broaden their area of attention by teaching these children to respond not only to concurrent cues, but to spatially separate cues, and cues presented in various spatial configurations. In addition, the autistics could be taught to switch their responses from one cue to another, alternate responding under conditions of extinction, and so on. If autistic children can be taught to sample their environment in this way, perhaps the natural environment will be more effective in teaching and maintaining new skills.

Note _____

Portions of the research reported in this chapter were supported by U.S. Office of Education Research Grant No. G007802084 from the Bureau for the Education of the Handicapped. The authors are grateful to the administration and staff of the Henry Wiseman Kendall Center and the Guilford County Developmental Center for their generous support of our experimental programs, and to Ken Berry, Rick Cook, Linda Eason, and Debbie Packard, who helped in treatment and data collection.

Motivational Techniques

O f the many descriptions and interpretations of autistic symptomatology, one characteristic is consistently evident: autistic children do not appear motivated to engage in socially appropriate activities. Indeed, autistic children are typically described as aloof, oblivious, or withdrawn (e.g., Koegel, Egel, and Dunlap 1980; O'Gorman 1967; Rimland 1964; Kanner 1943). They display little curiosity or exploratory behavior, are typically unresponsive, and show a singular disregard for most external events (Koegel and Schreibman 1976; Rutter 1966). In short, autistic children tend to display a virtual absence of goal-directed behavior. They are uniquely unmotivated to learn or perform the behaviors which are necessary for successful functioning in society.

Over the past few years, psychologists and educators have made great gains in understanding and treating the symptoms of autism (see Koegel, *et al.* 1980; Dunlap, Koegel, and Egel 1979). In order to make this progress, some initial understanding of the variables governing the motivation of autistic children was necessary. Thus, Ferster and DeMyer's early work (1962, 1961), which showed that the responding of autistic children could be lawfully controlled by the principles of reinforcement, served as the basis from which further gains were developed. The knowledge that carefully administered reinforcers could be used to build behavioral repertoires led to effective programs for the establishment of imitation (e.g., Metz 1965), speech and language (e.g., Lovaas 1977b; Carr, Schreibman, and Lovaas 1975; Stevens-Long and Rasmussen 1974; Hewett 1965) and numerous self-help and school-related behaviors (e.g., Rincover and Koegel 1977a; Rosenbaum and Breiling 1976; Koegel and Rincover 1974; Martin, *et al.* 1968; Marshall 1966). The techniques of reinforcement were used repeatedly during the 1960s and 1970s to significantly modify the condition of autism. Procedures involving positive, and occasionally negative reinforcers (e.g., Lovaas, Schaeffer, and Simmons 1965), were proven to be viable motivation techniques.

*This chapter was authored by **Glen Dunlap,** University of California, Santa Barbara and **Andrew L. Egel,** University of Maryland, College Park.*

While progress in treating autism over the past two decades has been very rapid, some limitations associated with the commonly used motivational techniques have become increasingly apparent. It has been necessary to employ very powerful reinforcing stimuli (such as foodstuffs) in relatively controlled settings, in order to produce behavior gains. Such situations have, until recently, comprised the essence of motivational strategy. This approach has been expensive in terms of the amount of reinforcement and professional time required to teach a particular response. In addition, such powerful primary reinforcers are subject to rapid satiation and, thus, their utility within an educational session can be short-lived. A further limitation of this approach to motivation is that the artificial nature of primary reinforcers in controlled settings has proven highly discriminable. Thus, while the autistic students may show impressive improvement in the treatment environment, the gains typically do not generalize or maintain in other settings (see Chapter 15). In summarizing over 12 years of research and treatment with autistic children, Lovaas (1977a p. 370); pointed to the above issues as the principal difficulties in his generally successful efforts, and attributed these difficulties to "our basic ignorance of motivation."

Recently, increased interest and research activity has focused on the problem of motivating autistic children. While we must still admit to a "basic ignorance," we are, nevertheless, beginning to identify some additional variables which are proving influential in heightening autistic children's motivation. Many of these motivational variables have been subject to investigation in other populations (e.g., MacMillan 1971), but have not been systematically studied with autistic children. This information is being translated into techniques which can be used successfully in classrooms, clinics, and other settings. The purpose of this chapter is to describe some of the recent work on applied, motivational research. In particular, it will focus on a number of recent studies conducted in a variety of schools and clinics, and will stress the applicability of these motivational techniques for teaching autistic children.

What is Motivation? _____

Before discussing the development of techniques for increasing motivation, it will be useful to briefly examine what is meant by the term. Traditionally, *motivation* has been described as an internal force or drive which is somehow intrinsic to an individual, and which spurs the individual to engage in particular behaviors. Motivation, in addition, has been viewed as an explanatory construct which helps define a person's *psychological identity*. From this perspective, psychologists, educators and philosophers have explored the development and vicissitudes of a variety of motives. Such investigations have been primarily theoretical because inferred entities, such as motivation, are not amenable to direct observation or measurement. Just as it is difficult to empirically study motivation as a hypothetical construct, it is similarly difficult (or impossible) to identify variables or techniques which might influence it.

For this reason, scientists have begun to question the utility of directly studying motivation as an inferred, mentalistic construct (Fantino 1973). Instead, the focus of motivation research has been turned to operationally defined response characteristics, such as latency and frequency, which may be considered to be manifestations of motivational states (cf., Teitelbaum 1966). For example, rather than attempting to determine whether a child is "motivated" to watch television or perform school work, an empirical approach would involve direct measures of the amount of time the child engages in such activities. Such measures, of course, cannot be construed as direct measures of motivation. However, they may be used as a starting point or baseline from which changes in the child's motivation to engage in such activities may be studied. Thus, if the child begins to spend increased amounts of time doing school work, we might claim that the child appears to be more motivated to do so. Further, if a particular intervention (such as changing to a new textbook) can be reliably associated with the increase in time spent with school work, it might be reasonable to suggest that the intervention was an effective motivational technique. It is important to remember, however, that this approach refers to motivation in terms of behavioral manifestations and not in terms of internal hypothesized constructs. In this sense, motivational techniques cannot be said to impinge upon "motivation" per se, but, rather, upon response characteristics which have come to be seen as indicative of motivation. Motivational techniques affect behavior in much the same way as language instruction affects observable verbal behavior. In this chapter, the term *motivation* will refer to those response characteristics which have been commonly known as reflecting motivation.

What, then, are the behavioral characteristics that can be considered indicative of motivation? More specifically, if the motivation of an autistic child to perform a particular behavior is modified, what kind of behavioral evidence might one expect to see? First of all, we must rely on measures of nonverbal behavior. Autistic children are often incapable of producing verbal reports and, at any rate, verbal reports frequently do not correspond with nonverbal behavior (cf., Risley and Hart 1968; Cromwell 1963). Second, the nonverbal characteristics of motivated behavior should be measurable and should contain face validity; that is, the target characteristics should conform to accepted notions of motivation. The rate, frequency, and duration with which a response is performed constitute such characteristics. For example, if a child's motivation to play with toys increases, one would expect to observe the child playing more frequently and for longer periods of time. Similarly, perseveration, or the number of attempts to solve a problem (e.g., a jigsaw puzzle), is a common indicator of motivation. If a child's attempts to complete a problem increase, one would say that the child is more motivated to perform the behavior. Response latency is another characteristic that can be associated with motivation. Children who respond quickly to instructions are typically considered more motivated than those who dawdle, delay, or engage in alternative behaviors. Applied researchers are also beginning to use observer judgments of aspects of children's behavior in efforts to validate the effects of their interventions (cf., Wolf 1978). For example, observers have been asked to rate the levels of enthusiasm displayed by children as they engage in particular activities. Such ratings, accompanied by the more objective measures described above, can be considered to offer information relevant to the goal of increasing motivation.

While most applied research on instructional procedures for autistic children has included techniques relevant to motivation (e.g., reinforcement), relatively few investigations have focused specifically on attempts to manipulate motivation per se. Rather, the bulk of this applied research has been concerned with the development of behavioral repertoires (e.g., procedures for teaching language skills), or with the investigation of particular learning characteristics (e.g., stimulus overselectivity). The rest of this chapter will focus on some recent studies which have explicitly investigated the effects of techniques designed to improve the motivation of autistic children to learn and perform appropriate behaviors. The studies involve positive procedures which can be readily applied by teachers in public classrooms and other education settings.

Research on Reinforcers _____

From a behavioral perspective, the issue of motivation has usually been addressed as a question pertaining to the power of reinforcers. Most of our behavior, and its development, is assumed to occur as a function of the numerous reinforcers prevelant in our environment. Even a cursory inventory would quickly turn up hundreds of reinforcing stimuli which daily serve to control (to motivate) our complex responding. While some of these reinforcers are arbitrary or programmed, such as pay checks, most occur naturally as we interact with out surroundings (Ferster 1967). The fact that most people are similarly motivated by natural reinforcers (e.g., smiles, social approval, warmth from putting on a jacket) probably helps to explain the commonalities in human development.

Unfortunately, autistic children do not appear to be motivated by many of these naturally occurring events. Social stimuli, such as smiles and frowns, generally do not affect them (Lovaas, *et al.,* 1966; Ferster 1961). Many treatment efforts have sought to overcome this problem by using powerful primary reinforcers, such as food. While this approach has been successful in producing the motivation required to teach many behaviors, the artificial nature of this motivational system is rarely matched in the normal environment and, as a result, treatment gains are not typically displayed outside the treatment settings (Lovaas, *et al.,* 1973).

Recognition of the problems associated with artificial reinforcers and the need to normalize autistic children's motivation was evident in some of the earliest behavioral writings on the topic of autism (Ferster 1961). Efforts were soon made to establish social stimuli, such as physical proximity to adults and the word *good,* as reinforcers. Successes were reported in two experiments (Lovaas, *et al.,* 1966; Lovaas, Schaeffer, and Simmons 1965); however, the effects were reported as stimulus-specific — that is, the social stimuli did not continue to serve as reinforcers beyond the controlled environments in which they were established. In the years since these findings were reported, essentially no additional work has been published, and we remain quite ignorant about the feasibility of establishing conditioned reinforcers. As other authors have argued (e.g., Rincover and Koegel 1977b), this issue of normalizing autistic children's motivation is one of the most critical areas awaiting future research.

While little is known about the exact mechanisms by which neutral stimuli become reinforcers, it, nevertheless, is certain that in some cases, autistic children become motivated by social reinforcers (e.g., Risley and Wolf 1967; Wolf, Risley, and Mees 1964). This suggests that teachers should continue to attempt the development of social reinforcers through continual pairing of social approval with functional primary reinforcers. In the future, research may suggest ways to expedite this process.

Reliance on food reinforcers is problematic for reasons beyond artificiality. Children tend to satiate on food relatively quickly and, thus, food may lose its reinforcing value by the end of a school day. In addition, some autistic children are finicky, disliking or refusing to eat all but a limited number of foodstuffs. For many children, and for many reasons, food (or liquids) may not always be a functional reinforcer. In order to provide the necessary motivation to conduct educational activities, creative teachers and psychologists have looked elsewhere for reinforcing stimuli. Since autistic children tend to spend most of their free time engaged in self-stimulation (Koegel, *et al.,* 1974; Lovaas, Litrownik, and Mann 1971), a logical place to seek reinforcers is in the realm of sensory stimulation. Sensory reinforcers such as lights and music have been used to teach autistic and retarded children a number of complex behaviors (e.g., Hung 1978; Bailey and Meyerson 1969; Fineman 1968). In particular, the work of Rincover and his colleagues (Rincover, *et al.,* 1979; 1977) has suggested numerous ways that motivation can be built through the contingent use of sensory stimulation. This work is discussed in detail in Chapter 8 where one point is clearly illustrated: Reinforcing stimuli, whether food or favored sensory events, are idiosyncratic, and individual children will be motivated to work (learn) for quite different reinforcers. A worthwhile strategy for identifying reinforcing stimuli is to observe individual children in free play activities. Favored and potentially reinforcing stimuli may quickly become evident. Teachers can then use these stimuli to increase children's motivation by presenting them contingently upon a target response. As Premack (1959) has described, access to high probability responses (e.g., sensory stimulation) can serve to reinforce low probability responses (e.g., school work).

Research on Variation

A great deal of theory and research has argued persuasively that organisms have a need for and are motivated by variation and novelty in their surroundings (Fowler 1965; Dember 1961; Maddi 1961; Berlyne 1960). Indeed, studies on deprivation have suggested that functioning may be severely impaired in the absence of novel and variable stimuli (Koegel and Felsenfeld 1977; Rosenzweig 1976; Zubek 1969). Common sense tells us that children, including autistic children, might be more motivated by situations that contain elements of change, variation, and novelty (as opposed to unchanging or monotonous situations). Innovative teachers have recognized this possibility and have attempted to program various surprises, schedule changes, and novel activities into their classroom curricula. Still, there has been little evidence regarding the effects that such manipulations might have on the motivation of autistic children. In order to

The power of sensory reinforcement can be seen here where the child is receiving reinforcement through the manipulation of a toy.

provide some information on this topic, recent studies have assessed the value of motivational techniques involving variation in reinforcing, as well as antecedent (instructional), stimuli.

Varying Reinforcers

While most research pertaining to stimulus variation has focused on manipulations of antecedent stimuli, a number of studies have looked at the motivational effects of varying the stimuli which are presented subsequent to a response. This body of research has demonstrated facilitative effects when variable or novel stimuli (reinforcers) are presented contingent upon responding. For example, Gullickson (1966) showed that preschool children produced more lever-pressing responses when novel (as opposed to familiar) auditory stimuli followed each response. Manley and Miller (1968) reported similar effects when the stimuli were in the visual mode. In a later study, Wilson (1974) found that children who were engaged in a two-choice discrimination task emitted significantly more responses to a button which produced novel, rather than familiar, stimuli. Results similar to these have also been found with nonhuman subjects (e.g., Fowler 1967; Butler and Woolpy 1963; Butler 1957; 1954).

The above studies, all of which employed sensory stimuli such as lights or sounds, have an analogy in the autism literature. As mentioned previously, Rincover, *et al.* (1977) found that contingent sensory stimulation was able to sustain high rates of responding by autistic children. They also found that repeated exposure to a particular sensory event (e.g., a particular song) eventually produced declines in the rate of responding (i.e., satiation). They further demonstrated, however, that the introduction of variation in aspects of the sensory presentations (i.e., changing the song) was sufficient to completely restore the high response rates. Even very slight variations of the reinforcing stimuli were sufficient to re-establish high levels of motivation.

These results suggest a plausible means of extending the effectiveness of not only sensory, but edible reinforcers as well. Fowler (1967), for example, explicitly suggested that satiation with edibles (or other stimuli) is less likely to occur if the reinforcer presentations incorporate a degree of novelty. An investigation was designed to assess the possibility that varying edible reinforcers would increase and prolong the motivation of autistic children.

The study was conducted in two phases. In the first phase, a basic research approach was adopted in which highly controlled conditions governed the experimental manipulations. The second phase extended the procedures to naturalistic, classroom environments. Both phases compared a method of presenting varied reinforcers with a strategy of employing a single, yet functional, reinforcer.

Ten autistic children participated in the first phase of the investigation (Egel 1980). They ranged in age from 4 years to 13–1/2 years and represented a broad range of autistic characteristics (cf., Ritvo and Freeman 1978). Experimental sessions were conducted in a quiet, partitioned area of a classroom which prevented visual distractions. This small (8' × 6') area contained a chair and a table, on top of which was a specially constructed box containing a response lever and a chute for automatic delivery of reinforcers. This apparatus was selected because sessions could be conducted, responses emitted, and reinforcers delivered in the total absence of interpersonal interaction, thus removing any possible effects of experimental bias or contamination. All sessions were videotaped in order to maximize accuracy and reliability of data recording.

Prior to the investigation, each child was taught to emit one lever-pressing response and collect (and consume) a reinforcer prior to making another response. The reinforcers used during this pretraining were not used during any experimental session. All reinforcers used for pretraining and experimental sessions were selected from teacher-prepared lists of functional, edible reinforcers specific for each child. These reinforcers were then randomly assigned to the constant and varied reinforcer conditions.

Each child participated in each condition, with the order of presentation balanced across the children. In the *constant reinforcer* condition, a child received the same reinforcer each time a response was made. The child was al-

FIGURE 7–1.   Total number of responses emitted by each child in the constant and varied reinforcer presentation conditions. (Figure reprinted from Egel, A.L., 1981 "The Effects of Constant vs. Varied Reinforcer Presentation on Responding by Autistic Children," *Journal of Experimental Child Psychology*. Copyright by Academic Press, Inc. Reproduced by permission.)

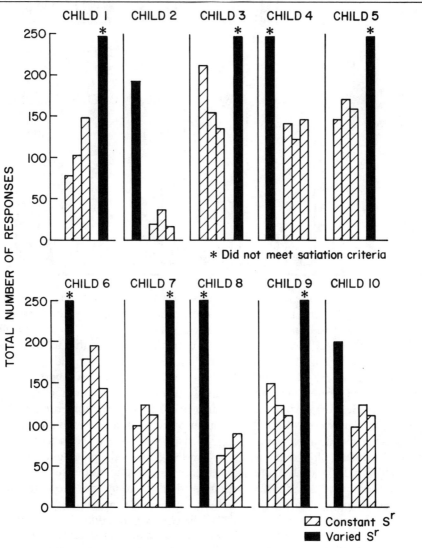

FIGURE 7–2.   Average interresponse intervals (sec.) for each child in the constant vs. varied reinforcer presentation condition.

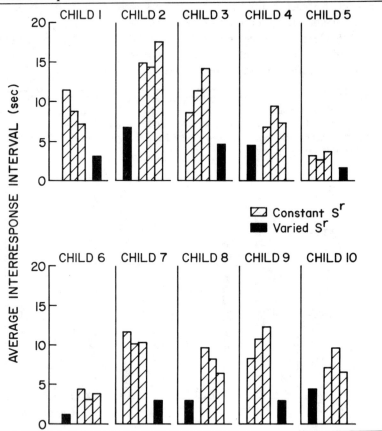

lowed to continue responding until satiation (three or less responses for each of three consecutive minutes) or 250 responses occurred. A second reinforcer was then presented until criterion was once again achieved. The *varied reinforcer* condition was conducted in the same manner, except that following approximately every third response, the child received a different one of the three reinforcers used in the context of the constant reinforcer condition. The specific order of presentation was randomly determined; however, a child never received less than two nor more than four of the same reinforcer in a row.

Data were collected on total responses emitted in each condition, as well as the speed (interresponse interval) with which the responses were produced. The results, plotted in Figures 7–1 and 7–2, proved highly significant (*probability* <.001) for each of the dependent measures; that is, the children emitted significantly more and faster responses when the reinforcer presentation was varied as opposed to when it was held constant. It is interesting to note that these results were consistent across all of the children studied.

The above findings are very encouraging and suggest an easily applied method for strengthening the utility of edible reinforcers. However, it remained to be seen whether or not a similar effect could be obtained in natural classroom environments. Therefore, in the second phase of this investigation (Egel 1981), methods similar to that of the first phase were applied in typical classrooms for autistic children. Specifically, the differential effects of constant versus varied reinforcer presentation on correct responding and on-task behavior were compared within the context of a reversal design. In the *constant* condition, the same reinforcer was presented by the classroom teacher until the child emitted 125 correct responses or had not responded for three consecutive trials. These criteria were chosen for two major reasons. The 125 correct responses were chosen as a criterion in order to "overtrain" the discriminations used in this investigation, since previous research has demonstrated that overtraining is an

FIGURE 7–3. The effects of constant vs. varied reinforcer conditions on percent correct responding and on-task behavior. The heavy solid line separates constant vs. varied conditions, while the dashed lines separate individual sessions. (Figure reprinted from Egel, A.L., in press. "Reinforcer Variation: Implications for Motivating Developmentally Delayed Children," *Journal of Applied Behavior Analysis.* Copyright by Society for the Experimental Analysis of Behavior, Inc. Reproduced by permission.)

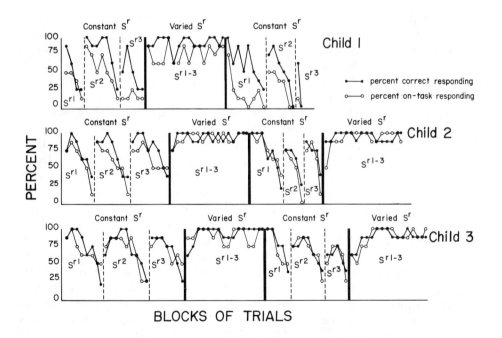

important variable in reducing stimulus overselectivity in autistic children (e.g., Koegel, *et al.,* 1979; Schover & Newsom 1976). The other criterion, failure to respond for three consecutive trials, was employed in order to indicate the occurrence of satiation. Following the presentation of the first reinforcer (and the occurrence of one of the criteria), a second reinforcer was delivered until one of the above criteria was met, at which time a third reinforcer was introduced. The *varied* reinforcer condition was conducted in exactly the same manner, except that the child received a different one of the three reinforcers used in the constant condition for approximately every third response.

The results obtained from this second phase (Figure 7–3) proved similar to the first phase in demonstrating the superiority of using varied reinforcers. The varied reinforcer approach produced much higher percentages of correct responding and less off-task behavior when compared to the constant presentation condition.

The results are significant in that they identify a relatively simple procedure which classroom teachers can employ to motivate autistic children. The results indicate that satiation can be delayed by varying the presentation of edible reinforcers. Clearly, it is likely that teachers (and children) will benefit from the incorporation of varied stimuli into their reinforcement contingencies.

Varying Antecedent (Instructional) Stimuli

In addition to the work on varied reinforcers, there have been frequent suggestions that varying antecedent stimuli can produce similarly facilitative results. Much of the early work in this area assessed the impact of antecedent variation or novelty on such motivational variables as orientation, responsivity, and approach behavior. For example, a number of studies with infra-human subjects found that novel environments or objects elicited increases in a variety of exploratory and observational responses (Berlyne and Slater 1957; Welker 1956; Berlyne 1955; Montgomery 1952; 1951). Very similar results also have been obtained with human adults (Berlyne and Ditkofsky 1976; Berlyne 1960; 1958; 1951) and children (Hutt 1975; 1967; Cantor and Cantor 1964a, 1964b; Fantz 1964).

Work on antecedent stimulus novelty and variation has also been conducted with developmentally disabled individuals. For example, O'Connor and Hermelin (1967) found that psychotic children showed a preference for novel, as opposed to familiar, stimuli. Similarly, Young (1969) demonstrated that novel stimuli attracted increases in the visual fixations of autistic children, while such fixations to familiar stimuli decreased. In a study involving discrimination learning, Zeaman, House, and Orlando (1968) found that the insertion of novel stimuli into otherwise unchanging discrimination tasks significantly improved the performance of retarded children. Other research has shown similarly facilitative effects from providing antecedent stimulus variation in a number of training contexts (Mulligan, *et al.* 1980; Panyan and Hall 1978; Granzin and Carnine 1977; Schroeder and Baer 1972; Bilsky and Heal 1969; White 1966; 1965; Greeno 1964).

While relatively little research has considered manipulations of antecedent stimuli in teaching situations with autistic children (e.g., Dunlap and Koegel, 1980b), the above research suggests that instructional variation might prove influential in improving the children's motivation, responsivity, and task performance. This possibility seems especially plausible in light of the observation that instructions for autistic children are typically presented in a serial and relatively unchanging manner where a particular task is presented separately throughout a session until a predetermined performance criterion is achieved, or until the session ends. Only then is a new task introduced. It is possible that this fixed-format approach may inadvertently serve to restrict motivation and, in effect, produce a boring interaction which the student may seek to avoid (Bijou 1978).

Task variation can have a dramatic effect on the children's emotions during learning. This child's happiness and enthusiasm for learning are readily apparent during this varied task teaching session.

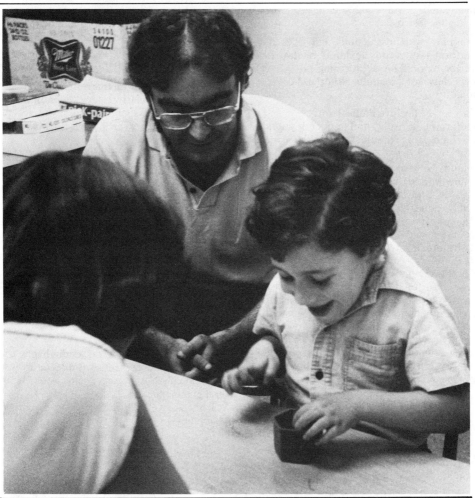

TABLE 7-1
Rating Scales for Child Enthusiasm, Interest, Happiness, and General Behavior.*

ENTHUSIASM
Negative Enthusiasm
Tries to leave the room, throws tantrums, kicks, screams, throws material around the room, cries, pushes the task away or refuses to perform the task   (Score 0)

Remains in chair, but generally does not comply with instructions; behavior consists primarily of vocalizations and motor behavior unrelated to the task — yawning, rocking, loud tapping, etc.   (Score 1)

Neutral Enthusiasm
Generally complies with instructions, but tends to get fidgety; moments of staring or inattention, "toying" with stimulus materials, wriggling feet, etc.   (Score 2)

Complies with instructions, but does not perform task readily; exhibits neutral behavior by occasionally focusing on (watching) clinician or stimulus materials between trials   (Score 3)

Positive Enthusiasm
Performs task readily and frequently attends to clinician or stimulus materials between trials   (Score 4)

Attends to task quickly, laughs or smiles while working on the task; predominantly watches clinician and stimulus materials intently; performs extra behaviors related to the task, and performs appropriate creative behaviors with stimulus materials   (Score 5)

GENERAL BEHAVIOR
Poorly Behaved
Child is disruptive, may tantrum, attempt to leave chair or room, interrupt teacher's instructions and/or show aggression towards teacher, self or objects; child is generally off-task, may fidget and squirm, show inappropriate vocal behavior (e.g., off-task laughter and noises) or motor behavior unrelated to task; shows little attention to task, and may be noncompliant
(Score 0 or 1, depending upon extent of disruptiveness)

Neutral Behavior
Child is neither very disruptive nor exceptionally attentive; child may fidget and appear inattentive, but is not aggressive or rebellious; generally complies with instructions, but may not do so readily

(Score 2 or 3, depending on extent of attentiveness)

Well-Behaved
Child sits quietly, attends to teacher and to task; responds to instructions; is compliant and appears to try to perform successfully; may laugh or show other emotional behavior under appropriate circumstances
(Score 4 or 5, depending upon extent of attention and compliance)

INTEREST
Disinterested
Child looks bored, noninvolved, not curious or eager to continue activity; may yawn or attempt to avoid (or escape) situation; spends much time looking around and little time attending to task; when child does respond, there may be a long response latency
(Score 0 or 1, depending on extent of disinterest)
Neutral Interest
Neither particularly interested nor disinterested; child seems to passively accept situation; does not rebel, but is not obviously eager to continue
(Score 2 or 3, depending on extent of interest)
Interested
Attends readily to task, responds readily and willingly; child is alert and involved in activity
(Score 4 or 5, depending upon level of alertness and involvement)

HAPPINESS   ### Unhappy
Cries, pouts, tantrums, appears to be sad, angry or frustrated; child seems not to be enjoying self
(Score 0 or 1, depending upon extent of unhappiness)
Neutral
Does not appear to be decidedly happy or particularly unhappy; may smile or frown occasionally but, overall, seems rather neutral in this situation.
(Score 2 or 3, depending upon extent of happiness)

Happy
Smiles, laughs appropriately, seems to be enjoying self
(Score 4 or 5, depending on extent of enjoyment)

The enthusiasm scale was taken from Koegel and Egel (1979), while the other three scales are from Dunlap and Koegel (1980a).

In order to test this possibility, a study was designed to evaluate the differential impact of two methods of delivering instructions on the motivation and task performance of autistic children (Dunlap and Koegel 1980a). In the context of a multiple baseline design, with a brief reversal for one child, two conditions were compared. In a *constant task* condition, a single task was presented separately for a consecutive number of trials throughout each 5– 10 minute session. All of the tasks were drawn from the children's regular curricula and were reported as being problematic. In a *varied task* condition, the same tasks were presented, but they were interspersed with a variety of other tasks, all drawn from the children's curricula. No task in this condition was ever presented more than twice in succession, and particular tasks averaged about one presentation out of every seven total trials. Reinforcement contingencies were identical in the two conditions, as was level of teacher competence.

Data were obtained on correct responding to each instruction throughout the experiment. In addition, for one of the children, data were obtained pertaining to the child's affect and general behavior as she engaged in the prescribed activities. The rating scales used by the observer were designed to reflect behavioral characteristics of motivation and are shown in Table 7– 1.

The results on correct responding were consistent across children, and showed that performance under the varied task approach was generally superior

FIGURE 7– 4.   The percentage of trials during which Child 2 gave no response to the task instruction. (Figure reprinted from Dunlap, G. and Koegel, R.L. 1980. "Motivating Autistic Children through Stimulus Variation," *Journal of Applied Behavior Analysis,* 13:619—627. Copyright by Society for the Experimental Analysis of Behavior, Inc. Reproduced by permission.)

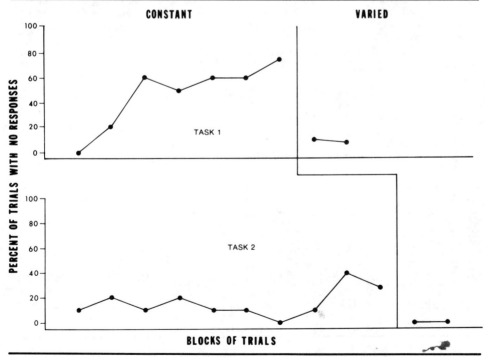

to performance under the constant task condition. In addition, and perhaps more significantly, trends in the varied task condition suggested continuous improvement in correct responding, while the constant task trends illustrated no improvement or declining performance.

When the data from the Dunlap and Koegel study are subjected to more detailed analyses, they become more striking and more clearly related to motivation. For example, as the constant task sessions progressed, one nonverbal child was observed to cease responding altogether, offering no attempt to respond at all. However, even with no change in reinforcement contingencies, the varied task approach apparently restored sufficient motivation for the child to at least attempt a response on virtually every trial. These data, shown in Figure 7–4, suggest that this child may have been "trying harder" when the instructions were varied.

Some confirmation of this hypothesis was obtained from additional analyses of the responding of another, higher functioning child. This child's sessions were all relatively long, permitting inspection of within-session trends in correct responding. These data, presented in Figure 7–5, show that as each constant task session progressed, the child made fewer and fewer correct responses. However, regardless of the length of the sessions or the number of total trials presented, the varied task session always produced trends which increased or

FIGURE 7–5.   Detailed within-session trends for Child 1. The heavy solid lines divide the varied vs. constant tasks conditions (in the multiple baseline design), and the dashed lines separate individual sessions within conditions. The asterisks indicate the block of trials during which the brief reversal occurred. The minus (–) and positive (+) signs indicate, respectively, declining trends and either increasing or constant trends in correct responding within a session. (Figure reprinted from Dunlap, G. and Koegel, R.L. 1980. "Motivating Autistic Children through Stimulus Variation," *Journal of Applied Behavior Analysis,* 13:619—627. Copyright by Society for the Experimental Analysis of Behavior, Inc. Reproduced by permission.)

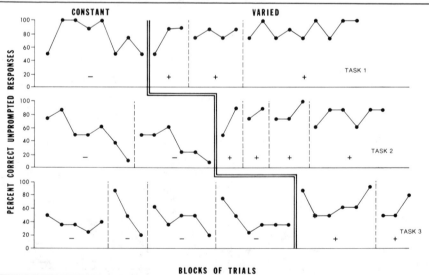

remained stable. (The dip in the first varied task session for Task 3 represents the point at which the brief return to the constant task session was conducted.) These data suggest even more strongly that the constant task approach may have produced boredom and apathy, and that variation may have generated a heightened and prolonged motivation and interest in the activities. It is interesting to note that these trends are very similar to those reported by Egel and discussed on page (000). This similarity strongly suggests that variation (whether antecedent or consequent) has a powerful effect on motivation as measured by level of correct responding.

As all of the sessions for this higher functioning child were videotaped, it was possible to obtain further data relevant to this possibility. After dividing each videotaped session into three-minute segments and transferring the segments in random order onto new videotapes, these taped segments were shown to two observers who were naive with respect to all aspects of the experiment, and who had no previous exposure to this syndrome of autism. The observers independently scored each three-minute segment on each of the four six-point scales shown in Table 7–1 (see page [000]). The scales assessed the child's level of *Enthusiasm, Happiness, Interest* (in the task) and *General Behavior* (on-task versus off-task behavior). The data obtained from the four scales showed very similar functions and have been combined in Figure 7–6. The figure is similar to Figure 7–5 in that it permits inspection of within-session trends. In this case, scale amplitudes (showing level of enthusiasm, etc.) are shown on the ordinate, and continuous, three-minute segments are on the abscissa.

The trends clearly reflect declining affect (or motivation) in the constant task sessions, with improved affect throughout the relatively lengthy varied task sessions. (Again, the dip in the first varied task session for Task 3 represents the brief reversal to the constant task approach.)

While these results indicate that varying instructions can serve to heighten motivation, it is not yet clear whether this approach will facilitate the acquisition of new behaviors. The tasks in the study described above may have been learned prior to or during early phases of the experiment. Thus, it is possible that variation may have facilitated motivation and task performance, but not necessarily aided in the process of task acquisition. An experiment is currently being conducted in order to clarify this issue.

The finding that task variation is an influential variable suggests that other methods of introducing variation might also be effective. For example, Dunlap and Koegel (1980b) attempted two additional strategies for providing change in educational activities. In the first, variation was provided by suddenly changing stimulus materials, and in the second, a change in routine was introduced by providing a four-week break before renewing activity on a specific task. Both approaches served to improve performance. Other methods may be similarly influential. For example, modulations of instructional intonation, changes in settings or occasional substitutions of teachers may be found to have similarly facilitative effects. While these questions are in need of further research, the results obtained thus far strongly indicate that task variation can be employed as a powerful technique to increase autistic children's motivation.

FIGURE 7–6.   The composite ratings by experimentally naive observers of Child 1's affect and general behavior. The ordinate shows the composite scales with 5 being very happy, very interested, very enthusiastic, and very well behaved, and 0 being extremely unhappy, disinterested, unenthusiastic, and poorly behaved. Consecutive 3-minute segments are shown on the abscissa. The heavy solid lines divide constant vs. varied task condition (in the multiple baseline design), and the dashed lines separate individual sessions. The asterisks indicate the 3-minute segments that contain the brief reversal of conditions. (Figure reprinted from Dunlap, G. and Koegel, R.L. 1980. "Motivating Autistic Children through Stimulus Variation," *Journal of Applied Behavior Analysis,* 13:619—627. Copyright by Society for the Experimental Analysis of Behavior, Inc. Reproduced by permission.)

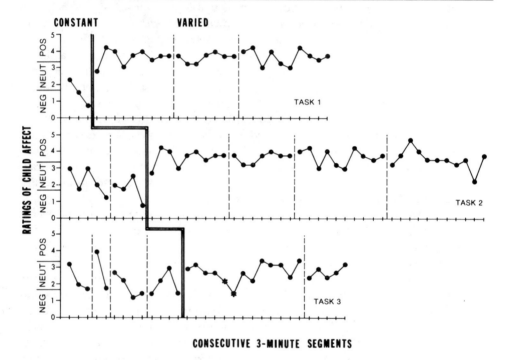

Research on Success versus Failure

A great deal of work in the area of motivation has considered the differential effects of success and failure experiences. A basic thesis of this work is that histories of failure may serve to dampen motivation, impair performance, and increase task avoidance (Clark and Rutter 1979; Rodda 1977; MacMillan 1971; Bradley 1970; Zigler and Butterfield 1968; Zigler 1966). Such effects may be especially conspicuous with handicapped persons whose motor and cognitive disabilities probably result in numerous and prolonged exposures to failure and frustration. Repeated failures may then reduce expectancies for success (MacMillan 1975), and future levels of motivation and perseverance may subsequently decline. In this way, a circular reaction may develop in which failure leads to impaired motivation that may increase the probability of additional failure, ad infinitum.

In recent years, a number of researchers have conducted experiments on the effects of failure with a variety of handicapped populations (e.g., Chan and Keough 1974; Gruen, Ottinger, and Ollendick 1974). For example, experimentally induced failure has been shown to significantly affect the situational expectations (MacMillan 1975) and probability learning (Ollendick, Balla, and Zigler 1971) of retarded children. Similarly, Brookshire (1972) found that exposure to difficult items interfered with adult aphasics' subsequent ability to name easy-to-name items. Zeaman and House (1963) found that, following a prolonged sequence of failure experiences, retarded subjects could not perform a simple discrimination problem which they had solved earlier.

In one of the first investigations of success versus failure with autistic and schizophrenic children, Churchill (1971) found that pathological behavior increased dramatically during exposure to failure. In this experiment, two classroom-like tasks were manipulated to ensure high rates (over 90 percent) of successful responding in one condition and very low rates (under 10 percent) of success in the failure condition. It was found that self-stimulation, frustration (tantruming, crying, etc.) and avoidance were significantly elevated in the failure condition.

Along these same lines, Koegel and Egel (1979) designed a study to assess the influence of success versus failure (correct versus incorrect task completion) on autistic children's motivation. In this study, motivation was defined in terms of the children's attempts to complete a task and the level of enthusiasm the children displayed (as defined by the enthusiasm scale of Table 7–1). In the first part of the experiment, the children were presented with tasks and instructed to complete them. The results showed that the children were generally unsuccessful, and that over the course of the instructional sessions, they spent less and less time attempting the tasks. These data are shown in the left-hand portion of Figure 7–7.

Apparently, as the children encountered failure, they became less motivated to complete the problems. Observer ratings of the children's enthusiasm during this phase indicated negative enthusiasm (ratings of zero to one on the six-point scale). Koegel and Egel related this finding to research on *learned helplessness*. Learned helplessness has been defined as a state in which the subject has learned that responding and reinforcement are independent (e.g., Miller and Seligman 1975; Overmier and Seligman 1967; Seligman and Maier 1967). The perceived independence of responding and reinforcement affects the subjects' behavior in two basic ways. First, reponse initation is slowed and may not occur at all. Second, subjects have greater difficulty learning the response-reinforcement contingency, even when their responses produce reinforcement (e.g., Seligman, Klein, and Miller 1976). The behavior of the autistic children in the Koegel and Egel study and of autistic children in general (Ferster 1974), is quite similar to the behavior of subjects in learned helplessness studies.

The second part of the Koegel and Egel study evaluated a treatment procedure designed to improve the children's motivation by increasing correct re-

FIGURE 7–7.   The percentage of intervals with attempts at responding to the task during pretreatment (when the children generally completed the task incorrectly) as compared with posttreatment, following a period of prompted correct responding (CR). (Figure reprinted from Koegel, R.L. and Egel, A.L. 1979. "Motivating Autistic Children," *Journal of Abnormal Psychology,* 88:418—426. Copyright by American Psychological Association, Inc. Reproduced by permission.)

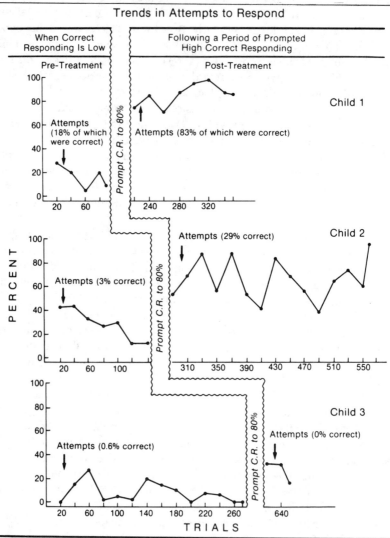

sponding. Verbal and manual prompts were used to encourage the children to continue working until the tasks were completed. These prompts were maintained until a criterion of 80 percent correct responding was achieved. The data shown in the right-hand portion of Figure 7–7 reflect the children's motivation following treatment. As the children experienced success, their perseveration increased such that they began to spend much of the time attempting to perform the tasks. Koegel and Egel's findings are supported by the post-treatment enthusiasm ratings which indicate that when the children were responding correctly, their enthusiasm was judged to be high (ratings of four and five on the six-point scale).

The implications of the research on success/failure ratios are numerous. First, it is clear that autistic children's characteristics of low-level correct responding (i.e., failure) can result in depressed levels of motivation. This is reflected in the Koegel and Egel study by reductions in attempts to complete tasks, as well as by low levels of enthusiasm. A second implication is that efforts designed to increase successful task completion can restore the children's motivation. These findings suggest that autistic children should be encouraged to maintain their responding until their tasks are completed and reinforcers are delivered. Repeated exposure to successful experiences in all areas of functioning may be essential if autistic children are going to "try" to achieve and, eventually, overcome their handicap.

Summary and Conclusion_____

Until recently, relatively little has been known about the variables which can influence autistic children's motivation. Educators have had to depend on primary reinforcers. While such stimuli continue to be important reinforcers (as they are for normal children), recent applied research has provided an increased armamentarium for heightening levels of interest and goal-directed motivation. The development of sensory reinforcement techniques, for example, has significantly expanded inventories of functional, easily applied reinforcers. Teachers may find that individual children will produce a great deal of appropriate behavior in order to receive favored sensory stimuli, such as music or tickling. Such reinforcers may have the advantages of being more resistant to satiation (cf., Devany and Rincover, this volume) and, perhaps, less artificial (Rincover and Koegel 1977b; Lovaas and Newsom 1976). The introduction of both consequent and antecedent variation has also been demonstrated to influence autistic children's enthusiasm. Teaching sessions which incorporate multiple reinforcers and varied tasks can produce more student responding, enthusiasm, and happiness than when all stimuli remain constant. Finally, studies have found that maximizing success and task completion can result in increased attempts and on-task behavior. When autistic children are encouraged to successfully complete the tasks which are assigned (e.g., academics, dressing, toileting), their motivation to perform such tasks in the future can be expected to improve.

The findings reported in this chapter are encouraging in light of the persistent problems educators have faced in motivating autistic children. Nevertheless, motivation continues to be an area that is poorly understood and in critical need of further research. As most of the symptoms of autism can be related in some way to inadequate motivation, it follows that the further development of powerful motivation techniques may be central to future treatment efforts. The normalization of motivation, such as through the establishment of functional conditioned reinforcers, represents one of the major challenges to contemporary research. In view of the recent projects and reinforced activity in this area, it is reasonable to expect additional gains and, concurrently, a brighter outlook for autistic children.

Note _____

The preparation of this chapter and portions of the research reported was supported by U.S. Office of Education Model Demonstration Grant No. G008001720 from the Bureau of Education of the Handicapped (Andrew L. Egel, principal investigator), U.S. Public Health Service Research Grant Nos. MH28210 and MH28231 from the National Institute of Mental Health (Robert L. Koegel and Laura Schreibman, principal investigators), and U.S. Office of Education Research Grant No. G007802084 from the Bureau of Education for the Handicapped (Robert L. Koegel and Arnold Rincover, principal investigators).

Self-Stimulatory Behavior and Sensory Reinforcement

T he problems discussed in Chapter 7 have prompted researchers to seek additional motivational tools to supplement and replace the use of food as a reinforcer. In searching for alternative reinforcers, it is noteworthy that autistic children engage in a great deal of self-stimulation. Since self-stimulation appears to be maintained by the sensory feedback it produces, an extremely powerful *natural* reinforcer may be sensory stimulation. Sensory reinforcement, the unconditioned characteristic of sensory events to increase the probability of events they follow, has been repeatedly demonstrated in various populations: primates and subprimates (Kish 1966), normal children (Stevenson and Odom 1961), infants (Siqueland and Delucia 1969), and even in decorticated subjects (Deiker and Bruno 1976). Recent experimental evidence suggests that sensory reinforcement may play a major role in motivating autistic children, both in motivating present pathological behaviors and as a potentially rich source of motivation in teaching new, appropriate behaviors.

This chapter will describe new findings concerning the motivation and treatment of self-stimulation and self-injurious behavior; the utility of a new procedure, *sensory extinction*; and the role of sensory reinforcement as an alternative motivational tool in treatment.

Self-Stimulatory Behavior

Self-stimulation is one of the most pervasive and formidable problems encountered by teachers of developmentally delayed children. Self-stimulatory be-

*This chapter was authored by **Jeanne Devany** and **Arnold Rincover,** University of North Carolina, Greensboro.*

haviors, repetitive, stereotyped mannerisms that seem to have no obvious functional relationship to the environment, have been found to occur in the majority of institutionalized developmentally disabled children (Berkson and Davenport 1962). Indeed, it is not uncommon to encounter children who spend nearly all of their free time engaged in stereotypic object manipulations (e.g., top spinning), body rocking, arm flapping, and the like.

These behaviors pose a serious challenge to treatment. It is known that self-stimulation interferes with attention and learning (Koegel and Covert 1972), disrupts previously mastered behaviors (Lovaas, Litrownik, and Mann 1974), and it may well interfere with observational learning (Varni *et al.* 1979). In addition, suppression of self-stimulation is associated with several positive changes in behavior. For example, decreases in self-stimulation have been associated with increases in both appropriate play (Epstein *et al.* 1974) and social behavior (Lovaas and Newsom 1976; Risley 1968). Excessive self-stimulation may also have an ostracizing effect; the child who publicly flaps his arms and fingers may frighten or repel people who might otherwise provide him with beneficial social or educational experiences.

Treatment alternatives.

For these reasons, the elimination of self-stimulation is considered a prerequisite to any serious attempt to educate developmentally disabled children. Unfortunately, few treatments for self-stimulation exist which produce a generalized and durable suppression, and several of the available treatments are considered undesirable or impractical by teachers and caretakers.

Self-stimulation is generally resistant to social extinction (Newsom, Carr, and Lovaas 1977) and the use of timeout is typically ineffective in reducing self-stimulation. Timeout, by removing the child from the task at hand and isolating him/her temporarily, affords the child the opportunity to self-stimulate without restraint. In some cases, the use of timeout may actually increase the target behavior, as the opportunity to self-stimulate during timeout may serve to *reinforce* the misbehavior (Solnick, Rincover, and Peterson 1977).

The two most frequently used procedures for self-stimulation have been punishment, such as a loud no, slaps, shock or overcorrection, and the *differential reinforcement of other behaviors* (DRO). DRO procedures involve reinforcing the child for going for brief time periods without emitting the target behavior. For example, if a teacher wishes to eliminate hand flapping and chose to use a DRO procedure, the teacher would initially reinforce the child for going for a very brief time (such as 5 or 10 seconds) without hand flapping. In effect, any *other* behavior besides hand flapping is reinforced during that time period. As the problem behavior decreases, the time requirement is gradually extended until the child is spending a period of 10 or 15 minutes without hand flapping.

Physical punishment with shocks or slaps produces a rapid decrease in self-stimulation (Forehand and Baumeister 1976) but is generally "the treatment of last resort", both because of ethical, legal restrictions and because the use of punishment has sometimes been associated with negative side effects, such as decreases in social behavior or increases in aggressive behavior (Mayhew and Harris 1978). In addition, behavior change obtained through the use of physical punishment often fails to generalize to other persons or settings; the gains are frequently limited to the setting or person who delivered the punishment or to the presence of the punishing stimulus itself.

An alternative deceleration procedure is *overcorrection* (Foxx and Azrin 1973). In this procedure, the occurrence of the undesired behavior is consequated by having the child perform a series of specified activities. Generally, two components are involved. First, the child overcorrects the environmental consequences of the target behavior by *restoring* the environment to its previous state. For example, a child who throws food on the floor at meal times might be required to clean the food off the floor. In the second phase, the child is required not only to rectify the results of the misbehavior, but to overcorrect by restoring the environment to a better-than-normal condition. In our example, the child who throws food on the floor, after cleaning the messy area, might be required to sweep and mop the *entire* floor as well. This combination of activities, designed both to correct and overcorrect the child's behavior, decreases inappropriate behaviors while at the same time teaching more appropriate behaviors. While it is often effective, overcorrection is not without some problems. Overcorrection is extraordinarily time consuming, often aversive for the staff, and is therefore less likely to be correctly and consistently applied. In addition, increases in untargeted, self-stimulatory behaviors may occur when overcorrection procedures are applied (Doke and Epstein 1975; Epstein *et al.* 1974).

The results of DRO procedures are mixed; some studies have demonstrated the successful use of DRO (e.g., Barkley and Zupnick 1976; Carroccia, Latham, and Carroccia 1976), while others have reported only marginal reductions in self-stimulation when DRO is used (e.g., Foxx and Azrin 1973). An additional problem is that DRO procedures are difficult to use successfully with extremely high-rate behaviors. In some children, self-stimulatory behaviors compose virtually all of the child's repertoire and the absence of self-stimulation, even for extremely short intervals, is difficult to observe and appropriately consequate.

Sensory extinction and self-stimulation.

Recently, a new procedure for the elimination of self-stimulation has been developed. This technique, known as *sensory extinction,* is based on the notion that self-stimulatory behavior is maintained by its sensory (e.g., auditory, visual, tactile, kinesthetic) consequences (Rincover 1978; Rincover *et al.* 1979; Rincover, Newsom, and Carr 1979). For example, repetitive arm flapping may be maintained by the visual feedback from watching the arms, and/or proprioceptive feedback from the arm movements themselves; delayed echolalia may be maintained by its auditory feedback. Treatment for self-stimulation then involves the identification and removal (or masking) of the functional sensory consequences for each targeted behavior.

In the initial evaluation of the use of sensory extinction (Rincover 1978), three psychotic children were observed, each with a different self-stimulatory behavior. One child, Reggie, constantly spun objects (such as plates) on a table top. Another child, Robert, engaged in excessive finger flapping in front of his face, while the third, Brenda, twirled various objects (such as feathers) in front of her eyes. Based on these observations, it was hypothesized that visual or auditory feedback could be maintaining the plate spinning and that visual or proprioceptive feedback could be maintaining the finger flapping and object twirling. Three types of sensory extinction procedures were therefore developed, corresponding to the three types of sensory feedback identified.

In order to eliminate the auditory feedback from the plate spinning, flat carpeting was installed over the entire surface of the table top. This covering did not prevent plate spinning from occurring, but successfully removed the sound of the plate spinning. The sensory extinction procedure designed to mask the proprioceptive consequences of the object twirling and finger flapping involved taping a small vibratory mechanism to the back of the child's hand; the vibrator generated a repetitive low-intensity pulsation but did not physically restrict self-stimulation. Finally, a snug blindfold placed over the child's eyes was used to eliminate the visual consequences for all three self-stimulatory behaviors.

The results of the sensory extinction procedures used with each child are shown in Figure 8–1. Each row represents the data for one child; the percentage of self-stimulatory behavior occurring in the session is plotted on the ordinate and sessions are presented on the abcissa.

For the first child, the introduction of the auditory sensory extinction procedure (carpeting) dramatically reduced the rate of plate spinning to near zero levels. When the carpeting was removed (second baseline condition), the rate of plate spinning returned to pretreatment levels. When the visual sensory extinction (blindfold) was introduced, the rate of plate spinning was unaffected, suggesting that visual stimulation was not reinforcing the spinning. The reintroduction of the carpeting successfully eliminated the plate spinning once again. Overall, these data support the hypothesis that Reggie's plate-spinning was maintained by its auditory consequences, not its visual consequences, and that it could be eliminated by removing the auditory stimulation.

Similar results were obtained for the second child, Robert. After baseline, the visual sensory extinction procedure was introduced but produced little behavior change. When the proprioceptive sensory extinction procedure (vibrator) was employed, finger flapping was almost completely eliminated. Although the change in behavior was not as dramatic, Brenda's data also show a decrease in self-stimulation produced by the proprioceptive (vibrator) sensory extinction. In addition, follow-up sessions revealed that the sensory extinction procedures produced long-term elimination of self-stimulation for two of the children.

In a later study, sensory extinction procedures were used to identify the sensory reinforcers maintaining the self-stimulation of four autistic children. Procedures were implemented in which the auditory, visual, or proprioceptive sensory consequences of the self-stimulation were systematically removed. If the self-stimulation decreased or was eliminated by removing one of these sensory consequences, that consequence was considered the child's preferred sensory reinforcer. After each child's preferred sensory consequence was identified, the chil-

FIGURE 8–1.   Percent occurrence of self-stimulatory behavior is plotted on the ordinate across sensory extinction and baseline conditions for all three children. Sensory Extinction: Auditory condition signifies the removal of the auditory consequences of the self-stimulation; Sensory Extinction: proprioceptive and visual conditions indicate the removal of the proprioceptive and visual sensory consequences, respectively. (This figure is reprinted from Rincover, A., Cook, R., Peoples, A., and Packard, D. 1979. "Using Sensory Extinction and Sensory Reinforcement principles for programming Multiple Treatment Gains in Autistic Children. *Journal of Applied Behavior Analysis* 12:221—33. Copyright by The Society for the Experimental Analysis of Behavior. Reproduced by permission).

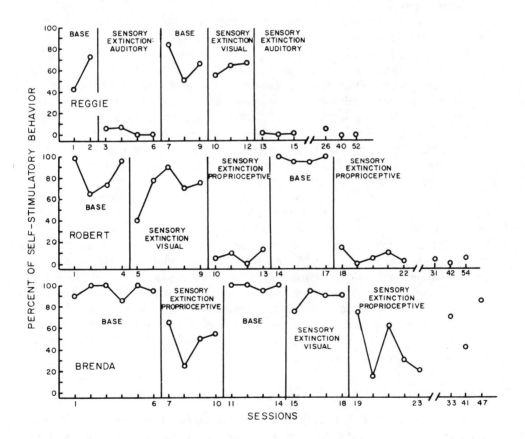

dren were taught to play with several toys, some of which produced the preferred consequence and some of which did not. Each of the children played extensively with the preferred sensory toys, while playing little, if at all, with the remaining toys. Even in the absence of constraints (i.e., sensory extinction) on self-stimulation, the children played with the preferred sensory toys and did not engage in self-stimulation. However, when the preferred toys were removed and only the nonpreferred toys were available, self-stimulation increased dramatically. The gains in play behavior and decreases in self-stimulation were durable over a period of months without external reinforcers for play or restraints on self-stimulation. These data illustrate how *multiple* treatment gains (i.e., decreased self-stimulation and increased toy play) may be obtained by identifying functional sensory consequences (via sensory extinction) and then selecting play materials which are a rich source of the child's preferred type of sensory stimulation.

When compared with other treatments for self-stimulation, sensory extinction procedures may have several advantages. For many children, removal of the appropriate sensory consequences leads to dramatic reduction in the rate of the targeted self-stimulation. This alone is a tremendous advance over most of the currently available treatments. Durable reduction is often achieved when the sensory extinction modification, such as a padded table, can be left in place. When this is not possible, as when a child is blindfolded to remove visual sensory consequences, durable reductions in self-stimulation may be obtained by using the results of the sensory extinction procedure as *assessment* data identifying powerful sensory reinforcers that can be used to teach appropriate competing behaviors, such as toy play (Rincover *et al.* 1979).

Sensory extinction has few known detrimental side effects; in fact, new spontaneous verbal and social behaviors have been observed in some children following its use (Rincover *et al.* 1979). Employment of sensory extinction requires little staff training or child supervision and only a small investment of time and money to be effective. These features make it admirably suited for use in classrooms and residential institutions where it is frequently impossible to provide a one-to-one child-therapist ratio, or where staff may be reluctant to learn or appropriately implement other sophisticated or time consuming behavioral techniques. In addition, no serious ethical objections to sensory extinction have been raised, as parents and teachers have generally been enthusiastic over its simplicity and effectiveness.

Sensory extinction with other deviant behaviors.

Other forms of pathological behavior, such as fetishes, compulsions, seizurelike activity, echolalia, and so forth, are often difficult to explain by currently popular motivational theories. In those instances where such behavior seems to have no external consequences, the question arose if they, too, might be operant behavior maintained by naturally occurring sensory reinforcers.

Compulsive rituals are generally thought to be maintained by anxiety reduction or avoidance. This has led to the use of treatments aimed at eliminating the maladaptive anxiety, such as extinction via response prevention or, more commonly, systematic desensitization. Yet, this approach has had only limited success. These mixed results might be due to the possibility that different compulsive rituals may involve different motivational mechanisms, and that anxiety-reduction techniques would not be effective in those cases where anxiety is not observed in a compulsive client. Take, for example, two developmentally disabled children who evidenced no anxiety before or during their light-switching rituals. These rituals were investigated to see if they could be maintained by sensory reinforcement. Interestingly, although the rituals of these children were topographically similar, each was found to be maintained by a different sensory consequence (Rincover, Newsom, and Carr 1979). For one child, light switching decreased when its visual consequences (illumination changes) were removed by disconnecting the light from the light switch. For the other child, light switching was not eliminated until its auditory consequences (the click of the light switch) were removed by carpeting the light switch. The results emphasize that one should not assume that behaviors showing a similar topography will necessarily share the same motivation. More importantly, these data support the notion that some compulsions may be maintained by sensory reinforcement rather than anxiety reduction.

In another case, sensory extinction procedures were found useful in eliminating the seizurelike behavior of a developmentally delayed child. There was no known organic basis for this child's "seizure" activity, which involved spastic contractions of the child's muscles, particularly his arms, legs, and head muscles, often accompanied by his falling to the floor (but no loss of consciousness). During baseline observation, these contractions occurred at a mean rate of eight per minute (range = 0–35). Treatment consisted of the attachment of a small vibratory mechanism to the child's arm, which did not impede the child's range of movement but did mask part of the kinesthetic feedback from the bodily contractions. Using a reversal (ABAB) design, it was found that the application of the vibrator did reliably and substantially decrease the rate of contractions; the rate of contractions fell to zero. While it was not methodologically possible in this study to separate a *distracting* function of the vibratory stimulation from a masking (i.e., extinction) function, it is notable that this device did not distract the child from normal classroom academic exercises, and other developmentally delayed children (and normal adults) quickly adapted to the vibrator, suggesting that sensory extinction would be the most feasible explanation of these data.

In the case of delayed echolalia, where children repeat words, T.V. commercials, songs, and other things, that they have heard previously, two motivational sources were observed. Some delayed echolalia appears to be sensory: In several cases, delayed echolalia has been eliminated by masking the auditory consequences, using ear muffs, ear wax, or white noise. Furthermore, it was found that after taping a child's echolalia it could be used as a reinforcer for other behaviors, lending support to the notion that the auditory consequences are, in fact, sensory reinforcers for delayed echolalia. It is notable, however, that some instances of delayed echolalia are not easily explained by sensory reinforcement. Such instances include "no," "don't do that," "do it right," and other verbalizations that seem to have been associated with aversive or demand-related situations in the past. In these punishment-related instances of delayed echolalia, sensory extinction has not been effective.

Sensory extinction has also proven useful for other behavior problems, such as self-injury (described in a subsequent section) and a fetish for stockings (by changing the texture, i.e., sewing in a coarse lining). While most of these data are quite recent and only now being prepared for publication, the generality of the procedure leads us to suspect that diverse topographies of maladaptive behavior may be sensory in nature and amenable to sensory extinction. This, of course, is not to say that sensory extinction is the treatment of choice for compulsions, self-injury, and the like; rather, when a particular maladaptive behavior has no observable external antecedents or consequences, and no anxiety appears, it is possible that the behavior is "intrinsically" reinforcing (via its sensory consequences) and may lend itself well to sensory extinction.

Despite these advantages, several caveats must be noted. First, in our own research there are instances in which sensory extinction has produced only a partial reduction in self-stimulation (cf., Rincover 1978; Rincover *et al.* 1979), perhaps because the proper sensory consequence to remove could not be identified, or perhaps because some instances of self-stimulation are not maintained by sensory reinforcement. Second, it is sometimes difficult to remove a sensory consequence once identified, particularly proprioceptive consequences. This is not a severe problem, though, if alternative play materials can be found or designed which are a rich source of that stimulation (cf., Rincover *et al.* 1979), in which case the self-stimulation can be replaced with play.

Sensory Reinforcement _____

The identification of the sensory consequences maintaining self-stimulation also identifies reinforcers that can be used to develop new appropriate behaviors (Rincover *et al.* 1979). Once a teacher or parent knows that certain forms of sensory stimulation may act as powerful reinforcers, similar sensory events can be programmed into treatment.

Historically, case reports or descriptions of the successful use of sensory reinforcement with autistic and retarded children date back to the early use of behavior modification with these populations. Several researchers (e.g., Lovaas 1966; Hewett 1965) describe the use of music, tickling, spinning, and other sensory events, in addition to food, to consequate correct responding. More detailed investigations of contingent sensory stimulation later appeared (Fineman 1968a, 1968b; Fineman and Ferjo 1969). For example, in one study (Fineman 1968b) a 4–1/2-year-old girl was taught to verbalize by consequating each of her verbalizations with visual (color) stimulation from a commercial color organ. This finding was later replicated with a deaf-mute schizophrenic child who was taught to produce over 100 sounds during training (Fineman and Ferjo 1969).

These early reports strongly suggested that the use of sensory stimulation could be a valuable adjunct to edibles in treatment. Later experimental analyses

have further confirmed this view. Rincover *et al.* (1977) assessed the reinforcement value of various sensory events for developmentally delayed children. In
this study, different types of sensory stimulation (brief intervals of taped music,
windshield wiper movement, or strobe light) were used to consequate bar pressing with autistic children. The rates of responding maintained by the three different sensory events are presented in Figure 8–2. In this figure, the responding is
presented on the ordinate and the sessions are presented on the abscissa. The
dark lines on each graph represent data from the sessions when the strobe light
was used to consequate bar pressing, while the dashed lines represent data from
the windshield wiper sessions and the lines with open circles represent responding for the music. With all four children, it was found that sensory events could indeed be used as reinforcing stimuli as evidenced by the high, steady rate of bar
pressing. However, the reinforcing function of the sensory events was idiosyncratic across children; what functioned as a reinforcer for one child did not necessar-

FIGURE 8 – 2.   Rate of bar pressing for three types of sensory stimulation. (This figure
is reprinted from Rincover, A., Newsom, C.D., Lovaas, O.I., and Koegel, R.L. 1977. "Some
Motivational Properties of Sensory Reinforcement in Psychotic Children, *Journal of Experimental Child Psychology*. 24:312—23. Copyright by Academic Press, Inc. Reproduced by permission).

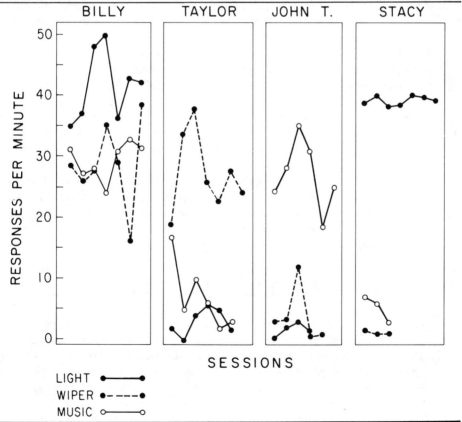

ily function as a reinforcer for another child. Two children clearly responded at a higher rate during the strobe light sessions, one clearly preferred the windshield wiper movement, and the fourth responded at a higher rate during the music sessions. The rate of responding for the preferred sensory event was consistently above the rate of responding for the others.

Additional sessions held with John and Tracy indicated further that the preferred sensory event could maintain responding for literally thousands of trials before satiation. Although satiation eventually did occur, in each case only a slight change in the stimulus (a change of music or wiper speed) was sufficient to recover the previous high levels of responding. One implication of these results is that one might maintain responding indefinitely by systematically varying the sensory consequences.

The above study suggests that sensory reinforcement may help solve the problem of rapid satiation which occurs when edibles are used in treatment. In order to test this, Rincover and Devany (in press) directly compared the relative satiation characteristics of food and sensory events. Three autistic children were consequated with either preferred edibles or preferred sensory events for correct responding on a variety of preacademic tasks, such as color and form discriminations. In one phase of the experiment, food sessions utilized a single preferred edible as the consequence, while the sensory sessions utilized a single preferred sensory event. In a second phase, five different sensory reinforcers were alternately used to consequate correct responding within each sensory session, while five different edibles were alternated in each food session. Responding and learning was roughly equivalent for all three children when a single food or a single sensory event was used to consequate responding. The children responded at a high rate for several hundred trials, after which responding suddenly dropped off. When a variety of foods and sensories were used, however, a different picture emerged. When multiple sensories were used, responding was much more durable than responding when multiple edibles were used. This was found to be replicable both within and across children. Thus, sensory stimuli seem as ineffective as edibles in maintaining responding when single reinforcers are used, and are clearly superior to edibles in maintaining responding when a variety of reinforcers are used. Consequently, it is possible that the problem of satiation during treatment might be, in part, resolved by using a variety of sensory reinforcers, such as tickling, music, games, caressing, and toys.

Self-Stimulation as a Reinforcer _____

If reinforcers are difficult to identify for a given child, then one may not wish to eliminate self-stimulation completely but instead use it as a reinforcer to teach other, more appropriate, behavior. Self-stimulation in some children is extremely pervasive and persistent and is, by definition, a powerful reinforcer (Premack 1959). It seems logical that a useful motivational alternative would be to harness the self-stimulation itself to teach and maintain adaptive functioning.

Theoretically, employment of self-stimulation to reinforce appropriate behavior is a sensible idea. We know from experimental work with animals and humans that if low-rate behaviors are consequated with the opportunity to engage in high-rate behaviors, the low-rate behaviors will increase in frequency (Premack 1959). Thus, if appropriate play or social behaviors (the low-rate behaviors) are consequated with the opportunity to engage in self-stimulation (a high-rate behavior), appropriate play or social behaviors should increase in frequency. The opportunity to engage in self-stimulation, in this example, will serve to reinforce the occurrence of play and social behavior.

Ethical concerns.   Teachers, parents, and professionals have expressed some concern that using an inappropriate behavior, such as self-stimulation, as a reinforcer could have detrimental side effects. Two major concerns have been that this procedure may lead to an increased overall rate of self-stimulation outside of treatment, and that using self-stimulation as a reinforcer may somehow strengthen it and make the self-stimulation more resistant to later treatment. Since self-stimulation is socially stigmatizing, interfering with play, attention, and new learning, these concerns deserve careful consideration and an empirical test. In an initial study (Rincover and Devany 1978), three children were immediately consequated for correct responding on a task (such as form or letter discriminations, sentence completion) by allowing very brief access to a preferred self-stimulatory object. These objects were, of course, idiosyncratic, including Kleenex, twigs, bubbles, keys, and lint. After every correct trial, the child was given his/her preferred object and permitted to self-stimulate for 5 to 10 seconds. The object was then removed and another trial presented.

When self-stimulatory reinforcers were used, children often worked for many trials (often 300 or more) before satiation occurred. Thus, the children worked for long periods without the frequent breaks needed when food is employed. Also, learning, as measured by the number of tasks mastered within a session, did occur when self-stimulatory reinforcers were employed. In fact, a systematic comparison of children's responding in sessions were either edible or self-stimulatory reinforcers were employed (Rincover and Devany 1979; Devany and Rincover 1979) showed that the children worked longer *and* learned more during the sessions when self-stimulatory reinforcers were used than when food reinforcers were used. In short, one benefit of using self-stimulation is that it is a powerful reinforcer more resistant to satiation than edible reinforcers. Similar evidence of the effectiveness of self-stimulation as a reinforcer has been obtained by other researchers (Hung 1978; Shilton and Fuqua 1979).

Regarding the rate of self-stimulation outside of treatment, it is noteworthy that no change in rate was apparent when self-stimulation was introduced as a reinforcer for either of two children (Rincover and Devany 1979). Finally, sensory extinction procedures worked quickly even after self-stimulation had been used as a reinforcer for thousands of trials over several months.

It is interesting to note that, for one child, self-stimulation eventually decreased to zero outside of treatment when it was used as a reinforcer, and sensory extinction was not needed at the end of the study. If permitted, this child spent nearly 100 percent of his free time before treatment toe rocking while rapidly flipping the pages of department store catalogs. Access to one catalog was used as a reinforcer for correct responding on preacademic tasks for 1,500 trials; the child was then observed again in the free play situation. Surprisingly, the rate of self-stimulation had fallen to zero and remained there. When the procedure was repeated with additional catalogs, the same dramatic decrease in self-stimulation was obtained with each catalog. It was as if the child did not value the behavior very highly once it had been externalized. The theoretical explanation of this decrease is not clear and further research is needed to determine the generality of the effect. But if replicated, the procedure of harnessing self-stimulation as a reinforcer could prove to be a valuable tool for the *elimination* of self-stimulation.

Self-injurious Behavior

Self-injurious Behavior (SIB) is probably the most bizarre and frightening behavior problem of developmentally disabled children. Prolonged self-injurious behavior, such as scratching, biting, and head banging, may lead to permanent scarring and disfigurement or, in very severe cases, the loss of a limb. Numerous treatment techniques have been used to eliminate SIB, primarily, extinction and various punishment procedures, such as response-contingent electric shock (Lovaas and Simmons 1969), aromatic ammonia (Tanner and Zeiler 1975), oral administration of lemon juice (Sajwaj, Libbet, Agras 1974), and overcorrection (Foxx and Azrin 1973; Harris and Romanczyk 1976).

Self-injurious behavior is sometimes maintained by positive reinforcement, such as parental care (Lovaas and Simmons 1969). In other cases, the occurrence of self-injurious behavior can lead to a release from task demands or terminate a therapy session; in these instances, SIB is maintained through reinforcement, i.e., escape (Carr, Newsom, and Binkoff 1976). It has recently been suggested that some SIB may be respondent, (elicited) rather than operant, in nature (Romanczyk and Kistner in press). However, sometimes there are no obvious external antecedents or consequences to SIB. In these instances it seems possible that the SIB could be maintained by sensory consequences.

Although the use of sensory extinction with self-injurious behavior has been limited, several studies provide experimental support for the role of sensory reinforcement in maintaining SIB. In one study, Dorsey (1979) examined three severely retarded, institutionalized adolescents who exhibited head hitting, eye gouging, and face slapping. The sensory extinction apparatus consisted of foam-padded gloves and a foam-lined football helmet designed not to physically restrain the subjects from engaging in self-injury but to attenuate the tactile consequences of the behaviors. Introduction of the sensory extinction procedure produced immediate and substantial decreases in SIB in each of the subjects. Differential reinforcement of other behaviors (DRO), using edibles and contingent access to toys providing stimulation in the same modality as the SIB, had previously been unsuccessfully employed with all subjects. In a later modification, application of the treatment procedure was made contingent on the occurrence of self-injury (i.e., was used as a punisher) and was combined with a DRO procedure using the selected sensory toys to maintain the reduced levels of SIB. This successful maintenance procedure kept the rate of SIB low and also permitted the subjects to go for periods without the gloves and helmets. A subsequent experiment demonstrated that the modified procedure (contingent application combined with DRO) produced long-term suppression of the self-injurious behavior.

In the Dorsey (1979) study, a punishment paradigm was used along with a DRO to program the generalization and maintenance of treatment gains. Other recent data illustrates the use of a sensory extinction procedure to program a generalized, durable reduction in SIB, which did not require the use of aversives, and which obviated the need to constantly monitor and consequate the subject (Rincover and Devany in press). In the research by Rincover and Devany, the subject was a 4-year-old retarded male who forcefully banged his head on the concrete walls, floors, or the tabletops in his classroom. When observations began, he was engaging in head banging or head hitting (with his fist) between 80 and 100 percent of the time. It was hypothesized that this child's head banging might be maintained by the tactile or auditory consequences of head banging and a procedure was designed to minimize both. Intervention consisted of covering an area of the classroom with foam-filled mats similar to those used for recreation and rest in elementary schools. The walls and floor of one corner of the room were covered with approximately two inches of matting. The subject's daily treatment sessions were conducted in this area by his regular therapists using the same curriculum, materials, and reinforcement procedures they had used before moving over to the padded corner. As in the pretreatment sessions, instances of head banging or head hitting were not verbally or physically punished by the therapists, and if an occurrence of SIB disrupted a training trial, that trial was presented again.

The introduction of the mats to the training setting produced a dramatic and durable reduction in the amount of time spent in SIB. When the mats were briefly withdrawn, the rate of SIB skyrocketed to its previously high levels. Reintroduction of the mats again produced suppression of the self-injury. Over time, the mats were faded out, first by reducing the size of the mat layer, and later by simply placing a mat over the classroom tabletop. Eventually, the mats were completely eliminated from the day-to-day therapy without a rise in the SIB. Similar results were obtained by placing a glove on a child who scratched her face severely, after which the glove was gradually faded.

These data support the view that sensory consequences may play an important role in maintaining some instances of self-injurious behavior. It would be a mistake to assume, however, that SIB is controlled only by sensory reinforcement. It appears that self-injurious behavior may be multiply determined; that is, it may be maintained by different motivational factors across individuals (Carr 1977 and chapter 10 in this volume) and even within one individual. This possibility of multiple motivations highlights the need for a vigorous assessment of all maintaining factors before intervention occurs. Failure to conduct a thorough assessment may lead to implementation of a treatment that may be useless or even harmful. For example, if attention is assumed to be the maintaining factor when the behavior is actually maintained by the negative reinforcement of escape from the therapy task, timeout would let the child out of the task and inadvertently reinforce SIB (Carr, Newsom and Binkoff 1976). Or, if sensory consequences are maintaining SIB, a treatment based on the withdrawal of adult attention, such as timeout or extinction, would be ineffective.

Final Considerations _____

The role of sensory reinforcement in motivation would seem to be a very profitable area of research. There is a great variety of human behavior which presently lies outside the scope of traditional theories of motivation. Historically, many authors have found it significant that much human behavior may not be maintained by external consequences. In other words, much human behavior seems to be based on *internal* motivation, or *internally produced* reinforcers. For example, some authors have postulated constructs such as *manipulation drive* (Harlow, Harlow, & Meyer 1950), *curiosity motivation* (Butler 1953), *need for recognitive familiarity* (Hunt 1965), *intrinsic motivation* (Deci 1975), and *self-reinforcement* (Herrnstein 1977a, 1977b), to account for behavior that appears to be internally motivated. At present, the concept of sensory reinforcement may provide an adequate explanation of this behavior (e.g., Scott 1975).

It is obvious that sensory events serve as potent reinforcers for human behavior, as people will spend an inordinate number of (wo)man hours of work on a stereo, television, movies, and so forth. What is less obvious are the perceptual events that serve as reinforcers for much of our behavior. If we can conceive of perceptual events as sensory reinforcers, much human behavior now perceived as self-reinforcing may lend itself well to the concept of sensory reinforcement.

To illustrate, one type of perceptual reinforcer might be physical beauty. Physical beauty is concerned with stimulus arrangements, such as symmetry, color, repetition, texture, scent, and the like, that are pleasing to the senses. Obviously, our society is very concerned with the perception of beauty, ranging from the clothes and make-up we buy, to the house and furniture we select, and the various art forms (singing, drawing) we try.

A second type of perceptual reinforcers that may maintain a great deal of behavior is proprioceptive consequences. Proprioceptive consequences come into play in athletics or hobbies and illustrate the reinforcement obtained from improving our own skill. We spend a great deal of our free time practicing our jump shot, bodysurfing, building a bookcase, sewing a sweater. It is (perhaps innately) reinforcing not only to do it with our own hands, but to get better and better. The proprioceptive "feeling" one gets from a great run down the slope, catching a wave just right, swimming faster and with less effort than ever before, may be a powerful (though idiosyncratic) consequence which reinforces our attempts to do more, do it better, and to sample other similar activities.

A third type of perceptual reinforcer might be labelled *preservation of sameness*. Interestingly, this perceptual reinforcer is common in autistic children and thought to be deviant. An autistic child may rage violently if the alignment of chairs is disturbed or the door is left open, and spend hours arranging blocks, toys, or furnishings into precise, repetitive patterns. Similarly, a normal child is shaped (reinforced) into having the same reinforcers as his/her parents; when the shaping has not been entirely successful, i.e., the more different the reinforcers between father and son, the poorer their relationship may be. On a broader scale, it seems that our society is very resistant to change. No matter what the cause, or how reasonable — ranging from civil rights and sexual equality to the Viet Nam war — there seem to be the inevitable large number of people who prefer to keep things the same, at least until other reinforcers (or punishers) gradually become more salient.

A final type of perceptual reinforcer is *cognitive*. Cognitive perceptual reinforcers refer to work and play that involves some creativity, problem solving, or a challenge. It is difficult to maintain a high rate of research activities, for example, if one does not enjoy the scientific enterprise — posing important questions, designing methodologies to clearly answer those questions, anticipating, interpreting, and reorganizing the data. The financial rewards are not great, the social rewards are few and far between — neither can account for the long hours over many years by many chemists, anthropologists, mathematical engineers, psychologists, and other scientists. The same is true of most other vocations: it seems that turnover is least, morale highest, and unpaid overtime most common and acceptable in those positions which offer individuals some challenge or problem to solve. Whether we are talking about inventions, vocations, filling in a crossword puzzle, or watching a mystery movie, the reinforcing properties of solving a problem maintains a great deal of our daily behavior.

The perceptual reinforcers described are subject to modification as new research findings become evident, and are not intended as comprehensive. Rather, the intent of this chapter was to illustrate how the concept of sensory reinforcement may be clinically useful in treating behavioral excesses, and how it may be more generally useful in accounting for much of human behavior that presently lies outside the scope of most learning theories. Research that investigates the conditions under which a sensory consequence becomes prepotent, (as well as techniques, such as sensory extinction, which might be used to treat the diverse behavior problems, e.g., aggressive, sexual, self-stimulatory, etc.), that seem to be, at times, motivated by sensory consequences) may be a valuable addition to both clinical and theoretical literature.

Sign Language

Many children with developmental disabilities have serious speech and language disorders. For example, a sizable proportion of *retarded children* whose IQs fall in the severe and profound range (Stanford-Binet IQ less than 35) do not learn to talk (Baroff 1974). Since approximately 5 percent of retarded persons have IQs in this range (Grossman 1973), there are literally many tens of thousands of nonverbal retarded children living in the United States. More important for the present chapter is the fact that 75 percent of *autistic children* have IQs in the retarded range, the majority being severely or profoundly retarded (Rutter 1968). About 50 percent of autistic children fail to acquire speech (Rutter 1966; Rimland 1964). With an incidence rate for autism of 4 to 5 per 10,000 births (National Society for Autistic Children 1978), this means that there are approximately 90,000–110,000 autistic individuals in the United States and, of these, approximately 45,000–55,000 are nonverbal.

The seriousness of this problem is underscored by the fact that if an autistic child has not acquired speech by the age of five, the prognosis is generally poor (DeMyer *et al.* 1973; Rutter 1968; Eisenberg and Kanner 1956). In fact, follow-up studies suggest that the most probable outcome for such children is lifelong institutionalization (Lotter 1974). It is also important to note two additional facts: (1) exposure to a structured education experience is correlated with a more positive outcome (Rutter, Greenfield, and Lockyer 1967), and (2) it is much more difficult to educate a child who is nonverbal. Thus, if a means could be found to teach such children an effective form of communication, it is likely that they would be in a better position to profit from structured education and therefore improve their chances of not being institutionalized.

This chapter was authored by **Edward Carr,** *State University of New York, Stony Brook.*

Numerous attempts have been made to teach nonverbal autistic children to speak. The most widely used methodology has been that of operant conditioning (Risley and Wolf 1967; Lovaas 1966). The operant method is divided into four phases. In Phase 1, the child is taught to *attend* to the teacher on request. In Phase 2, the child is taught a series of gross motor imitations. This *nonverbal imitation* training gradually progresses to the point of practicing more refined motor imitations centering on the mouth region. In Phase 3, *verbal imitation* training is introduced. This procedure consists of the following sequence: (a) reward all vocalization; (b) reward vocalization occurring within six seconds of the model's vocalization; (c) reward vocalization which occurs within six seconds of the model's vocalization and that approximates vocalization of the model; and (d) introduce a new sound randomly interspersed with the sound from step (c). Finally, in Phase 4, *functional language* training is introduced. Initially, the child's verbal imitative ability is used to teach simple labeling through a fading procedure in which the child's speech is shifted from being under imitative stimulus control to being controlled by the relevant environmental referent for his/her speech.

Using operant methods such as those described above, researchers have been able to teach autistic and retarded children a wide variety of speech and language skills, including the use of plurals (Guess, Sailor, Rutherford, and Baer 1968), prepositions (Frisch and Schumaker 1974), declarative sentences (Garcia, Guess and Byrnes 1973), verb tenses (Lutzker and Sherman 1974), adjectival inflections (Baer and Guess 1971), compound sentences (Stevens-Long and Rasmussen 1974), complex sentences (Odom, Liebert, and Fernandez 1969), and interrogative sentences (Twardosz and Baer 1973).

The results of operant speech and language training procedures have not been uniformly positive, however. Some children require tens of thousands of trials before mastering a simple discrimination (Lovaas *et al.* 1971). Others fail to acquire speech altogether or make only minimal gains (Mack, Webster, and Gokcen 1980). Thus, there remains the problem of how to deal with those children who have been unable to acquire speech in spite of systematic training efforts. One possibility is to attempt to refine the speech training techniques (see Chapter 4). Sign language has been suggested as another alternative means of communication for this group of autistic children (Carr 1981a; Creedon 1975). There are several reasons why this form of communication might prove useful. First, it has been suggested that for some children, the use of *simultaneous communication* (i.e., the adult speaks while signing) might trigger or facilitate speech development (Creedon 1973). Second, it appears that although many autistic children have a great deal of difficulty understanding spoken words, they appear somewhat better at comprehending gestures (Rincover and Koegel 1975; Webster *et al.* 1973; Pronovost, Wakstein and Wakstein 1966). This is consistent with the literature which demonstrates that whereas autistic children show poor skills in the area of speech comprehension, they show much better skills on visual discrimination tasks (Hermelin and O'Connor 1970). A third consideration is that a teacher or parent can easily mold (i.e., manually prompt) the child's hands into the appropriate sign configuration. This advantage is particularly beneficial during the difficult period of initial language acquisition when much prompting is necessary (Bonvillian and Nelson 1976; Creedon 1973). Fourth, for many signs, there is a concrete relationship between the sign and its referent. For example, the sign for banana consists of "peeling" the extended index finger of one hand with the fingers of the other hand. Since the cognitive functioning of these children is typically described as being concrete (Hermelin and O'Connor 1970), the iconic or pictorial quality of many signs is likely an additional teaching advantage. Preliminary research (Konstantareas, Oxman, and Webster 1978) provides support for this assertion in demonstrating that signs which are highly iconic are more readily learned than noniconic signs. Fifth, and finally, it can be noted that even though the children with whom we work are not deaf, a child who *has* acquired sign language can potentially be placed in a classroom and/or community for the deaf thereby providing additional opportunities for academic, vocational, and social development.

Several attempts have been made to teach nonverbal autistic children to sign. Again, operant conditioning as described above has been used extensively in the training procedure (e.g., Carr *et al.* 1978; Konstantareas *et al.* 1977; Schaeffer *et al.* 1977; Creedon 1973), although other methodologies involving cognitive and multisensory approaches have also been used (e.g., Benaroya *et al.* 1977; Miller and Miller 1973).

The results of sign training efforts have been both promising and contradictory. Following sign training, some children develop speech (Fulwiler and Fouts 1976; Creedon 1973) while others do not (Salvin *et al.* 1977; Bonvillian and Nelson 1976; Miller and Miller 1973). Some children develop abstract sign language including prepositional and pronominal concepts (Creedon 1973) while others do not (Konstantareas *et al.* 1977; Fulwiler and Fouts 1976). Several investigators have reported that some children can acquire complex syntax and that their pattern of sign language development mirrors the pattern of vocal language development seen in young normal children (Bonvillian and Nelson 1976; Fulwiler and Fouts 1976; Creedon 1973). Through operant conditioning procedures, some children have acquired *generative* signing skills (Carr and Kologinsky 1978); that is, the ability to create new sign combinations that had not been specifically taught to them. Finally, a number of investigators have reported general improvement in adaptive functioning following the acquisiton of sign language. These changes have included a reduction in self-stimulatory and disruptive behaviors (Carr 1979; Casey 1978; Creedon 1973) as well as an increase in the level and complexity of special behaviors (Benaroya *et al.* 1977; Konstantareas *et al.* 1977; Creedon 1973).

The results just described are very promising. However, the vast majority of studies involved complex treatment packages. Thus, sign training was frequently accompanied by specific instruction in play skills, special programs for controlling undesirable behaviors, extra sessions devoted strictly to vocal speech training, and a host of other interventions. When multifaceted treatment packages are used, one must be wary of attributing all of the gains that occur solely to one element of the treatment package. In other words, the changes reported following sign training may be due to such training but then again, they may be due to other interventions that accompanied the training. There is no way of replicating most of the studies reported in the literature because of this general emphasis on *outcome* rather than *process* (Carr 1979). What is most needed is the systematic delineation of a model that pinpoints which gains are attributable to the signing procedures per se. That is, the model should detail in a *step-by-step fashion* the kinds of procedures necessary to produce the desired gains. Only when this task has been completed will we be in a position to offer parents and educators a *replicable* technology for producing some of the more notable achievements reported in the initial sign language studies. Further, once such a model has been constructed, it could then be written up in the form of a manual to be disseminated to all those concerned with teaching sign language to nonverbal autistic children. Although the field has produced manuals for teaching *vocal* language to the severely handicapped (Lovaas 1977; Guess, Sailor, and Baer 1976; Kozloff 1974), no similar manual exists for teaching *sign* language. For this reason, more widespread use of this promising language training model has been preempted and practitioners are left on their own to guess what the best method of intervention might be. It should be noted that such a manual could also be of use to those parents and educators who are concerned with teaching the nonverbal retarded how to sign. This is particularly true in the light of growing evidence that retarded as well as autistic individuals can profit from sign training (Hobson and Duncan 1979; Smeets 1978; Kiernan 1977; Kopchick, Rombach, and Smilovitz 1975; Topper 1975; Wilson 1974; Berger 1972; Larson 1971; Hall and Talkington 1970). In sum, the current literature suggests the need to develop a sign training model which details the teaching process in a step-by-step fashion. Such a model could then be written into manual form for dissemination to all those parents and educators who wish to teach their nonverbal autistic (or retarded) children how to communicate with sign language. In what follows, we shall begin to effect the construction of such a model by attending closely to a number of intertwined theoretical and clinical issues that must be addressed so that a meaningful approach to the problem of language learning in nonverbal children can be constructed.

Perceptual dysfunction and sign language acquisition

The first skill area to be taught involves expressive and receptive labeling. In researching this area, we have isolated some important perceptual variables that are pertinent to understanding language acquisition in autistic children. To begin with, we will describe the procedures that are effective in teaching labeling skills. Then, we will describe the interface between perceptual and linguistic factors.

The procedures that have proven successful in teaching expressive signing bear a striking resemblance to those that have proven effective in teaching expressive speech (cf., Lovaas 1966). Specifically, a three-step procedure is used (cf., Carr *et al.* 1978). In Step 1, the object to be labeled is presented to the child and the teacher *prompts* the child to make the appropriate sign label. Two kinds of prompts are used depending on a given child's behavioral repertoire. Nonimitative children are *manually* prompted to make the correct sign. That is, the adult molds the child's hands into the correct sign configuration and then reinforces the correct response. Children who are capable of imitation are *imitatively* prompted. That is, the adult makes the correct sign and then when the child imitates that sign, the adult delivers a reinforcer. In Step 2, all prompts, whether manual or imitative, are gradually *faded out* so that by the end of this step, the adult has merely to hold up the object and the child will label it with the correct sign. In Step 3, a new object is introduced and the sign for it is trained by recycling Steps 1 and 2. Also, during Step 3, trials involving the previously mastered sign are interspersed with trials involving the new sign in a ratio of one trial per old sign for every three trials of the new sign. This method of *stimulus rotation* serves to help the child practice the old sign and at the same time facilitate the child's learning to discriminate between the two signs. Step 3 is typically repeated for a number of signs until the child has a repertoire of 15 to 20 expressive sign labels. Initially, the signs that are chosen for training are *functional* for the child; that is, they involve events that are reinforcing, such as foods, toys, and favorite activities. Only after a child has mastered a number of these kinds of signs are more arbitrary objects (e.g., clothing, school materials, names of animals) introduced. The rationale for the above selection process relates to the fact that autistic children are much more motivated (and therefore learn more quickly) when the initial training objects are functional reinforcers

The teacher gives an imitative prompt for a sign and the child responds with the same sign.

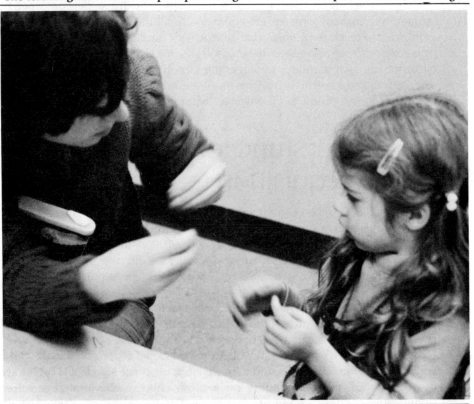

rather than arbitrary stimuli. This point is taken up again below in the section on language use.

The procedures just described for expressive sign labeling have also proven effective in teaching receptive sign labels. That is, a combination of prompting, fading, and stimulus rotation has been demonstrated to be useful in producing sign comprehension as well as sign production (Carr and Dores in press).

During the course of teaching expressive and receptive sign labels, we investigated the impact of certain perceptual variables on language acquisition. In order to understand this research, one must note at the outset that the typical method used for teaching sign language to autistic children involves *simultaneous communication* (Smith 1975), a procedure in which the therapist accompanies each sign with the corresponding spoken word. Thus, if one were to ask a child to pick up a shirt off the floor, the sign for "shirt" would be accompanied by the spoken word "shirt." This simultaneous communication paradigm is of particular interest because it relates to a number of other studies published prior to the current surge of research on sign language acquisition. These studies suggested that when two or more stimuli are presented simultaneously to an autistic child, the child will very frequently attend to only one of the stimuli (Lovaas and Schreibman 1971; Lovaas, *et al.* 1971), a phenomenon referred to as "stimulus overselectivity." (see Chapter 6). Therefore, it is logical to expect that if signs are presented at the same time as spoken words, a child may in fact learn about only one of the stimuli presented. The key question then becomes which stimulus, sign or spoken word, will a given child attend to? To answer this question, we carried out a detailed experimental analysis of the nature of language acquisition on a receptive labeling task following simultaneous communication (Carr and Dores in press). More specifically, we trained several autistic children on a series of four-way receptive object discriminations using the procedures already described. It is important to emphasize that each time that the adult asked the child for an object, both sign and speech were used simultaneously. Thus, if the objects in front of the child were a truck, car, ball, and cup, and the adult wished the child to pick up the ball, the adult would simultaneously sign and say "ball." Over a number of trials, each child acquired the four-way discrimination. However, since simultaneous communication was used, it was an open question as to *what* the child had learned. That is, the child may have acquired some receptive speech (i.e., attended to and learned the spoken words), or the child may have acquired some receptive signing (i.e., attended to and learned the signs), or the child may have acquired both receptive speech and receptive signing. Other children had acquired receptive signing, but *not* receptive speech. There is no way of knowing what has been learned unless one performs a *stimulus control analysis* in which signs and spoken words are presented alone on probe trials following mastery of the four-way discrimination. When we performed this analysis, we discovered not one pattern of language acquisition but rather *two*. Some children had acquired *both* receptive speech and receptive signing. Our data in fact represented a controlled experimental confirmation of results reported previously in uncontrolled studies in the literature. Specifically, some investigators had found improvements in receptive signing and receptive speech following simultaneous communication (Konstantareas, Webster, and Oxman 1979; Miller and Miller 1973); whereas other investigators had found improvements only in receptive signing (Salvin *et al.* 1977; Bonvillian and Nelson 1976; Webster, *et al.* 1973).

The above results raise an important question, namely, is there a way to predict whether a given child will acquire receptive speech as well as receptive signing following exposure to simultaneous communication? Our data suggest this question is indeed answerable. Specifically, we discovered that the two patterns of language acquisition described above were directly related to a given child's verbal imitation skill. Although the children with whom we worked were nonverbal in the sense that they lacked functional speech, some children were capable of simple verbal imitation (e.g., imitating on request a sound such as "ma" or "oo"). These children acquired receptive speech as well as receptive signing. In contrast, children who had poor verbal imitation skill acquired only receptive sign. Why should verbal imitation ability predict whether or not a given child will acquire receptive speech? We believe that the answer rests on the assumption that a high score on a verbal imitation task can be taken as an indicator that the child is proficient at attending to and discriminating among auditory stimuli, including potential speech stimuli. On the other hand, children who are poor at this task may be ignoring speech stimuli and otherwise failing to discriminate among such stimuli in general.

The study just described raises an intriguing question, namely, how would the two identified subgroups perform if taught using sign *alone* versus speech *alone*? Recall that up until now we have been describing language performance following *simultaneous* communication. The data that have been presented on the simultaneous communication procedure might suggest that the good verbal imitation group would perform well in either the speech or sign modality. However, the poor verbal imitation group might perform well only in the sign modality. These predictions were confirmed in a direct experimental test (Carr 1981b; Carr and Pridal unpublished). Specifically, we identified ten autistic children, five of whom had good verbal imitation skill and five of whom had poor verbal imitation skill. We taught each child a number of two-way receptive label discriminations using either speech alone or sign alone. Each stimulus pair that was presented was trained in both the speech modality and the sign modality with the order of modality presentation being counter-balanced across children and stimulus pairs. The resulting findings are best illustrated by the data of selected children. E.M. was representative of children in the poor verbal imitation group. Consider a stimulus pair such as "comb" versus "glasses." After 1,000 trials of training in the speech modality, she was correct on 48 percent of the trials; that is, she was still functioning at chance. In sharp contrast, after only 59 trials in the sign modality, she reached mastery criterion on the same pair. Consider now the performance of S.W., who was representative of children in the good verbal imitation group. After 25 trials of training in the speech modality, he reached the mastery criterion. In the sign modality, he reached criterion after only 125 training trials. (The differences between the number of trials to reach criterion in the two modalities were not significant for the good verbal imitation group taken as a whole.) In sum, then, there appear to be two different subgroups of nonverbal autistics such that one subgroup acquires language with equal facility in either the sign or speech modality, and the other subgroup acquires language only in the sign modality. Apparently, these two different patterns of language acquisition can be predicted from a knowledge of the child's verbal imitation ability.

Currently, we are investigating the factors responsible for the rapid acquisition of signs by the poor verbal imitation group (Carr 1981b; Pridal and Carr unpublished). One variable of importance concerns the fact that many signs have an iconic or pictorial quality. That is, the sign is related to some aspect or function of the object. Once again we use the sign for banana, which consists of "peeling" the extended index finger of one hand with the fingers of the other hand. This iconicity may be particularly important in view of the fact that most autistic children have great difficulty processing all but the most concrete information (Hermelin and O'Connor 1970). Iconic stimuli, of course, are quite concrete. Since speech stimuli cannot by definition be iconic, the superiority of sign over speech for many autistic children may relate to the iconicity of sign language. A second variable concerns the oft reported phenomenon wherein autistic children imitate the signs of the adult prior to making an appropriate response (cf., Creedon 1973). It may be that such "echopraxia" serves a mnemonic function. Specifically, by imitating a sign, the child maintains the language stimulus in the environment for a period of time, thereby permitting extended study of the cue. Speech stimuli in contrast are ephemeral and there is no way for a nonverbal child to maintain the cue for further study since such a child is incapable of repeating the speech stimulus the way an echolalic child might (cf., Carr, Schreibman, and Lovaas 1975). Thus, sign may be superior to speech because the nonverbal child can use sign-based echopraxia as a mnemonic to aid discrimination learning. We are presently studying each of the above variables systematically by varying the iconicity of the sign and by controlling the degree to which echopraxia occurs. Should either or both of these variables be found to facilitate sign acquisition, another important step will have been taken in learning how best to help autistic children acquire sign language.

The above studies make clear some of the factors that help bring about sign language acquisition and aid in the process of identifying children for whom this language modality is most appropriate. An important question remains, however, namely, can these children learn more complex forms of language than the simple labeling skills discussed thus far? We address this issue next.

Generative aspects of sign language ___

Young normal children quickly progress from one-word utterances to two-word utterances. Thus, from a developmental perspective, it is rational to teach autistic children who have mastered one-word sign "sentences" how to combine signs into more complex two-word sentences. One useful sentence type is that involving description. Descriptive sentences may, for example, answer a question such as "What am I doing?" signed by an adult who is engaging in some activity. By teaching a child how to respond to such a question, we are building the basis for simple conversational skills.

When we begin to teach description, we find that a child has a strong set (due to prior object training) to label everything as a noun. Consider a situation in which an adult moves a toy car across a table and asks the child (in sign), "What am I doing?" We would like the child to respond with the two-word sign sentence, "Move car," meaning, "You are moving the car" (the extra words and the participial ending are not taught until a much later stage of sign training). Typically, the child responds with the single sign "car," indicating that he or she has not yet learned to attend to and label the action "move." We have developed a program designed to deal with this problem (Carr 1981a). Our basic strategy is to begin by making the verb action more salient by removing all noun objects and accentuating the motion implied by the verb. Thus, in the example described, the adult would pantomime, in an exaggerated fashion, moving an (imaginary) car across the table. The child is then prompted to make the sign for "move" in response to the adult's actions. Over trials, the prompts (i.e., exaggerated movements) are faded until the child eventually signs "move" whenever the adult makes the "moving" action and then asks "What am I doing?" At this point, the intervention can proceed in either of two ways. Either a new action can be introduced (e.g., "pick up"), or the noun object can be reintroduced with the old verb (e.g., "move car"). If the choice is to introduce a new verb, the adult will teach the discrimination between the two verbs (i.e., "move" versus "pick up") through the stimulus rotation procedure described above (cf., Carr *et al.* 1978). A third verb (e.g., "point to") is then taught using the stimulus rotation procedure. Once a three-way discrimination among the verbs has been established, a single noun object (e.g., "car") is introduced and the adult performs the three actions with respect to this object. Typically, the adult will now have to prompt the child to make the noun sign in addition to the verb sign, but after a number of trials the prompts can be faded out. The procedure is then recycled in the stimulus rotation format with a number of different noun objects (e.g., "truck," "boat"). As noted above, there is a second way of proceeding once the child has acquired his or her first verb sign. This way is somewhat different from what we have just described. Specifically, a noun object (e.g., "car") is introduced immediately and the prompting and fading procedures are carried out (with respect to the noun label) until the child can sign the verbnoun combination (e.g., "move car"). At this point, new noun objects are introduced via the stimulus rotation format (e.g., "move truck," "move boat"). Once these new combinations have been mastered, the whole procedure is recycled with new verbs (e.g., "pick up," "point to").

Irrespective of which of the above two teaching strategies is adopted, the outcome is the same. After the child has been taught a number of verb-noun sign combinations, he/she becomes capable of producing new sign combinations that have *never been taught*. For example, after a child has been taught to combine the verbs "move," "pick up," and "point to" with several nouns such as "car," "truck," and "boat," new verb-noun combinations such as "pick up doll" or "move train" can be introduced and the child will produce the correct sign combination *immediately* without any training. This skill has been referred to as *generative signing;* that is, the children generate or create new combinations from signs they already know in order to describe new situations. Such skills are a common feature of the verbal repertoire of young normal children and the fact that autistic children can also acquire this skill, given appropriate remediation, is a significant finding. The observation that autistic children are capable of generative signing means that they do not have to be taught every possible sign combination. Instead, under appropriate conditions, they can rearrange signs that they have already mastered in order to meet new communication challenges.

Verbs and nouns are concrete parts of language. Although they are useful to know, a child must learn abstract language forms as well in order to function adaptively. Abstractions define relationships among people, objects, and events and include prepositions, pronouns, and time concepts, as well as a host of other concepts, such as color, size, shape, yes and no, "same" and "different." These relationships are shared by many different objects, and therefore, before a child can be said to have mastered such concepts, he/she must be able to "abstract" or discriminate what all the objects have in common. Thus, "brown" can be characteristic of wood, chocolate, cars, leaves, and many other objects. The child must learn that brown is not a characteristic of one specific object, but rather a characteristic of a wide variety of objects otherwise differing in many dimensions, such as height, weight, surface texture, etc. Concepts represent one of the greatest challenges in teaching language to developmentally disabled children.

We will describe a sample program that we have used to teach a representative concept, namely, yes and no. This concept is particularly important since it is used so commonly in everyday conversation. There are two different types of yes and no situations. The first refers to object identification as represented by the question, "Is this a (n) _____?" The second refers to personal feelings, for example, "Do you want _____?"

To teach object identification, we begin by presenting two objects for which the child knows the sign labels, for example, a spoon and a cup. In Step 1, the adult points to the spoon and signs, "Is this spoon?" or "Is this cup?"; likewise, with respect to the cup, the adult would sign either "Is this cup?" or "Is this spoon?" At this stage, the child will likely respond to all four of these questions simply by labeling the object. Therefore, the adult must manually (or imitatively) prompt the yes and no signs as appropriate. The four questions are randomly intermixed from the start of training and, over trials, the adult gradually fades out the prompts. With this procedure, the child cannot learn to give the correct response merely by looking at the sign label which the adult is making or merely by looking at the object to which the adult is pointing. Instead, the child must learn to *compare* the sign which the adult is making with the sign label for the object being pointed to. If the two are identical, the child signs yes; if not, the child signs no.

In Step 2, a new pair of objects is introduced and the above procedures are repeated. As successive pairs of new objects are presented in this step, the child learns the yes/no discrimination in fewer and fewer trials. After many different pairs have been trained, the child will begin to sign yes and no to new pairs immediately without having been trained on those pairs. At this point the child can be said to have mastered the yes/no concept.

The skill required to answer the other type of question, namely, "Do you want _____?" is best taught to begin with by using pairs of foods, one of which the child likes a great deal and the other which he/she dislikes. For example, a child may like orange juice but dislike spinach. Two types of training trials are conducted. On trial 1, a glass of orange juice is displayed and the child is asked, "Do you want orange juice?" The child is prompted to sign yes and then receives a sip of orange juice for doing so. On trial 2, a small plate of spinach is displayed and the child is asked, "Do you want spinach?" The child is prompted to sign no and then the spinach is removed. These two types of trials are randomly intermixed. Over trials, the prompts are gradually faded out. If later in training the child should sign yes for spinach, he/she is given some. Likewise, if he/she signs no for orange juice, the adult removes the juice and thus the child loses a reinforcer by signing incorrectly. The above consequences generally serve to discourage the child from making the same errors again and thus help discrimination learning. Once the first pair has been mastered, a new pair is introduced and the above procedures are repeated. Again, we find that after a number of pairs have been learned, the child will begin to sign correctly to new pairs that have not been trained. In this manner, the child shows that he/she has acquired a general yes/no concept.

It should be clear from what has been said above that abstract concept formation is another example of *generative* signing. At first, the child acquires a limited repertoire of yes/no exemplars that have been explicitly trained. However, as more and more exemplars are trained, each child becomes capable of correctly signing yes and no to new exemplars that have *not* been trained. Clearly, the procedures that we have been describing produce changes in each child's language repertoire that generalize far beyond the original teaching situation. By using their newly acquired skills "generatively," these autistic children are displaying language behavior that parallels that shown by normal, speaking children.

Pragmatics of sign language _____

In working with autistic children, one finds that a recurrent problem relates to the fact that even after these children have acquired a large repertoire of signs, they typically do not use their signs to communicate. Pragmatics is that area of psycholinguistics concerned with language *use* or, more broadly, *communication*. This problem area is likely to dominate language research more and more in the future, particularly, as we shall see below, because it relates directly to the important issues of generalization and maintenance of language gains.

Communicative language is both functional and spontaneous. Such language helps the individual to have an effect on others, to the individual's own advantage. Yet, very little systematic work has been done on this problem although there are some general descriptions available (e.g., Lovaas 1977; Kozloff 1974). Interestingly, the most comprehensive and systematic effort has been made with disadvantaged, normal preschool children (Hart and Risley 1978, 1976, 1975.

1974, 1968). The procedure used is referred to as incidental teaching in order to distinguish it from the structured teaching (i.e., drill format) described above. The procedures that constitute incidental teaching are of interest since they appear readily modifiable for use with nonverbal autistic children. The basic premise of incidental teaching is that the child's language should be useful (i.e., functional) for him/her (see Chapter 1 for an extended discussion of this point). Thus, one would not begin by teaching a child labels such as "chair" or "nose" since the labels have no functional utility. Instead, one might begin by teaching labels such as "cookie" or "ball" since these labels are related to reinforcers and are therefore potentially functional for the child. Each instance of teaching is child-initiated (rather than adult-initiated as in the operant speech procedures described above). That is, the child approaches the adult and indicates (by pointing or looking) that he/she is interested in obtaining a particular item. The adult uses the child's momentary interest in order to teach the child to use the appropriate word(s) to request the item of interest. For example, in one variant of this procedure, Hart and Risley (1968) taught children to use color labels in requesting various toys. If a child requested a toy truck, the teacher would prompt the child to name the color of the truck when making the request (i.e., to ask, "Can I have the red truck?" rather than simply, "Can I have the truck?"). Following this procedure, children showed increased usage of color adjectives in their *spontaneous* speech. In fact, following extensive use of this procedure in many language learning situations, these children showed widespread improvement in the variety and complexity of their spontaneous *sentences* and *conversation* (Hart and Risley 1978). Although this technology has not been systematically applied to nonverbal autistic children, it might be particularly useful with this population since it emphasizes the *functional* (i.e., reinforcer-getting) aspects of verbal behavior. In short, incidental teaching may be one method for overcoming the lack of functional and spontaneous verbal behavior on the part of autistic children.

We have adapted the method of incidental teaching in order to facilitate the acquisition of spontaneous sign language. In order to understand the problem at hand, one must consider a typical situation such as the following. A child who has an extensive repertoire of signs for powerful reinforcers (e.g., cookie, candy, a music box) is brought into a room in which such reinforcers are available. The child attempts to seize one of these reinforcers, but the adult intercedes, preventing the child from obtaining the reinforcer. The adult is, however, prepared to give the child the reinforcer contingent on an appropriate sign. Instead of signing, though, the child immediately loses interest in the reinforcers and retires to a corner of the room to engage in self-stimulatory rocking. Why should a child who knows what the signs for various reinforcers are fail to use these signs to communicate? We conceptualize the problem as one of *narrow stimulus control*. If one were to hold the reinforcer in front of the child's face and sign, "What do you want?", the child would invariably give the correct sign. It appears that sign use is under the control of a complex but narrowly defined stimulus situation: (1) the adult must sign, "What do you want?", and (2) the relevant reinforcer must be clearly visible to the child and in close proximity to him/her. We have attempted to resolve this problem by taking steps designed to *broaden* stimulus control

(Carr 1981a). To begin with, we had the adult therapist refrain from asking the child what he/she wanted. Further, we concealed the reinforcers so that they were present in the teaching situation but not visible to the child. Next, we began the training procedure proper. We selected a strong reinforcer, such as a cookie, and had the adult make the sign for "cookie." When the child imitated this sign, he/she was given a cookie. Thus, our training procedure relied on *imitative prompting*. Over trials, the adult gradually fades out these prompts and waits for the child to initiate the sign before the reinforcer is dispensed. By the end of this phase, the child will spontaneously initiate the sign for "cookie" whenever the adult appears. At this point, the adult recycles the procedure described above using a wide variety of food, toy, and activity reinforcers. Now, whenever the adult appears, the child spontaneously signs any of a number of different reinforcer labels. That is, signing is no longer under narrow stimulus control: the child does not have to be asked what he/she wants, nor does the reinforcer itself have to be visible or in close proximity to the child. The mere presence of an adult is sufficient to act as a discriminative stimulus for signing. This situation resembles that existing between a normal, speaking child and his/her parents.

The procedure that we have been describing generally produces high levels of spontaneous signing. Further, we have found that after a child has been taught in this manner by several adults in several different settings, spontaneous signing appears in novel settings and in the presence of adults not originally associated with the training procedures. That is, the spontaneous use of sign language generalizes across a variety of settings and a variety of adults. Interestingly, the pattern of language use has a naturalistic quality. Children who had signed for and received salty foods, such as pretzels and potato chips (and were presumably thirsty) would invariably begin signing for fluids. A child who had eaten alot (and was presumably satiated) stopped signing for foods and began signing for various toys and activities.

One of the most important consequences of the acquisition of spontaneous signing relates to certain consistently observed *response generalization effects*. That is, as we taught the children to sign spontaneously, we observed concurrent changes in other behaviors that we had not directly intervened upon. For example, as spontaneity increases, dramatic decreases in self-stimulatory behaviors are commonly observed (Carr 1981c; Carr 1979). A child who used to spend 50 percent or more of his time rocking and hand gazing may virtually cease such activities, and, instead, attend to the adult and request various reinforcers. Perhaps such changes occur because sign language provides the child with access to reinforcers that are more powerful than those inherent in psychotic self-stimulatory behaviors. Thus, sign language comes to compete with and eventually sharply reduce the frequency of self-stimulatory behaviors.

Another interesting response generalization effect concerns an apparent reduction in aggressive behavior following the training of a specific adaptive manual sign (Carr, Newsom, and Binkoff 1980). A 14-year-old boy who became extremely aggressive whenever difficult demands were placed on him was taught a manual sign that prompted the adult to discontinue briefly the teaching episode. Gradually, the child began to use the sign as a means of temporarily escaping the demand situation rather than using aggressive behavior to do so. Thus, aggressive behavior was reduced not by a direct intervention, but rather by teaching the child a communicative equivalent for the undesirable behavior. This study can serve as a prototype for larger-scale investigations. For instance, it appears that many severe behavior problems have a communicative function (Carr and Lovaas in press; Carr, Newsom and Binkoff 1980, 1976; Carr 1977). Some behaviors serve as escape responses. Thus, a child who is compelled to carry out a difficult academic task may strike the teacher as a way of communicating the message, "Let me out of here" or "This task is too difficult for me." Other behaviors serve as attention-getting functions. Thus, a child who is being ignored by an adult may strike the adult as a way of communicating, "Pay attention to me." It is quite probable that many children, particularly those who are nonverbal, may "use" their inappropriate behaviors to communicate. There is a clear treatment implication that can be deduced from this reconceptualization of behavior problems. Specifically, it may be possible (as we have already shown, in a preliminary way, in the case of the aggressive boy described above) to provide the nonverbal child with signs that can be substituted for the disruptive behaviors. Thus, following a careful functional analysis designed to determine the communicative function of the problem behavior, a therapist can proceed to teach the child the communicative "sign equivalent" of the disruptive behavior. Once the child has acquired the relevant sign or signs, the problematic behavior no longer serves a function and may therefore disappear. Our results in this area, described above, appear promising and we are now following up in detail on this method of analysis and treatment.

Most of the gains in spontaneous sign language that we have thus far described were produced during relatively limited periods of the day, generally restricted to 15 minute "free time" intervals during which the special reinforcement contingencies were in effect. Recently, we have begun to extend the incidental teaching method across large periods of the day in an attempt to produce spontaneity that will occur in many situations and at many different times. We have begun to work in a group home setting in which we can structure a large number of incidental teaching episodes to ensure more widespread gains (Carr and Posner unpublished). Thus, many times each day, adults conduct spontaneity training sessions in which children receive reinforcers for initiating signs having to do with food, toys, and activities. Our work on this problem has only just begun, but several issues have already become clear. First, the maintenance of spontaneous signing is basically a problem of environmental design. The environments in which autistic children live and are educated are frequently lacking powerful reinforcers. The more institutional the environment, the fewer the reinforcers there typically are. Thus, there is no "reason" for these children to use the language they have learned. To alleviate this problem, we must restructure the environment so that a wide variety of reinforcers are available but inaccessible unless the child initiates the appropriate sign. For this purpose, foods and materials may have to be placed in locked cabinets, behind glass cases, or visible but out of reach. Another part of environmental design involves developing better "on the spot" assessment methods for determining a given child's momentary reinforcer preferences. Staff must be trained to recognize the subtle behavior changes that a child engages in when he/she becomes interested in a particular object or event and is therefore potentially "rewardable" for initiating the appropriate sign. A child may, for example, simply stare at an object or he/she may point, gesture, place the adult's hand on the object, or make an idiosyncratic sound. Less subtle children may lunge for the object or try to "steal" it from another child. All of these behavior patterns are suggestive of the reinforcing nature of the object, and unless an adult is trained to recognize their significance and capitalize upon them by conducting an incidental teaching episode, spontaneity is unlikely to be promoted.

A problem related to that described above concerns the fact that autistic children often do not seem to have any reinforcers that they desire. But even here, it is the case that they are always doing *something* with their time and it is that "something" that can be used as a reinforcer. One child with whom we worked would sit for large portions of the day, simply staring into space. Our strategy in his case was to ask him to stand and then permit him to sit only if he made the appropriate sign. Or, we would take him outside and have him sign "in" (meaning, "I want to go into the house"). Following that, he would have to sign "chair" (meaning, "I want to go over to the chair"). Finally, he would have to sign "sit" once again after we brought him to the chair. In this manner, we induced him to use a greater portion of his repertoire of signs. By recycling this procedure across several other activites that he would periodically engage in, we were able to increase the number and variety of his spontaneous signs, and bring him into communicative contact with more and more aspects of his environment.

In working in the natural environment, we have identified a second issue that is worth some attention. Specifically, we have found that over time the child's spontaneous sign repertoire becomes *constricted* so that the child comes to use only a few of the many signs that he/she knows. This perseverative signing pattern can, however, be broken by withholding reinforcement for those signs that have been repeated too often during a given time period. When reinforcement is withheld in this manner, sign use typically becomes more varied.

A third issue concerns the holophrastic nature of spontaneous sign output; that is, the children will typically use only one sign per communicative episode. Some investigators have suggested what amounts to a "critical mass hypothesis," namely, that once the child learns a large number of signs, he/she will *automatically* begin to combine them into short phrases. We have not observed this outcome consistently, and, therefore, we have now adopted the strategy of *teaching* sign combination using procedures analogous to those described above under generative sentence formation, modified to fit an incidental teaching format. Basically, the adult *prompts* the child to make additional signs whenever possible. Thus, after the child has consumed a piece of cake, he/she would be prompted to sign "more cake" rather than simply "more" or "cake." After some training, it is only necessary for the adult to *delay* the prompt following the child's single-sign request and then the child will, on his/her own, sign again using a two-word request. After further training, the prompts can be dropped altogether.

In sum, following only a brief incursion to date into the area of spontaneous sign training, we have identified three issues that are worth pursuing: environmental design, perseverative signing, and holophrastic sign usage. Doubtless, other issues of theoretical and clinical importance will emerge. What is clear, even at this early juncture, however, is that naturalistic language training will demand the development of many new research strategies and conceptualizations. It is this area of inquiry that is likely to become one of the dominant foci for research in the coming years.

Note

I, Edward Carr, would like to thank Dr. Martin Hamburg, Executive Director, Suffolk Child Development Center, for his generous support of this research, and the teachers of Suffolk Center for their kind cooperation. Most of all, I want to acknowledge my students who have taught me a great deal: Jody Binkoff, Paul Dores, Eileen Kologinsky, Marjorie Pelcovits, Donna Posner, Cathryn Pridal, and Sally Thomason. The work described was supported in part by U.S.P.H.S. Biomedical Research Support Grant 5 S07 RR07067–11 to SUNY at Stony Brook.

The Motivation of Self-Injurious Behavior

10

S elf-injurious behavior is perhaps the most dramatic and extreme form of chronic human psychopathology. Self-injurious behavior involves any of a number of behaviors by which the individual produces physical damage to his/her own body (Tate and Baroff 1966). Some individuals engage in scratching, biting, or head banging to the point at which bleeding occurs and sutures are required. Others may engage in self-inflicted punching, face slapping, or pinching, thereby producing swelling and bruises over large areas of their bodies.

Self-injurious behavior is most frequently reported in individuals labeled autistic, schizophrenic, retarded, or brain damaged. The frequency of occurrence of such behavior has been reported to be about 4-5 percent in psychiatric populations (Frankel and Simmons 1976; Phillips and Alkan 1961). Interestingly, self-injurious behavior, particularly head banging, is also seen in young normal children (Ilg and Ames 1955). Here, the frequency of occurrence has been reported to be 11-17 percent at ages 9-18 months and 9 percent at 2 years of age (Shintoub and Soulairac 1961). De Lissovoy (1961) reported the incidence of self-injurious behavior to be 15.2 percent in a normal population aged 19-32 months.

Despite the relative infrequency of self-injurious behavior, the behavior has commanded a great deal of attention from clinicians because of its life-threatening nature and because of the barrier it poses to normal social and intellectual development. Treatment efforts, which have been numerous, have been sum-

This chapter was authored by **Edward Carr,** *State University of New York, Stony Brook.*

This chapter previously appeared as Carr, Edward G., *The Motivation of Self-Injurious Behavior: A review of some hypotheses.* Psychological Bulletin, 1977, 84: 800-11. Copyright by the American Psychological Association, reprinted by permission.

marized in comprehensive review articles by Smolev (1971), Bachman (1972), and Frankel and Simmons (1976).

The focus of the present chapter is on the motivation, rather than the treatment, of self-injurious behavior. The major reason for this focus stems from the fact that treatment interventions have not always been successful (e.g., Romanczyk and Goren 1975; Seegmiller 1972). It is very likely that self-injurious behavior, like most complex human behavior, may be under the control of a number of motivational variables and that different treatment interventions may be required to eliminate each source of motivation. For this reason, it would be important to identify what the different motivational variables might be. With this consideration in mind, a review of several hypotheses pertaining to the motivation of self-injurious behavior is undertaken.

A search of the literature indicates that the most noteworthy hypotheses, in terms of frequency of citation and/or amount of empirical support, are the following: (a) self-injurious behavior is a learned operant, maintained by positive social reinforcement (positive reinforcement hypothesis); (b) self-injurious behavior is a learned operant, maintained by the termination or avoidance of an aversive stimulus (negative reinforcement hypothesis); (c) self-injurious behavior is a means of providing sensory stimulation in the absence of adequate levels of tactile, vestibular, and kinesthetic input (self-stimulation hypothesis); (d) self-injurious behavior is the product of aberrant physiological processes (organic hypothesis); and (e) self-injurious behavior is an attempt to establish ego boundaries or to reduce guilt (psychodynamic hypotheses). The evidence bearing on each of the hypotheses is reviewed and evaluated, and some directions for future research are discussed.

Positive Reinforcement Hypothesis

This hypothesis states that self-injurious behavior is a learned operant, maintained by positive social reinforcement, which is delivered contingent upon performance of the behavior (Lovaas *et al.* 1965). This hypothesis suggests that the frequency of self-injurious behavior should decrease when the social consequences that presumably maintain the behavior are withdrawn. There is a substantial body of literature indicating that the complete removal of social consequences can in fact greatly reduce or eliminate self-injurious behavior (Bucher and Lovaas 1978; Jones, Simmons, and Frankel 1974; Lovaas and Simmons 1969; Hamilton, Stephens, and Allen 1967; Wolf *et al.* 1967; Tate and Baroff 1966; Wolf, Risley, and Mees 1964; Ferster 1961). In a representative study, Hamilton, Stephens and Allen (1967) treated several severely retarded institutionalized individuals, using a time-out procedure. This procedure prescribes that access to all forms of reinforcement be removed from an individual for a fixed period of time, contingent upon the emission of a response. In the present example, the procedure consisted of confining the individual to a chair for a fixed period of time, contingent upon each instance of self-injurious behavior. Because the chair was located in an isolated area of the ward, the procedure effectively removed all opportunity for reinforcement (including social reinforcement) for the fixed period. Under these conditions, self-injurious behavior decreased precipitously to negligible levels. One interpretation of these data is that self-injurious behavior decreased because social reinforcement, the variable maintaining the behavior, was removed each time the behavior occurred. Curiously, in this study and others like it, there was no measurement of the frequency of occurrence of social reinforcement. There was thus no demonstration that ward staff, for example, were in fact attending to such behavior at any time. Yet, when self-injurious behavior occurs at a high frequency, the assumption is often made that somebody must be attending to such behavior, thereby reinforcing it. Because this assumption is a prevalent one, it would be important, in future research, to include measures of the frequency of adult social reinforcement before, during, and after treatment intervention. In this manner, the role of social reinforcement in maintaining self-injurious behavior could be more adequately assessed.

Another methodological point pertaining to time-out studies relates to the possibility that time-out procedures may actually constitute aversive stimuli, that is, self-injurious behavior decreases, not because of the removal of social reinforcement, but because of the punishing aspects of being confined to a chair or being forced to wait in a barren room. From this standpoint, time-out studies are poor tests of the positive reinforcement hypothesis because reinforcement withdrawal and punishment are confounded. A purer test can be found in those studies involving the use of extinction. Extinction is a procedure in which the reinforcement for a previously reinforced behavior is discontinued. In the present example, extinction would involve the brief discontinuation of social reinforcement contingent upon each occurrence of self-injurious behavior. Since the extinction procedure does not involve placing the individual in a physically aversive situation, punishment effects are presumably minimized, and any reduction in self-injurious behavior can be attributed directly to the removal of social reinforcement. Interestingly, Lovaas *et al.* (1965) and Tate and Baroff (1966) found that simple extinction had no effect on the frequency of self-injurious behavior. Superficially, it would thus appear that social reinforcement is not an important variable. The results are difficult to interpret, however, because no measure of adult attending behavior was reported in either study. It is entirely possible that the adults inadvertently attended to the self-injurious behavior on an intermittent basis. This situation is likely because of the difficulty of ignoring an individual when that individual is engaging in dangerous high-frequency head banging or face slapping.

Because of the above problems, many researchers have employed a noncontingent time-out procedure to study self-injurious behavior. In this procedure, the individual is placed in an isolation room. The isolation, however, is not contingent upon the occurrence of self-injurious behavior. Instead, each day, a period of time is set aside during which the individual is physically and socially isolated. Since the procedure is noncontingent, the punishment aspect is controlled for, while at the same time, inadvertent social reinforcement (such as might occur during simple extinction) is eliminated because no adult is present. Using this procedure, several investigators (Jones, Simmons, and Frankel 1974; Lovaas and Simmons 1969) have reported that self-injurious behavior gradually declined to negligible levels. Corte, Wolf, and Locke (1971), however, reported that noncontingent social islolation did not change the rate of self-injurious behavior for their two subjects. But, as the authors themselves pointed out, the procedure was in effect for a sum total of 12 hours, probably too short a time for any effect to show. On balance, then, the above evidence is consistent with the hypothesis that social reinforcement may play a role in maintaining self-injurious behavior.

Finally, on the topic of noncontingent social isolation, Lovaas and Simmons (1969) and Romanczyk and Goren (1975) presented data, both anecdotal and experimental, showing that at the beginning of isolation, there was an increase (over pretreatment levels) in the intensity and frequency of self-injurious behavior. This increase is apparently identical with the *extinction burst* phenomenon, frequently reported in the animal literature (Skinner 1938, p. 74). Skinner noted that in rats, following the discontinuation of reinforcement for a previously reinforced response, there was typically an initial but temporary increase in the frequency and/or magnitude of that response. Thus, the demonstration of a self-injurious behavior extinction burst at the start of the isolation procedure may also be taken as support for the positive reinforcement hypothesis. Parenthetically, it might be noted that a frequent byproduct of extinction is aggressive behavior (Azrin, Hutchinson, and Hake 1966). The occurrence of aggressive behavior during the extinction of self-injurious behavior would thus be noteworthy, since such a finding would tend to support the positive reinforcement hypothesis. Such research remains to be done.

Another corollary of the positive reinforcement hypothesis is that self-injurious behavior should increase when positive reinforcement is made contingent upon the behavior. Lovaas *et al.* (1965) and Lovaas and Simmons (1969) demonstrated that when comforting remarks or preferred activities were made contingent on the occurrence of self-injurious behavior, self-injurious behavior increased dramatically. Such evidence supports the above hypothesis. In addition, the fact that activities may also serve to reinforce self-injurious behavior suggests that social reinforcement is not the only variable maintaining self-injurious behavior. Thus, the positive reinforcement hypothesis may have to be broadened to include activity reinforcers or perhaps even material reinforcers as sources of motivation for self-injurious behavior.

Another property of self-injurious behavior, consistent with the positive reinforcement hypothesis, is that such behavior can come under rather powerful stimulus control. Several studies have shown, for instance, that self-injurious behavior rates may be rather low when the child is alone but very high when adults are present (Romanczyk and Goren 1975; Bucher and Lovaas 1968; Hitzing and Risley 1967). These findings are predictable within the framework of the positive reinforcement hypothesis: The children, over time, discriminate that self-injurious behavior results in positive reinforcement in the presence of adults but not in their absence and thus engage in self-injurious behavior primarily when adults are present. This notion might be tested further by measuring self-injurious behavior rates in the presence of familiar versus unfamiliar adults. One expectation would be that the rates might be higher in the presence of the familiar adults, since the child presumably has a history of social reinforcement for self-injurious behavior in their presence (but not in the presence of the unfamiliar adults).

Several other studies in the literature are pertinent to a discussion of the stimulus control of self-injurious behavior. Lovaas *et al.* (1965) demonstrated that for one child, the withdrawal of positive social reinforcement (i.e., adult attention) for singing and dancing to a set of songs was discriminative for high rates of self-injurious behavior. Similarly, Corte, Wolfe, and Locke (1971) and Peterson and Peterson (1968) demonstrated that high rates of self-injurious behavior occurred when a blanket or mittens were taken away from the children whom they were treating. There was some indication that the blanket and mittens functioned as positive reinforcers. These three studies taken together suggest that the operation of reinforcement withdrawal can be discriminative for high rates of self-injurious behavior. Lovaas *et al.* (1965) suggested a way to understand this type of stimulus control in the context of the positive reinforcement hypothesis. They speculated that, over time, a child can learn that when a positive reinforcer is withdrawn, it may be possible to get the reinforcer reinstated, simply by emitting a bout of self-injurious behavior. Parenthetically, it might be noted that such speculation has a close conceptual similarity to the notion that self-injurious behavior is a learned response to frustration, frustration being operationalized in terms of reinforcement withdrawal (Baumeister and Forehand 1973; Dollard 1939, pp. 46-49). To test the hypothesis, it would be necessary to arrange experimentally for a variety of positive reinforcers to be reinstated each time a child engaged in self-injurious behavior. The child should soon learn to engage in high rates of self-injurious behavior in the reinforcement withdrawal situation. Such a demonstration has never been made because, of course, it is ethically indefensible. Perhaps the relationship between frustration and self-injurious behavior could best be studied experimentally by using lower organisms, such as monkeys. In this regard, recent demonstrations that self-injurious behavior occurred in some monkeys following frustration produced by extinction of a lever-pressing response are noteworthy (Gluck and Sackett 1974).

If self-injurious behavior depends on positive social reinforcement for its maintenance, one would expect that deprivation and satiation of social reinforcement should influence the rate of self-injurious behavior. The small amount of data pertaining to this question is equivocal. Lovaas and Simmons (1969) found that following 1-day periods of either social reinforcer satiation (the child had been given continuous attention) or social reinforcer deprivation (the child had been left alone in his room), no systematic changes in the rate of self-injurious behavior were observed. On the other hand, Lovaas *et al.* (1965) found that following several sessions of social extinction (a deprivation operation), reinstatement of social attention contingent on self-injurious behavior produced the highest rates of that behavior recorded in their study. This situation presumably arose because the deprivation operation enhanced the potency of the social reinforcement. Perhaps the conflicting results obtained in these two studies were a function of procedural differences. In the Lovaas and Simmons (1969) study, the effects of the deprivation and satiation operations on self-injurious behavior were studied while the child was in isolation. No adult was present. By contrast, in the Lovaas *et al.* (1965) study, the child's self-injurious behavior was examined while an adult was present. Thus, it may be that the sensitizing effects of the deprivation and/or satiation operations are not apparent unless an adult is present to dispense social reinforcement.

If the positive reinforcement hypothesis has merit, the reinforcement schedule applied to self-injurious behavior might also be expected to influence the rate of this behavior. As a test of this notion, Lovaas *et al.* (1965) delivered supportive remarks on either a continuous reinforcement schedule (each instance of self-injurious behavior was reinforced) or on a variable-ratio schedule (every fifth instance of self-injurious behavior, on the average, was reinforced). There was some indication that the variable-ratio schedule generated higher rates, but no direct comparisons of the two schedules were made. Other studies have demonstrated that the differential reinforcement of behavior other than self-injurious behavior (i.e., a DRO schedule) can produce a decrement in the rate of self-injurious behavior (Repp, Deitz and Deitz 1976; Weiher and Harman 1975; Corte, Wolfe, and Locke 1971; Peterson and Peterson 1968). Weiher and Harman, for example, delivered reinforcement only after a given amount of time had elapsed during which there were no instances of self-injurious behavior. They found that on the DRO schedule, the rate of self-injurious behavior decreased dramatically to negligible levels, a finding that parallels the effects of DRO reported in the animal learning literature (Reynolds 1961). One possible danger of using a DRO schedule should be noted: This schedule does not specify that a particular, desirable response should be reinforced, but only that reinforcement must be withheld until a given time period has elapsed during which self-injurious behavior has not occurred. Therefore, it is conceivable that on this schedule one could potentially reinforce some other undesirable high-frequency behavior, such as tantrums, a behavior that might well be occurring after the specified DRO time interval has elapsed. The clinician must be wary of this pitfall when using DRO to treat self-injury.

A potential avenue for future research might be to explore the use of differential reinforcement of low rates (DRL) schedules to produce decreases in self-injurious behavior frequency. That is, one might explicitly reinforce only low rates of self-injurious behavior, with the goal of making the behavior occur so infrequently as to be relatively innocuous. This strategy might be particularly desirable when the complete elimination of self-injurious behavior by other means has proven impossible. DRL schedules have already been used successfully to control various classroom misbehaviors in retarded and normal populations (Deitz and Repp 1974, 1973). Extending the use of DRL schedules to the control of self-injurious behavior would have clear clinical and theoretical significance. Taken as a whole, then, the literature reviewed above does suggest that the rate of self-injurious behavior can be influenced by changes in the reinforcement schedule applied to that behavior. This fact is consistent with the positive reinforcement hypothesis.

There is evidence that the topography of self-injurious behavior, at least in the case of lower organisms, can be shaped by using positive reinforcement (as one might expect if reinforcement were an important controlling variable). Schaefer (1970), for example, successfully shaped head hitting in two rhesus monkeys by using food reinforcement. The only attempt at influencing the topography of self-injurious behavior in humans was reported by Saposnek and Watson (1974). By utilizing positive reinforcement procedures, these investigators were able to shape a child's head slapping into the more benign behavior of slapping the therapist's hands. Of course, hand slapping can be an aggressive behavior and might well become a clinical problem in itself. An alternative tactic that might be clinically useful (as well as providing data on the validity of the positive reinforcement hypothesis) would be to shape the intensity of self-injurious behavior into a low-magnitude and therefore less dangerous response. Herrick (1964) and Noterman and Mintz (1962) have shown that with lower organisms, the intensity of an operant can be shaped by differential reinforcement procedures. Perhaps it might also be possible to alter the intensity of self-injurious behavior, that is, low-intensity self-injurious behavior would be reinforced while high-intensity self-injurious behavior would be subjected to extinction. Such research remains to be done.

In summary, the positive reinforcement hypothesis receives considerable empirical support from studies demonstrating that (a) self-injurious behavior rates can be reduced when social reinforcers are withdrawn, (b) self-injurious behavior rates can be increased when positive reinforcement is made contingent upon the behavior, and (c) self-injurious behavior can come under the control of stimuli in whose presence self-injurious behavior is positively reinforced. Data on the effects of deprivation and satiation variables, reinforcement schedules, and shaping procedures on the rate of self-injurious behavior are equivocal or incomplete. Considerable additional experimentation (possibly utilizing lower organisms when ethically required) therefore remains to be done.

Despite the power of the positive reinforcement hypothesis in accounting for much self-injurious behavior, there remain many instances in which the behavior appears to be a function of different variables. Some of these motivational variables are discussed next.

Negative Reinforcement Hypothesis

This hypothesis states that self-injurious behavior is maintained by the termination or avoidance of an aversive stimulus following the occurrence of a self-injurious act (Carr, Newsom, and Binkoff 1976). The small amount of literature on this topic centers almost exclusively on the role of escape motivation in the maintenance of self-injurious behavior, and the present discussion therefore focuses on escape factors.

There are several anecdotal reports concerning children who injure themselves, presumably to terminate an aversive situation. Freud and Burlingham (1944, pp. 74-75), for example, described one institutionalized girl who would bang her head against the bars of her crib when put to bed against her wishes. She did so presumably to escape from the crib. Similar cases have been cited by Goodenough (1931, p. 139). More recently, Jones, Simmons and Frankel (1974),

Myers and Deibert (1971), and Wolf, *et al.* (1967) noted that demands were very likely to set off self-injurious behavior in children. Following such behavior, the adult therapists who were working with the children would typically stop making demands. Reports such as these imply that demands may constitute aversive stimuli and that self-injurious behavior may be an escape response, maintained by the termination of such stimuli. The experimental evidence relevant to this problem is reviewed next.

Carr, Newsom, and Binkoff, (1976) demonstrated that levels of self-injurious behavior were high in demand situations (such as a classroom) and low in conversational and free-play situations (which did not contain demands). If demands are aversive stimuli and self-injurious behavior is an escape response, one would expect that (a) self-injurious behavior should cease upon the onset of a stimulus correlated with the termination of demands (i.e., upon the presentation of a so-called safety signal) and (b) self-injurious behavior should, under certain circumstances, show the schedule properties exhibited by other behaviors under aversive control. Both of the above features were observed by Carr *et al.* First, when the child was presented with the safety signal, "O.K., let's go," a stimulus that normally terminated the classroom (i.e., demand) period, the child abruptly stopped hitting himself. In contrast, when the child was presented with a neutral stimulus such as "The sky is blue" (a stimulus that was never used to terminate the classroom sessions and therefore could not have become a safety signal), the child's rate of self-injurious behavior remained high. Second, the child's rate of self-injurious behavior during the demand sessions showed a scalloped pattern, that is, the rate gradually increased during the course of a given session. This is the pattern of responding that is generally obtained on fixed-interval schedules of escape with lower organisms (Azrin *et al.* 1965; Hineline and Rachlin 1969). The scalloping was thought to evolve as follows: Each demand session was of fixed length (10 min.); hitting that occurred at the end of the session would be negatively reinforced, since such hitting would be correlated with the termination of the demands. Conceptually, this situation corresponds to a fixed-interval schedule of escape, a schedule that typically generates a scalloped pattern of responding.

Demands may not be the only aversive stimuli that can function to maintain self-injurious behavior. Ross, Meichenbaum, and Humphrey (1971) reported a case in which an adolescent girl would wake herself up each night, whenever she was having nightmares, by banging her head against the bed. (Oswald 1964, cited a similar case). Ross *et al.* assumed that the self-injurious behavior was maintained by the negative reinforcement that resulted from the termination of the aversive dreams. On the basis of this assumption, they proceeded to desensitize their patient to the content of her nightmares and by this procedure were able to eliminate her self-injurious behavior altogether. It should be noted that covert stimuli other than dreams, for example, hallucinations or compulsive thoughts, might also play some role in escape-motivated self-injurious behavior. At present, however, this remains an unresearched area, except for a brief report (Cautela and Baron 1973) of an individual whose self-injurious behavior was always preceded by a compulsive thought that he must poke or bite himself.

The above studies support the hypothesis that self-injurious behavior can be motivated by escape factors and also suggest several additional studies for future research. First, if the frequency of self-injurious behavior is controlled by the termination of aversive stimuli, one would expect that counterconditioning and desensitization procedures that were applied with respect to such stimuli should reduce the rate of self-injurious behavior. The desensitization study by Ross, Meichenbaum, and Humphrey (1971) was a preliminary test of this notion. In addition, Carr, Newsom and Binkoff (1976) reported that counterconditioning procedures (e.g., presenting the demand stimuli in the context of a positive, entertaining conversation known to be discriminative for appropriate social behaviors) could also be used to reduce escape-motivated self-injurious behavior. These two studies, though preliminary, suggest that additional research with these procedures might yield effective management techniques. Second, if self-injurious behavior is escape behavior, then it should be possible to eliminate it by ensuring that the occurrence of self-injurious behavior no longer has the consequence of terminating the aversive stimulus. That is, the demands would not be withdrawn as long as the child was engaging in self-injurious behavior. This procedure corresponds to *escape extinction* as reported in the animal literature (Catania 1968, p. 187). Finally, the notion of self-injurious behavior as escape responding suggests some plausible research that is relevant to the role of restraints in the control of self-injurious behavior. Many children exhibiting self-injurious behavior are put in physical restraints to protect themselves from injury. Removing such a child from restraints usually sets off a bout of self-injurious behavior (e.g., Romanczyk and Goren 1975; Tate 1972). It is plausible that restraints could, over time, become a safety signal for such children, indicating that few or no demands will be placed on them. Typically, a child in restraints is allowed to lie passively, spread-eagled on a bed, or to sit alone, hands bound. Although such a child is unlikely to receive much social reinforcement, the social isolation is, in a sense, more than compensated for by the absence of even the most minimal demands. It is only when demands need to be made on the child (e.g., the child must be fed, clothes must be changed, or he must be taken to the washroom) that the child is taken out of restraints. An important research problem, with clear treatment implications, centers on the question of whether the safety signal value of the restraints could be altered by making them discriminative for high levels of demands. That is, as long as the child is restrained, he would be showered with demands; when unrestrained, he would be permitted to sit or lie passively, free to do anything he wished. Under this condition, one might predict that the restraints should lose their positive value. The above three questions, though not exhausting the research possibilities relevant to the negative reinforcement hypothesis, would provide some significant tests of such a hypothesis.

Self-Stimulation Hypothesis _____

This hypothesis holds that a certain level of stimulation, particularly in the tactile, vestibular, and kinesthetic modalities, is necessary for the organism, and that, when such stimulation occurs at an insufficient level, the organism may engage in stereotyped behaviors, including self-injurious behavior, as a means of providing sensory stimulation (Baumeister and Forehand 1973; Green 1968, 1967; Cleland and Clark 1966; Silberstein, Blackman, and Mandell 1966; Rutter 1966, p. 80; Cain 1961; Kulka, Fry, and Goldstein 1960; Lourie 1949). Kulka, Fry and Goldman (1960) postulated the existence of a kinesthetic drive and on this basis predicted that overrestriction of motoric activity would result in self-injurious behavior. In support of this prediction, Levy (1944) noted several cases of head banging among institutionalized orphans who were restricted to their cribs without toys. When the infants were given toys to play with, self-injurious behavior disappeared, presumably because of the increased tactile and kinesthetic stimulation. Similarly, Dennis and Najarian (1957), working with a group of institutionalized orphans left to lie alone in their cribs because of understaffing, observed self-injurious behavior, such as self-slapping, in several children and attributed such behavior to "stimulation hunger" (p. 11). Collins (1965) reported head banging in a restrained, isolated, retarded adult. Treatment consisted of exposing the adult to a great deal of sensory stimulation in the form of toys, activity, and radio. The consequent elimination of self-injurious behavior was attributed to the increase in tactile and kinesthetic stimulation during treatment. De Lissovoy (1962) and Kravitz *et al.* (1960) noted that the normal young children in their sample banged their heads primarily at bedtime, before falling asleep. To the extent that lying in bed in a dark room, alone, and without anything to do, represents a state of diminished stimulation, the above observations are consistent with the self-stimulation hypothesis. The studies cited thus far, though suggestive, are limited by the fact that they are based solely on anecdotal or correlational accounts. The experimental evidence bearing on the self-stimulation hypothesis provides a more meaningful test and is reviewed next.

Some of the more interesting data relating to the hypothesized self-stimulatory nature of self-injurious behavior come from the animal analogue experiments conducted by Harlow and his associates (Harlow and Harlow 1971, 1962; Cross and Harlow 1965; Harlow and Griffin 1965). Monkeys were studied under two rearing conditions. One group was reared with their mothers, in a playpen situation in which other young monkeys were also present. A second group was reared in partial social isolation. They could see and hear other monkeys but could not make physical contact with them. They were thus deprived of the opportunity to play with their peers and to cuddle with their mothers. In addition, they were raised in small cages and thus had limited opportunity to move around. The typical finding was that many of the partially isolated monkeys engaged in a variety of repetitive, stereotyped acts, such as rocking, cage circling, staring into space, and most importantly, self-injurious behavior in the form of self-biting. Monkeys reared with their mothers in the playpen situation rarely exhibited such behaviors. One interpretation of the anomalous behaviors is that the cage-reared isolates, being deprived of tactile and kinesthetic stimulation, generated their own stimulation through self-injurious behavior and other repetitive, stereotyped behaviors.

An implication of the self-stimulatory hypothesis, supported by the animal literature cited above, is that a barren unstimulating environment would be much more conducive to the maintenance of self-injurious behavior and other stereotyped behaviors than would an environment that provided opportunities for stimulation in the form of play activities. Several studies with mental retardates are relevant to evaluating this implication. Berkson and Mason (1964) studied the stereotyped behaviors (e.g., head banging, rocking, and complex hand movements) of mental retardates under two conditions. In the no-objects condition, the subject was brought into a room, barren except for an observer, and his behavior was recorded for a period of 400 sec. The objects condition was identical with the preceding, except that several objects (e.g., a rubber ball, plastic train, string, furry toy dog) were left lying on the floor of the room. Stereotyped behaviors (including head banging) occurred at a higher level in the no-objects condition than in the objects condition. Furthermore, there was a negative correlation between frequency of object manipulation and frequency of stereotyped behaviors. This negative correlation, which has been found in several other studies as well (Berkson and Mason 1963; Davenport and Berkson 1963; Berkson and Davenport 1962), led Berkson (1967) to conclude that such stereotyped behaviors may be self-stimulatory in nature, occurring primarily in the absence of adequate stimulation. When adequate stimulation is provided (e.g., in the form of play activities), the stereotyped behaviors are no longer required as a source of stimulation, and disappear.

The self-stimulation hypothesis is, on occasion, evoked as an explanation of self-injurious behavior when no other explanation is available. It should be clear that this argument by exclusion does little to advance our understanding. An adequate evaluation of the self-stimulation hypothesis must take into consideration several methodological problems inherent in the above research. First, the data on self-injurious behavior were typically grouped together with the data on other stereotyped behaviors, and we therefore do not know how self-injurious behavior per se changed as a function of the different experimental conditions. In the few studies in which data on self-injurious behavior have been reported separately from data on other stereotyped behaviors (Hollis 1965a, 1965b), the frequency of self-injurious behavior did not change as a function of the different conditions of stimulation. We cannot be certain whether or not this relationship was also obtained in the other studies noted above. Second, in all of the reported studies, only group data on self-injurious behavior were presented, and we therefore do not know how an individual subject's self-injurious behavior changed across stimulus conditions. Third, the self-stimulation hypothesis is particularly open to the criticism of circularity. If a subject is engaging in self-injurious behavior, there is said to be a lack of adequate stimulation, but if the subject is not engaging in self-injurious behavior, the amount of stimulation is said to be adequate. One way out of this tautology is to define adequate stimulation in terms of the physical parameters of the stimulus rather than in terms of the occurrence or nonoccurrence of self-injurious behavior. Myerson, Kerr, and Michael (1967), for example, studied the effects of vibration (as a source of sensory stimulation) on the level of self-injurious behavior of their autistic patient. They suggested that the child engaged in self-injurious behavior because he was deprived of tactile stimulation. They reasoned that if an alternative form of tactile stimulation (such as vibration) were provided, self-injurious behavior would decrease. There was some indication that the sensory stimulation that they used decreased the duration of self-injurious behavior from what it was at baseline, but their results were inconclusive because they ran only two treatment sessions. The study is noteworthy, however, in that the authors defined the level of sensory stimulation provided in physical terms (i.e., the amount of vibratory stimulation), as opposed to inferring the level of stimulation from the level of self-injurious behavior. Finally, in many of the reported studies, social attention from adults was introduced simultaneously with toys and other sources of physical stimulation. Such a procedure, of course, confounds the effects of social reinforcement with the effects of sensory reinforcement. These two sources of reinforcement must be separated for an adequate test of the self-stimulation hypothesis.

The review of the literature thus suggests that future research should (a) stress the measurement of self-injurious behavior independently of other stereotyped behaviors, (b) attempt to present data on individual subjects rather than continuing to report only group means, (c) specify the level of sensory stimulation provided in terms of physical parameters, and (d) separate social reinforcement effects from sensory reinforcement effects. Until such research is carried out, the self-stimulation hypothesis of self-injurious behavior remains plausible but untested.

Organic Hypothesis

The organic hypothesis states that self-injurious behavior is the product of aberrant physiological processes. Available evidence implicates either a genetically produced aberration (as in the Lesch-Nyhan and de Lange syndromes) or a nongenetic aberration (possibly involving elevated pain thresholds or such medical problems as otitis media, a middle ear infection). Data bearing on each of these conditions are reviewed next.

Lesch-Nyhan syndrome is a rare form of cerebral palsy that is X linked and found only in males (Seegmiller 1972; Nyhan *et al.* 1967). The syndrome results from a genetic flaw in purine metabolism that results in a deficiency of the enzyme hypoxanthine-guanine phosphoribosyltransferase. Manifestations of the disease include muscle spasticity, choreoathetosis, mental retardation, and hyperuricemia (Lesch and Nyhan 1964). More pertinent to the present review is the observation that self-injurious behavior is also part of the syndrome and almost invariably takes the form of compulsive repetitive biting of the tongue, lips, and fingers (Dizmang and Cheatham 1970; Nyhan *et al.* 1967; Seegmiller, Rosenbloom and Kelley 1967; Hoefnagel 1965; Hoefnagel *et al.* 1965; Nyhan, Oliver, and Lesch 1965; Lesch and Nyhan 1964). Because of the homogeneity of symptoms across cases, it has been proposed that the self-injurious behavior is directly produced by the specific biochemical abnormality (Seegmiller 1972; Seegmiller, Rosenbloom and Kelley 1967). On this basis, one might expect that a chemical cure would be possible. In support of this viewpoint is a recent report (Mizuno and Yugari 1975) of the apparently successful elimination of self-injurious behavior in Lesch-Nyhan disease with L-5 hydroxytryptophan. Unfortunately, the report had several methodological flaws: There was no measurement of interobserver reliability, the recording procedure was inadequately specified, and the nurses who acted as observers were not blind to the drug condition in effect. Further, there was considerable variability in the frequency of self-injurious behavior during the treatment intervention. Finally, Nyhan (1976) reported discouraging results using L-5-hydroxytryptophan to control self-injurious behavior. More promising results were obtained using a combination of carbidopa and L-5 hydroxytryptophan, but no systematic data were presented. Successful treatment using the combination of drugs would tend to support the organic hypothesis.

Also relevant to the organic hypothesis is a proposal by Hoefnagel (1965) that the proximal cause of self-injurious behavior in the Lesch-Nyhan syndrome may be the irritation produced by an elevated uric acid level in the saliva, a fact that might explain why the self-injurious behavior is directed to the area of the mouth. Hoefnagel's hypothesis seems unlikely, however, in light of data demonstrating that prevention of elevated uric acid levels through early administration of allopurinol did not block the eventual appearance of self-injurious behavior (Marks *et al.* 1968).

Several lines of evidence mitigate against a purely organic explanation of the motivation of self-injurious behavior. First, there are reports that self-injurious behavior may be lacking altogether in Lesch-Nyhan (Seegmiller 1972, 1969; Nyhan 1968) or that it may take atypical forms, such as head banging or eye gouging (Duker 1975; Dizmang and Cheatham 1970; Hoefnagel *et al.* 1965). Second, operant treatment techniques such as extinction, time-out, and differential reinforcement of behavior other than self-mutilation can be effective in eliminating the self-injurious behavior (Anderson and Herrmann 1975; Duker 1975). One would not expect such procedures to be effective if self-injurious behavior were directly controlled by a biochemical abnormality. Finally, there are observational reports that self-injurious behavior can be brought under stimulus control, becoming more likely in the presence of certain adults (Anderson and Herrmann 1975; Duker 1975). These authors intimated that the children learned to mutilate themselves more frequently in the presence of adults who attended to such behavior. The organic hypothesis would have predicted that, since self-injurious behavior is biochemically determined, its occurrence should therefore be relatively independent of external stimulus conditions. It is possible, of course, that a behavior can be brought under stimulus control and yet still have organic involvement. Nevertheless, these observations on stimulus control, if verified experimentally, would be significant insofar as they are consistent with the other evidence cited above, evidence that suggests that self-injurious behavior, even in Lesch-Nyhan syndrome, may have an operant component.

Another organic condition, of possibly genetic origin (Jervis and Stimson 1963) and involving self-injurious behavior (Bryson *et al.* 1971), is the de Lange syndrome. The self-injurious behavior in the two cases reported by Shear *et al.* (1971) took the form of self-scratching and biting of the fingers, lips, shoulders, and knees. One child could dislocate his hips while standing. Shear *et al.* (1971) reported that for one of the children, an operant therapy program including aversive stimulation was useful in controlling the self-injurious behavior. On this basis, it seems again unlikely that self-injurious behavior is simply the product of aberrant physiological processes.

Several reports in the literature have described an association between self-injurious behavior and certain other problem conditions. Goldfarb (1958), for example, reported on the pain reactions of 31 schizophrenic children observed over a 1- to 3-year period. Twenty-three of the children showed aberrant pain reactions (e.g., failing to show defensive behavior when a finger was caught in the door and bleeding). Seven of the children also exhibited self-injurious behavior with no evidence of apparent pain behavior. One child would bite his hand until it bled and another mutilated his hand using scissors, but neither child gave any indication of a pain reaction. It was suggested that perhaps such children had elevated pain thresholds, This hypothesis seems unlikely in view of the fact that the children's pain reactions to a pin prick test were normal. Also, it is clear that even if such children have elevated pain thresholds, that fact'alone would not explain what motivates self-injurious behavior, but only why there is an absence of pain reaction.

A study involving nongenetic organic pathology was carried out by de Lissovoy (1963). He compared the incidence of painful middle ear infection (otitis media) in a group of 15 head bangers with that in a control group (matched for age, sex, etc.) of 15 children who did not engage in self-injurious behavior. There was a higher incidence of otitis in the head-banger group (6 out of 15) than in the control group (1 out of 15). De Lissovoy (1964, 1963) concluded that head-banging was a form of pain relief. The data are difficult to interpret, however, because the question remains as to why nine of the children in the head-banger group, who did not have otitis, banged their heads anyway. Despite this difficulty, a recent study of self-mutilation in mice lends some credibility to de Lissovoy's hypothesis. Harkness and Wagner (1975) found that many mice in their colony produced severe head lacerations as a result of self-scratching. They discovered that all mice engaging in such behavior suffered from otitis media. The interpretation was somewhat complicated by the fact that some additional mice who had otitis did not mutilate themselves. The authors suggested that self-injurious behavior was most likely to occur when the otitis was severe enough to inflame sensory nerve fibers. Such inflammation acted as a painful stimulus that elicited self-injurious behavior, a behavior that functioned as a form of pain relief. Parenthetically, it might be noted that this suggestion, if verified by further research, would lend additional support to the negative reinforcement hypothesis discussed above. This study also serves to emphasize the utility of animal research in testing hypotheses concerning the motivation of self-injurious behavior.

Taken as a whole, the evidence reviewed above indicates that self-injurious behavior is sometimes correlated with a number of conditions of demonstrated or plausible organic origin. The available studies on humans have suffered from too heavy a reliance on subjective, anecdotal, or retrospective accounts. There have been no conclusive demonstrations of a causal relationship between organic pathology and self-injurious behavior. Where systematic observations have been made, the evidence suggests that self-injurious behavior may be an operant. Adequate experimental analyses of self-injurious behavior that is correlated with organic conditions have yet to be made. Perhaps when they are made, the organic pathology may turn out to be a contributing factor to the initial development of self-injurious behavior, a behavior that, at a still later period in its development, is maintained by social reinforcement in the form of adult attention.

Psychodynamic Hypotheses

A number of hypotheses concerning the motivation of self-injurious behavior can best be grouped together under the term psychodynamic. Several theorists, for example, have suggested that some individuals have difficulty in distinguishing the self from the external world (Hartman, Kris, and Loewenstein 1949) and that self-injurious behavior arises as an attempt to establish "body reality" (Greenacre 1954, p. 38) or to trace the "ego boundaries" (Bychowski 1954, p. 67). No attempt is made here to review such viewpoints in depth. The interested reader can consult Cain (1961) for a review of the psychoanalytic literature on self-injurious behavior. The major problem with such theories lies in the difficulty of operationalizing constructs such as "body reality" or "ego boundaries." This difficulty might account for the lack of empirical tests of these hypotheses. One exception to this lack of testing comes from a study by Lovaas *et al.* (1965) that sought to evaluate the psychodynamic hypothesis that individuals attempt to alleviate their guilt through self-injury (Frankl 1963; Beres 1952). Lovaas *el at.* (1965) reasoned that on the basis of the guilt hypothesis, it should be possible to reduce self-injurious behavior by making guilt-alleviating statements such as, "I don't think you're bad," each time that the child hit herself. What they found, however, was that such statements actually increased the frequency of self-injurious behavior, a fact that suggests that the comments were functioning as social reinforcers. The guilt hypothesis would thus seem to be disconfirmed. Of course, it could be argued that such statements as those mentioned above are not adequate to alleviate guilt. Such arguments, however, only serve to emphasize the difficulties inherent in operationalizing constructs such as guilt or guilt alleviation. Until some consensus can be reached on how best to operationalize these constructs, empirical testing of psychodynamic hypotheses remains all but impossible. In the absence of such tests, the utility of these hypotheses in understanding the motivation of self-injurious behavior is moot.

Treatment Implications

This review of the literature on self-injurious behavior suggests that such behavior is multiply determined, that is, it seems unlikely that a single factor is responsible for the motivation of all self-injurious behavior. Instead, one could profitably make a distinction between two broad sets of motivational factors underlying the maintenance of self-injurious behavior. On the one hand, there are several forms of *extrinsic reinforcement* for the behavior. Both social and negative reinforcement, as described in this article, are examples of extrinsic reinforcement. The occurrence or nonoccurrence of such reinforcers are controlled by individuals other than the client. On the other hand, there are several forms of *intrinsic reinforcement* for self-injurious behavior. Specifically, the self-stimulation and organic hypotheses seem to imply that the source of reinforcement for self-injurious behavior may be inherent in the behavior itself. Individuals other than the client himself cannot directly control the occurrence of such sources of reinforcement.

The dichotomy between extrinsically and intrinsically motivated self-injurious behavior has several important treatment implications. First, to the extent that self-injurious behavior appears to be extrinsically motivated, treatment would consist largely of redefining the contingencies of reinforcement. For example, if the self-injurious behavior is being maintained by social reinforcement, then one might expect that techniques such as extinction or time-out would be effective, in that these techniques result in a removal of the social reinforcers maintaining the behavior (Lovaas and Simmons 1969; Hamilton, Stephens, and Allen 1967). These same techniques, however, should be ineffective in dealing with intrinsically motivated self-injurious behavior, for which the maintaining variables are presumably biochemical or sensory. As a further example, if the self-injurious behavior is an escape behavior in response to demands, the treatment would again consist of redefining the reinforcement contingencies, in this case, so that the client would not be permitted to escape from demands simply by engaging in self-injurious behavior (Carr, Newsom and Binkoff 1976). In this manner, the extrinsic negative reinforcement resulting from escape would be terminated.

Whereas the treatment strategy for dealing with extrinsically motivated self-injurious behavior would center largely on redefining the contingencies of reinforcement as described above, the strategy for dealing with intrinsically motivated self-injurious behavior would consist of an attempt to negate or attenuate the reinforcers themselves. Thus, if it is thought that a child is injuring himself in an attempt to reduce the pain inherent in a middle ear infection (otitis media), one might expect that a direct medical intervention designed to cure the infection and thereby attenuate the pain should result in a decrease in self-injurious behavior. Sometimes, of course, it is not possible to attenuate the reinforcers for self-injurious behavior. For example, some children might be hitting themselves to generate tactile and kinesthetic stimulation (Berkson 1967). A technology does not currently exist for attenuating the reinforcement inherent in such stimulation. In such cases, the therapist could consider an alternative tactic, one that would involve providing reinforcers to compete with the reinforcers maintaining the self-injurious behavior. The use of toys as a source of competing tactile and kinesthetic reinforcement has been explored by Berkson and Mason (1964). Presumably, toys might be effective in two ways: first, by providing a competing source of reinforcement, and second, by setting the occasion for play behaviors that compete with the occurrence of the self-injurious behavior itself.

Clearly, the treatment issues described above are complex, but the present review of the literature does suggest a plausible sequence of steps that the clinician may wish to follow in determining the possible motivation (and therefore the treatment) of self-injurious behavior. Table 10–1 lists the screening sequence. As the psychodynamic hypotheses do not currently rest on a firm data base, they have not been included in the table.

The outlined screening procedure is by no means definitive, but it does re-

---
TABLE 10–1
A Screening Sequence to Determine the Motivation
of Self-Injurious Behavior

STEP 1

Screen for genetic abnormalities (e.g., Lesch-Nyhan and de Lange syndromes), particularly if lip, finger, or tongue biting is present.
Screen for nongenetic abnormalities (e.g., otitis media), particularly if head banging is present.
If screening is positive, motivation may be organic.
If Step 1 is negative, proceed to Step 2.

STEP 2

Does self-injurious behavior increase under one or more of the following circumstances:
   (a) When the behavior is attended to?
   (b) When reinforcers are withdrawn for behaviors other than self-injurious behavior?
   (c) When the child is in the company of adults (rather than alone)?
If yes, motivation may be positive reinforcement.
Does self-injurious behavior occur primarily when demands or other aversive stimuli are presented?
If yes, motivation may be negative reinforcement.
If Step 2 is negative, proceed to Step 3.

STEP 3

Does self-injurious behavior occur primarily when there are no activities available and/or the environment is barren?
If yes, motivation may be self-stimulation.

---

flect our current, rudimentary state of knowledge. As a guide for assessment, it should provide a useful beginning and a basis for deciding which treatment procedures might be appropriate. Reviews of some current treatment interventions for dealing with self-injurious behavior have been provided by Azrin *et al.* (1975), Bachman (1972), Frankel and Simmons (1976), Seegmiller (1976), and Smolev (1971).

Summary and Evaluation _____

This review has suggested the possibility that self-injurious behavior may be multiply determined. One important direction for future research would seem to center on the question of what, if any, are the relationships between the different motivational sources of self-injurious behavior. De Lissovoy (1964, 1963, 1962) observed that a large percentage of head bangers had, early in life, engaged in certain rhythmical activities such as rocking and head rolling. Green (1967) hypothesized that during the course of such activities, the infant might accidentally strike his head. In this manner, the sensory stimulation of rocking, for example, would become associated with self-injurious behavior, endowing the latter with self-stimulatory properties. However, as Green noted, other factors soon come into play: Parents observing the head banging are likely to attend to the child. Over time, the behavior may come under the control of social stimuli and the associated positive reinforcement (i.e., adult attention). Empirical studies should be carried out to determine if such sequential relationships, as described above, do indeed exist between the various motivational sources of self-injurious behavior.

Yet another example implying a sequential progression is that concerning the organic control of self-injurious behavior. Children suffering from the Lesch-Nyhan syndrome may, at least initially, mutilate their fingers and lips as part of a reaction to a biochemical abnormality (Seegmiller 1972). In time, however, such behavior evokes much attention from parents and nursing staff. At this point, the behavior may be, at least partially, under social control (Duker 1975; Anderson and Herrmann 1975; Dizmang and Cheatham 1970). Again, a sequential relationship among the different sources of motivation is intimated. Developmental studies, now lacking, could provide information on such relationships.

Research into the motivation of self-injurious behavior could also profit from an increased use of animal analogue experiments. Such studies avoid the ethical problems stemming from human experimentation and at the same time provide useful information on motivational hypotheses. A start has already been made in this direction. For example, head banging in monkeys has been shaped, brought under stimulus control, and extinguished using operant conditioning procedures (Schaefer 1970). Pigeons have been taught to peck a key in order to receive mild punishment, provided that such punishment has, in the past, been correlated with food reinforcement (Holz and Azrin 1961). (Here, the analogy to humans is clear: Perhaps some individuals engage in self-injurious behavior because such behavior has, at one time, been correlated with positive reinforcement.) Frustration in monkeys (Gluck and Sackett 1974) and certain organic factors in mice (Harkness and Wagner 1975) have been demonstrated to be potentially important in the control of self-injurious behavior. Finally, a number of bizarre and stereotyped behaviors (including self-injurious behavior) have been observed in monkeys who have had a history of prolonged social and sensory isolation (Harlow and Harlow 1971; Cross and Harlow 1965). It should be possible to manipulate positive reinforcement variables, level of sensory stimulation, and length of social deprivation, as well as organic and frustrative factors, to study the effects of each of these variables on the frequency, intensity, and topography of self-injurious behavior in lower organisms. The results of such studies could help to form a basis for assessing the validity of the various hypotheses pertaining to the motivation of self-injurious behavior and thereby bring us closer to eradicating this dangerous form of human psychopathology.

Notes _____

Portions of this manuscript were written while the author held a Medical Research Council of Canada Postdoctoral Fellowship at the University of California, Los Angeles. The preparation of this manuscript was also supported by National Institute of Mental Health Grant 11440.

The author gratefully acknowledges the helpful comments made by Crighton Newsom and Ivar Lovaas on earlier drafts of this paper.

Section

3

Classroom Integration and Teacher Training

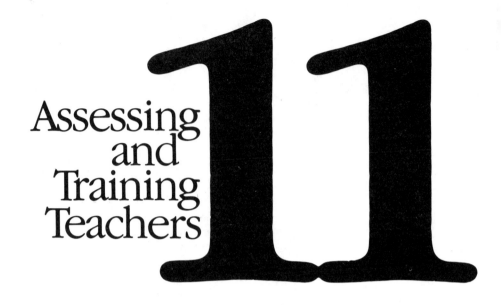

Assessing and Training Teachers

The studies reviewed throughout this volume point out that it now seems abundantly clear that: (1) behavior modification has been used to produce considerable treatment gains in autistic children; and (2) these results have been replicated in numerous experimental laboratories. It should also be noted, however, that it is not at all certain that any given teacher or therapist could replicate these results (cf., Lovaas *et al.* 1973). This conclusion is based primarily on the fact that in most schools and clinics there are no empirical criteria employed for measuring whether or not a given individual is adept at using the techniques which have been proven to be successful in teaching autistic children. The purpose of this chapter is twofold: (1) to summarize objective behavioral guidelines which have been employed successfully by teachers for the treatment of autistic children; and (2) to summarize the results of empirical validations of the use of some of these techniques and the effects they have had on children's behaviors. The guidelines listed below can be used by themselves as a core for assessing and training teachers; or, they can be used as an outline for the development of additional assessment criteria in a comprehensive teacher training/assessment program.

Such criteria become particularly important when one considers that the formal criteria for teacher certification in special education do not include any empirical measures of a teacher's ability to teach such children. Furthermore, many autistic children are still excluded from school programs on the grounds that the teachers are unable to provide instruction for such children. Therefore, four autistic children were randomly selected from a pool of 29 such children

This chapter was authored by **Robert L. Koegel,** *University of California, Santa Barbara.* **Dennis C. Russo,** *Harvard Medical School,* **Arnold Rincover,** *University of North Carolina, Greensboro, and* **Laura Schreibman,** *Claremont Men's College.*

who had previously been excluded from every public school program they applied for, including special education classes. These four children were then placed in new public school classrooms for systematic observation. In all cases the results were similar. Over the four-week measurement period the percent occurrence of appropriate behaviors (verbal and nonverbal responses to commands and questions) remained consistently below 10 percent. Further, there was a very high percentage of inappropriate behaviors (self-stimulation, screaming, running around the room, etc.) during the four-week period.

The assumption generally made by school administrators was that the teachers were teaching correctly, and that the children were unable to learn. There was no assessment of whether or not a teacher was using the procedures which have been empirically demonstrated to be effective in teaching such children. Thus, the cause of the failure of these children to respond appropriately in school may have been inappropriately attributed to the children. It seems just as plausible that the problems could have been a function of using ineffective teaching procedures, rather than a function of an inability of the child to learn.

Therefore, before excluding autistic children from school, or even from a given classroom it seems important to: (1) empirically assess whether or not the child's teacher is using the teaching techniques correctly; and (2) assess the necessity and feasibility of training teachers to effectively teach autistic children.

The following investigation (Koegel, Russo, and Rincover 1977) focused on the establishment of a procedure for assessing and training a teacher's use of behavior modification techniques with autistic children. Especially important to such an investigation is the simultaneous measure of both teacher and student behavior and the recording of measurable improvement in the responses of the child as a function of appropriate use of these techniques. Specifically, this study addressed itself to the following questions: (1) Can one empirically specify whether or not a given teacher is correctly using behavior modification techniques (i.e., as their behavior relates to improvements in autistic children)? (2) If any given teacher does not use these procedures in teaching a child, is it possible to train that person to use these procedures correctly?

Eleven teachers participated in this investigation. Ten were under 30 years of age. Four resided in cities of Southern California; the other seven in New Jersey. At the time of this study, nine teachers had at least two years of previous teaching experience with autistic children. None of the 11 teachers had any formal training in behavior modification but all had read in the area. All the teachers were employed in special-education classrooms. However, the selection was not random, in that all of the teachers requested training, and all of them generally appeared eager to participate. No teacher was denied participation. Twelve autistic children also participated. They were randomly selected either from a participating teacher's classroom, or from one of the training sites. Five of the children were enrolled in an experimental classroom at the University of California at Santa Barbara, four were enrolled in the pilot classroom for autistic children in Orcutt, California, the other three were enrolled in the Princeton Child Development Institute in Princeton, New Jersey. The children ranged in chronological age from 5 to 13 years. Ten were reported to be untestable on standardized IQ tests; the other two had reported IQ scores of 28 and 32. The results of standardized social maturity tests placed all of the children between 2 and 4 years. All the children had been excluded from existing public school classrooms, and had been diagnosed as autistic by agencies not associated with this study. They engaged in little appropriate play or social behavior and had almost no appropriate speech. Six children were essentially mute, and the others were primarily echolalic. They evidenced little, if any, self-help behaviors (e.g., feeding themselves, dressing themselves, etc.), and frequently engaged in tantrum and self-stimulatory behaviors. In general, they were probably representative of children in the more severe half, with regard to severity of autism.

During each session, one teacher was seated facing one child at a 50.8- by 76.2-cm table. All the stimuli necessary to teach the behavior assigned, such as different color blocks, different pictures, etc., and a supply of food reinforcers were present on the table.

Target behaviors were selected for each child according to the individual level of academic skill. Also, some target behaviors were assigned that had already been learned by a child, so that we could determine if the teacher could maintain correct responding. A total of 27 target behaviors was selected. Each was selected from one of the following categories: self-help skills (e.g., shoe tying); arithmetic skills (e.g., "1" versus "2"); writing skills (e.g., tracing letters); picture labelling (e.g., "bear" versus "horse"); abstract language skills (e.g., "big" versus "small"); speech skills (e.g., verbal imitation — "Say 'mama' ").

Teacher Training Procedure _____

The teachers first were asked to read a training manual that described examples of correct and incorrect use of five categories of behavior-modification procedures. Each teacher also was shown videotapes illustrating correct and incorrect use of each of the procedures. The essence of the training procedure, as used for both parents and new teachers, is described below.

Behavioral Treatment Guidelines

In order to provide a generalized therapy program, it appears to be necessary to train therapists in the general procedural rules of behavior modification rather than in many individual treatment programs (Schreibman and Koegel 1981; Koegel, Glahn, and Nieminen 1978; Koegel, Russo, and Rincover 1977; Schreibman and Koegel 1975). When implementing a treatment program for autistic children, it appears to be important to take care to maximize the clarity with which stimuli are delivered. The training format usually followed in executing clinical programs helps present stimuli in a clear manner and seems to maximize the rate at which the children acquire new skills. The generalized format for a training trial is as follows:

1.   The teacher (parent) presents a clear stimulus (command or question) to the child who is quietly attending to the teacher or the task at hand.

2. This stimulus may optionally be followed by a prompting cue designed to evoke the desired response.
3. The child responds correctly or incorrectly.
4. The teacher consequates (with a reward, extinction or punishment).

Problems can take place at any point within a trial. For purposes of clarity, it is probably best to describe each component separately.

Discriminative Stimuli A trial begins by presenting a signal for the child to respond. This signal, a discriminative stimulus (S^D), is a stimulus which one desires to establish as discriminative for the child to respond. In explaining this to new therapists, it is pointed out that questions and commands are both examples of S^Ds; that when therapists say, "touch your nose," or ask, "What color is this?," they are presenting an S^D.

In order for an autistic child to learn, it is desirable that the S^D be presented in a certain way. The S^D should be: (1) presented when the child is attending; and (2) easily discriminable. Each of the characteristics of an effective S^D is considered separately.

Therapist is ensuring that the child is attending to the task while learning the concepts *open* and *close*.

CHILD ATTENDING   Frequently, the autistic child does not attend to the learning situation. He/she may be jumping around on the chair, pulling the therapist's hair, screaming, etc. In many cases it turns out to be practically useless to present the S^D while the child is not attending. All "off-task," nonattending behavior must be eliminated before the S^D is presented. Eliminating off-task behaviors is done in the same way as working with any other behavior. In other words, before attempting to teach the child the S^D "touch red," it would be better first to make sure that the child responds appropriately to the $S^D s$ "look at me," "hands down," "sit quietly," "no screaming," etc. In any case, the major point here is that the S^D should preferably not be presented if the child is engaging in self-stimulatory or other off-task behavior, since it often takes much longer for the child to learn under such conditions (see Koegel and Covert 1972; Risley 1968).

EASILY DISCRIMINABLE   This means that the S^D must be presented in such a way that it stands out from everything else. The S^D is the stimulus that eventually is to acquire control over the child's behavior. Eventually, the child is going to learn the *meaning* of the S^D. Therefore, in the case of autistic children, it is frequently necessary for the therapist to take considerable precautions to ensure that the child does discriminate the specific S^D that the therapist desires to become meaningful.

The reason for taking care in presenting S^D s is that there is a growing literature suggesting that autistic children have difficulty responding appropriately when multiple stimuli are presented (see Chapter 6 for a discussion of this problem). Under such conditions the children typically respond to only a restricted portion of the total stimulus complex. This characteristic has been called *stimulus overselectivity* (Lovaas *et al.* 1971). In the first study showing this finding, autistic and normal children were taught to respond to a complex stimulus display containing three elements: (1) a moderately bright visual stimulus (consisting of a 160-watt red floodlight); (2) an auditory stimulus consisting of white noise at a moderately high (65 db level) intensity; and (3) a tactile stimulus on the child's leg delivered by a pressure cuff at 20 mm mercury. These stimuli appeared quite noticeable to the children since they often oriented to them (e.g., turned around to look at the light, touched their legs when the cuff was inflated). This complex S^D was presented to the child and he/she was reinforced for responding (bar pressing) in the presence of the display, and not reinforced for responding in its absence. After training had established this stimulus display as functional for the children's response, single-cue test trials were presented where each component (auditory, visual, tactile) was presented separately.

The results showed that the normal children responded to each of the components equally. In other words, each of the separate cues became equally functional in controlling the child's behavior. The performance of the autistic children was quite different. Each child responded primarily to only *one* of the component cues. (The retarded children responded at a level between these two extremes.) Three of the autistic children responded primarily to the auditory component while two of the children responded primarily to the visual cue. None of the autistic children responded to the tactile stimulus. It was striking to observe the autistic children attentively respond to one of the component cues (e.g., the sound) only to remain motionless in the presence of the other (e.g., the light) even though that stimulus had been presented as discriminative for reinforcement.

Subsequently, two of the autistic children were trained to respond to the component which had remained least functional for them during test sessions. Both children quickly learned to respond to the previously nonfunctional component, *when that component was presented alone.* This helped to ensure that the problem was not one of some relatively "simple" sensory deficit (as in the case of being blind or deaf), but rather was a problem in responding to the cue in the context of other cues.

It was concluded from this first study that the data could best be understood as the autistic child's difficulty in responding to stimuli in context, a problem pertaining to the quantity rather than to the quality of stimulus control. The data failed to support any notion that a particular sense modality was impaired in autistic children or that any particular sense modality was a "preferred" modality.

The finding that autistic children respond overselectively has been replicated with auditory and visual cues (Koegel and Schreibman 1977; Rincover and Koegel 1975; Lovaas and Schreibman 1971), with multiple visual cues (Koegel and Rincover 1976; Schreibman 1975; Koegel and Wilhelm 1973; Schreibman and Lovaas 1973), and with multiple auditory cues (Koegel and Rincover 1976; Schreibman 1975; Reynolds, Newsom, and Lovaas 1974).

While responding to selective aspects of a complex situation is a normal adaptive, and necessary response, autistic stimulus overselectivity is much more restrictive. There is now a large corpus of data indicating that stimulus overselectivity might be the basis for much of the impoverished behavioral repertoire of these children and for the difficulty they have in learning new behaviors.

For example, restrictions on the number of stimuli which acquire control over behavior can cause serious problems in stimulus generalization, i.e., the extent to which a behavior learned in one environment transfers to other new environments. This relates to the familiar problem of "under generalization" of therapeutic gains — the failure of a behavior, acquired in a therapeutic setting, to transfer to a new "outside" environment.

This problem of limited generalization has been clinically observed in all our work on autistic children. It was shown in a study by Rincover and Koegel (1975) where stimulus overselectivity seemed directly to limit generalization (see Chapter 15). In this experiment, one teacher taught autistic children to perform a simple behavior upon request (e.g., "touch your nose"). Immediately after each child had learned this behavior, a second teacher took the child into another environment and made the same request. Four of the ten autistic children did not perform the relatively simple behavior in the new environment. Tests showed that the children had failed to generalize the learned behavior because they had selectively responded to irrelevant stimuli during training. In one case, for example, the child's responding was controlled by incidental movements of the first teacher's hand. Subsequently, when the second teacher simply raised his hand in a similar way in the outside setting, the child responded appropriately. That is, generalized responding occurred only after the systematic

Stimulus overselectivity can be a pervasive problem in teaching some autistic students. The picture above shows a child attending appropriately to the stimuli. The picture below shows the same child incorrectly attending to extraneous cues (eye movements) in the therapist's face, and not looking at the training stimuli while responding.

exploration and isolation of relevant "stimuli" in the treatment environment and the introduction of these stimuli to new (outside) environments.

In order to prevent such problems from occurring in the first place, the number of irrelevant stimuli present is reduced when teaching the children, even when verbal S^Ds are presented. This is easily done if the S^D is short and has a clear start and end. Examples of such discriminable S^Ds are "touch red" and "sit down."

Examples of presenting S^Ds which are hard for the child to discriminate follow.

"Okay, now we are going to learn all about colors: reds, greens, blues, oranges, and other pretty colors. What you are supposed to do is touch the color I name. Don't touch any other color, only the one I name. If I say touch red, then you touch red, not green or blue. Okay? Now touch red. Remember what I told you, now."

In this example, the words which are supposed to signal the child's response (touch red) are easily lost in the barrage of other stimuli. That is, one might readily expect the autistic child to overselect on the wrong word(s). A much better S^D might be simply to say "touch red."

Another example: "First, I'm going to put down a square block, and then I'm going to put down a round block. Now you tell me which block I put down first." This S^D contains too many cues and again is likely to result in overselectivity to the wrong cue. A better S^D would be to say, "Which is first?" or in the case of a nonverbal child, the S^D might be "touch first."

Prompts There are many occasions when the clinician wishes to teach a behavior that is not elicited by the S^D nor is likely to occur spontaneously. On these occasions it is advisable to use a *prompt* to bring about the correct response. A prompt, as we are using the term, is a stimulus presented along with the S^D that guides the child to the correct response. In behavior modification, prompts are very frequently used in teaching situations of all kinds. For example, if the S^D "touch your nose" is presented and the child does not respond, the therapist may prompt the response by manually moving the child's hand to his nose while presenting the S^D "touch your nose." Or if the therapist is trying to teach the child to imitate the sound "mm" but the child is not responding correctly, the therapist may prompt by holding the child's lips together as the S^D "mm" is presented. This could very likely lead the child to say the "mm" sound. If the child is echolalic and the therapist holds up a red block and says "What color is this?", the child may echo the S^D, saying "What color is this?" In this case the therapist can prompt a correct response by holding a hand over the child's mouth during the S^D presentation, preventing the echo. Then, immediately after the S^D, the therapist can say "red" and uncover the child's mouth permitting the echo "red." Thus, the prompt would look like this: therapist (with hand over child's mouth): "What color is this?" One second pause. "Red." (Therapist then uncovers child's mouth.) Child's response: "Red."

In the use of prompts at least two things are critical. First, a prompt is only a prompt if it works. That is, it *must* bring about a correct response. In the above examples, if the child pulls away when the therapist attempts to hold closed the child's lips or if the child echoes the entire sequence, "What color is this? Red.", then the prompts are ineffective and must be abandoned in favor of other, more effective prompts. One of the most common errors therapists make is to try an ineffective prompt repeatedly merely because it seems logical, or because it worked with another child.

The second major point to remember in prompting is that the prompt must eventually be removed. That is, once the prompted response has been established, the therapist seeks to reduce the child's dependency on the prompt by gradually "fading" the prompt until the child responds solely on the basis of the S^D. For example, in the above example where the therapist manually places the child's hand on his nose to prompt the response to "touch your nose," the prompt may be faded by gradually reducing the manual guidance. Thus, the therapist may lift the child's hand halfway to the nose while saying "touch your nose" so the child completes the response on his own. When the child will do this reliably, the therapist may merely lift the child's arm slightly. Then he may just touch the child's arm, etc. It is not just that the therapist is doing less guiding, but also as the prompt is faded the child is doing more and more on his own. Eventually the prompt is completely faded such that the child correctly touches his nose when the verbal S^D is presented. It appears to be important to fade the prompt slowly enough that the child makes few errors (cf., Terrace 1963). Yet it is important to fade the prompt completely so that the child's response comes under the control of the S^D and does not remain under the control of the prompt.

SPECIAL POINTS TO REMEMBER IN PROMPTING WITH AUTISTIC CHILDREN
This last point, total removal of the prompt, can be problematic in the case of autistic children. Whereas prompt-fading procedures have proven effective with normal children (e.g., Cheney and Stein 1974; Storm and Robinson 1973; Taber and Glaser 1962), retarded children (e.g., Dorey and Zeaman 1973; Touchette 1971, 1969, 1968; Sidman and Stoddard 1967, 1966), and autistic children (e.g., Koegel and Rincover 1974; Risley and Wolf 1967; Metz 1965; Ferster and DeMyer 1962), many studies have pointed out difficulties encountered when trying to fade the prompt completely with autistic children (e.g., Koegel and Rincover 1976; Schreibman 1975; Lovaas, *et al.* 1971; Sidman and Stoddard 1967, 1968; Acker 1966).

It appears that many autistic children do not learn with typical prompt-fading procedures. The reasons for this failure to learn may be due to the stimulus overselectivity phenomenon discussed earlier. This can be seen when one considers that the use of a prompt typically requires response to two simultaneous cues, the prompt stimulus and the training stimulus (S^D) (Fields, Bruno, and Keller 1976). The child must shift responding from the prompt to the training stimulus and in doing so, must associate the two cues. One can readily see that if the child responds only to one cue the necessary association of the two cues will not take place. More likely, since the prompt is the only reliable cue for reinforcement at the start of training, the autistic child overselectively responds to this cue and fails to respond to the training stimulus. In working with these children several investigators have indeed found that autistic children,

FIGURE 11—1.   An example of a within-stimulus prompt fading progression to teach the discrimination ✕ vs. ✗. (a) Fade in S−. (b) Fade out size and position prompts. (c) Fade in redundant components. (Redrawn from Schreibman 1975. Copyright by the Society for the Experimental Analysis of Behavior. Used by permission.)

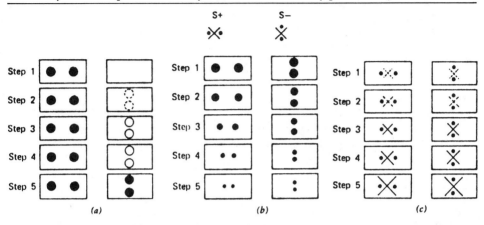

when presented with a discrimination task involving prompt fading, typically responded only to the prompts and did not learn the discrimination (e.g., Rincover 1978; Koegel and Rincover 1976; Schreibman 1975). For example, if the therapist first trained the child to respond to the color blue, and then prompted response to a particular word by underlining the word with a blue line, the child might continue to respond to very faded color cues as the prompt was faded, but never respond to the word when the color was completely absent.

However, since prompt fading is such a useful technique for bringing about correct responding, it is a tool the therapist can ill do without. Thus, some investigators (Schreibman 1975; Rincover 1978) have approached the problem by developing prompts which allow the autistic child to be overselective yet transfer from the prompt to the training stimulus when the prompt is removed. These investigators have developed "within-stimulus" and "distinctive feature" prompt-fading procedures.

For our purposes, these procedures can be discussed together. The basic principle is that rather than providing an extra stimulus as a prompt (thus requiring response to two cues), the therapist exaggerates the one component stimulus that is relevant for distinguishing S+ from S− in a discrimination task. This exaggeration is then slowly faded until the child can reliably respond correctly to the final discrimination. Figure 11–1 illustrates fading steps for such a prompt. In looking at the original discrimination (Part c, Step 5 in Fig. 11–1), the only relevant component of the discrimination is the position (horizontal or vertical) of the dots. The X is redundant. Thus, if the child is to learn the discrimination, he/she must respond to the orientation of the dots and *not* exclusively to the X. The first step in within-stimulus prompting involves pretraining an exaggerated presentation of the S+ relevant component; the horizontal dots (Fig. 11–1, Part a, Step 1). In this step only the horizontal dots are presented, ensuring that the child can only respond on the basis of this cue. Once the child learns

FIGURE 11—2.   An example of a within-stimulus, distinctive feature prompt fading progression to teach the discrimination JAR vs. SON. (Redrawn from Rincover, 1978. Copyright by the American Psychological Association. Used by permission.)

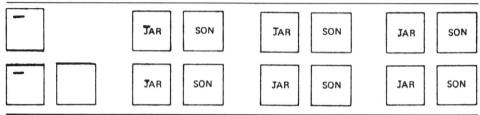

this step, the S— component (vertical dots) are slowly faded in (Steps 2–5). The child is now reliably discriminating S+ and S—. The exaggerated size of the dots is now gradually faded to their normal size (Part b of Fig. 11–1). At this point (Part c, Steps 1–5) the redundant component of the discrimination *(X)* is slowly faded in.

Schreibman (1975) reported that using this procedure, autistic children were able to learn discriminations they had failed to learn either without a prompt or with an extra-stimulus (therapist pointing to S+ card) prompt. The strength of this within-stimulus prompting procedure lies in that the child is *never required to respond to more than one cue* (in this case, dot orientation) and response to this cue is guaranteed by the initial prompt steps. Rincover (1978) elaborated on this work and pointed out the necessity of exaggerating the "distinctive feature" of the discrimination. Figure 11–2 presents a possible fading progression for teaching the discrimination "JAR" vs "SON." Note the emphasis on (1) exaggerating the distinctive feature of the discrimination (here there is a cross bar on "J" and none on "S" while the bottom curve on both letters is the same), and (2) exaggerating within that component as a prompt, and fading within that component.

While within-stimulus and distinctive feature fading have proven to be effective in teaching autistic children certain types of discriminations, their use is definitely limited. They cannot be used to teach all types of discriminations. For example, when attempting to teach a discrimination involving multiple modalities, a within-stimulus distinctive feature prompt may be impossible. Another limitation is that although the autistic children are learning with the prompts, they are still over-selective in their approach to learning situations. Thus, the basic learning deficit is unchanged and the children still fail to learn from their normal environment as do children who are not overselective.

Recent research, however, has suggested that autistic children *can* learn to respond to discriminations on the basis of multiple cues (Koegel and Schreibman 1977). In this study, autistic children were presented with a conditional discrimination task necessitating response to two cues. All of the children learned the task (although it took them much longer than it did for the normal controls). Further, preliminary data for one child suggested that after training on a series of successive conditional discriminations, this child ceased to be overselective on new tasks. Thus, it appears that the child learned to approach new tasks on the basis of multiple cues. The implications of this finding for prompting are obvious. If we can teach an autistic child to respond on the basis of multiple cues, then the child should then learn with traditional (extra-stimulus) prompting procedures. This possibility is currently being investigated and preliminary findings suggest that we can teach autistic children to learn with traditional prompts.

Gradual Approximations – Shaping and Chaining   The techniques of shaping and chaining are invaluable tools for a therapist working with autistic children. The basic principles of these procedures are relatively easy to communicate to new practitioners. To illustrate, here is how parents are instructed in the use of these procedures.

There are many behaviors that a therapist would want to teach an autistic child that do not lend themselves to some of the techniques we have discussed thus far. Some behaviors would be unlikely to occur spontaneously, and thus the frequency of their occurrence could not be increased by differential reinforcement of the response. An example of such a behavior is putting on a shirt. One could conceivably wait forever for the child to emit this reponse spontaneously. Thus, there are some complex behaviors that are best trained by breaking down the target behavior into smaller, graduated steps. Such procedures are called *shaping* (if the therapist breaks down a response into rough approximations that are emitted by the child) and *chaining* (if the therapist breaks down a complex response into a series of component responses which, when performed in sequence, lead to the target behavior).

SHAPING   Shaping is a procedure whereby a complex response is taught by rewarding successive approximations to that response. Initially, even the smallest approximation to the desired behavior is reinforced. Gradually, reinforcement is withheld until the child emits a response that more closely approximates the target response. When the child reliably performs this response, reinforcement is again withheld until the child emits an even closer approximation, etc. It is essential that the child only be rewarded for responses at least as good as those made on previous trials. This ensures forward progress. If the child seems to perseverate for several trials at a particular level without progress, the therapist should not back up and reward a less-accurate response. Instead, a more familiar task should be utilized for a few trials to allow the child to receive reinforcement and thus remain motivated. Then the therapist may return to the shaping sequence.

The use of shaping can be illustrated by an example. If the therapist desires the child to imitate the vocalization "ah," the response could be shaped in the following manner. The child is seated opposite the therapist, is exhibiting no off-task behavior, and is attending to the therapist's face. The therapist then says "ah." Initially the child will probably make no response. Since in shaping we begin by reinforcing even the smallest approximation to the goal behavior, we may wish to begin by reinforcing *any* vocalization the child makes, even if it is a grunt, babble, cough, etc. Sometimes initial vocalizations can be prompted or elicited by tickling or fondling. As soon as a sound is emitted, the child is reinforced. This rewarding of sounds is continued until the child's rate of spontaneous vocalization is quite high (about one every five seconds). When the child reliably vocalizes, reinforcement can now be withheld so that only vocalizations occurring right after the therapist's vocalization ("ah") are reinforced. All other vocalizations are not reinforced. When the child reliably vocalizes (with any sound) only after the therapist's "ah," the demands can be increased so that reinforcement is withheld until the child's vocalization more closely resembles "ah." For example, if the child has been saying "gee," reinforcement might be withheld until the child's vocalization is closer to the sound "ah." This procedure is continued until the child says "ah" after the therapist's "ah."

CHAINING   We can conceive of any complex behavior as being made up of a chain of simpler responses. To teach a behavior using chaining we break down a complex behavior into smaller progressive component parts and teach the parts one at a time. We begin by rewarding the first response in the chain, selecting a first response that is so simple that the child can successfully perform and thus be reinforced. The first step may be a long way from the target behavior, but we are building a foundation for the progression toward that behavior. Once the child reliably performs this first response, we slightly increase the demand by progressing to the next step. Now reinforcement is available only for successful performance on the next step. Ideally, the next step will be such that, again, the child is likely to be successful. (By breaking the behavior down into these small steps we minimize the number of errors the child makes during the chaining procedure.) When the child is proficient at this step, the therapist uses the same method to require advancement to the next step, and so on. (Note the close similarity to the shaping procedure.)

Of great importance to the success of the chaining procedure is the determination of when the child is proficient enough at one level before progressing to the next. A good rule of thumb for the therapist is to make sure that the child can perform consistently well on several consecutive trials on a step before advancing; however, if the child happens to emit a response that is a closer approximation than the present level, the child should be immediately reinforced. The child is now at this new level. As with shaping, the emphasis is always on progress since only responses that are at least as good as those made previously are reinforced.

EXAMPLE OF CHAINING   Dressing is a behavior that is unlikely to be spontaneously emitted by the child and is one that is often taught by a chaining procedure. To begin, only a very simple response is required as the first step in the chain. For example, the child may be presented with the verbal S^D "pants up" while being handed a pair of underpants. If the first step of the chain is "holding the pants," the child is rewarded for taking the pants from the therapist and holding them. When the child will hold the pants each time, the therapist increases the requirement to the next step which may be holding the pants with both hands before the child is reinforced. When this is done reliably, the next step may be requiring the child to hold them right side up. Further steps might include: (1) bending over, holding the pants close to feet; (2) placing one foot in leghole; (3) placing foot in correct leghole; (4) placing first one foot, then the other in the appropriate legholes; (5) raising pants to ankles; (6) raising pants to midcalf; (7) raising pants to knees; (8) raising pants to waist.

Sometimes a *backward* chaining procedure is employed. In this procedure, the steps are taken in reverse order so that the last step in the behavior sequence is the first trained and the therapist moves backward down the sequence of steps. In the previous example, the same behavior ("pants up") could be taught using backward chaining by placing the pants on the child and reinforcing him for touching the waistband when the S^D "pants up" is presented. After the child has reached criterion at this step, the therapist may pull the pants down a few inches and require that the child pull the pants to the waist when the S^D "pants up" is presented. Next, the child may be required to pull the pants up from the knees, etc. Note that the sequence of steps here may be identical to those used in forward chaining.

There are two essential points the therapist must recognize when using a chaining procedure. First, each of these steps is *cumulative,* meaning that to get rewarded at step 7, the child must correctly perform the entire previous sequence (steps 1-6). Second, the size of step increments will ultimately be determined by the child's performance. If he/she is having great difficulty, the step increments will have to be smaller than if progress is rapid. If the child begins to make errors (which do not seem to be due to inattention or lack of motivation), it will be necessary to back up to the previous step at which the child was successful. After the child performs correctly at this level, he/she should be again advanced, but at a smaller step increment then before the error.

SHAPING AND CHAINING WITH AUTISTIC CHILDREN   Therapists working with autistic children will find that whereas the *principles* involved in shaping and chaining are relatively simple and logical, the *practice* can be more difficult with some of these children. The training session may not always go as smoothly as described in the procedural description. Some of the problems frequently encountered when attempting to use shaping or chaining with autistic children follow.

First, the children often progress so slowly that improvement increments are infrequent and small. This, in turn, makes it very difficult for the therapist to discriminate the occurrence of these improvements. For example, if the therapist is shaping the sound "ga" and the child is saying "gee," the therapist needs to listen for any sound that is a closer approximation to "ga." Yet if the child has gone several trials with no improvement, the therapist may have trouble remembering the last best approximation and thus be unable to tell if the next one is indeed a further improvement.

Another problem is that a child may be progressing along at an early stage of the shaping process, when he/she, by chance, happens to make a response that is very close to the target behavior. By principle, the child should now be moved up to this more advanced level, yet the therapist knows that the child may not spontaneously make this response again for thousands of trials, and is therefore likely to cease responding long before another reward can be presented. What does the therapist do then — reinforce the response, but go back to the child's previous best approximation to continue shaping, or advance the child to the new high level? In practice, therapists have developed their own plans for handling this situation. One way seems to be to reinforce the good response and end the session for the day as an extra reward. (This also reduces the immediacy of allowing the child to be reinforced for less-accurate responses.) Others just treat the response as a lucky fluke and go back to the earlier stage of shaping where the progress had been more gradual and steady.

These situations point to a glaring hole in our knowledge of the use of gradual approximations with autistic children. We do not have a solid empirical basis for *how* to use these procedures, and we rely heavily on clincial intuition to handle these problems. What we need is some research on just how to do shaping and chaining. Hopefully, the use of shaping and chaining will be treated in the same manner as the prompting research discussed earlier. In that case, problems with prompting were identified and research conducted to understand causal variables and to design alternative, more effective, prompting procedures. This is the kind of research needed to help in developing more effective shaping and chaining procedures.

Consequences   The most important determinant of an individual's behavior may be the consequences the environment presents for that behavior (cf., Skinner and Ferster 1957). Thus, the therapist's most powerful tool for accomplishing behavior change is the effective use of *consequences*. This, in turn, requires that the therapist possess a sophisticated knowledge of the principles involved in consequating behavior. This is particularly essential in the case of autistic children since we know that the typical rewards and punishments that are effective with other children often do not work with autistic children. In this section we will discuss techniques of behavioral consequences as they relate to the treatment of these children.

The use of consequences can be broadly divided into two main areas: first is the *type* of consequence, second, is the *manner* in which the consequence is presented.

TYPE OF CONSEQUENCE   Behaviorally, the type of consequence is defined solely by the effect its presentation has on the behavior immediately preceding it (Skinner and Ferster 1957). If the strength of a behavior is increased when a particular stimulus is presented contingent upon its occurrence, the stimulus is defined as a *positive reinforcer*. Typically we see the use of positive reinforcement when someone says, "good boy," or gives the child a cookie when the child does something desirable. In the case of autistic children, one often needs to be particularly resourceful and imaginative when trying to find potent positive reinforcers. This is the case because, as discussed earlier, these children typically are socially unresponsive and, consequently, typical social reinforcers such as "good boy/girl" or a hug may be ineffective. With these children, the therapist often must resort to primary reinforcers, such as edibles (Lovaas, Freitag, Kinder, and Rubenstein, 1966). Sometimes even food is not a potent enough reinforcer and the therapist must seek alternatives (cf., Rincover *et al.* 1977).

This process can be difficult. For example, one boy with whom the authors worked presented a particularly difficult motivational problem. He was not socially responsive and rejected any attempts to use social approval as a positive reinforcer. He was also a poor eater and would not work for food. He did not play, thus ruling out the use of toys as a reward. Finally, it was discovered that he loved a particular song. On the possibility that the song might serve as a reinforcer, it was recorded on a cassette tape. During therapy sessions, 5-second intervals of the song were presented to the child contingent upon correct responding. Indeed, correct responding increased dramatically using this procedure.

A therapist must also be able to identify positive reinforcers that may not be intuitively obvious and, indeed, may seem very unlikely. It is often the case with autistic children that stimuli we may consider aversive have positively reinforcing effects on the child's behavior. For example, verbally chastising a child (e.g., "no," "stop that") may lead to an increase in the undesirable behavior even though the opposite effect is intended. But the therapist *is* attending to the child and attention like this can be reinforcing, especially if the child has few other sources of reinforcement, and/or if the child has some minimal social behavior. A particularly good example of an unexpected positive reinforcer was recently demonstrated by Favell, McGimsey, and Jones (1978). These investigators reported on three self-abusive subjects for whom physical restraint served as a positive reinforcer. When physical restraint was presented contingent upon increasing periods of time with no self-abuse, the self-abuse was eliminated.

The use of *negative reinforcement* has also proven to be effective with autistic children, particularly in those instances where an appropriate positive reinforcer cannot be found. Since a negative reinforcer is a stimulus that when removed or avoided serves to strengthen a behavior, we are typically dealing with an aversive stimulus. Thus, if the therapist cannot identify a positive reinforcer for which the child will work, an alternative is to use a negative reinforcer that the child will work to escape or avoid. For example, if trying to teach the child to look at the therapist, one method is for the therapist to hold a piece of food up in front of his/her eyes while saying "look at me." If the child cannot be enticed by the food (positive reinforcer), the alternative is to say "look at me" and hold the child's head firmly. Most likely this will be unpleasant to the child. When he looks at the therapist, the head is released. The child should quickly learn that the way to avoid or escape the head holding is to look at the therapist when asked.

Besides applying negative reinforcement to increase a desirable behavior, one needs to be alert to the possibility of negative reinforcement operating to maintain undesirable behavior. An example will serve to illustrate this problem. Carr, Newsom, and Binkoff (1977) presented the case of an institutionalized psychotic boy, Tim, with a long history of severe self-abuse. Tim's teacher was reporting that his self-abuse was interfering with his treatment. During his treatment sessions, he would slap his face repeatedly. The teacher, being careful not to present attention (positive reinforcement) to him when he self-abused, immediately stopped speaking to him and turned away. Soon Tim would stop hitting himself. Yet when the teacher resumed her instruction (which consisted of having Tim respond to commands and questions), his self-abuse recurred. Carr *et al.* hypothesized that the commands and questions constituted an aversive situation that Tim was escaping by engaging in self-abuse. A systematic analysis confirmed the hypothesis. Thus, Tim could avoid having to work by hitting himself. The teacher had inadvertently negatively reinforced the self-abuse (see Chapter 10 for an additional discussion of this point).

Extinction is a frequently used consequence and one of the most effective tools in a therapist's repertoire. Basically, extinction means that a stimulus known to be a reinforcer is no longer presented contingent on a behavior. If a child has been receiving attention for tantrums and if the attention has been maintaining the tantrums because it is a positive reinforcer, an effective way to eliminate the tantrums is to no longer provide the attention. Since there is no longer any reinforcement forthcoming for the disruptive behavior, the child will cease to tantrum. As another example, we can discuss the Carr, Newsom, and Binkoff (1977) study involving the child whose self-abuse was being maintained by the negative reinforcement of avoiding the teacher's commands. One would suspect that this behavior could be put on extinction by no longer presenting the negative reinforcer (teacher stopping the commands) when self-abuse occurred. Thus, in this case a potentially effective treatment procedure would be to *continue* the commands when the child self-abused so that he would learn that hitting himself would not lead to escape from the work situation. This would remove the payoff for such behavior.

This last point serves to bring us to some important characteristics of the extinction procedure. First, extinction is effective, but it typically involves a gradual reduction in the strength of the behavior rather than a sharp, dramatic drop (as is more characteristic of punishment). In the case of Tim, his self-abuse consisted of fairly mild self-abuse, and thus extinction might be used since he would not really do serious damage to himself. However, a child with more severe self-abuse might not be a good candidate for extinction because of the serious harm that might be inflicted during the extinction process. Second, at the onset of extinction there is usually an initial *increase* in the strength of the target behavior as the child "tries harder" to reinstate the reinforcer. Thus, the child might cry harder during a tantrum or nag harder for a cookie. After this initial extinction "burst" the behavior graudally extinguishes. It is important that the therapist expect this initial increase in the strength of the behavior or he/she may prematurely abandon an effective treatment procedure. Third, the therapist can expect an increase in the variability of the response at the onset of extinction. Thus, the child may be more creative in his/her attempts to gain attention during a tantrum by kicking the door or throwing himself on the floor, etc. Again, it is important to anticipate the occurrence of these effects during the initial stages of extinction.

Punishment refers to the presentation of a (usually aversive) stimulus contingent upon an undesirable behavior with the effect of reducing the strength of that behavior. Forms of punishment can range from a mild verbal no to a spank or other physical aversive. Punishment has been shown to be an effective means of decreasing problem behaviors.

Punishment with autistic children has received much attention over the years, both pro and con. Punishment has proved necessary with these children in instances where it would not be necessary with normal children. This is primarily due to the fact that autistics are typically nonverbal and rather than verbally describing the contingencies to the child ("Don't engage in self-stimulation because it interferes with your learning") the contingencies must be directly applied. Further, punishment has been demonstrated to be effective with forms of behavior that are very resistant to other forms of treatment, such as self-abuse (e.g., Lichstein and Schreibman 1976; Lovaas and Simmons 1969; Baroff and Tate 1968; Tate and Baroff 1966).

It is important for the therapist to remember that punishment serves only to suppress a behavior temporarily. If the child is not taught another, more acceptable behavior, then the undesirable behavior will recur after the punishment is removed. Thus, one of the advantages of punishment is that it suppresses an undesirable behavior, allowing the therapist to reinforce concurrently (increase the strength) of an incompatible, desirable behavior. For example, if a child is receiving attention for self-abuse and this attention is maintaining the behavior, the therapist may elect to punish the self-abuse. While this behavior is suppressed, the child can be taught another, more appropriate response that will similarly serve to gain attention. Perhaps the child can be taught to talk. Under these conditions, the child should and typically does not revert to self-abuse for attention.

The use of punishment should be governed by several considerations. First is the nature of the response suppression desired. Punishment is often the treatment of choice when it is deemed undesirable to allow the behavior to continue any longer. Such would be the case of a severe self-abusive child or a very aggressive child. Second is the fact that punishment may be used when other procedures such as extinction or rewarding incompatible behaviors have failed. Third is the fact that some therapists are more comfortable with one approach than another. If the therapist is not comfortable with punishment or with the particular punishing stimulus being used, he/she probably will not be consistent with the procedure. This would, of course, render the procedure ineffective. Fourth, one would typically opt for the mildest punishment that will prove effective for a particular behavior.

Time-Out is a form of punishment that is often used with autistic children. This procedure involves removing the child from the opportunity to receive reinforcement. This is done contingent upon engaging in an undesirable behavior. For example, if a child is engaging in disruptive behavior in a classroom or therapy setting, the therapist may remove the child to another small room where there are no toys, people, or other potentially reinforcing objects or activities. In addition, the child is no longer in the treatment environment where reinforcement is available. After the child has ceased the undesirable behavior, he is again brought back to the treatment setting.

While time-out can be a very effective procedure, it is only effective when the time-out environment is less reinforcing than the environment the child is being removed from (cf., Solnick and Rincover 1976). For example, removing the child from the classroom to another playroom will probably not be effective because the child might prefer to be in the playroom rather than the classroom. In fact, the child may be engaging in the undesirable behavior just to get to the playroom.

When using consequences, the therapist must remember that a particular consequence may not always be identified beforehand. A consequence is defined by the *effect* it has on the behavior and by no other definition.

MANNER OF PRESENTING CONSEQUENCES   As mentioned earlier, the manner in which a consequence is delivered is as important as the type of consequence. One can look at four basic rules when applying consequences.

1. *The consequence must be contingent upon the behavior.* This means that to be effective a consequence must follow *only* the specific target behavior and be presented *immediately* upon the behavior's occurrence. Thus, if the therapist is using candy to reinforce a child positively for saying "mama," he/she should be careful to present the candy immediately when the child says "mama" and not after other responses.

2. *The consequence delivery must be consistent.* If a consequence is to be effective it must be presented in the same manner and contingent upon the same behavior across trials. For example, one must be careful not to punish some instances of a behavior while allowing the child to "get away" with the behavior on other occasions just because the therapist is tired or occupied elsewhere.

3. *The consequence must be delivered in an unambiguous manner.* The nature of the consequence must always be clear to the child. If the reinforcer is positive, it whould be delivered in a positive fashion. For example if the child gives a correct response, the therapist might say, "Good boy!", smile, present a piece of candy, and sound happy. Thus, several positive cues are being delivered, and even if the child is responding to only one of the cues, he will know it was positive. On the other hand, an example of an ambiguous positive consequence would be where the child has made several errors and finally responds correctly only to have the therapist feed him and angrily state, "Well, it's about time!" The food is positive but the affect and verbal statement are negative. Similarly, another ambiguous consequence would be one in which a punisher is delivered simultaneously with a sympathetic statement (e.g., "No, no, no, but I know you're trying, you cutie you").

4. *The consequence should be easily discriminable.* The therapist must make the consequence obvious to the child. The best way to do this is to present the stimulus strongly and to minimize extraneous cues at the time. For example, if the consequence "good boy" is presented amid a running conversation, it is unlikely the child will discriminate it as a consequence. Again, this may be because of stimulus overselectivity (see 3 above). A good idea is to keep the consequence short, present it in a stronger tone than the regular conversation, and minimize other interactions at that time.

Practice with Feedback

After reading about and observing correct and incorrect examples of all of the above procedures, each teacher then attempted to teach a child a new target behavior. About once every five minutes, the trainer would interrupt the session and provide feedback as to whether or not the teacher was conducting the teaching according to the following operational definitions. If errors occurred in any category, the trainer (either an author or a university student familiar with these procedures) so informed the teacher, and then modeled the procedure according to its operational definition. Feedback was very brief, usually taking only a few seconds, in order to produce minimal interference with the session. For example, the trainer might say, "You are using good prompts, but your S^D s are too long. Try saying, 'Touch red.'" Approximately once every half hour, the teachers were given more elaborate feedback. These sessions continued until the trainer was subjectively satisfied with the teacher's performance. All the teachers completed training within less than 25 hours (usually either five days of 5 hours per day, or ten days of 2.5 hours per day). None of the teachers reported either training schedule to be excessively demanding.

Validation of Procedures

The design of this experiment was a modified multiresponse baseline (Birnbrauer, Peterson, and Solnick 1974). For a predetermined number of baseline sessions (one, three, or four sessions) each teacher attempted to teach one to four randomly assigned target behaviors. In each session, one teacher worked with one child on one behavior. During successive sessions, a teacher might be assigned to a different child and/or a different target behavior. After training, the teacher again attempted to teach one to three behaviors. The tasks assigned both before and after training were always different from those used during training. During each session, the correctness of the teacher's procedures was simultaneously measured with the learning of the child to assess whether changes in the children's behavior were a function of changes in the teacher's behavior and whether the training produced the teacher's generalized use of behavior-modification procedures across (autistic) children and tasks.

Assessment of Teacher Use of Behavior Modification Procedures

In each session, at least one observer recorded data on the teachers' use of five aspects of behavior-modification procedures. Each observer, whether familiar or naive with respect to the conditions of the experiment, had completed at least one college level course in behavior modification. The observers scored the teachers behaviors according to the same operational definitions described in the "scoring instructions" section of Chapter 14.

Measurements of the Child's Performance

In each session, data were recorded continuously on the correctness of the child's performance of the target behavior. On each trial, an observer recorded whether the child's response was correct, incorrect, prompted, or an approximation of the target behavior. If an approximation was performed, the observer noted whether or not it was a closer approximation to the target behavior than the last reinforced response. If a prompt was used to bring about a correct response from the child, the observed noted whether the prompt was faded over the course of training.

In addition to these trial-by-trial measures of student improvement, a summary measure was obtained to determine whether or not a child was learning in each session. A " +" was recorded if the child's responding during the last 10 trials of the session was improved (i.e., a closer approximation, a reduced prompt, or a higher percentage of correct responding) as compared to the first 10 trials of the session. Conversely, a "0' was recorded if responding during the last 10 trials showed no improvement, or a deterioration, when compared to the first 10 trials.

Reliability

Reliability of recording the teachers' use of behavior-modification procedures was assessed by the following procedures. Two observers (usually one trainer and one naive observer) independently (data sheets shielded from each others' sight) recorded data for 24 of the 47 sessions in this experiment. In addition, two naive observers independently recorded data from 16 video-taped sessions shown to them in a randomized order. An agreement or disagreement between observers was recorded for each of the five procedures in each 30-second interval. An agreement was counted if both observers marked the same square on their data sheets, and a disagreement was counted if only one observer marked a given square. Reliability for each session was calculated by dividing number of agreements (summing across categories) by the total number of agreements plus disagreements for that session. The mean percent agreement for these sessions was 94.6 percent. The range (82 – 100 percent) of reliability percentages was identical for both the *in vivo* and videotape recordings.

For child responses, one trainer and one naive observer independently and continuously recorded the child's behavior in 24 (of 47) randomly selected sessions. The observers were in agreement if, on a given trial, they both recorded the response as correct, incorrect, prompted, or a successive approximation. Reliability was calculated for each session by dividing the number of agreements by the number of agreements plus disagreements in that session. The mean reliability for these measures was 91.7 percent, with a range of 84 – 100 percent. For the summary (improvement versus no improvement) measure recorded in each of these 24 sessions, the observers were in complete agreement.

Results

Measurement of Teacher Behavior Before and After Training

Data for all 11 teachers, showing their use of behavior-modification procedures during baseline and posttraining sessions, are presented in Figure 11-3. Each point represents a composite score based on the average percent correct use of the five categories of behavior-modification procedures during a given session.

FIGURE 11—3. The session-by-session percent of correct use of behavior modification procedures by teachers before and after teacher training. (From Koegel, Russo and Rincover 1977. Copyright by the Society for the Experimental Analysis of Behavior. Reprinted by permission.)

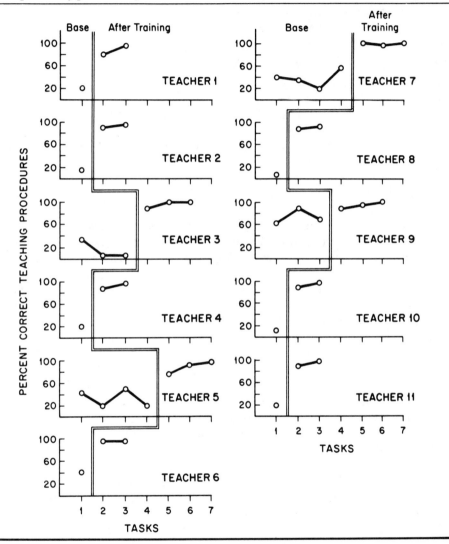

The ordinate shows the percent correct use of the behavior-modification procedures; sessions are presented on the abscissa.

During the baseline sessions, all 11 teachers evidenced low percentages. The percentages for 10 of the 11 teachers were consistently below 58 percent, and in two instances were as low as 0 percent. The remaining teacher achieved scores of 63, 91, and 71 percent during three baseline sessions.

In the posttraining sessions, the 11 teachers scored between 90 and 100 percent correct use of behavior-modification procedures for 25 of the 26 sessions.

For each teacher, this change represents both a decrease in the frequency of incorrect intervals, and an increase in the frequency of correct intervals, the number of recording intervals per session remaining constant. All 11 teachers showed considerable increases in their correct use of behavior-modification procedures after the training program. Furthermore, after training, teacher behavior generalized to new tasks.

Measurement of Children's Behavior Before and After Teacher Training

To determine whether correct performance of the five techniques of behavior modification was sufficient for teaching autistic children, the child's (unprompted) correct responses during each session were assessed. During 20 of the 21 baseline sessions, the children showed either no improvement or a decrease in correct responding. In marked contrast, after the teachers were trained, the children improved their level of correct responding during each of 26 posttraining sessions.

Figure 11-4 shows all of the data for four representative teachers. Percent correct responses performed on the particular task being taught to a given child during a given session is shown on the ordinate, and blocks of 10 training trials are shown on the abscissa. Single vertical lines separate different sessions; double vertical lines signify the time at which the teacher was trained. Since different behaviors were being taught to different children in each session, the number of trials varied (from 20 to 100 trials) over sessions.

The first teacher (Teacher 3 in Figure 11-4) attempted to teach three different behaviors to three different children during the baseline sessions. In all three instances, the data are similar; the children showed no improvement. In fact, during these sessions all children evidenced a lower percentage of correct responding at the end of the session than at the beginning. The results for the other three teachers during baseline sessions are similar. Out of a total of 14 baseline sessions, 13 showed either no improvement or a reduced level of correct responding by the end of the session.

After the four teachers had been trained, the children's correct responding increased. Every child showed large increases in the percent of correct responses during each of 12 sessions conducted after teacher training. In four sessions, the teachers introduced new prompt, shaping, or reinforcement-schedule fading techniques (marked in the figure by asterisks). Although temporary drops in correct responding occurred in these cases, each child quickly regained at least 90 percent correct responding.

Generalized Use of Behavior Modification Procedures

The teachers were not specifically trained to teach the particular behaviors used in the posttraining assessment; these results show that the training procedures produced generalized correct applications of the procedures taught during training. In addition, it may be important to note that posttraining Sessions 2 and 3 for

FIGURE 11—4. The percent of correct responding by the children before and after teacher training. Percent correct responses are plotted for each block of 10 trials within a session. (From Koegel, Russo and Rincover 1977. Copyright by the Society for the Experimental Analysis of Behavior. Reprinted by permission.)

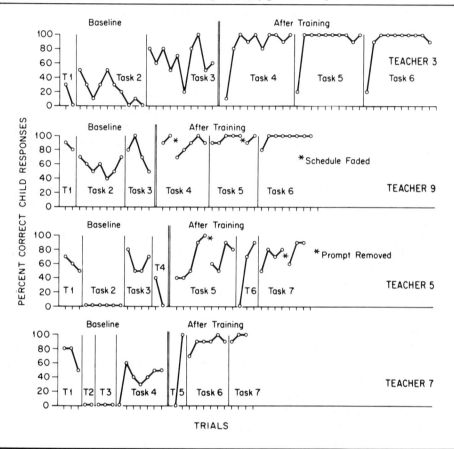

two teachers (Teachers 5 and 7) were conducted two and four months after training, leading us to feel optimistic about the durability of the results of training.

Discussion

The results showed the following:

(1) The assessment procedure reliably differentiated between teachers with respect to their correct use of defined behavior-modification procedures. Generally, when teachers failed to use the procedures correctly, efforts to teach the children produced no measurable improvement. Conversely, when the teachers showed consistently high percentages of using the procedures correctly, their teaching was effective in producing gains in the children's responding.

(2) The training procedure was effective, for all teachers, in increasing the

correct use of the procedures. Further, after training, the teachers' correct use of these procedures generalized to new target behaviors and new children.

The training procedure was a package involving the use of modeling, feedback, and training manuals. A component analysis was not done, and as such, it is not definite which components contributed to each aspect of the results. It is possible that certain components influenced acquisition of the techniques and other influenced generalization. A component analysis of this or any other teacher-training program might lead to interesting results (Koegel, Glahn, and Nieminen 1978; Bandura 1976; Kazdin and Moyer 1976).

There was no attempt to determine correlations between intermediate levels of teaching proficiency (e.g., 50 percent, 70 percent, etc.), and the rates of change in correct responding of the children. A 90 percent proficiency on the five procedures was almost always sufficient to ensure effective modification of the behavior of these severely autistic children. It may, however, be interesting to note that, during one of the baseline sessions for Teacher 9, there was no improvement in child performance with a high level of correct teacher performance. Thus, other categories of teacher behavior may be important to measure and some categories may be more important than others. Possibly some other variable, such as consistency in teacher behavior across sessions, may to some extent influence the results (note that this teacher worked with the same child in every session). As Parsonsen, Baer, and Baer (1974) and Herbert and Baer (1972) pointed out, there can be value in improving the overall performance of someone who is already moderately competent.

The five categories measured and trained in this investigation are not the only ones that could be studied. Several investigators (e.g., LeLaurin and Risley 1972; Sailor and Taman 1972) have suggested that the physical configuration of the teaching environment may be an important variable influencing learning. Various procedures that are effective for teaching a group of autistic children in a classroom setting have been investigated (Koegel and Rincover 1974). As these or other new categories are discovered, they perhaps should also be included in the assessment and training procedures. It is also suspected that subjective teacher characteristics, such as tact, sensitivity, ability to develop rapport, etc., should also be more carefully defined and measured. The contribution that the present empirical evaluation offers at this time is not in providing an all-inclusive list of procedures to measure but, rather, in suggesting that it is important to measure carefully both the behavior of the teacher and the behavior of the child in order to discover functional relationships between the two.

Classroom Management: Progression from Special to Normal Classrooms

R esearch in the area of classroom management with autistic children has progressed enormously over the past decade. The field has moved from the point of asking questions such as, "Is it possible to teach autistic children in school?," to questions such as, "What are the optimal teaching techniques?" and, "Might children in general best profit from educating autistic children among normal children in normal classrooms?" The purpose of this chapter is to describe this development, and to highlight issues and procedures which appear especially important if one is to achieve optimal progress in classrooms with autistic children. These issues and procedures are described in detail below.[1]

Teaching Autistic Children in Large Groups

Prior to the 1970s a large majority of the research investigating variables in the treatment of autistic children utilized a one-to-one teacher-child ratio (Lovaas and Koegel 1973). For example, a one-to-one teacher-child ratio was employed with autistic children by Wolf, Risley, and Mees (1964) to modify tantrum behavior; by Hewett (1965), Lovaas (1977a, 1969, 1966), and Risley and Wolf (1967) to establish

*This chapter was authored by **Robert L. Koegel,** University of California, Santa Barbara, **Arnold Rincover,** University of North Carolina, Greensboro, and **Dennis C. Russo,** Harvard Medical School.*

This chapter presents a summary of the experiments conducted by Koegel and Rincover (1974), Rincover and Koegel (1977a), and Russo and Koegel (1977). They are presented here together in order to emphasize the important inter-relationships between the procedures, and to illustrate the step-wise progression toward the children's education in a normal classroom.

functional speech; by Lovaas, *et al.* (1967) and Metz (1965) to condition generalized imitation; by Hewett (1964, 1966) to teach reading skills; and by Marshall (1966) to establish self-help skills. While the results of these studies showed that behavior modification procedures in one-to-one treatment had been extremely productive in a variety of situations and with diverse behaviors, such procedures had not been systematically investigated in the classroom setting.

However, at that time, research in classroom design with normal, culturally deprived, and retarded children was progressing enormously (cf., Kazdin and Bootzin 1972; O'Leary 1972; O'Leary and Drabman 1971). Several investigators were also suggesting guidelines for the development of classrooms for autistic children (Hamblin *et al.* 1971; Halpern 1970; Martin *et al.* 1968; Rabb and Hewett 1967; Elgar 1966).

However, no published studies had systematically investigated procedures for simultaneously teaching a group of autistic children in a classroom. As a result, few public-school classrooms were in operation for autistic children. In fact, lawsuits against the Department of Education were in progress in numerous states in the U.S. for failure to provide school programs for autistic children. It appeared that numerous educators still felt that educating autistic children within an actual classroom was still an impossibility.

In 1974 Koegel and Rincover published a study which examined some of the issues involved in this controversy. The study asked two major questions: First, would basic classroom behaviors taught in one-to-one sessions be performed consistently in eight-to-one (eight children and one teacher) classroom sessions? Second, without special intervention, would autistic children show any new learning in a classroom of eight children with one teacher?

Eight autistic children participated in the following experiment (Koegel and Rincover 1974). All were severely psychotic, displaying minimal, if any, intelligible verbal behavior, large amounts of self-stimulatory behavior (stereotyped arm and hand movement, rhythmic rocking, etc.), and minimal responsiveness to verbal instruction. Four of the children were mute, evidencing only a limited set of vowel sounds and no words. The other four children were echolalic, repeating what was said to them either immediately or after a delay. Five children were reported to be untestable when administered the Stanford Binet Intelligence Scale by an independent testing agency. The other three children attained IQ scores of 28, 32, and 38. Social development, as measured by the Vineland Social Maturity Scale was between 2 and 4 years for all of the children. The average chronological age of the children at the beginning of this project was 7.3 years (range 4.5 to 13 years). All of the children had been denied admission to, or expelled from existing public-school programs (including special education classes), and were living at home during the course of this investigation.

All sessions were conducted in a 20' × 30' classroom containing one large table (34" × 60"), two smaller tables (24" × 36"), and eight chairs. The classroom contained a variety of educational materials (e.g., Peabody Language Development Series, Distar Arithmetic Series, maps, clocks, picture charts of animals and objects) and play materials (e.g., balls, trucks, blocks, and record player).

In order to assess whether behaviors taught in a one-to-one treatment setting would be performed in larger group sizes, each of the children was initially taught, with a one-to-one teacher-child ratio, various verbal and non-verbal behaviors that would be appropriate in a classroom situation and then tested for performance of the behaviors in "groups" of one child with one teacher, two children with one teacher, and eight children with one teacher. Starting the first week of the study, the children were also tested in weekly classroom sessions in which a single teacher attempted to train a variety of *new* verbal and nonverbal behaviors to eight children simultaneously in order to measure novel learning in a group environment.

One-to-One Treatment Procedures

All children participated in one-to-one treatment sessions once per day, five days per week, each session lasting 50 minutes. Primary reinforcement (food) was used throughout one-to-one treatment. These sessions were directed toward teaching basic verbal and nonverbal skills believed necessary for learning to take place in a classroom-sized group of children. Table 12-1 presents representative examples of the stimuli used during the one-to-one treatment.

Appropriate nonverbal responses were shaped by first rewarding the child for establishing eye contact with the teacher until the child would consistently (90 percent correct trials for three consecutive days) look at the teacher for a period of at least five seconds when the teacher gave the instruction, "Look at me." Then, nonverbal imitation was gradually established by prompting and reinforcing imitation behaviors until the child could consistently imitate all of the following trained behaviors: nose touching, head touching, hand clapping, feet touching, elbow touching, and block stacking; and all of the following novel (not specifically trained) behaviors: standing, sitting, jumping, holding hands, and raising one arm. Imitation was then used as a prompt to teach other nonverbal responses to instructions. For example, the teacher would say, "Touch your nose" and prompt the correct response by saying "Do this" and modeling the correct response. The prompts were then faded until the child could perform all of the following commands without prompts: touch your nose, touch your elbow, clap your hands, sit down, hands on your lap, touch your feet, etc. (Detailed descriptions of similar treatment procedures have been provided by Lovaas *et al.* (1967) and Metz (1965).) Following this training, each child would remain seated in his/her chair, would look at the teacher when requested to do so, would imitate the teacher upon request, and had acquired some elementary receptive language.

The procedure used for establishing appropriate verbal behaviors in the mute children followed four steps. First, the teacher rewarded the child for all vocalizations emitted during the session, thereby increasing the frequency of vocalizations. Second, stimulus control was established by rewarding the child only for vocalizations made within five seconds of the teacher's vocalizations. Third, the child was rewarded only for gradually closer approximations to the teacher's speech. Finally, meanings were established for each of the words by differentially reinforcing use of the word in the appropriate stimulus conditions. For example, the child would be prompted and receive reinforcement for the target response "cookie" in response to the question "What is this?" when a cookie was presented. (Detailed descriptions of similar procedures have been

TABLE 12–1. Examples of stimuli presented during experimental sessions.

ONE-TO-ONE TRAINING OF BASIC CLASSROOM SKILLS	ACQUISITION OF NEW BEHAVIORS IN THE CLASSROOM
General Class of Stimuli I. Attending to the teacher **Examples** A. "Look at me" B. "Sit down" C. "Hands on the table"	**General Class of Stimuli** I. Discrimination Training: body parts, colors, people, animals, clothing, household and classroom objects and activities, etc. **Examples** A. "Touch your ____" (pants, finger, etc.) B. "What color is this?" (red, blue, green, etc.) C. "Who is that?" (Mommy, Polly, Lynn, etc.) D. "What does the bird do?" (fly, etc.) E. "What do you eat with?" (fork, knife, etc.) F. "What clothes are you wearing?" (shirt, pants, shoes, etc.)
II. Imitation A. "Do this"—teacher touches nose, feet, elbow, head, etc. B. "Do this"—teacher stands up, jumps, claps hands, picks up pencil, stacks blocks, hangs up coat, etc.	II. Basic writing skills A. "Pick up the pencil" B. "Draw a ____" (A, B, etc.) C. "Trace the lines" (cat, elephant, etc.) D. "Write your name" (Eddie, etc.)
III. Speech A. "Say m," "b," "c," etc. B. "Do this"—teacher holds lips in position to say "mm" etc. C. "Say cat," "mama," etc.	III. Basic reading skills Distar Reading series A. "This is ____; say ____" (mm, aa, etc.) B. "When I point to the sound, tell me what it says." (d, i, t, etc.) C. "What is this" (e.g., th), "and this" (a), "and this" (t). "Say it fast" (that) D. "What word is this?" (feed, rock, etc.)
	IV. Basic arithmetic skills: Distar Arithmetic series A. "What number is this?" (1, 2, 3, etc.) B. "Count to ____" (10, 20, 50, etc.) C. "How many balls do you see?" (1, 5, 10, etc.)

From Koegel and Rincover (1974). Copyright by Society for the Experimental Analysis of Behavior. Reprinted with permission.

presented in written form by Hewett (1965) and Lovaas *et al*. (1966) and are also available on film (Lovaas 1969).)

Speech was taught to the echolalic children by showing them pictures of objects and asking, "What is this?," and then prompting the correct response, which the child would echo. The prompt was gradually faded until the child responded with the correct answer without any prompt. (Detailed descriptions of similar procedures have been provided in written form by Risley and Wolf (1967) and Lovaas (1977), and on film by Lovaas (1969).) During the course of one-to-one sessions, both mute and echolalic children acquired basic skills of verbal imitation and labelling pictures (e.g., food objects, clothing objects, toys, people, and body parts). When a child completed this speech training, he/she could verbalize any word upon presentation of the instruction, "Say ＿＿＿," and could label at least three objects.

Throughout the one-to-one sessions, disruptive verbal and nonverbal behaviors were treated with extinction, or the application of contingent aversive stimuli (abruptly saying "No!" or slapping the child briskly). Since some self-stimulatory behaviors appear to interfere with learning (Koegel and Covert 1972), such behavior was also treated with contingent aversive stimulation.

Assessment of Performance in Various Group Sizes   After each child achieved a criterion of at least 80 percent appropriate responses in the one-to-one treatment sessions, performance of those behaviors was measured in groups of eight-to-one, two-to-one, and one-to-one. One-to-one training sessions were continued once per day throughout the testing. In each of the test sessions, the children were seated around the rectangular table, with the teacher seated at the head of the table. Each child was within arm's reach of the teacher. No primary reinforcement was used, in order to ensure that no new learning took place during the test trials.

Control for the order of group sessions was accomplished in the following way: with three group sizes there are six different sequences of testing (8, 2, 1; 1, 2, 8; 2, 1, 8; 1, 8, 2; 2, 8, 1; 8, 1, 2). Each subject was tested in three randomly selected sequences of group sizes. Since there were eight subjects and three sequences per subject, a total of 24 test sequences was used.

When the children reached the 80 percent criterion in the one-to-one training sessions, they were tested in all three group sizes on each of the next three days. Fifteen different stimuli were presented in each group size. For each session, these stimuli were randomly selected from each of the three classes of stimuli given in Table 12-1. Variability in the number of trials presented was eliminated by recording responses to only the first 15 different stimuli. The children received a total of 45 test trials in each group size. A child's companion was randomly selected for testing in a group of two. However, different children had to serve as companions for each test session.

In these test sessions, the teacher presented one trial to each child in the group before proceeding to the next stimulus. For example, the teacher would say, "Say mmm" once to each child starting from left to right. After each child in the group had received one trial, a new stimulus was presented in the same way. This procedure continued until each child had received 15 different stimuli.

Assessment of New Learning in the Clasroom   To assess learning of new behaviors in a classroom environment, classroom sessions with eight autistic children and one teacher were videotaped once per week. Each session was conducted for 50 minutes, with videotape time samples recorded during three randomly spaced 4-minute segments of each session. At the start of each session, the eight children were seated around the rectangular table, with the teacher seated at the head of the table. All children were within arm's reach of the teacher. The teacher then followed a training curriculum based upon the California State Department of Education Curriculum guidelines for kindergarten/first-grade children. These guidelines were selected because the children had no prior academic skills (as they had little or no previous school experience). The teacher presented approximately 125 (range: 70–150) stimuli per session. Table 12-1 presents representative examples of the stimuli used. Fifty percent of the stimuli were commands, and 50 percent were questions. Also, 50 percent of the stimuli required verbal responses, and 50 percent required nonverbal responses. Both questions and commands were presented to the children individually and as a group. For example, the teacher would first say, "Everyone, tell me what this is" and then, "John, tell me what this is," "Eddie, tell me what this is," etc. No primary reinforcement was used during these sessions. However, appropriate responses were reinforced socially in order to approximate normal classroom conditions.

For each weekly videotape, two observers selected from a pool of seven naive observers recorded the occurrence of both appropriate verbal and appropriate nonverbal responses as defined below in the instructions to the observers.

Appropriate verbal responses consisted of verbal responses which were clear and distinct and relevant to the question or command given by the teacher. The child's response needed to occur within 10 seconds of the teacher's stimulus. For example, if the teacher held up a blue card and asked, "What color is this?" and the child responded "blue" within 10 seconds, an appropriate verbal response was recorded. The response was recorded as inappropriate if it occurred more than 10 seconds after the teacher's question or command, or if it was irrelevant to the teacher's stimulus. For example, screaming, echoing the teacher's question, or answering the question, "What color is this?" with the response "square turtle," were all recorded as inappropriate. For each session, the percentage of appropriate verbal responses was defined as the number of appropriate verbal responses per session divided by the total number of stimuli that required verbal responses directed to the child in that session. For example, if the teacher presented 25 questions and commands requiring verbal responses from the child, and the child responded appropriately 20 times, he received a measure of 80 percent appropriate verbal responses for that session.

Appropriate nonverbal responses consisted of nonverbal responses that were relevant to the stimulus command or question and occurred within 10 seconds of the teacher's stimulus. For example, if the teacher said, "Touch your nose," and the child touched his nose within 10 seconds, it was recorded as an appropriate nonverbal response. A response was recorded as inappropriate if it occurred more than 10 seconds after the stimulus, or if it did not correctly answer or follow the stimulus command or question. For example, if the child engaged in self-stimulatory behavior, hit another child or himself, did not respond at all, or emitted any other response which did not relate to the question or command, it was recorded as inappropriate. The percentage of appropriate nonverbal responses was defined as the number of appropriate nonverbal responses emitted by the child divided by the number of stimuli which required nonverbal responses directed toward that child. For example, if the teacher directed 30 questions and commands requiring a nonverbal response by a given child, and the child responded appropriately 15 times, he/she received a measure of 50 percent appropriate nonverbal responses for that session.

Reliability   Measures were recorded from videotapes for the assessment of new behaviors learned in the classroom, and *in vivo* for the assessment of responding in the three group sizes. Two of seven naive observers independently recorded the teacher's instructions as well as the children's responses for each session. (Examples of the stimuli presented by the teacher in the classroom and group testing sessions are reviewed in Table 12-1.) Responses to each stimulus were recorded as appropriate or inappropriate as defined above. If both observers recorded a particular response as appropriate or inappropriate on a given trial, they were said to be in agreement. If one observer recorded a response as appropriate and the other recorded it as inappropriate, they were said to be in disagreement. Either an agreement or a disagreement was computed for each individual trial in the session.

Reliability between the two observers for each session was calculated according to the following formula:

$$\text{Reliability} = \frac{\text{number of agreements per session}}{\text{agreements and disagreements}} \times 100$$

All reliability measures were above 95 percent.

Comparison of Children's Behavior in Various Group Sizes

The children required an average of 3.2 weeks (range: two to four weeks) to acquire the behaviors in one-to-one treatment. After the children achieved a crite-

FIGURE 12–1.   Performance of learned behavior in various group sizes. Percent correct responses are plotted individually for each child during test sessions in groups of one, two, or eight children with one teacher. (From Koegel and Rincover 1974. Copyright by the Society for the Experimental Analysis of Behavior. Reprinted by permission.)

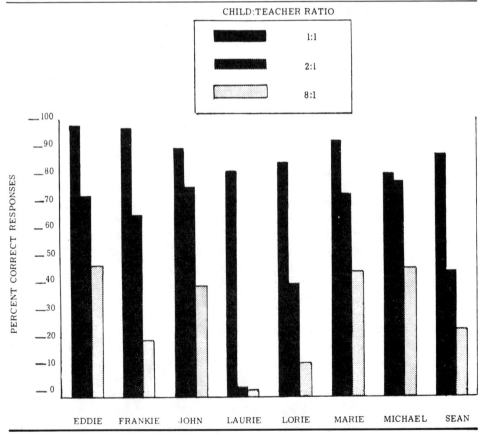

rion of 80 percent appropriate responding in one-to-one treatment sessions, their behavior was measured in groups of one, two, and eight children with one teacher. Data for each of the eight autistic children, showing their performance of learned behaviors in the various group sizes, are presented in Figure 12-1. Since verbal and nonverbal behaviors showed the same results, their data have been combined to obtain the percentages given in the figure. The ordinate represents percent of appropriate responding for each of the eight children separately. In this figure, the black bar depicts responding in two-to-one treatment sessions, and the light gray bar depicts responding in eight-to-one sessions. Each bar represents a percentage obtained in 45 trials. The figure reveals that each of the eight children responded appropriately to at least 80 percent of the stimuli presented by the teacher in the one-to-one situation. However, appropriate responding decreased when another autistic child was added to the one-to-one group size. That is, every child showed a decrease in correct responding when tested in a group of two children with one teacher. The decrease, however, was highly variable, ranging from a 3 percent decrease (Michael) to a 78 percent decrease (Laurie). Test trials in the eight-to-one sessions revealed an even greater decrease in appropriate responding for each subject. Again, the amount of decrease was variable. The decreases from one-to-one to eight-to-one ranged from 34 percent (Michael) to 81 percent (Laurie). There was no systematic change during the course of the test sessions.

Assessment of Appropriate Responding in the Classroom   Weekly classroom sessions were conducted to assess new learning in a classroom environment. The results presented below refer to the children's behavior in the classroom of eight children with one teacher. Data showing the amount of appropriate verbal and nonverbal responding in the classroom, for the mute and echolalic children separately, are presented in Figure 12-2. The dependent variable is percentage of appropriate responding. Each data point represents responding during one weekly session.

Consider the verbal responding first. Each of the four mute children showed absolutely no change from 0 percent appropriate verbal responding in the classroom throughout four weeks of daily one-to-one treatment sessions. Although each of these children performed appropriately on more than 80 percent of the trials in one-to-one sessions, not a single appropriate verbal response was emitted by any of the children in four weeks of classroom sessions. The echolalic children also displayed minimal appropriate verbal responding ranging from 25 percent (John) in Session 2 to 0 percent in at least one session for every child. No trends were apparent for any child.

Analysis of nonverbal responding reveals results similar to that of verbal responding. In brief, there was essentially no change in appropriate nonverbal responding for either mute or echolalic children. Nonverbal responding was minimal, ranging from 24 percent (Eddie) in Session 2 to 0 percent in at least one session for seven of the eight children. No trend was evident throughout the four weeks for any of the children.

In summary, the results showed that the performance of behaviors learned in one-to-one sessions was greatly reduced in a classroom-sized group of eight

FIGURE 12–2. Percent correct responding of new verbal and nonverbal behaviors being taught in the classroom. Behaviors are plotted for each child individually. Graphs for the mute children are presented on the right half of the figure; graphs for the echolalic children are plotted on the left. The ordinate represents the mean percent correct for one weekly session. (From Koegel and Rincover 1974. Copyright by the society for the Experimental Analysis of Behavior. Reprinted by permission.)

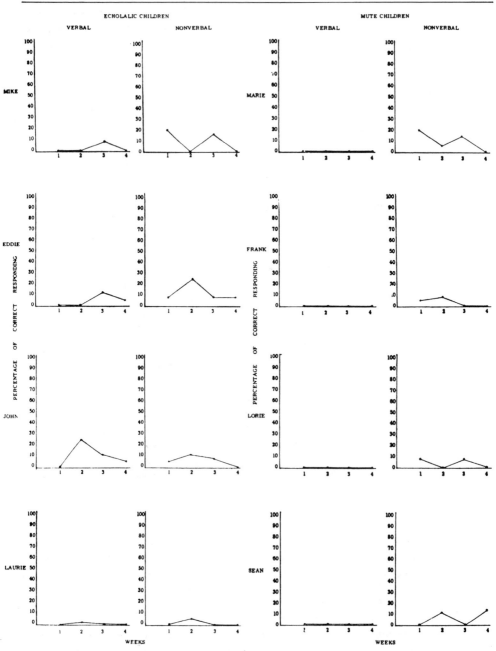

children with one teacher. Furthermore, the performance of these behaviors was also greatly reduced in a group of only two children. In conjunction with these findings, there was also no evidence of acquisition of new behaviors in classroom sessions conducted over a four-week period. These results made it somewhat easier to understand why educators were concerned about trying to teach autistic children within a public-school setting. Similar results for each of the eight autistic children directed us to the following experiment, which attempted to arrange conditions that would facilitate appropriate responding in the classroom.

The behaviors learned in one-to-one sessions above (speech, attending to the teacher upon command, imitation, labelling parts of the immediate classroom environment) seem essential for even minimal learning to take place in the classroom. However, it was found that the transfer of appropriate responding from one-to-one sessions to larger groups was minimal and variable. Also, it was found that no subsequent learning occurred in the classroom sessions. Therefore, it was necessary to develop a procedure that would facilitate a transfer of appropriate responding to the classroom. Since the children's appropriate responding in one-to-one training sessions did transfer to a "group" of one child with one teacher, but did not transfer to groups of two children or eight children with one teacher, it was decided to begin with a small "classroom" of one teacher and one child, and gradually fade in more children until a classroom-sized group was consistently performing the basic behaviors originally taught in one-to-one sessions. Using this procedure, it could also be assessed whether the children would then acquire new behaviors in the classroom.

Method

Design   To assess changes in the classroom behaviors of autistic children as a function of the treatment procedures (gradually increasing the group size and thinning the reinforcement schedule), a multiple baseline design was employed across behaviors. For each child, baseline measures were recorded on both verbal and nonverbal responses in the classroom. The treatment procedures for reducing the teacher-child ratio were then introduced for one class of behaviors (nonverbal), while the other class of behaviors (verbal) remained on the baseline. Treatment of nonverbal behaviors was initiated first because it was judged that such behavior might be useful in establishing verbal behavior (e.g., nonverbal imitation could be used to prompt the child in the placement of his/ her tongue, etc.). Treatment for reducing the teacher-child ratio on verbal behaviors was initiated at a preestablished later date. One-to-one treatment on the basic classroom behaviors was continued as a constant throughout the experiment.

Measurement of Classroom Behavior   Throughout the experiment, data continued to be recorded on the performance of each child in the classroom with eight children and one teacher once per week. Each of these sessions was conducted in exactly the same manner as the classroom sessions described above. That is, data were obtained on appropriate verbal and nonverbal classroom responses. Only social reinforcement was provided during these measurement sessions, since maintaining correct responding by "natural" reinforcers, rather than food, was the eventual goal. Procedures for computing reliability measures were the same as those used in the first experiment. All reliability measures were above 93 percent.

Treatment Procedures for Reducing the Teacher-Child Ratio

At the designated point in the multiple baseline design, the procedures for reducing the teacher-child ratio in the classroom were introduced. These sessions were conducted once per day, five days per week, and lasted 50 minutes each. The treatment sessions took place at a different time of day than the classroom measurement sessions discussed above. The treatment proceeded as follows.

> ***Step #1.*** First, two children were brought together to form a small class of two children, with one teacher and two teacher's aides. The children sat facing the teacher, with the aides seated directly behind the children. All procedures described in the one-teacher-one-child training sessions were followed here, except that in these sessions, only teacher's aides provided the necessary prompts and reinforcers. For example, the teacher would say, "Touch your ear," and an aide would prompt the child to touch his/her ear (by moving the child's hand), and then give him/her a candy.

> ***Step #2.*** When both children reached a criterion of 80 percent or more appropriate responses (without prompts), the reinforcement

Many school personnel report difficulty in teaching autistic children in groups. This photograph illustrates one of the steps in a sequence which eventually results in autistic children being able to work in groups of eight or more children with one teacher.

schedule was reduced to a fixed ratio 2, in which a given child was rewarded after performing two correct responses, and then one aide was faded out.

Step #3.   At this point, these two children were grouped with two other children who had achieved the same criterion, to form a class of four children, one teacher, and two teacher's aides. As each child was now responding twice for one reinforcer, the teacher's aides could then provide prompts and reinforcers for two children. The children were again brought to an 80 percent appropriate response criterion, and the reinforcement schedule was gradually thinned to a fixed ratio 4, in which a child received reinforcement after every fourth correct response, and again, one aide was faded out.

Step #4.   These children were then grouped with four others who had reached the same criteria to form the final class size of eight children. When all of the children again achieved the criteria, the reinforcement schedule was further thinned to a variable ratio 8, in which a given child received reinforcement on the average of every eight correct responses.

Step #5.   Both teacher's aides were then gradually removed from the classroom to work on other assignments (preparation of stimulus materials, etc.).

Results

Seven of the eight children completed the treatment for reducing the teacher-child ratio, eventually performing the basic skills (taught in one-to-one sessions) at a rate of 80 percent or higher in a group of eight children with one teacher. The number of trials required to achieve the 80 percent criterion varied considerably (approximately 400 to 2,100 trials).

The effect of the treatment procedures upon subsequent learning in the classroom is shown below for each of the eight children, including the one child (Laurie) who did not complete the treatment. All of the results presented refer to the children's behavior in the classroom of eight children with one teacher. Figure 12-3 shows the data for the mute children and echolalic children separately. The ordinate depicts percent of appropriate responses for new verbal and nonverbal behaviors taught in the classroom. Two-week intervals are presented on the abscissa.

Consider the verbal behavior first. Although all of the children were receiving one-to-one therapy throughout the baseline sessions, three of the four mute children never evidenced any appropriate verbal responses in the classroom during the baseline condition. Similarly, three of the four echolalic children displayed only minimal appropriate verbal behavior during the baseline sessions. That is, for six of the eight children, neither the one-to-one treatment sessions, nor repeated exposure to the classroom environment, had any observable effect on performance in the classroom. This is particularly dramatic in the case of Frankie, who never displayed any appropriate verbal responding in the

FIGURE 12–3.   Percent correct responding of new verbal and nonverbal behaviors being taught in the classroom. Behaviors are plotted individually for each child. The double line on each graph signifies the introduction of treatment (fading) sessions. Data for mute children are plotted on the left; data for echolalic children on the right. The ordinate represents the mean percent correct for two weekly sessions. (From Koegel and Rincover 1974. Copyright by the Society for the Experimental Analysis of Behavior. Reprinted by permission.)

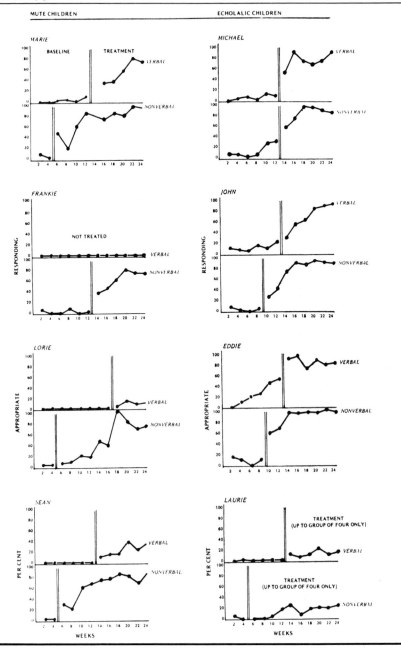

classroom over a six-month baseline condition (Frankie received no treatment on verbal behavior at the time of this experiment because of his participation in another study not associated with this research). Only one child (Eddie) showed any large degree of improvement in the classroom environment during the baseline conditions. It is difficult to determine whether the improvement was a function of transfer from one-to-one training or a function of repeated exposure to the classroom.

With the introduction of treatment, all of the children began to show increased appropriate verbal behavior, and continued to show levels of responding above the baseline level throughout treatment. In general, the echolalic children showed larger increases in appropriate responding than the mute children. Three of the echolalic children (Eddie, John, and Michael) reached levels above 80 percent appropriate verbal responses by the end of this investigation. Only one of the three mute children to receive treatment (Marie) approached this level of success (79 percent appropriate verbal responses in the 21- to 22-week interval). The one notable exception (Laurie) to the success of the echolalic children was also the only child participating in this study who did not complete the treatment procedure. In fact, Laurie never achieved the criterion of 80 percent in the group of four children (within 6,000 trials). Her performance of the basic behaviors previously acquired in one-to-one sessions did not exceed 69 percent appropriate responding in the group of four children, and, therefore, it was never possible to fade her into the treatment in a group of eight children. It is noteworthy that her performance in the classroom sessions was much less appropriate than that of any other echolalic child.

The effects of treatment on nonverbal behavior followed a pattern similar to that of the verbal behavior. In general, the percentage of appropriate nonverbal responses was very low throughout the baseline sessions. Seven of the eight children averaged less than 10 percent appropriate nonverbal responses per session. With the initiation of treatment, however, all of the children showed large increases in appropriate responding. Seven of the eight children attained levels of 80–100 percent appropriate nonverbal responses per session by the end of the investigation. No obvious differences were observed between mute and echolalic children.

In summary, the results showed that: (1)   although the children were receiving one-to-one treatment during the baseline condition, there were minimal appropriate verbal or nonverbal behaviors in the classroom before treatment, and (2)   treatment procedures based upon gradually thinning the reinforcement schedule and gradually increasing the number of children in the group did produce large increases in both appropriate verbal and appropriate nonverbal behaviors in the classroom (on both previously learned basic classroom skills, and on new behaviors learned in the classroom).

Implications for the Development of Classroom Programs for Autistic Children   These results directly contradict the notion that one can simply bring together a group of autistic children and begin academic instruction. Even repeated exposure to the classroom for extended periods of time does not appear to produce much change in the children's behavior. Eleven of the 16

baseline measures recorded for the eight children in this investigation showed either no change at all or deterioration during the baseline conditions. That is, the combined effect of one-to-one treatment and repeated exposure to the classroom environment, for periods of up to six months, produced very little change in the children's behavior in a classroom of eight children with one teacher. Perhaps this is why so few classroom programs existed for autistic children.

However, these results did show that classroom programs for autistic children could be both feasible and productive. Certain elementary classroom skills such as speech, attending to the teacher, imitation, etc. could be taught with behavior modification procedures in one-to-one sessions. Then, these skills could be evoked in successively larger group sizes approaching the size of a classroom group. Simultaneously, the schedule of reinforcement could be systematically thinned so that the teacher was able to supply sufficient reinforcers in the final classroom to provide for subsequent learning. Once this was accomplished, academic progress followed. By the end of the investigation, the children were (among other behaviors) learning to perform various classroom activities such as telling time, reading first-grade books, printing the letters of the alphabet, and solving simple arithmetic problems.

Responding Without Direct Teacher Supervision

Even with a solution to the major problem of developing appropriate group responding, additional problems have been encountered. The behavioral repertoires of autistic students are often extremely heterogeneous, and when the classroom instruction is paced to a particular student, or a few students, the remaining children learn very little. It would seem more efficient to individualize each child's instructions so that every child could work at his/her own rate, and on those skills most beneficial for his/her individual development. This approach has been suggested for various populations of exceptional children (cf., Bijou, Birnbrauer, Kidder, and Tague 1966; Birnbrauer, Kidder, and Tague 1964). The problem, particularly for autistic children, is how to individualize instruction without providing a teacher for each child.

One aspect of individualized instruction which seems troublesome for exceptional children is the amount of direct teacher supervision given to students. Individualized instruction in a group requires the teacher to move from child to child, leaving individual children to work by themselves for various periods of time. Therefore, in order for individualized instruction to be effective in a classroom of exceptional children, each child must continue working in the absence of the teacher.

The following experiment (Rincover and Koegel 1977a) was designed to assess the feasibility of using individualized instruction in a classroom of autistic children, without providing continuous one-to-one instruction. To alleviate the concern that the amount of unsupervised responding might be a variable which would influence the effectiveness of individualized instruction in a group, a treatment program was designed to increase the unsupervised responding of each child. In order to assess the effect of this variable, both the amount of unsupervised responding and the amount of academic progress which occurred were measured, before and after treatment, during sessions of individualized instruction in a group.

Four autistic children, ages 4, 7, 10, and 13, participated in this experiment. Each of the children had been denied admission to or expelled from, existing

When teaching unsupervised responding, tasks should be selected which will leave a record of the child's responses made during the teacher's absence. In this example, an autistic child is being taught using sets of pictures which he places in temporal sequences. When the teacher returns, the location of the pictures provides an indication of the child's unsupervised responding.

public school programs (including special classes). At the time of this investigation, all the children were students in an experimental school for autistic children and were living at home. Three of the students were echolalic, repeating words or phrases said to them either immediately or after a delay. The fourth student was originally mute, but by the time of this investigation, had acquired a functional vocabulary of slightly more than 100 words.

Sessions were conducted for 30 minutes each, once per day, five days per week. The children were seated around a horseshoe-shaped table across from the teacher, who was within reach of each child. Since the children were going to need to respond in a teacher's absence, it was necessary for them to work in a manner which would leave a record of their responding for the teacher to examine upon her return. Such tasks might include placing a certain number of objects into a specific container (according to specified printed instructions; writing the answers to arithmetic problems; coloring figures in a coloring book according to a specified model; printing; tracing, etc.) In this particular experiment, written responses were heavily relied upon. Since, however, most of the children could not write, it was necessary to simultaneously teach them to write as part of this experiment. Pencils and an ample supply of paper were provided for each child at the beginning of each session. Each paper (e.g., a page in an arithmetic book) was partitioned to allow 12 written responses per page. Since the learning rates and behavioral repertoires of the four children varied considerably, the particular tasks and materials assigned to a given child were determined by the child's personal level of academic skill. The tasks and materials for each individual child are described below. Figure 12 – 4 illustrates the sequencing of worksheets used to teach some of the tasks.

David. At the start of this study David could not trace a straight line. Specifically, he would start at one end and finish at the other, but he did not stay on the line between the end points. Therefore, the first worksheet contained one straight line for him to trace in each of the 12 squares. If he met criterion on this worksheet, a second and then a third line were included in each square on subsequent worksheets (see Figure 12 – 4, row 2). If he learned to trace the straight lines, he would then go on to the task of printing the letter 'A' using materials identical to those described for John.

John. John had already learned to trace a variety of straight lines. He was therefore assigned the task of combining straight lines in order to print letters of the alphabet. The first letter, consisting of three straight lines, was an 'A'. A succession of worksheets was designed to first shape tracing the letter A (see Figure 12 – 4, row 2). Subsequently, the tracing prompt was gradually removed so that John was eventually required to print the letter 'A' without any prompt (see Figure 12 – 4, row 3).

Sean. Since Sean had already learned to trace the letter 'A' correctly, he was assigned the task of printing. His sequence of worksheets was designed to gradually fade out the prompt, i.e., the lines to be traced (see Figure 12 – 4, row 3), until only an 'A' was at the top of each page for him to model. Since Sean started at a more advanced stage than the first two children, a second behavior was also selected for treatment. Sean did not trace curved lines correctly: he

FIGURE 12–4.   Illustrations of several types of programmed materials that can be used to teach printing. (From Rincover and Koegel 1977a. Copyright by Plenum Publishing Corporation. Reprinted by permission.)

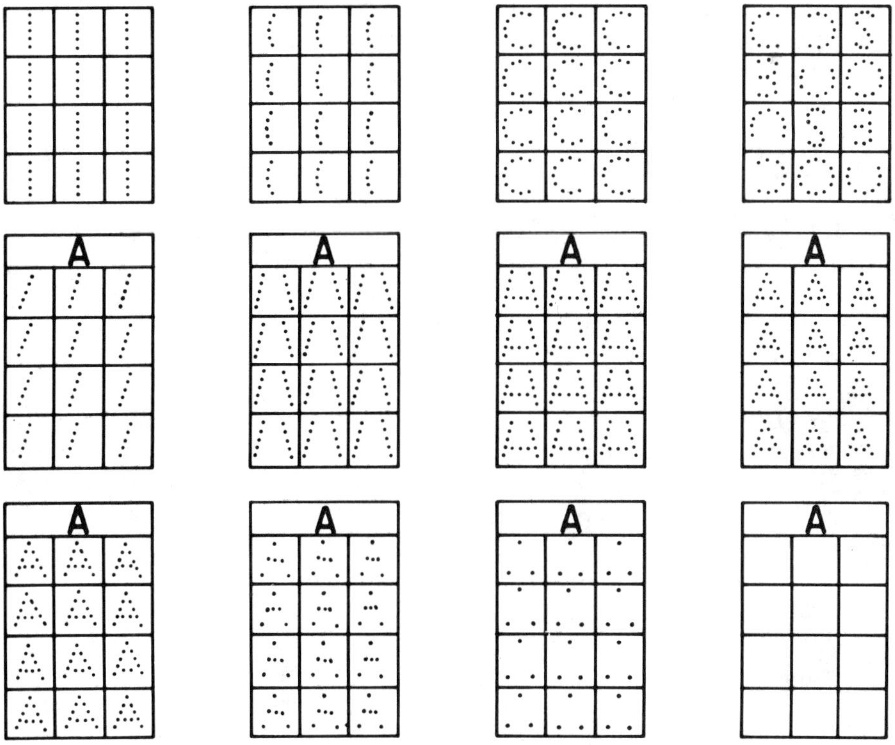

constantly crossed over the line, drew straight lines through some points, and sometimes left the line entirely in connecting only the start and end points. Therefore, worksheets were constructed to teach Sean to trace a variety of curved lines which are found in printed letters (see Figure 12–4, row 1). Specifically, the first worksheet contained the same straight line in each square. If Sean achieved criterion on that line, then the points making up the line were changed on succeeding worksheets, in a gradual stepwise fashion, to form a curved line. If he eventually mastered this curved line, a variety of new curves were introduced on later worksheets.

Eddie. As Eddie had previously learned to draw a variety of straight and curved lines, he was assigned the task of printing the letters 'A' and 'B'. Since he would already copy lines from a model, no tracing prompt was necessary. Eddie's worksheets had one letter ('A' or 'B') at the top of the page, and 12 blank squares underneath. These worksheets were used throughout the treatment (to shape progressively more legible responses) for Eddie's printing. Eddie was also assigned a second task. By the start of this experiment, he had learned to solve simple arithmetic problems in the Sullivan Mathematics Series, Book 4. In order to continue Eddie's progress in arithmetic, the materials selected for his teaching were the next 50-plus pages of Book 4 in the Sullivan Arithmetic Series.

A child worked on duplicated copies of the same worksheet until he performed 12 consecutive correct responses, at which time he would start working on the next worksheet in his particular sequence. The important point for each sequence was that a gradual change was made in a systematic step-wise manner, progressing from a type of response the child was already able to make toward the eventual goal response.

Design and Procedures for Teaching Unsupervised Responding

Each child participated in a predetermined number of baseline sessions. In a multiple baseline design, each child then participated in a treatment procedure designed to facilitate unsupervised responding.

Baseline Sessions   During these sessions all four children were simultaneously seated at the table across from the teacher. The teacher first presented each student with his own worksheet and a pencil, and then provided each student, in turn, with his particular instructions. When all of the children had received their instructions, the teacher returned to the first child, in order to provide reinforcers and additional instructions, then to the second child, and so forth. As a result of this procedure, the period of time in which a student was not supervised varied considerably, according to the amount of time that was required to instruct, prompt, and reinforce each of the other students. The teacher was naive with respect to the experimental hypothesis and design, in order to eliminate the possibility of teacher bias.

Treatment Sessions   The treatment was designed to build gradually longer chains of student behavior in response to a single instruction from the teacher. In order to provide reinforcement for the number of responses, rather than correct responses, only a worksheet which had already been mastered by the particular student was used during this treatment condition.[1] All treatment sessions were conducted in a one-to-one setting.

After a child made one correct response to the teacher's instruction on 12 consecutive trials, the criterion for reinforcement was increased so that the child was required to make two responses (e.g., trace two lines) before a reward would be presented. If the child stopped after one response, a prompt was given to evoke a second response in the adjacent square on the worksheet, and then the prompt was faded on subsequent trials. The procedure of prompt fading and increasing the number of responses per reinforcer continued until the child was performing at least 12 responses after each instruction from the teacher. Two kinds of data were recorded. First, the amount of unsupervised responding was recorded before, during, and after treatment. In addition, academic progress was assessed before and after treatment.

Unsupervised Responding   The following procedures were used to measure the amount of responding each child would perform after a given in-

struction from the teacher. Each time the teacher provided the child with his instruction (e.g., "trace the lines"), the number of on-task responses which followed was recorded. A trial ended when a child ceased responding and began to
engage in off-task behavior, as determined by the (experimentally naive)
teacher. This procedure of recording the number of unsupervised, on-task responses was repeated for each instruction in a session. A new worksheet was
given to the child on each trial, which provided an easy way to measure the average number of responses the child made per teacher instruction directly from a
child's worksheets in each session.

Academic Progress   For each session, it was assessed whether or not a
child progressed to a new (advanced) worksheet. To progress to a new worksheet, a child first had to meet criterion on the initial worksheet used in that session. The criterion used was 12 consecutive correct written responses, responses
which appropriately followed the instruction of the teacher. For example, if the
task was to trace straight vertical lines, then a correct response would be a line
which was recognizable as vertical and straight, and which did not extend beyond the upper or lower dots of the line to be traced. It did not matter if the 12
correct responses occurred all on one trial (after one instruction) or over a
number of trials. As long as the child made 12 consecutive correct written responses, he would proceed to the next worksheet.

Reliability   One of the two naive observers and the teacher independently
recorded responses as correct or incorrect directly from the students' worksheets provided on each trial. The observers were not told from which session a
child's worksheets were obtained. An agreement or disagreement was noted for
each individual trial. An agreement was recorded on a particular trial only if both
the teacher and the observer recorded the child's responding as either correct
or incorrect. The observers also recorded the total number of responses performed on each trial. For this measure, the observers were said to be in agreement only if they recorded the same number of responses by the student on a particular trial. The reliability between observers for a particular session was computed by dividing the number of agreements by the number of agreements plus disagreements in a session and multiplying by 100. Reliability measures were
obtained for each session in this study. The mean reliability for recording
whether or not a response was correct was 96 percent (range: 87–100 percent).
The average reliability for recording the number of responses per instruction
was 99 percent (range: 96–100 percent).

Results

For purposes of clarity, it may be helpful to first look at the data obtained in the
treatment setting, where individual children were taught to respond without
teacher supervision, before examining the effect of this intervention on classroom functioning.

Number of Responses per Instruction During Treatment   For each
of the six behaviors treated, it was found that the child learned to provide a large

number of responses per trial during the treatment phase. Figure 12–5 shows the results of treatment for each of the four children. The vertical line in each graph represents the start of treatment. It should be noted that a child entered the treatment setting *after* the number of responses per instruction was assessed in the baseline sessions. Therefore, the staggered introduction of treatment in Figure 12–5 reflects both the different number of baseline sessions conducted before treatment and the different number of baseline sessions conducted in the treatment setting.

First, looking at Eddie's performance, there were very few responses per instruction during the baseline sessions in the treatment setting. He averaged 1.7 responses per instruction during the baseline session for Behavior 1 (printing 'A' and 'B'), and .9 and .8 responses per trial during the two baseline sessions for Behavior 2 (arithmetic problems). When treatment began for Behavior 1, Eddie's responding immediately increased to 3.6 responses per instruction, and continued to increase to a high of 17 responses per instruction in Session 10.

FIGURE 12–5.   The average number of responses per instruction, in the treatment. The vertical line in each graph represents the beginning of the treatment procedures. (From Rincover and Koegel 1977a. Copyright by Plenum Publishing Corporation. Reprinted by permission.)

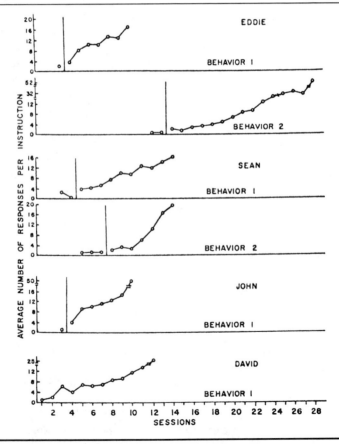

When treatment was subsequently introduced for Behavior 2, his rate of responding gradually increased to a high of 52 problems per instruction within 15 treatment sessions.

Sean's behavior follows the same general trend. During baseline for Behavior 1, Sean averaged 2.2 and .1 responses per trial. When treatment was initiated (Session 5), his rate of responding steadily increased to 16 responses per trial in Session 14. Sean's performance on tracing curved lines (Behavior 2) follows a similar pattern. During three baseline sessions he averaged less than one response per trial, yet, by the seventh treatment session Sean was performing an average of 19 responses per trial.

John's and David's data are also similar. John averaged 1.2 responses per instruction before treatment, which increased to 50 responses per instruction during treatment. In order to rule out order of conditions as a variable, David received no baseline sessions and started treatment immediately. David's average number of responses per trial steadily increased during treatment, reaching 25 responses per instruction during the final session.

FIGURE 12—6.   The average number of responses per instruction by the teacher during individualized instruction in a group, before and after treatment. The vertical line in each graph represents treatment. (From Rincover and Koegel, 1977a. Copyright by Plenum Publishing Corporation. Reprinted by permission.)

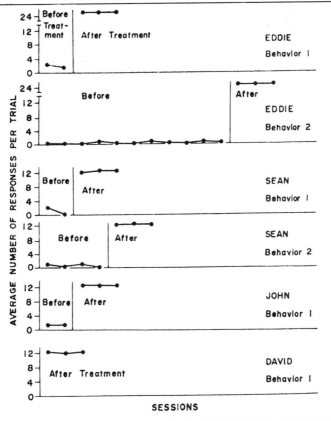

In summary, it was initially found that the children would not continue working in the absence of teacher supervision; however, each child did learn to work with minimal supervision during treatment. The teacher could then present an instruction to any child and leave him alone until he had finished at least one worksheet (i.e., 12 responses).

Number of Responses per Trial During Classroom Group Sessions

Figure 12–6 shows the average number of responses per instruction in the classroom group, before and after treatment. The vertical line in each graph represents the treatment.

The data presented in Figure 12–6 show that the large number of responses per trial which occurred during treatment also transferred to the sessions using instruction in a group. Before treatment, the children responded approximately once per trial. However, after treatment each child averaged at least 12 responses (i.e., completed at least one worksheet) per trial. Eddie was consistently completing 2 worksheets per trial. In other words, after treatment, the teacher was able to instruct, prompt, and reinforce each child individually, while at the same time the other children were continuing to work on their assigned task.

FIGURE 12–7. Academic progress in each session of individualized group instruction, before and after treatment. (From Rincover and Koegel 1977a. Copyright by Plenum Publishing Corporation. Reprinted by permission.)

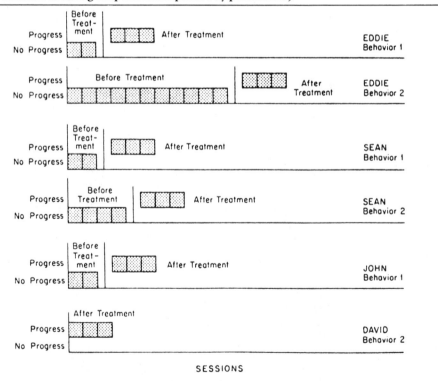

Academic Progress During Instruction in a Group   Figure 12–7 shows the amount of progress occurring during instruction sessions in a group, before and after treatment. No progress was evident with instruction in a group before treatment. That is, none of the children met criterion on any worksheet, and therefore did not progress to any new worksheets. After treatment, however, it was found that all of the children were benefiting from instruction in a group. In fact, progress occurred for each behavior in every session after treatment. In short, not only did the children continue responding when not continuously instructed by the teacher (Figure 12–6), but only under these conditions did academic progress occur (Figure 12–7).

Implications for Teaching

The purpose of this study was to assess the feasibility of providing individualized instruction simultaneously to a group of autistic children. It was found that unsupervised student responding was a variable which significantly influenced the effectiveness of instruction in a group. The students generally gave only one response per instruction of the teacher before treatment and, during this time, no progress through the programmed instructional materials was observed. However, whenever a child was taught to provide a large number of responses per instruction of the teacher, the individualized instruction in a group then produced academic progress for each child. For example, Eddie was working consistently for more than 15 minutes after each instruction from the teacher, and had progressed from page 1 to page 57 in the programmed text, *M.W. Sullivan Mathematics: Book 4*. Since the completion of this study, he has finished this and many other series and will work alone for periods well over 45 minutes without supervision.

Despite some obvious differences, the individualized instruction described in this classroom is similar to the Personalized System of Instruction (PSI) described by Keller (1968). By the end of treatment, the children: (1) worked on their own task; (2) worked at their own pace; (3) perfected one worksheet before being assigned another; (4) utilized writing in teacher-student communication; and (5) received feedback and supervision after a specified amount of work was completed. An additional benefit which seems worthy of note is that the teachers appeared to be very pleased with this change in the classroom program. That is, teaching these children was reported to be a less "hectic" and more pleasant experience.

It must be pointed out that the treatment procedure described for using individualized instruction is a package consisting of specific shaping, chaining, and prompting procedures. In addition, these children had participated in previous research on programming transfer from a one-to-one setting to a group setting (Koegel and Rincover 1974).

One part of this package, the sequencing of worksheets for each child, may deserve special emphasis. After treatment, there was no reduction in unsupervised responding, from one worksheet to the next, when each new worksheet was an extension of the one previously mastered. For example, since Sean was able to trace straight lines at the start of this study, it was possible to change the points on the straight line to be traced, in a gradual stepwise manner, into a curved line, with no reduction in responding. On the other hand, the data show that there was *no transfer* of unsupervised responding across larger changes in stimulus materials. For example, although Eddie was responding for extended periods of time on Behavior 1 (printing), there was no evidence of continued responding on Behavior 2 (arithmetic) until treatment was introduced for the second behavior. Thus, it seems that there was little transfer of responding from one worksheet to the next when the worksheets were not systematically changed in small steps. Perhaps additional research in the areas of stimulus generalization (e.g., Rincover and Koegel 1975) and response generalization (Rincover and Koegel 1977b) may help clarify variables influencing the development and effectiveness of programmed instructional materials.

The generalizing of the results of this study to other environments where continuous supervision is difficult awaits further research. However, the importance of such research cannot be overemphasized. For example, some investigators have suggested that segregating handicapped children into special classes according to a disability label may actually hinder learning (Quay 1968; Johnson 1962). Yet, if every child in a class is working on his/her own instructional materials and at his/her own pace, with minimal supervision from the teacher, it may not be necessary to segregate children according to specific handicaps (cf., Russo and Koegel 1977; Nedelman and Sulzbacher 1972), particularly if these procedures are combined with techniques for modifying other classroom behaviors, such as generalized instruction following (Craighead, O'Leary, and Allen 1973), basic classroom skills (Koegel and Rincover 1974), and motivation training (see Chapter 7).

Parents often report difficulties due to the continuous supervision required for their autistic child. It is therefore important to teach autistic children to engage in appropriate unsupervised responding to both alleviate the stress on caregivers and to encourage the autistic individual's independence from constant supervision. These autistic boys are shown engaging in two types of unsupervised activities at home. The left panel shows an autistic child who is being taught to occupy himself with toys when he is alone. The right panel shows an autistic child in the early stages of learning to play unsupervised with other children. Here he is being encouraged (prompted) to go and join his playmates in a game.

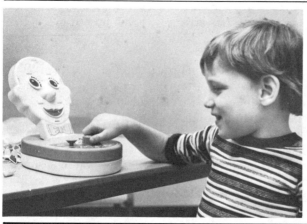 

A second setting in which continuous supervision is difficult is in the home. In fact, some of the most pressing problems reported by the parents of autistic children seem to stem from having to watch their child continuously all of his/her waking hours (Greenfeld 1972). Therefore, research focused on the development of treatment procedures requiring minimal direct supervision appears to be of benefit, both in teaching autistic children directly and in reducing the emotional stress and isolation often reported by those persons responsible for the care and welfare of such children.

A Method for Integrating Autistic Children into Normal Classrooms ____

While special classes for autistic children have been effective and are becoming more widely available, they still present a potential problem, in that in most cases they are composed solely of autistic children. Thus, such classes may provide merely another form of exclusion. By placing every autistic child in a classroom made up entirely of autistic children, we may deprive those children of several possible benefits, including the influence of appropriate role models and the exposure to a nonautistic curriculum taught in regular classrooms.

Therefore, once the steps of group learning and unsupervised responding have been accomplished, the next step we advocate is to place the child in a normal classroom. The following study (Russo and Koegel 1977) systematically investigated the feasibility of integrating an autistic child into a normal public-school classroom.

A 5-year-old girl, who had received a primary diagnosis of autism from two independent agencies, served as the primary subject. She evidenced a relative lack of appropriate verbal behavior, rarely initiating verbal interactions with the teacher or the other children in her public-school kindergarten class, and generally failing to respond to the questions or commands of others. When she did engage in speech, it was generally out of context with her activity, or characterized by pronoun reversal. For instance, when asking for a drink of water, she would say, "You want a drink of water."

The child's classroom behavior consisted of a small repertoire of generally inappropriate actions. She would often stand up in the middle of a work period and walk about the room, twirling a large feather, a flower, or a handkerchief that she persistently carried with her. When she did interact with the teacher, she would ask, repetitively and without regard to classroom activities, to get either a drink of water or a tissue. If these requests were not met, a tantrum ensued, with screaming and physical withdrawal from the other people in the room.

In general, the child remained aloof, rarely interacting with anyone. Her behavioral repertoire consisted primarily of bizarre autistic mannerisms and stereotyped behaviors. She engaged in frequent repetitive finger manipulations in front of her eyes and rhythmic manipulations of the objects she carried. She would also frequently masturbate in class. The baseline data reported below give a more empirical measurement of the child's pretreatment behavior.

Although the child's verbal and social behaviors were minimal, the fact that such behaviors were evidenced at all by an autistic child suggested that she would show relatively good response to treatment. Nevertheless, because of her relative lack of appropriate behavior and relative abundance of inappropriate autistic mannerisms, school officials had made the decision that typifies the fate of autistic children: to exclude her from the school system. The child was, however, allowed to remain in school for the course of this investigation.

The entire investigation was conducted in the kindergarten and first-grade classrooms of an elementary school in Santa Barbara, California. In addition to the child and the therapist, present in both classrooms were an observer to record data, a teacher, a teacher's aide, and 20 to 30 normal children. The children attended school from 9:00 A.M. to 2:30 P.M., five days a week. Each classroom was equipped with tables and chairs, and a rug on which all of the children sat during story and discussion times. The rooms, each 9.1 by 9.1 m, contained toys, blocks, and other usual materials.

A multiple-baseline design across behaviors was employed to assess the effects of treatment by the therapist on the behavior of the child in each classroom. Implementation of the treatment program by the classroom teachers was instituted simultaneously across behaviors. A brief reversal on social behavior was also instituted to assess the maintenance of treatment gains by the untrained kindergarten teacher.

Three target behaviors were selected on the basis of the following criteria: (1) that school officials demanded the behaviors be modified if the child was to remain in school, and (2) that they were characteristic deficits of autistic children. The definitions and instructions used by the observers for recording target behaviors are listed below.

Social Behavior   Any response involving direct interaction with another person. The major criterion for including a response in this category was that the behavior would not be occurring if another person were not present. Examples of the behavior were saying "hello" to another student, borrowing a toy from a child, sharing candy, etc. Social behavior was measured by frequency of occurrence during the session, with each instance recorded by a check on the data sheet.

Self-stimulation   Any stereotyped movement, e.g., rocking, repetitive finger movements, rhythmic manipulation of objects (feather, flower, handkerchief, etc.), and gazing at objects such as pencils or lights. Much of the child's self-stimulatory behavior was of a subtle nature, such as repetitive finger movements in the lap, and persistent, repetitive scratching and pulling of socks and other clothing. This behavior was measured by duration: every time an incidence of self-stimulation was observed, the observer started a stopwatch and allowed it to run until the offset of the behavior. Seconds of self-stimulation were kept cumulatively for each observation session and divided by the total session time to obtain the percentage of session time occupied by self-stimulatory behavior.

Verbal Response to Command Any appropriate verbal response to a verbal stimulus presented by the teacher or therapist. A verbal stimulus was any statement (e.g., "What color is this?") that required a verbal response from the child. This stimulus may have been directed to the child individually, or toward the entire class, requiring a group response. An appropriate verbal response was any verbal statement made within five seconds of the verbal stimulus that provided the type of response requested (e.g., the name of a color, "I don't know"), whether correct or incorrect. Each verbal stimulus, the response or lack of response, and whether or not the response was appropriate were recorded on the data sheet. This behavior was measured by the percentage of verbal stimuli responded to appropriately in each session.

Observation and Measurement

All observers had previous training in the general observation and recording of behavior, and had successfully completed one undergraduate course in the area of autism. Before observation in the classroom, observers were taught the definitions and scoring procedures, as well as the procedures for and the importance of unobtrusive observation. None of the observers was informed of the purpose of the study.

Measures were recorded in three 4-minute time samples per session, each separated by nine minutes of no recording, giving a total measurement time of 12 minutes per session. Two measurement sessions were conducted each week throughout all conditions. Measurement sessions began at 9:30 A.M. All three target behaviors were recorded simultaneously during each session. Observers indicated each occurrence of social behavior, kept a cumulative record of self-stimulation on the stopwatch, and recorded each verbal stimulus and the child's response during each 4-minute sample.

The procedure for evaluating the child's behaviors, therapist treatment, and transfer of the program to the kindergarten teacher is presented below.

Baseline Measurements were taken of the child's behavior in the kindergarten classroom with 20 to 30 other children present, before any intervention. The teacher was instructed to continue regular classroom activities. No attempt was made to manipulate reinforcement contingencies. At the start of this condition, the therapist was introduced to the class as another teacher who would be visiting often in the future. During the class period, the therapist sat next to the child in the last row of children, to habituate both the child and the rest of the class to his presence, but he interacted with neither the child nor her classmates.

Procedures for Integrating the Child into a Normal Classroom_____

Step #1. In order to dispense rewards easily and unobtrusively within the classroom, it was decided to employ a token economy (Kazdin and

Bootzin 1972; O'Leary and Drabman 1971). The child received three 1-hour pretraining sessions to establish tokens as reinforcers. These sessions were conducted after school during the third week of the baseline condition, in a small room (1.8 by 2.4 m) at the University of California, Santa Barbara. During the sessions, the child was intermittently handed a white poker chip and prompted to exchange it for a food reward (one piece of candy, one potato chip, etc.). Token deliveries were not contingent on any specific behavior by the child. When she began to trade tokens for food without prompting, and saved at least three tokens for 10 minutes, the token program was implemented in the classroom during subsequent treatment conditions.

Step #2. The tokens could then be used in the classroom to teach each of the three target behaviors. Treatment of social behavior in the classroom was begun in Week 4. Each occurrence of social behavior by the child during a session was followed by the presentation of a token and appropriate verbal feedback (e.g., "Good girl!") by the therapist. As in the previous condition, the therapist sat quietly next to the child and interacted with her only when social behaviors occurred. One-hour treatment sessions were carried out twice a week, beginning at 9:20 A.M., while the teacher continued to conduct the class according to her regular procedures. During the session, the child saved tokens in a cellophane bag attached to her dress. After the session, she was able to redeem her tokens at the "store," a small area at the rear of the classroom. (After three weeks of treatment of social behavior by the therapist, the baseline condition was reinstated during Weeks 7 and 9, and treatment by the therapist was begun again in Week 10. This reversal was used to assess the effects of therapist treatment on social behavior.)

Treatment of self-stimulation was begun in Week 10, concurrently with the second treatment of social behavior. During this condition, each occurrence of self-stimulatory behavior was followed by the removal of tokens and an abrupt verbal statement, "No." The absence of self-stimulatory behavior for progressively longer intervals produced the contingent presentation of a token and the verbal statement, "Good sitting." In the early stages of treatment, a prompting procedure was used to control self-stimulation. The therapist restrained the child from this behavior by placing his hands on the child's when she began to self-stimulate. The restraint was then faded gradually, and longer and longer periods (ultimately about 15 minutes) of no self-stimulatory behavior were shaped. The close physical proximity of the therapist, the use of a systematic shaping program, and the position of the child and therapist in the back of the room allowed the procedure to be conducted with a minimum of disruption to the class.

Beginning with Week 13, treatment was begun on verbal response to command. The therapist awarded the child a token every time she answered a question requiring a verbal response, whether the question was directed specifically toward her or toward the class as a whole, and regardless of whether the response was correct or incorrect. At first, the therapist prompted the child with the command, "Answer the question!" If she did not respond within five seconds, she was prompted with the correct response and rewarded for repeating it. The prompt was then faded by increasing the interval between the teacher's verbal statement and the therapist's prompt. While initially the procedure required 15 to 20 seconds to produce a response, the necessity of waiting for a response or prompting it was also a common occurrence among the other pupils in the class.

Step #3. Training of the teacher by the therapist. The teacher was trained during Weeks 14 and 15, while regular morning measurement and treatment sessions by the therapist were continued. The teacher-training procedure included several components (general instruction, practice, and feedback) reported by Koegel, Russo, and Rincover (1977) as effective in training teachers in generalized behavior-modification skills with autistic children. These components, demonstrated effective in one-to-one teaching situations, were adapted for use in the public-school classroom in the present study. (These procedures are reviewed in Chapter 11.) Training of the teacher involved four steps:

(a) The teacher received general training in behavioral techniques. The following materials were used to acquaint the teacher with the behavioral approach, define terms, and present behavior-change strategies: *Teaching/Discipline* (Madsen and Madsen 1970); *Parents are Teachers* (Becker 1971); and Volumes I, II, and III of the *Managing Behavior Series* (Hall 1971). Three 1-hour sessions were required for the teacher and therapist to discuss the materials and review test questions. (The interested reader may also wish to consult the H&H Enterprises "How to Work with Autistic and Other Severely Handicapped Children" Eight Volume Series — e.g., see Koegel, in press, and Koegel & Schreibman in press).

(b) The therapist discussed with the teacher the operational definitions and specific contingencies operative on the child. During two 1-hour sessions, the therapist and teacher discussed each of the definitions, the teacher was asked to describe examples of the child's behavior, and the therapist provided feedback and questions. At this time, the teacher also received a complete explanation of the token economy.

(c) With the therapist present, the teacher identified occurrences of the child's target behaviors. While an aide ran the class, the child was observed during three 1-hour afternoon periods of free play and story time. When the teacher observed one of the target behaviors, she explained the behavior, how it fit the definition, and the applicable token administration procedure. The therapist provided feedback and pointed out instances of target behaviors that the teacher had missed.

(d) The teacher, under the therapist's supervision, began administering social reinforcement. During these additional afternoon periods, the teacher provided verbal praise to the child for social behavior, quiet sitting, and verbal responding.

Step #4.   During Week 14, concurrent with the training of the teacher, the therapist began systematically to reduce the density of token reinforcement. From an initial rate of one token given for every occurrence of appropriate behavior, as defined, and the removal of one token for each instance of self-stimulation, the therapist began giving tokens on an intermittent basis. Social reinforcement (e.g., "Good girl") and saying no contingent on self-stimulation were continued at each occurrence of the target behaviors. As the fading of tokens continued, the therapist maintained behaviors by social reinforcement, while providing tokens for intervals of appropriate behavior (e.g., sitting quietly for 10 minutes, playing for several minutes with another child, responding appropriately to questions during a class activity).

Step #5.   During Week 15, under the therapist's direction, the teacher began to provide social reinforcement and tokens for appropriate behavior, and to remove tokens contingent on self-stimulation. The child was moved to the front of the classroom to facilitate these interactions, with the therapist initially remaining close to her. The therapist was present at least four days each week during the fading of tokens and transfer of the program to the teacher (Weeks 14 and 15), to ensure a smooth transition. By putting the aide in charge of the class during parts of the school day, the teacher was able to spend more time with the child during the transfer. The therapist provided feedback to the teacher during each break in school activities.

Step #6. Treatment by the trained kindergarten teacher without the therapist's assistance.   Beginning with Week 16, the teacher totally took over treatment, carrying out the token program throughout the school day. The teacher was told to remain in close proximity to the child and to provide frequent, specific social feedback, with periodic tokens during breaks (about every 30 to 45 minutes). Instances of self-stimulation continued to be consequated by the immediate removal of tokens. On a sheet she kept with her, the teacher was asked to note why she had given tokens and the times at which they were administered. She reviewed this information with the therapist each day, either in person or by telephone. While maintaining control of the child's behavior with social feedback, the teacher increased the response requirement for tokens over a 14-day period by lengthening the time between token presentations. Eventually, the teacher was able to dispense tokens twice a day (once before lunch and once before the day ended) with a brief explanation to the child as to why she was receiving them. However, verbal feedback continued to be presented immediately after appropriate behaviors.

Observations during this condition were made twice each week on selected weeks, in the manner previously described. The therapist continued to visit the classroom at least twice a week during the first five weeks and once a week during the remaining five weeks.

Reliability Over the course of the experiment, 135 reliability measures were obtained. At least two reliability sessions occurred in each condition for all of the three target behaviors. In each reliability session, observations were made independently by two observers during three 4-minute blocks spaced nine minutes apart. Observers were said to be reliable if agreement on each behavior recorded within a given 4-minute block was 80 percent or better. Reliability was calculated by dividing the lower number of units (occurrences or seconds) recorded for a particular behavior by the higher number of units recorded for the behavior, and multiplying the quotient by 100. Forty-four of the 45 measures for social behavior were above 80 percent (mean reliability = 89.2 percent per session; range = 67–100 percent). All of the reliability measures for self-stimulation were above 80 percent (mean = 92.1 percent; range = 85–99 percent), as were those for verbal response to command (mean = 93.2 percent; range = 83–100 percent).

Results

Figure 12–8 shows the results of Experiment 1 across conditions for each of the three behaviors measured in the kindergarten classroom. The data reveal changes in the child's classroom behavior on all measures. First, consider the child's social behavior. During the three weeks of baseline, she consistently emitted fewer than four social behaviors per session. When the therapist introduced token reinforcement in Week 4, the child's social behaviors immediately increased, with a mean of 11.5 recorded during Week 6. Beginning with Week 7, a brief reversal (Baseline 2) was instituted to assess the reinforcing effects of the tokens. The child's rate of social behavior dropped to 5.5 per week in Week 7, and remained consistently below the treatment rate during the three weeks of this condition. In Week 10, when the therapist reinstituted token reinforcement (Retreatment), the child's social behaviors again increased, reaching an average of 13 per session, and a high of 17.5 in Week 14. Measurements of the child's behavior in the Trained Teacher condition occurred in Weeks 16 to 25. Throughout the 10 weeks of this condition, the child's rate of social behavior remained as high as or higher than during treatment by the therapist.

The child's self-stimulatory behavior was measured during the same period. The occurrence of self-stimulation ranged from 27 percent to 54 percent during the nine weeks of baseline. It decreased to 19 percent during the first session of treatment by the therapist (Week 10), and continued to decrease to a low of 3 percent during Week 14. During the Treatment by the Trained Teacher condition, the child's rate of self-stimulatory behavior was maintained at a level similar to that achieved during the Treatment by the Therapist condition (range = 8–14 percent).

FIGURE 12–8.   Social behavior, self-stimulation, and verbal response to command in the normal kindergarten classroom during baseline, treatment by the therapist, and treatment by the trained kindergarten teacher. All three behaviors were measured simultaneously. (From Russo and Koegel 1977. Copyright by the Society for the Experimental Analysis of Behavior. Reprinted by permission.)

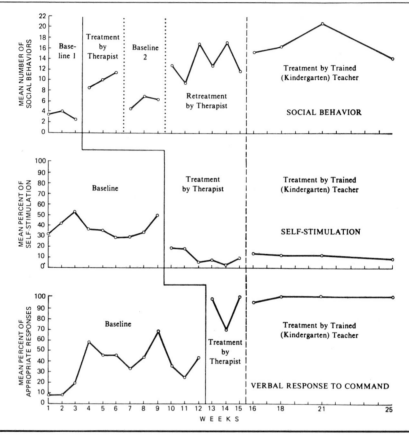

The child's verbal response to command also showed systematic improvement. During baseline, appropriate verbal responses showed great variability, ranging from 8–68 percent, with a mean of 35 percent appropriate responses per session. Beginning with the first session of Treatment by the Therapist, in Week 13, the child's percentage of appropriate verbal responses rose to 97 percent and ranged between 68 percent and 100 percent during the three weeks of treatment. A steady high rate of appropriate responses was maintained during the Treatment by the Trained Teacher condition. The child's rate of appropriate verbal responses was low during baseline, improved during treatment by the therapist, and reached a consistent level of 100 percent for the final eight weeks of treatment by the trained teacher.

On the kindergarten teacher's recommendation, the child was graduated at the end of the term to the first grade and a new teacher. However, during the first week of the new term, the school reported that the child's classroom behavior was again unmanageable, and requested additional treatment for her. In order to ascertain whether the changes induced in the kindergarten classroom had, in fact, not been maintained after the summer vacation and the introduction of a new teacher and class, measures were again taken on the three target behaviors. Definitions of target behaviors, design of the investigation (with the exception of a reversal on social behavior), and recording and observation procedures were identical to those described previously.

Baseline in the First Grade   This condition was procedurally identical to the Baseline 1 condition described above. Measurements of the child's classroom behavior were begun during the second week of the first-grade term.

Retreatment by the Therapist   Retreatment of social behavior by the therapist was begun in Week 40 (as measured from the start of the experiment). The procedures utilized were identical to those described above, except for the fact that no token pretraining was given.

Treatment of self-stimulation, begun in Week 43, was conducted concurrently with treatment of social behavior. The procedures for treatment of self-stimulation were the same as those described above.

A high, steady rate of appropriate verbal responses was observed between Weeks 37 and 46. Since this percentage was within the range of responses achieved during treatment of this behavior as described above, no further treatment of verbal response to command was undertaken.

Training of the First Grade Teacher by the Therapist   The first-grade teacher was trained under the same procedure as the kindergarten teacher. During Week 46, she was trained to recognize the occurrences of the target behaviors in the classroom, to present and remove tokens, and to provide social feedback.

Treatment by the Trained First-Grade Teacher without the Therapist's Assistance   Beginning in Week 47, the first-grade teacher took over treatment. Since treatment by the therapist in Experiment II involved re-establishing previously functional contingencies, the first-grade teacher took over on the final contingencies, using social reinforcement to provide immediate feedback to the child and dispensing tokens twice daily (before lunch and at the end of the school day). Otherwise, procedures were identical to those described above.

Reliability   At least two reliability sessions were held in each condition. Reliability, calculated as before, was over 80 percent for each category.

Results in the First Grade

Date on treatment during the child's first-grade year are presented in Figure 12–9. Baseline measures indicated that the child's social behaviors had decreased and her rate of self-stimulation had increased since treatment in kindergarten. Verbal response to command, however, had remained stable at previous treatment levels.

Retreatment by the therapist on social behavior and self-stimulation, using previously established contingencies, was sufficient to restore improved levels of the behaviors. Social behavior increased to over 12 responses per session, and self-stimulation decreased to 3 percent by Week 46.

The child was monitored for 10 weeks after the training of the first-grade teacher (Weeks 47 to 55). Her behaviors were maintained in the same range as during the Retreatment by the Therapist condition, with social behavior ranging between 12 and 16 responses per session and self-stimulation remaining below 10 percent.

Discussion

The present results may be summarized as follows. First, the child showed considerable improvement in classroom performance for each of the three behaviors treated. Her final performance on each of these behaviors was more than adequate, as judged by school officials, to ensure her continuation in the public schools. Second, training the kindergarten teacher in behavior-modification techniques seemed sufficient to enable her to maintain all of the treatment behaviors over a 10-week formal measurement period, which was the remainder of the academic year. The concreteness of the token procedure, coupled with the increased response requirement for obtaining a token, appeared to provide a means for maintaining strong behavioral control without constant teacher attention. Third, recurrence of problems with two of the target behaviors at the onset of the first-grade year was rapidly remediated by the therapist and maintained after the training of the first-grade teacher. No further problems were reported by the school through the remainder of that year, nor during the child's second- and third-grade years when she had different teachers.

It may be important to note that the behavior change induced by the therapist was maintained after the training of the teachers. The brief return to baseline in the kindergarten, and the lack of maintenance of two target behaviors that necessitated retreatment in the first-grade classroom lend additional support to the notion that training facilitated maintenance. The introduction of the therapist in a one-to-one situation within the broader context of the classroom allowed for intensive treatment to bring the child's autistic behaviors under control. After such control was established and the teacher was trained, the child's behavior was maintained with little disruption to classroom routine.

A previous study has shed some light on the importance of the development of maintenance environments to the long-term success of behavior modification with autistic children. Lovaas, Koegel, Simmons, and Long (1973) provided extensive follow-up data which show that when autistic children are discharged from a behavior-modification treatment program, their continued improvement is to a large extent a function of the posttreatment environment. Children who were discharged to state hospitals regressed. Children who were discharged to their parents' care (after the parents received some training in basic principles of behavior modification) continued to improve. The results imply that in this

FIGURE 12–9. Followup data in the normal first-grade classroom during baseline, retreatment by therapist on social behavior and self-stimulation, and treatment by the trained first-grade teacher. All three behaviors were measured simultaneously. (From Russo and Koegel 1977. Copyright by the Society for the Experimental Analysis of Behavior. Reprinted by permission.)

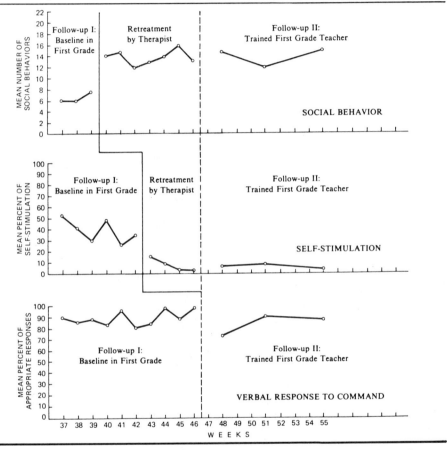

experiment training classroom teachers contributed to the maintenance of treatment behaviors. This is particularly true because two of the three behaviors deteriorated when the child entered the first grade with a new teacher. However, it is also possible that the thin partial-reinforcement schedule used during the final stages of treatment may have contributed to the maintenance results (cf., Koegel and Rincover 1977). Research on variables contributing to treatment durability is still in its infancy, and continued research in this area will undoubtedly prove very important (see Chapter 15).

Generality of Results   Autistic children have previously been excluded from public-school programs, or in some cases are given only the option of a "special" autism class. The significance of this study lies in its suggestion that school teachers can easily learn to teach at least some autistic children in regular classrooms. Although much research is still necessary, a fairly large number of

TABLE 12–2. Characteristics and placements of four additional autistic children placed in normal classrooms.

Child	Pre-treatment*	Age at Placement	Verbal Behavior at Placement	Placement	Curriculum Level	Duration of Placement
1	1 yr	5 yr	Some Conversational Speech (3- to 5-yr level)	Kindergarten	Same	1 yr
2	2 yr	10 yr	Able to express simple one sentence demands—e.g., "I want candy," or "I want bathroom."	Fifth Grade	First-Second Grade	1 yr
3	2 yr	6 yr	Some Conversational Speech (3- to 5-yr level)	Kindergarten	Same	1 yr
4	2 yr	6 yr	Able to express simple one-sentence demands—e.g., "I want outside," or "I want candy."	Kindergarten	Same	1 yr

*Procedures used were identical to those described in this chapter.

(From Russo and Koegel 1977. Copyright by the Society for the Experimental Analysis of Behavior. Reprinted by permission.)

autistic children may be able to benefit from the treatment described here.

Using the procedures outlined here, numerous additional autistic children have now been placed in normal public-school classes. Table 12–2 describes the characteristics and placements of four of these children. All were fairly advanced, in that they had some minimal social and verbal behavior at the time of their placements. In each case, the abilities of the particular child were matched to those of the class, and deficits remediated with one-to-one training in the classroom before the program was transferred to the teacher. Each of the four children was given extensive pretreatment, using the procedures described earlier in this chapter (Rincover and Koegel 1977a; Koegel and Rincover 1974), before placement was attempted. Therefore, this study suggests that, in addition to higher-level autistic children, some lower-level autistic children trained in a class composed solely of autistic children, might upon "graduation" (achievement of a minimal appropriate behavioral repertoire) be placed in a normal classroom among children who may provide more appropriate role models.

Summary _____

The research and techniques discussed in this chapter highlight two major points. First, there are existing procedures available for educating autistic children within regular school classrooms; and second, training in the use of the procedures appears to be necessary in order for most teachers to be able to successfully work with autistic children in a classroom environment. Once teachers have been trained in basic behavior modification procedures, it appears to be relatively easy for them to teach autistic children to: (1) learn in group situations; (2) work independently on tasks designed for their personal level of achievement; and (3) function successfully in classrooms composed predominately of normal children. This approach to the treatment of autistic children within normal community schools will work in several ways to benefit the children. The opportunity for 12 or more years of systematic programming should, by itself, produce a very high level of functioning. In addition, autistic children's continual interaction with normal members of the community will also serve to enhance development through both appropriate role modeling (see Chapter 13) and through the identification of maximally relevant target behaviors (see Chapter 1) for optimal community functioning.

Note _____

The preparation of this chapter was supported by USPHS Research Grant # MH28210 from the National Institute of Mental Health and by U.S. Office of Education Research Grant # G007802084 from the Bureau of Education for the Handicapped.

After this training is completed, and the children are responding for lengthy periods of time per instruction, some children will begin to "rush" through the worksheets, making very sloppy responses. If this happens, it may be necessary to require the child to erase and re-do each sloppy response before providing the reinforcer. In the beginning stages of treatment, however, it is most important to establish a contingency for increased numbers of responses per instruction, and that is why previously mastered target responses are employed at that stage.

Integration of Autistic Children with Normal Children

13

As discussed in the previous chapter, the past ten years have seen a tremendous proliferation of instructional technologies for teaching appropriate classroom skills to autistic and other severely handicapped children (e.g., Koegel, Egel and Dunlap 1980; Sailor, Wilcox and Brown 1980; Sontag, Smith, and Certo 1977; Rincover and Koegel 1977b; Brown *et al.* 1976; Brown and Sontag 1972; Hamblin *et al.* 1971; Martin *et al.* 1968). These developments, together with the advent of legislative/social mandates requiring public education for handicapped children in the least restrictive environment, have generated a need for additional research to determine the efficacy of integrating these children into regular education environments. The intent of this chapter is to discuss in greater detail issues and research related to the integration of autistic and other handicapped children with their nonhandicapped peers. First, legislative and social trends that have resulted in the current move toward integrating handicapped and non handicapped children will be reviewed. Next, an examination of the potential benefits of integration will be made, with special emphasis on the role of nonhandicapped peers in the integration process. Issues specific to the integration of autistic children will then be discussed, again emphasizing the role of nonhandicapped peers as instructional models. Finally, a discussion of directions for future research will be presented.

*This chapter was authored by **Andrew L. Egel,** University of Maryland, College Park, **Gina S. Richman,** Florida State University, and **Christopher B. Button,** University of Maryland, College Park.*

Legislative Rationale _____

Prior to the passage of Public Law 94-142, the Education for All Handicapped Children's Act in 1975, an exclusionary posture was frequently taken by public schools in relation to educating autistic and severely handicapped children. An examination of court decisions relating to exclusion of handicapped children reveals that such a posture was frequently based on subjective measures. For example, an 1874 decision in the *Ward vs. Flood* case awarded the principal of a public school the right to refuse admittance to children deemed to have "insufficient education" (48, Cal., 36). In a similar ruling, the Supreme Court of Wisconsin ruled that an otherwise nonthreatening cerebral palsied child be excluded from school because his "condition produced a depressing and nauseating effect on the teachers and school children and . . . he required an undue portion of the teachers' time" (*Beattie vs. State Board of Education* 1919).

Cases of exclusion from public schools are not, however, relegated to the pre-1930s "forget and hide" period (Caldwell 1973). In fact, while Congress estimates that there are eight million handicapped children in the U.S., the 1976-77 child count showed that only 3.5 million were receiving services, and estimated that one million were still excluded entirely from public educational facilities (BEH 1979).

The passage of P.L. 94-142 thus marks the beginning of a new era in terms of educational opportunities for autistic and other handicapped children (Council for Exceptional Children 1977). In fact, the impact of P.L. 94-142 implementation is clearly evident in comparing the above child count data with the indicated number from the most recent Report to Congress (U.S. Office of Special Education 1980). According to this report, special education and related services are now being provided to approximately 4.03 million handicapped children. This increase represents concerted effort on the part of states to identify handicapped children who were previously not receiving services. In addition, this most recent report indicates that approximately 94 percent of these school-aged handicapped children are receiving their educational and related services within a regular public school environment as compared with the 92.6 percent indicated by the 1976-77 child count. In order to fully understand the impact of such legislation, it is important to briefly trace the development of legislative incentive leading to this mandate which challenges the educational mainstream to accommodate a broader range of exceptional children.

Right-to-Education: Legislative History

The century separating the 1874 *Ward vs. Flood* decision and the 1975 passage of P.L. 94-142 saw gradual movement from the philosophy of screening, exclusion and segregation, to one of identification and provision of equal opportunity to handicapped individuals. Forged from the demands of parents and educators, and based on the promises of the Fifth and Fourteenth Amendments to the Constitution, the evolution of legislative actions protecting handicapped individuals can be viewed as an extension of the civil rights movement.

The civil rights movement took its challenge of segregation and exclusion into the domain of public education with the historic 1954 Supreme Court decision of *Brown vs. the Board of Education.* This decision stated:

> "It is doubtful that any child may reasonably be expected to succeed in life if he is denied the opportunity of an education. Such an opportunity, where the state has undertaken to provide it, is a right which must be made available to all on equal terms."
> (345 U.S. 483, 493)

The Brown decision related to public school desegregation on the basis of race. However, the basic concept it expressed — that "separate" is not "equal" — can be seen in future decisions on the educational treatment of handicapped individuals.

In spite of the 1954 Brown decision, a current examination of the roots of legal actions in education provides evidence that the legal system did not, until recently, question the administrative policies of school systems (Budoff 1978). Legal requirements of the public schools were however enumerated in the classic *Pennsylvania Association for Retarded Children (PARC) vs. Commonwealth of Pennsylvania* decision of 1972. This decision was the first to result in the requirement that due process protection be afforded handicapped children. the *PARC* decision indicated that:

> "No child who is mentally retarded or thought to be mentally retarded can be assigned initially or re-assigned to either a regular or special education status, or excluded from a public education without a prior recorded hearing before a special hearing officer."
> (PARC Consent Agreement, 343 F. Supp. 279)

While this decision clearly related to children who were deemed mentally retarded, such protective measures were extended to all handicapped children in the subsequent Mills (1972) decision. Thus, where handicapped children could previously be arbitrarily excluded from public school, due process guarantees stipulated by these decisions mandated that the school system must instead justify its removal of children from regular classroom environments.

The impact of right-to-education litigation can be further seen in the passage of Public Law 93-380, The Education Amendments Act of 1974. This law added additional protective measures to handicapped children by mandating their education within the least restrictive educational environment — or that environment closest to the regular education mainstream which is appropriate to the child. P.L. 93-380 also mandated that State Departments of Education submit a state plan delineating those procedural safeguards afforded handicapped children to protect their educational rights.

These Constitutional rights were firmly reiterated by Congress with its passage of P.L. 94-142, the Education for All Handicapped Children's Act in 1975. This act refined the due process guarantees provided by P.L. 93-380, and reaffirmed that educational decisions must include consideration of placement of handicapped students in the least restrictive environment. P.L. 94-142 in fact solidified these guarantees since it is legislation which contains no expiration date.

The emphasis on instructional integration is clearly evident in several major components of P.L. 94-142. The *Least Restrictive Environment* criteria, for example, requires that handicapped children be educated in as close proximity as possible to nonhandicapped children. This requirement, based on the assumption that a continuum of placement options should be available to each child, does not mandate that every child be "mainstreamed" into regular classroom environments. Rather, it ensures that each child's unique needs be considered in planning a school program, and that the placement which allows the most normalized appropriate environment be selected.

Some consideration of public school placement and participation in the regular education program is evident in the development of the *Individual Educational Program* (IEP). The IEP is a written educational plan which outlines services to be delivered to a handicapped child. Developed in concert between parents and educators, this plan provides an individually tailored educational program which must specify, among other components, the extent to which a child participates in a regular educational program.

The IEP component, in combination with the requirement that handicapped children be placed in the least restrictive educational environment, provide the force behind the *integration imperative* discussed by Gilhool and Stutman (1978).

Social Trends

P.L. 94-142, according to Gilhool and Stutman, creates a mandate which requires that handicapped students be integrated into public school settings. Indeed, such an integration movement is clearly evident when one considers the number of philosophical forces which have been developing over several years. These forces represent changes in societal assumptions regarding handicapped individuals — assumptions which previously had been based on a doctrine of limitations regarding their abilities (Sontag, Certo and Button 1979), and which served to continue their isolation from the mainstream of society.

Normalization

One such change in society's attitude is reflected in the principle of *normalization*. Normalization refers to a cluster of beliefs and experiences which make available to handicapped individuals a pattern of existence which is as close as possible to the mainstream of society (cf., Wolfensberger 1980). Nirje (1980) has outlined a number of components to the principle of normalization which imply needed changes in all aspects of opportunities provided to the handicapped population. According to Nirje, the components include making available to the handicapped population a normal rhythm of the day (such as being involved in meaningful activities, eating under normal circumstances, and having opportunities for interaction with others), a normal rhythm of the week (with differentiation between home, work, and leisure environments), and a normal rhythm of the year (including the celebration of holidays and other days of personal importance). In addition, the normalization principle implies that handicapped individuals will participate in those normal experiences of the life cycle which the nonhandicapped population encounters; specifically those transitions which affect how and where they live, as well as what they do. For example, nonhandicapped school age children have their day partially structured for them through school activities where they encounter many social experiences and much stimulation. In the transition to adulthood, the nonhandicapped population moves away from the shelter of their family into more independent living situations. In their transition into old age, nonhandicapped individuals typically remain in familiar surroundings with friends, relatives, and/or other individuals of personal significance. The principle of normalization advocates that the handicapped population should be given these same opportunities. Finally, Nirje (1980) indicated that normal respect, normal economic and environmental standards, and the opportunity to live in a heterosexual world should all be included in the realization of this principle. Wolfensberger (1980) has further described the normalization principle through three closely related definitions. He indicates that normalization includes:

1. the use of culturally valued means, in order to enable people to live culturally valued lives;
2. the use of culturally normative means to offer persons life conditions at least as good as that of average citizens, and to as much as possible enhance or support their behavior, appearances, experiences, status and reputation;
3. the utilization of means which are as culturally normative as possible, in order to establish, enable or support behaviors, appearances, experiences and interpretations which are as culturally normative as possible (p. 7-8).

Several individuals have suggested that realization of the goal of normalization will have the effect of changing society's attitudes toward the handicapped population. The effect of this change in attitude should prove beneficial not only to the handicapped population, but to society as a whole (Wolfensberger 1980). Nirje (1980) also noted that normalization will necessitate integration of handicapped people at many levels, including those physical, functional, social, personal, societal, and organizational levels on which the nonhandicapped population function in their daily living.

Deinstitutionalization

Hand-in-hand with the movement towards normalization is the movement to *deinstitutionalize*. Deinstitutionalization is a term which embodies both a remedial and a preventive component. It is remedial in the sense that it advocates that large numbers of institutionalized individuals be brought into more normalized, community-based settings (e.g., community integration). It is preventive in its support of providing initial placements of handicapped persons within a variety of community-based settings rather than in existing institutional facilities (BEH

1980). Certainly a significant impetus towards deinstitutionalization was the publication of a number of exposes on the deplorable conditions perpetuated by institutional settings (Blatt, Ozolins, and McNally 1979). Schreibman, Koegel, Charlop and Egel, (in press) noted several problems associated with institutionalization. According to these authors, children may acquire behaviors in the institutional environment which may not be appropriate for successful functioning in natural environments such as the home. In addition, the contingencies encountered by individuals within institutional settings are usually very different from the natural environment contingencies with the result that behavioral improvements are not likely to generalize to environments outside of the institution. A third problem is the distance institutionalization creates between the children and their natural parents. Finally, the reliance of three shifts of staff creates problems in trying to provide and maintain consistent programming. Other investigators have provided empirical support demonstrating that institutional environments typically interfere with the acquisition and maintenance of appropriate behavior (e.g., Horner 1980; Lovaas *et al.* 1973; Ball, Seric and Payne 1971).

As a result of these problems, many researchers have begun to develop alternatives to institutionalization which significantly enhance the quality of life for institutionalized individuals. One new and exciting alternative for autistic and retarded children, incorporating the concepts of normalization, integration and deinstitutionalization, has been the development of *teaching homes* (Lovaas *et al.* in press; McClannahan and Krantz 1979).

This type of program typically involves training professional parents to care for autistic and/or retarded children in a family setting within the child's community. The teaching homes usually include both autistic and nonautistic children, thus enhancing the opportunity for the autistic children to learn through peer social interaction and modelling. The "teaching parents" who staff the family residences are adults who have been specifically trained to work with autistic and/or retarded individuals.

Such teaching homes provide an environment which helps rectify some of the major problems of institutionalization. The children learn, for example, home-appropriate behaviors, such as cleaning their rooms, preparing meals, money exchange, and community shopping, rather than behaviors typically learned within institutional environments. In addition, the teaching home model provides a set of contingencies that are more likely to be encountered in the child's natural home and community settings. As a result, there is greater likelihood that the skills learned in the teaching homes will generalize to outside environments.

Teaching homes may thus be a viable alternative to institutionalization. It may be possible to use the teaching homes as the initial treatment setting for autistic children who cannot live at home. If followed by training of natural or foster parents, the necessity of institutional placement may be eliminated (Schreibman, Koegel, Charlop and Egel in press).

For some adolescents and adults, teaching homes may also serve as an intermediate treatment setting prior to community placement. Many of the behaviors emphasized in teaching homes represent basic skills necessary for independent functioning in the community. A number of investigators have developed programs for teaching community living skills such as money handling (Cuvo *et al.* 1978), community mobility (Page, Iwata, and Neef 1976; Neef, Iwata and Page 1978), and appropriate eating in public places (Van der Pol *et al.* in press).

Clearly, this technology could be applied much more efficiently and effectively in a teaching-home environment rather than the typical institutional-ward setting.

Integration

Integration seems to be a concept central to reaching both the goal of normalization and deinstitutionalization. In terms of instructional environments, integration refers to a belief that handicapped individuals should be placed into educational environments which facilitate interactions with nonhandicapped peers (Brown *et al.* 1977).

Until recently, instructional integration seldom occurred since most autistic and severely handicapped children were served in self-contained classrooms. These classrooms were "self-contained" in the sense that they serve only handicapped students. While this arrangement has at times proven to be an effective learning environment, there is a growing body of literature which questions the efficiency of the self-contained classroom (Sontag, Certo, and Button 1979; Brown *et al.* 1977; Sailor and Horner 1976; Sontag, Burke, and York 1973). Some investigators have suggested that in many ways segregated placements may actually interfere with learning (Russo and Koegel 1977; Quay 1968; Johnson 1962). Brown *et al.* (1977) noted several disadvantages inherent to segregated classes. These included:

1. absent or minimal opportunity for interactions to occur between handicapped and nonhandicapped children;
2. the tendency for handicapped children to learn "handicapped" behaviors; and
3. the tendency for teachers to establish performance criteria based on the extent of the handicapping condition.

These inherent problems, in combination with the evidence of viable alternatives for autistic and other handicapped children, has caused the move to integrate such individuals to proceed rapidly.

Benefits of Integration — The Role of Nonhandicapped Peers —

The legislative and social mandates reviewed earlier provide a compelling rationale for integrating handicapped and nonhandicapped children. Recent research has added support to the social and legislative positions by providing empirical evidence demonstrating that, in many cases, handicapped children can benefit from integration (see Karnes and Lee 1979 for a review of this research).

Autistic children may be increasingly handicapped by limited socialization experiences. In these photographs, an autistic child is provided with the opportunity (and instruction) to play with her sister and other neighborhood peers.

One area of particular interest has been the role of nonhandicapped peers in promoting the development of appropriate behaviors in handicapped children. Guralnick, for example, conducted several studies designed to examine the use of nonhandicapped peers to facilitate social development of handicapped children. In his first study, Guralnick (1976a) instructed nonhandicapped peers to reinforce all positive behavior exhibited by a severely withdrawn, behaviorally disordered child. The results demonstrated that the close proximity of the nonhandicapped children and reinforcement of positive social behaviors in the withdrawn child dramatically increased positive social interactions of the handicapped child.

In a second study, Guralnick (1976b) assessed the role of nonhandicapped peers in effecting changes in the appropriate social play behavior of handicapped children. In this study, nonhandicapped peers were instructed to model and encourage appropriate toy play, and to reinforce only appropriate social behaviors exhibited by the handicapped child. The results demonstrated that through modelling and reinforcement, the peers were effective in increasing cooperative play in the handicapped child.

The integration of handicapped and nonhandicapped children also provides opportunities for handicapped children to learn appropriate behaviors through imitation. Extensive work by several investigators examining observational learning has demonstrated that peer models for nonhandicapped children have effected change in a variety of behaviors. These behaviors have included sharing (Igelmo 1976; Elliot and Vasta 1970; Hartup and Coates 1967), sex role behaviors (Miran 1975; Kobasigawa 1968), self-reinforcement (Bandura and Kupers 1964), problem solving (Debus 1970; Ridberg, Parke, and Hetherington 1971), and emotional behaviors (Bandura, and Menlove 1968; Bandura, Grusec, and Menlove 1967).

Research with handicapped children has shown that they also can learn through peer imitation. A number of investigations addressing the role of nonhandicapped peers have been conducted by Apolloni and his colleagues (see Snyder, Apolloni, and Cooke 1977 for a review of this literature). Apolloni, Cooke, and Cooke (1976), for example, designed a training procedure to teach developmentally delayed children to imitate (in a structured situation) the motor responses of a nonhandicapped peer. Their results demonstrated that, under structured conditions, handicapped children learned to imitate the nonhandicapped peer. The study, however, did not demonstrate generalization of imitation responses to unstructured settings.

As a result, Peck *et al.* (1978) designed a study to assess the effects of a peer-imitation training procedure on the behavior of nonhandicapped and handicapped children in a nontraining, free play setting. The investigation demonstrated that peer-imitation training resulted in the handicapped children imitating the free play behavior of the nonhandicapped children, and that these increases generalized and were maintained under nontraining conditions.

Peer-imitation training procedures have also been used to teach handicapped children vocal imitation. Raver, Cooke, and Apolloni (1978) trained two handicapped children to verbally imitate nonhandicapped peers, and found that the handicapped children's imitative verbal behavior increased as a result of the training procedure. In addition, the data further demonstrated that verbal peer imitation generalized to words that were not directly trained.

A final study demonstrating the effectiveness of peer models in promoting appropriate behavior was reported by Talkington, Hall, and Altman (1973). In this study, receptive language skills of severely retarded children were trained either by peer models demonstrating the correct response or with verbal instruction provided by the teacher. The results showed that the group exposed to the peer models responded correctly to significantly more verbal instructions than the teacher-directed group.

Overall, these studies provide compelling evidence that handicapped children can learn from their nonhandicapped peers. These data tend to support the trend toward integrating handicapped and nonhandicapped peers, since the ability to learn from observation is probably a prerequisite for successful integration (Koegel, Egel and Dunlap 1980).

Integrating Autistic Children

All but one of the studies reviewed above were conducted with mild to moderately handicapped preschool children. Fewer studies have examined the possibility of integrating autistic children.

Russo and Koegel (1977) indicated that research on the education of autistic children has largely been of two types: that which requires teaching on a one-to-one basis, and that which places the autistic child in a self-contained, special education classroom. While both of these arrangements have proved effective in terms of behavioral and academic growth, both serve to extend segregated placements by continuing to isolate such students from the mainstream of public education and from contact with their nonhandicapped peers.

The integration of autistic children into educational programs necessitates an understanding of behavior problems that could interfere with successful placement in public schools. Fortunately, the last decade has seen a proliferation of instructional techniques which increases the feasibility of integrating autistic children into the educational mainstream (for reviews of much of this literature see Koegel, Egel and Dunlap 1980; Dunlap, Koegel, and Egel 1979; Rincover, Koegel, and Russo 1978; Lovaas and Newsom 1976). For example, as discussed in Chapter 12, a behavioral technology now exists for teaching autistic children to respond to instructions in a group situation (i.e., one teacher and eight children), and to work independently within the group without continuous supervision (Koegel and Rincover 1974; Rincover and Koegel 1977a). The extent of the technology has led some professionals to suggest that a moral obligation exists to intensively explore an integrated treatment approach (e.g., Dunlap, Koegel, and Egel 1979; Christoplos 1973; Rutter 1970).

With the possibility of placing autistic children successfully in the educational mainstream, an important consideration is whether or not, with this population, nonhandicapped peers can serve as role models for appropriate behavior. Although only a few studies have been conducted which systematically examine observational learning with autistic children, there has been some suggestion that normal peer models might be helpful for this population. Coleman and Stedman

(1974), for example, described a case history in which a normal peer seemed to serve as a model to modify voice loudness and increase the labelling vocabulary of an autistic child. Other studies have suggested, however, that such positive benefits may not be possible for all autistic children or with all types of models. For example, in a systematic assessment of observational learning with 15 autistic children and adult models, Varni *et al.* (1979) found that very low functioning autistic children acquired only a small portion of adult modelled responses. Varni *et al.* suggested that stimulus overselectivity in lower functioning autistic children may have accounted for those children's failure to learn through observation. They also suggested the possibility that this problem may be less severe for higher level autistic children. In view of the above studies, it seems likely that at least some autistic children should be able to benefit from exposure to normal peer models.

Recently, Egel, Richman, and Koegel (1981) completed a study designed to systematically assess the question of whether or not autistic children could learn from observing nonhandicapped peers model correct responses. The authors worked in the classrooms of four autistic children and employed teaching procedures commonly used in special education classrooms to teach discrimination tasks. The children had to be sitting quietly and attending before an instruction was presented. Correct responses were rewarded with edible reinforcers and/or verbal praise, while incorrect responses were followed by a mild, verbal no. Prompt-fading techniques were also utilized when it was evident that the child was having difficulty acquiring the task (the criterion was incorrect responding for three consecutive trials). For example, the prompt used to teach one child color discrimination was manually guiding the child's hand to the target color requested. This was faded out by directing the child's hand to a lesser extent on each successive trial. It was found that even when prompt fading techniques were used, the children still had difficulty acquiring the tasks and were responding at around chance level when the prompts were removed. For example, the child learning a color discrimination continued to haphazardly point to a color without discriminating among the colors present.

At this point, the possibility of introducing nonhandicapped peers into the instructional setting was investigated. It was reasoned that the likelihood of integrating some autistic children into classrooms with nonhandicapped peers would be increased if it was demonstrated that they could learn from observing nonhandicapped children model the correct response. The modelling situation was set up so that a normal peer, seated to the side of or across from the autistic child, modelled the appropriate response to the teacher's instruction. The teacher then reinforced the peer's behavior, and immediately presented the same instruction and stimulus materials to the autistic child. The autistic child's responses were consequated by the teacher in the manner previously described.

The results are presented in Figure 13–1, and demonstrate that in the no modelling condition, correct responding was typically at or below chance level. The introduction of the peer models dramatically improved correct responding for all of the children. Each child reached the predetermined acquisition criterion (80 percent) within 10–20 trials. To ensure that the children had in fact learned the task and were not merely echoing the model's response, the normal peer

FIGURE 13–1. The multiple baseline analysis of the influence of peer models on the autistic children's behavior (From Egel, A.L., Richman, G.S., and Koegel, R.L., "Normal Peer Models and Autistic Children's Learning," *Journal of Applied Behavior Analysis,* 1981. Reproduced by permission.)

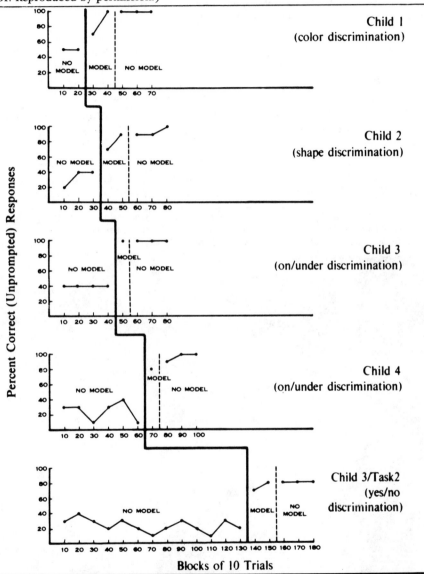

models were removed for the last 30 trials of each task (conducted two days later). When the models were removed, all of the children maintained high levels of correct responding. Each child continued to respond correctly for 80–100 per-cent of these last 30 "no modelling" trials.

The results were very encouraging in that they suggested that at least some autistic children can benefit from exposure to peer models. It should be noted, however, that the autistic children in this investigation differed significantly from those autistic children in previous studies on observational learning. For example, the children in the Varni *et al.* (1979) investigation were described as functioning at a level of severe behavioral retardation, exhibiting very minimal expressive or receptive speech, and engaging in high rates of self-stimulation. The children who participated in the Egel, Richman, and Koegel (1981) investigation, while having serious learning impairments, were not among the most severe of the autistic population. All of the children had well-developed imitative repertoires, were beginning to acquire a small, functional, expressive vocabulary (with the exception of one, nonverbal child), and had relatively large basic receptive language abilities (e.g., were able to follow two and three part commands). Thus, it is possible that certain types of pretraining may be necessary before autistic children can benefit from exposure to normal peer models (cf., Russo and Koegel 1977).

A related consideration is that the children in this investigation had IQ scores ranging from 50 to 87. When one considers this fact in light of articles relating observational learning to IQ and/or maturational level (e.g., Lovaas,

The beneficial effects of peer integration can often be very subtle yet very significant. In this series of pictures we can see an autistic child learning the concept of "down" in a game of "ring around the rosie" with her normal playmates.

Koegel, and Schreibman 1979; Varni, *et al.* 1979; Ross 1976), it seems conceivable that the possibility of autistic children learning through observation may need to be qualified in terms of these children's level of functioning. That level, however, is typical of a very large proportion of the autistic population currently being excluded from interactions with normal peers.

Other factors may also have influenced the results. For example, in this investigation, the models were all approximately the same age as the autistic children. Several investigators working with other populations of children have noted that, for some responses, peers may be more effective models than adults (e.g., Barry & Overman 1977; Kornhaber and Schroeder 1975; Kazdin 1974; Hicks 1965). It is thus possible that such variables as the age and sex of the model and observer may directly affect the probability of the model begin imitated (Hartup and Lougee 1975; Rosenkrans 1967; Bandura, Ross, and Ross 1963). This may explain why, in the baseline, the therapists' prompts were ineffective, while the use of the peer models facilitated correct responding. Similar facilitative effects have also been found when peers were used as tutors (Strain, Kerr and Ragland 1979; Norris 1978; Ragland, Kerr, and Strain 1978). In these studies, however, observational learning was not assessed.

The initial data, even with the above qualifications, imply that there will be benefits from placing some autistic children with normal peers. Many researchers have also recognized this potential and have begun to examine other important integration variables such as teacher training.

One such effort (described in detail in Chapter 12) has been conducted by Russo and Koegel (1977). They examined the feasibility of placing five autistic children in public school classrooms composed of one teacher and 20 to 30 normal children. The results demonstrated that increases in appropriate verbal and social behaviors and decreases in disruptive behaviors (e.g., self-stimulation) were maintained by training the kindergarten teacher in behavior modification techniques. This training also enabled the first-grade teacher to maintain the gains when the child progressed to first grade. Russo and Koegel (1977) noted that the importance of the study was its demonstration of an effective procedure for integrating autistic children in regular classes when appropriately utilizing behavior modification techniques.

Attitudes of nonhandicapped children towards autistic children have also recently been examined. McHale and Simeonsson (1980) evaluated the attitudes of second and third graders toward autistic children before and after playtime interactions. The results indicated that the normal children's attitudes at each time were highly positive. The authors suggested that their findings were significant in that they helped to dispel the often stated assumption that integration will not be beneficial to handicapped children because of the negative attitudes of the normal peers (e.g., Burton and Hirshoren 1979).

Overall, it appears that evidence is mounting in favor of integrating autistic and other severely handicapped children into more normalized educational environments. The data presented in this chapter urge the continuation of efforts to evaluate such placements in a serious and comprehensive manner. Variables such as the child's language abilities, the children's overall functioning level, and the level of the classroom teacher's sophistication may be important areas for future research if significant gains are to be expected from placing autistic and other severely handicapped children into integrated settings.

Note

The preparation of this chapter was supported by U.S. Office of Education Model Demonstration Grant #G008001720. The authors are grateful to Dr. Robert L. Koegel, Richard C. Lee, and Nick Certo for their helpful comments.

Section

Generalization and Maintenance of Treatment Gains

4

A Comparison of Parent Training to Direct Child Treatment

T he previous chapters in this book clearly show that over the past 20 years a large body of literature in the field of behavior therapy has shown that autistic children can make substantial treatment gains through a direct clinic intervention program (cf., Schreibman and Koegel 1980; Keith *et al.* 1976; Lovaas and Newsom 1976; Gunderson *et al.* 1973; Mosher, Gunderson, and Buchsbaum 1972). While proving to be effective, these programs have typically required large expenditures of therapist time and effort since the treatment procedures have been implemented primarily by professionals and specialized therapists. Thus, these treatments largely excluded parents from the treatment process, and thereby ignored a potentially valuable clinical resource. In recent years, however, increasing emphasis has been placed on training the parents of autistic children to implement the principles and procedures of behavioral intervention (e.g., Koegel, Egel, and Dunlap 1980; Koegel, Glahn, and Nieminen 1978; Freeman and Ritvo 1976; Kazdin and Moyer 1976; Kozloff 1975; Koegel and Rincover 1974; Kozloff 1973; Lovaas, Koegel, Simmons, and Long 1973; Nordquist and Wahler 1973; Watson 1973; Wing 1972; Schopler and Reichler 1971). It may be that when the parent becomes the therapeutic agent in the child's natural environment, treatment gains will be maintained and generalize to multiple settings and people.

The importance of training parents of autistic children was clearly illustrated by the results of an intensive follow-up investigation conducted by Lovaas *et al.* (1973). These investigators compared the follow-up results of two groups

This chapter was authored by **Robert L. Koegel,** *University of California, Santa Barbara,* **Laura Schreibman,** *Claremont Men's College,* **Karen R. Britten,** *University of Kansas, Lawrence,* **John C. Burke** *and* **Robert E. O'Neill,** *University of California, Santa Barbara.*

of autistic children who had each received one year of intensive behavior therapy. One group of children was treated by trained clinicians, without any parental involvement. The other group of children, in addition to receiving clinic treatment, had their parents trained to carry out the behavior therapy. Follow-up measures, obtained one to four years after termination of treatment, indicated that those children whose parents were trained continued to improve. In contrast, the children who were returned to nontrained parents or to institutions lost the gains they had achieved in treatment. Lovaas *et al.* (1973) suggested that clinic treatment alone (unsupplemented by parent training) does not lead to durable treatment gains. That is, the effects of clinic treatment alone may not be successful in producing results that will be maintained over time, or aid in the transfer of these gains to novel behaviors, persons, and situations.

Programs aimed at using parents as delivery agents must be acceptable to them, and must have a positive impact on the entire family. The acceptability of a program to consumers (e.g., parents, teachers, society at large) is important, as well as the direct treatment results. In addition to analyzing treatment gains made by the children as a result of parent training, it is also essential to determine the effects of such a program on other family members as well. While collateral effects of behavior modification have been investigated in terms of the target subject (e.g., Sajwaj, Twardosz, and Burke 1972; Wahler *et al.* 1970; Buell *et al.* 1968; Risley 1968), very little data have been reported relating to the collateral effects of parent training. A considerable amount of research is directed at determining the differential effects of parent training and direct clinic treatment upon a wide variety of child and family variables related to autistic children.

Briefly, in this research the families were divided on a random basis into two groups. For one group, the children were treated by trained clinicians, while the parents received no training in behavior modification. For the second group, the parents were trained to treat their own children and no in-clinic treatment was provided. In the preliminary analyses of the results, two sets of measures served as dependent variables. One set focused on changes in the children's behavior and included: 1) measures of changes in psychotic and appropriate behaviors; 2) measures of durability and generalization of these changes; and 3) measures of social maturity. The other set of measures focused on potential changes in the family and included measures in the following specific areas: 1) parental psychological and marital adjustment; 2) the family environment; 3) parental time allocation for daily activities; and 4) family members' interactions.

Subjects

The subjects represented families who had children with a reliable diagnosis of autism. Referrals came from schools, development centers, and regional agencies serving the developmentally disabled.

All the children were diagnosed autistic using the National Society for Autistic Children criteria for the diagnosis of autism (Ritvo and Freeman 1978). This assessement was conducted by two independent outside agencies not associated with this research. The children participated in this research through either the University of California at Santa Barbara, or Claremont Men's College.

The children ranged in age from 2 years to 10 years ($\bar{x}$ = 5 years). They represented a broad range in terms of the severity of their handicap. Social age scores on the Vineland Social Maturity Scale ranged from less than one year to almost 6 years ($\bar{x}$ = 2.7 years). Most of the children were mute or echolalic, engaged in self-stimulation behaviors, and had minimal social and self-help skills.

The majority (approximately 85 percent) of the parents were the biological parents (14 percent of these were single parents) of their children and the remaining were step parents. The majority of the families were in the middle to upper middle socioeconomic range. Most of the parents were high school or college graduates, while a small percentage had less than a high school education.

Parent Training Procedures _____

The parents of the children in this group received training in the same type of treatment (behavior modification) as was used in the clinic treatment group (see below). The difference between the clinic treatment and parent-training groups is that in the parent-training group the child's treatment was conducted by the parents (instead of by the clinician), with the therapist serving essentially as a parent trainer and consultant. The basic goals, sequence, and content of the treatment were identical for both groups. The parents received an average of five hours per week of training until they reached a criterion level of mastery of

---

This photo sequence illustrates the transfer of stimulus control over the child from the parent trainer (Frame 1) to the parent (Frame 4), which occurs during the parent training program.

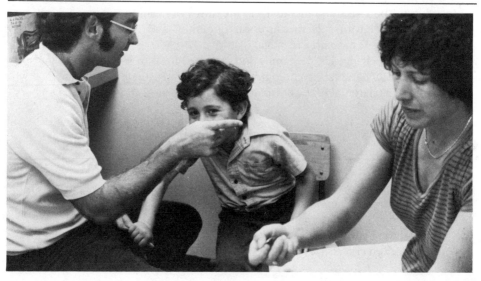

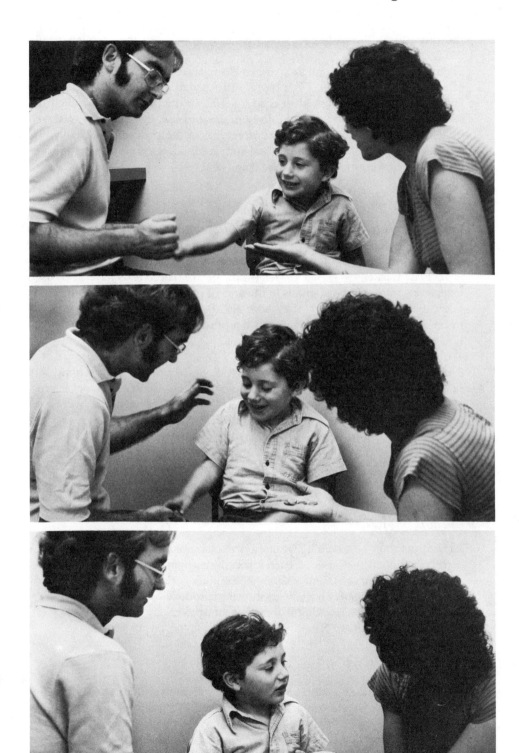

the procedure. The average parents typically completed this training within 25–50 hours.

The procedure used to train the parents is similar to that used to train teachers (discussed in Chapter 11). The program proceeded along the following lines. First, the parents were asked to read a series of training manuals which described the procedures they were to be trained to use. Second, they observed models engaging in correct and incorrect use of the procedures. Finally, the parents engaged in a series of practice with feedback sessions where they performed the procedures they read about and observed.

Training Manuals

General Behavioral Texts.   The purpose of reading these texts was to give the parents a general familiarity with the terminology and an overview of the various procedures of child management with behavior modification (Baker *et al.* 1976; Becker 1971; Hall 1971a, 1971b, 1971c). These texts have been used extensively in research programs in the area of parent training with populations other than autistic children. They have also been widely used as introductory material for nonprofessionals who have a practical interest in the implementation of behavior modification programs.

Autism Parent-Training Manuals.   Since autistic children present problems requiring specialized skills, the parents also read additional instructional materials specifically related to autism. Though these materials were written in laymen terms, they were based directly on the results of pilot data and other research efforts (e.g., Kozloff 1973). They consisted of descriptions of each of the procedural rules summarized in the Scoring Instructions section. These rules are a detailed paraphrasing of the procedures discussed in Chapter 11 (see also Koegel and Schreibman, in press).

Observation of Models

Each parent then observed a 35-minute videotape of therapists engaging in the correct and incorrect use of each procedure (presentation of instructions, prompts, consequences, and shaping techniques). These general procedures were taught because they have been shown to produce a generalized level of efficiency for parents in teaching many different types of target behaviors (Koegel, Glahn, and Nieminen 1978).

Practice with Feedback

The parents were then asked to work directly with their children on specific behaviors of their own choosing. They were asked to attempt to teach these behaviors one at a time to their child. Periodically, the therapist provided the parent with feedback regarding their correct or incorrect use of the techniques. The therapist modelled the correct use of any technique the parent performed incorrectly, and then asked the parent to continue the session. Parent training was terminated when they completed a session at the criterion level of 80 percent or higher correct use of the procedures.

Support and Maintenance

In order to provide the parents with support and to indicate the experimenters' concern, included in the parent-training package was the provision of a "hot-line" for parents to contact the parent trainer in times of stress. The parents were also visited at home once a month over the course of the year.

Measures of Parental Acquisition of Procedures

In order to determine the extent to which parents could use the procedures effectively, structured tests in the laboratory were set up where parents were asked to demonstrate their competence in using the behavioral principles in teaching their children. For each session a particular task (e.g., colors, prepositions, verbal imitation) was selected from a pool of tasks which the child had not yet learned. The parent was then given all the materials necessary and was requested to begin teaching the task. These 15-minute structured teaching sessions were videotaped, and each parent was scored on their use of specific techniques of behavior modification. Using a 30-second interval data recording procedure, the parents' teaching techniques were recorded as correct or incorrect for each interval during the 15-minute session.

Parent Behavior   The parents' behavior was recorded in each of the following five skill areas, with the respective scoring instructions given to the observers.

Scoring Instructions

Using the following definitions, observers were asked to make a decision about the adequacy of each aspect being assessed. (If they did not see an S^D , etc., in a given 30-second interval, the initials "NA" were recorded.)

1. The S^D should be *clear and discriminable;* that is, it should stand apart from anything else that the parent says. A good S^D has a distinct beginning and a distinct end.
2. The S^D should be *appropriate* to the task. If parents are teaching their child to point to a red card, they should not mistakenly say, "point to the blue card," or "hand me the red card."
3. The S^D should be *consistent* with that given on the previous trial. Exception: The S^D can appropriately vary when a discrimination task is being taught.
4. The S^D should be *uninterrupted.*
5. When the S^D is presented, the child should be *attending.* The child

The child's mother uses prompting (Frame 1) and prompt fading (Frame 2) to teach the child how to tie his shoes.

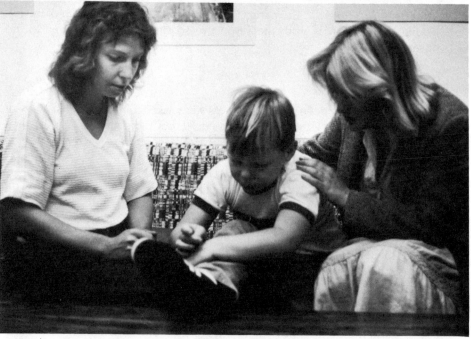

should not be engaging in off-task behavior. The child should be sitting quietly, not engaged in any overtly disruptive behavior when the verbal component of the S^D is presented. The child should be looking either at the task at hand or at the parent.

Prompts   The prompt must be *effective;* that is, it must evoke a correct response.

Shaping   Shaping involves the correct reinforcement of successive approximations. In order to have a good shaping procedure, each reinforced response should be at least as good as the last one. (Score shaping with reference to responses actually observed during the scoring period.)

Consequences

1. Consequences should be delivered *immediately* after the response. "Immediately" is defined as within three seconds.
2. Consequences should be *contingent;* that is, reinforcement only for correct responses, and nonreinforcement or punishment only for incorrect responses.
3. The consequences should be *unambiguous.* A no said with a smile or a "Good boy" given with a frown are ambiguous.
4. Consequences should be *consistent.* Reinforcement should follow each correct response, unless the child has reached an advanced level, in which case the reinforcement may be scheduled. Similarly, once the parent begins to punish, the punishment should occur every time the child engages in a particular behavior.
5. Consequences should be *effective.* They should be tailored to each child. Reinforcements should be something the child is eager for, and punishments something the child attempts to avoid.

Discrete Trials   The session should consist of *discrete trials;* that is, trials which have a distinct beginning and end, and a discrete intertrial interval. An inter-trial interval consists of a (usually *very short*) period of time in which no on-task responding is required of the child (cf., Koegel, Dunlap, and Dyer 1980).

Raters scored each of the five categories for each 30-second period as "Correct" (fulfilled all aspects of the definition of the technique for all of the trials occurring in that interval), "Incorrect" (did not fulfill the definition in some way during any trial(s) within the interval), or "NA" (not applicable — technique was not observed in the 30-second period).

At the end of the session, a percentage score was obtained of correct use of the five categories. The scores were obtained as follows:

$$\text{Percent Correct} = \frac{\text{Number of 30-sec. intervals in which "Correct" was scored}}{\text{Total number of scored intervals in session}}$$

(Note: "Scored intervals" were those in which "Correct" or "Incorrect" was scored. Intervals scored "NA" were omitted).

Measurement of the Child's Performance

For each session, continuous data were recorded on the child's performance of the target behavior. On each trial an observer recorded whether the child's response was correct, incorrect, prompted, or an approximation of the target behavior.

In addition to these trial-by-trial measures of student improvement, a summary measure of whether or not a child was learning in each session was obtained. A "+" was recorded if the child's responses during the last 10 trials of the session were improved (i.e., a higher percentage of correct responses) as compared to the first 10 trials of the session. Conversely, a "−" was recorded if responses during the last 10 trials showed no improvement, or a deterioration, when compared to the first 10 trials.

Reliability   Reliability of the parents' correct use of behavior modification procedures was assessed according to the following procedure. To control for any possible observer drift as a function of familiarity with the experiment, two naive observers independently recorded data from each videotaped session shown to them in randomized order. Percentage of agreement was calculated by dividing agreement (identical scores for each pair of observers for a given 30-second interval) by the total number of agreements plus disagreements for the total session. The mean percent effective agreement (excluding recordings in the "NA" category) for all sessions was always above 80 percent.

For child responses, the two naive observers independently and continuously recorded the child's behavior in each of the sessions. The observers were in agreement if, for a given block of 10 trials, they recorded exactly the same percent of unprompted correct responses. Reliability was calculated by dividing the number of agreements by the number of agreements plus disagreements per session. The mean realiability for these measures was always above 90 percent. For the summary (improvement *versus* no improvement) measure recorded for the child's behavior in each of these sessions, these observers were in complete agreement.

Direct Clinic Treatment Procedures _____

As with the parent training procedure, clinic treatment consisted of the most effective package that could be put together based on available literature and previous research experience. This group received the same type of treatment (behavior modification) as the children in the parent-training group. For each child there were two primary therapists, each having at least two lecture and two practicum courses in the use of behavior modification with autistic children. The children were seen in the clinic for 4-1/2 hours per week for one year. This treatment has been extensively described in numerous published articles, and a review of the treatment (Schreibman and Koegel 1981) is summarized here.

Simultaneously with the suppression of self-stimulatory behaviors, teachers generally begin their work by attempting to establish some early forms of

A child receiving treatment in the clinic. Initially, he was very difficult to motivate until the therapist discovered his liking for music, which was then employed as a reinforcer in his language-training program.

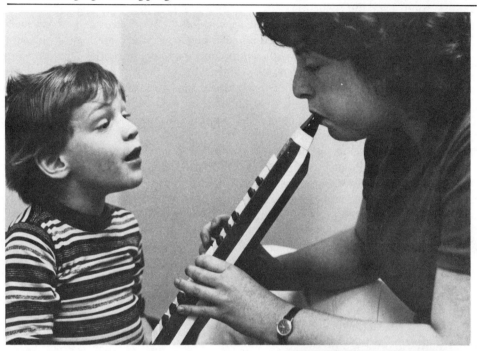

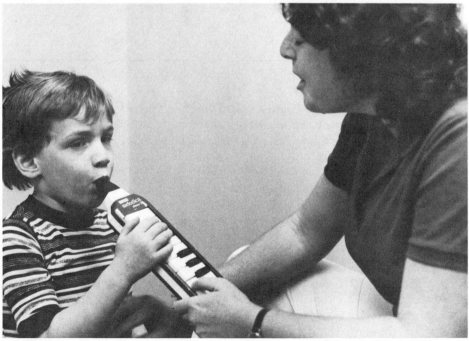

stimulus control. The teacher may request some simple behavior, such as the child's sitting quietly in a chair. Since even such a minimal request often evokes tantrums or self-destructive behavior, the establishment of this basic stimulus control and the reduction of aggression and self-destructive behaviors generally proceed together. It is impossible to work on the acquisition of appropriate behaviors until one has achieved some reduction of the pathological behaviors. New behaviors are taught with reinforcers which are functional. One can always use basic reinforcers such as food, and as one works with any child, one discovers idiosyncracies in his/her motivational structure, such as a particular liking for a certain piece of music, a toy, etc., which can be used in various ways and delivered to the child contingent upon certain desirable behaviors. The acquisition of new behaviors is accomplished in a step-by-step program. The procedures used to teach language illustrate how these programs work (see Chapters 1 and 4).

Throughout both treatment programs (parent training and clinic treatment) there is an emphasis on teaching the child behaviors which are both socially desirable and useful to him/her. Thus, while a great deal of research has focused on attempts to build language, there have also been several attempts to facilitate social and self-help skills. Lovaas *et al.* (1967) published a procedure for building nonverbal imitation which proved particularly useful for the purpose of developing such skills. It includes methods for building behaviors that make the child easier to live with, such as friendly greetings and shows of affection, dressing him/herself, feeding him/herself, brushing his/her teeth, and so on.

In summary, both groups received very similar behavior modification treatment; the difference was in who provided the treatment (parent versus clinician).

Measures

Child Measures

These measures focused on changes in the children's behavior and included the following: (1) *Structured laboratory observations,* which involved an adult attempting to engage the child in a series of interactions in a playroom setting. Multiple response recordings were obtained to provide for a reliable, quantitative description of the degree to which appropriate and inappropriate behaviors (appropriate play, appropriate speech, social nonverbal behavior, tantrums, self-stimulation, psychotic speech, and non-cooperation) were present or absent. Data were recorded from videotapes made of each structured laboratory observation. The videotape equipment was concealed behind a one-way mirror. The observations were conducted with the child's mother, therapist, and a stranger (at separate times) to assess the durability and generalization of treatment gains. (2) *Unstructured home observations* were employed to determine the childrens' appropriate responses to parental questions and instructions. Data were recorded from videotapes made during each family's dinner hour, a time when the entire family was together. (3) the *Vineland Social Maturity Scale* was used to assess the Social Quotient (social age divided by chronological age) of each child.

Family Measures

This set of measures focused on changes in the families' attitudes, adjustment, and interaction, and included the following: (1) The *Minnesota Multiphasic Personality Inventory* (MMPI) was administered to measure the parents' personality characteristics. It was chosen because it is one of the most widely used measures of personality adjustment. The booklet form of the MMPI was used and the response sheets were numerically coded and scored by the National Computer Systems Scoring Company (Minnesota) for the three validity scales (*L,F,K*), eight major clinical categories, and the *Mf* and *Si* interest scales. (2) The *Dyadic Adjustment Scale* (Spanier 1976) was used to measure each parent's happiness and satisfaction within the marital relationship. This scale was chosen because it is an empirical composite based on the most widely-used measurements of marital adjustment (e.g., Orden and Bradburn 1968; Locke and Wallace 1959; Nye and MacDougal 1959; Burgess and Cottrell 1939). In addition, this measure has been shown to have good validity, high scale reliability, is very brief, and can be administered in a minimum amount of time (Spanier 1976). (3) The *Family Environment Scale* (FES) (Moos, Insel, and Humphrey 1974) was administered to obtain an indication of the atmosphere of the whole family system. The long form (Form R, 90 questions) was used and scores were obtained for all 10 FES subscales. (4) In addition to the FES, *daily activity diaries* kept by the parents were used to assess how each family spent their time during the day.

These four measures were individually administered to the parents under standard conditions, as prescribed by the test authors to control for experimenter bias and possible demand characteristics. All behavioral measures were repeated at one year (posttreatment) and at three months follow-up.

Preliminary Results _____

The following data are from the families who participated in the first two years of the research project. While more extensive analyses are in progress with larger groups, several clear trends are apparent in the data analyzed to this point.

Child Measures

Figure 14–1 depicts the results of the structured laboratory observations during the condition when the children were with their mothers. It can be seen that by the time of the followup measures (three months after the end of treatment) the children in the parent-training group evidenced more progress than the children in the clinic-treatment group. In contrast, the children in the clinic-treatment group showed a decrease from posttreatment to follow-up.

Figure 14–2 shows results for the condition when the children were with their treatment providers. Both groups showed improvement from pre- to post-

FIGURE 14–1. Structured laboratory results when the children were with their *mothers*. The ordinate shows the change (improvement or deterioration) in the percent of appropriate behaviors performed during the videotaped playroom sessions, from pre- to posttreatment, and from pretreatment to follow-up.

FIGURE 14–2. Structured laboratory results when the children were with their *treatment provider* (i.e., clinic group with therapist; parent-group with mother). The ordinate shows the change (improvement or deterioration) in the percent of appropriate behaviors performed during the videotaped playroom sessions, from pre- to post-treatment, and from pretreatment to follow-up.

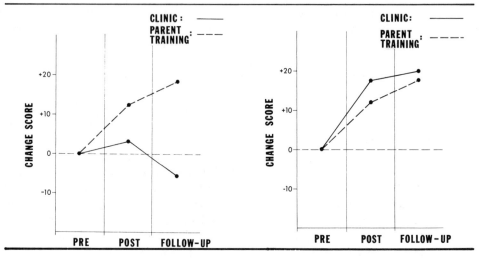

treatment assessments, and continued to show improvement at follow-up. This suggests that the improvement with the parent-training mothers in Figure 14–1 may have been because the mothers were also the treatment providers.

It can be seen that when the children were in the presence of a stranger (Figure 14–3), there was little improvement, and essentially no differential improvement between the children in clinic treatment versus those in parent training by the time of follow-up. Thus, in the absence of a treatment provider, improvement was not evident

Relating these results back to those in Figures 14–1 and 14–2, the data suggest that there was little generalization for either group of children, even though the children in the parent-training group appear to have had an advantage in that their treatment provider was also their parent. Thus, their treatment gains were evident with their parents.

Results for the unstructured home observations show similar trends. The data plotted in Figure 14–4 show the children's percent correct appropriate responses to parental questions and instructions. Consistent with the structured laboratory results, by the time of follow-up the children in the parent-training group were responding more appropriately than the children in the clinic treatment group. Also consistent with the structured laboratory measures, these home observations showed that the major difference between the groups occurred between posttreatment and follow-up. Although all of the parents in the parent-training group reached mastery criterion in a structured setting at a much earlier date, it may take a longer period of time for the effects of their training to

FIGURE 14—3.   Structured laboratory results when the children were with *strangers*. The ordinate shows the change (improvement or deterioration) in the percent of appropriate behaviors performed during the videotaped playroom sessions, from pre- to posttreatment, and from posttreatment to follow-up.

FIGURE 14—4.   Unstructured home observations. Percent appropriate responses to parental questions and instructions are plotted on the ordinate for pre- and posttreatment, and follow-up measures.

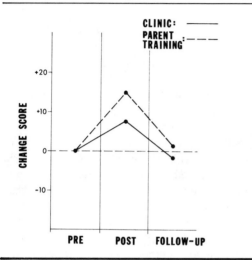

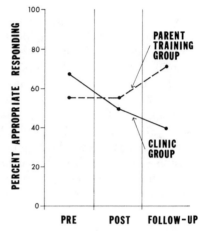

generalize to an unstructured home setting.

Data from the Vineland Social Maturity Scale are presented in Figure 14—5. Both groups of children showed improvement in their Social Quotient (social age divided by chronological age) from pre- to posttreatment, and both groups maintained their gains at follow-up. These data, based upon interviews with par-

FIGURE 14—5.   Vineland Social Maturity Scale results. Social quotients are plotted on the ordinate for pre- and posttreatment, and follow-up measures.

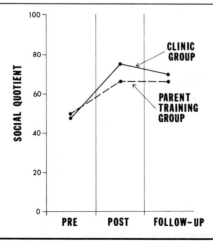

ents and teachers, suggest that the children did evidence gains. Relating these results to other measures, these data are consistent in that they suggest both groups of children did improve. A difference can be seen between these results and those of the direct behavior measures in that the behavior measures suggested improvement may only be evidenced with people and settings similar to those in the original treatment environment.

Family Measures

Data for the MMPI are presented in Figure 14–6. It can be seen that at both pre- and post-assessments the parents scored well within the normal range in all scales. These results are highly consistent with other results in the literature on families of autistic children (cf., McAdoo and DeMyer 1978). Thus, this population of parents does not appear to be different from other populations reported in the autistic literature. In addition, the parents' psychological adjustment does not appear to be differentially affected by either treatment.

The results for the Spanier Dyadic Adjustment Scale are plotted in Figure 14–7. Consistent with the MMPI data, these results show that the parents scored within the range of happily married couples, both at pre- and posttreatment.

Results from the time activity diaries are shown in Figure 14–8. These data represent the first activities that were selected for analysis. These particular activities were selected because they relate to frequent reports from parents that they feel "chained to their child" or "trapped in their house." Therefore, the investigators went through the diaries and tabulated the number of minutes each family engaged in: (1) having friends over to their home; (2) outside recreation

FIGURE 14–6.   MMPI results. The upper portion of the figure shows the pre- and posttreatment results for the clinic group. The lower portion shows the results for the parent-training group.

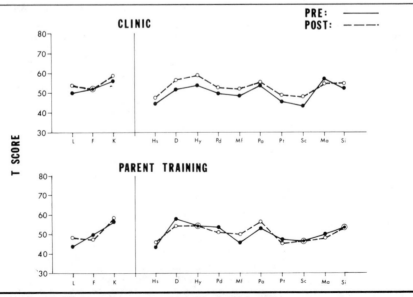

FIGURE 14–7.   The marital adjustment results for pre- and posttreatment. (The horizontal dashed lines indicate the normative results for happily married versus divorced couples.)

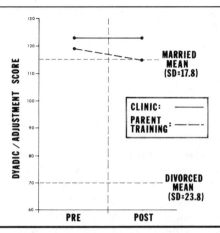

with the family; and (3) quiet leisure time alone in their home. The average number of minutes spent in these activities was almost identical at pretreatment, and well below normal, for both groups. By posttreatment, however, there was a large difference (of 115 minutes) between the two groups. That is, the two treatments differentially affected the parents' leisure time activities, with the parent-training group showing significantly greater increases by posttreatment. These results are consistent with those obtained on the Moos Family Environment Scale. The three subscales on this measure which showed the greatest difference between the groups were "Expression," "Intellectual-Cultural Orientation," and "Active Recreational Orientation." Each of these measures greatly favored the parent-training group, with the posttreatment scores very near to the standardized scores for normal families, as opposed to the pretreatment scores, which were well below normal for both groups.

FIGURE 14–8.   The amount of time the families devoted to leisure time activities at pre- and posttreatment for parent-training versus clinic treatment.

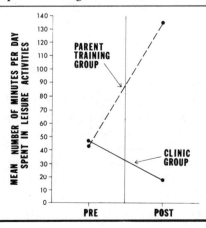

Overall, it can be seen by the measures of marital and psychological adjustment that these parents of autistic children are well within the normal range, and that their overall personalities appear to be unaffected by either type of treatment. The behavioral measures, however, indicate that the two treatments differentially affected the children, as well as the interactions of the entire family.

Social Validation

These studies demonstrate changes in objective as well as observable behaviors in the autistic subjects and their parents. However, as noted in Chapter 5, in recent years concern has been focused on whether treatment effects that are empirically demonstrated are seen as socially important to consumers (Wolf 1978). Determining the social acceptance of intervention has been termed *social validation,* and has been studied by a variety of investigators (Wolf 1978; Maloney *et al.* 1976; Minkin *et al.* 1976; Phillips *et al.* 1973).

To obtain information about the social validation of these objective measures, a study was conducted to explore the relationship between systematically measured behaviors of autistic children and the subjective impressions formed of these children by untrained, naive judges (Schreibman, Koegel, Mills & Burke, in press). In particular, investigators were interested in determining whether naive judges subjectively perceived the same degree and direction of change in the children's behavior as their objective measures, and, if the behaviors that the subjective judges chose to evaluate were the same behaviors that were assessed in their objective measures.

Videotapes were made of the first 14 children and their mothers in a play setting at pretreatment and after six months of treatment. Video equipment was concealed behind a one-way mirror. Objective measures of behavioral changes were scored by trained observers using previously published operational definitions (Lovaas *et al.* 1973). [These were the structured laboratory observations described earlier.] In addition, 182 undergraduate students with negligible knowledge of autism and behavior therapy subjectively evaluated the video tapes.

In order to assess the subjective impressions of these naive judges, a reaction scale was developed based on written essays by 10 undergraduate students. These students were asked to describe the characteristics of the children that they felt were important. These characteristics were reduced to short, descriptive phrases, which resulted in the rating scale.

In addition to the items generated by the essays, the scale contained five questions about the extent to which the judges liked the children and the extent to which the child appeared normal (Gottlieb and Gottlieb 1977; Siperstein and Gottlieb 1977). These items were arranged in a seven-point Likert scale anchored by "very little" to "very much."

Results showed that there were three types of correspondence between the objective measures and naive judges: (1) the naive undergraduates detected the same changes in the children's behavior as the objective measures; (2) there were highly significant correlations between certain behaviors for both the objective observers and the subjective evaluations; and (3) the more favorable

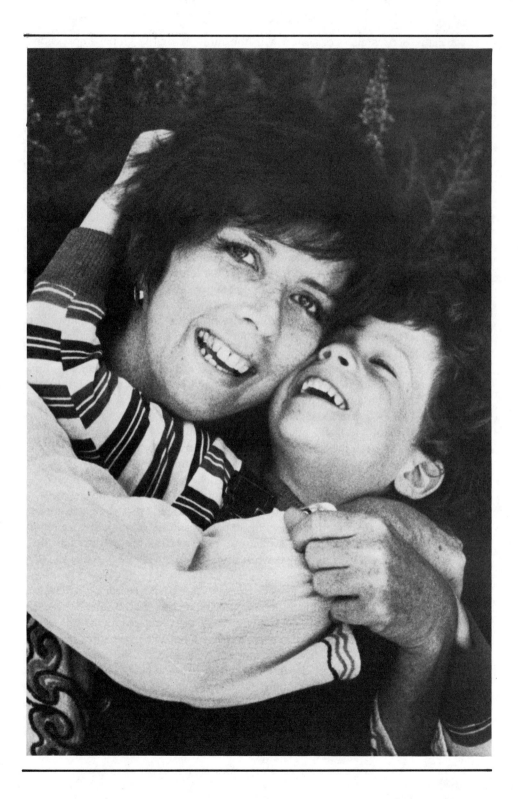

objective scores also correlated with the more favorable global impressions, such as how much the observers liked the children.

These findings show a high degree of correspondence between the ratings of naive judges and the objective behavioral observations, lending support to the belief that the measures of treatment outcome are socially relevant. That is, objective measures of change appear to be measuring changes which are readily apparent to members of the community.

Summary

Results to date:

1. On almost every individual measure (standardized tests and behavioral measures) we are seeing as much initial improvement and more durable improvement with 25–50 hours of parent training as compared with 225 hours of direct treatment in the clinic.
2. Parent training appears to be superior to clinic treatment to a large extent, because the parent (treatment provider) is present in many different settings. However, data indicate that generalization to strangers may still present problems.
3. With respect to daily activity measures (FES and daily diaries), preliminary results show essentially no change for the clinic group, but for the parent-training group significant increases in recreational/leisure activities appear to be taking place.
4. Psychological and marital adjustment measures (MMPI and DAS) are well within the normal range for both groups and do not appear to be significantly affected by either type of treatment.
5. A significant degree of correspondence was found between the subjective ratings made by naive judges and eight objectively observed components of the children's behavior, indicating that the measures of treatment outcome are readily apparent and meaningful to community members. This and other measures (e.g., parents' leisure time activities) suggest that the objective measures have a high degree of social validity.

Thus, the results to date provide evidence that parent training is a plausible means of increasing the availability, intensiveness, and cost effectiveness of the treatment of autistic children as compared to direct clinic treatment. This is true with respect to direct measures of the children's behavior, measures of parent-child interactions in both home and laboratory settings, and measures of parent psychological and marital adjustment. The data also indicate, however, that lack of generalization may be one of the most important factors limiting the success of treatment with autistic children. Parent training is perhaps superior to clinic treatment because the parent (treatment provider) is present in many different settings and at many different times. Data on the behavior of the children with nontreatment providers suggest that even though parent training may be superior to clinic treatment, generalization is still a problem. Therefore, even within a parent-training program, it is necessary to analyze the variables influencing acquisition and generalization of new behaviors. Current research (see Chapter 15) is aimed at meeting these goals.

Note

This research was supported by U.S. Public Health Service Research Grants MH28231 and MH28210 from the National Institute of Mental Health, and by U.S. Office of Education Research Grant G007802084 from the Bureau of Education for the Handicapped. The authors are grateful to Drs. Andrew L. Egel, Ray E. Hosford and Scott Moss and to Jack Mills for their assistance in earlier portions of the research.

Programming the Generalization and Maintenance of Treatment Gains

Virtually every chapter in this book has noted that, while a child may perform a particular skill in the clinic or classroom, the same skill may not be performed in other environments, or for that matter, be maintained over time. The severe limitations created by the failure of skills to *generalize* and *maintain* becomes apparent when one considers the number of settings, persons, and stimuli encountered by autistic children.

For years applied researchers have concentrated primarily on developing a technology for promoting behavior change in classrooms or treatment environments while devoting less attention to ensuring that newly learned behaviors were performed and maintained outside of treatment settings. This reflects a widely held belief that skills learned in the treatment environment will automatically generalize to and be maintained in extra-therapy settings. Recently, however, several investigations have been conducted to assess the parameters of generalization and maintenance. Taken together, these studies have clearly demonstrated that generalization to and maintenance in extra-therapy settings rarely occurs without special intervention (Kazdin and Bootzin 1972; Baer, Wolf, and Risley 1968).

One problem with earlier research on generalization was a failure to separate generalization from maintenance effects. Typically, these studies initiated treatment in a therapy setting, and then assessed responding to another environment. If no improvement was observed in the extra-therapy setting, it was typically reported as a lack of generalization. Koegel and Rincover (1977), however, suggested that there may be potential problems with this interpretation. They noted that with the experimental procedures employed in previous investigations, it is difficult to determine whether or not the behavior did not

*This chapter was authored by **Andrew L. Egel,** University of Maryland, College Park*

FIGURE 15–1.   Percent correct responding measured concurrently in the therapy environment and the extra-therapy environment, Experiment I. (Reprinted from Koegel, R.L., and Rincover, A. 1977. "Research on the difference between Generalization and Maintenance in Extra-Therapy Responding" *Journal of Applied Behavior Analysis,* 10:1—12. Copyright by the Society for the Experimental Analysis of Behavior, Inc. Reprinted with permission.)

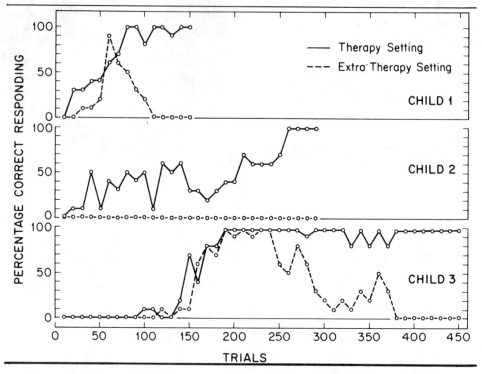

generalize, or whether generalization occurred, but responding was not maintained in the extra-therapy setting.

These differences are exemplified in Figure 15–1. Responding in the therapy setting is represented by the continuous line while extra-therapy responding is represented by the broken line. The data show that all three children acquired the target behaviors and maintained high correct responding in the therapy room. A close examination of *extra*-therapy responding, however, produced some notable differences. The responses of two of the children (Child 1 and 3) initially generalized to the extra-therapy setting but were *not maintained.* The other child *never* responded correctly in the extra-therapy setting, reflecting a lack of *generalization.*

The distinction between generalization and maintenance becomes critical if each is influenced by a different set of variables and thus requires different treatment strategies. As a result, it is important for teachers and clinicians to have a relatively thorough understanding of the variables that influence generalization and maintenance of treatment gains.

This chapter is designed to provide such an understanding, and falls into four sections. The first examines studies (both general and specific to autism) describing how learned behavior can come under the *control of stimuli* specific to the treatment (or classroom) environment. In this situation, the child typically emits the target behavior only in the presence of a particular stimulus or arrangement of stimuli, and as a result, responding fails to generalize to situations which do not share the controlling stimuli. For example, a child may respond appropriately to the instruction "touch green" when a green crayon is presented, but not when the stimulus is a green cup. This section concludes with a discussion of how teachers can manipulate controlling stimuli to promote generalization of treatment gains.

The second section discusses how *reinforcement* contingencies may influence response *maintenance.* In this case a child who, for example, learns that a particular behavior is reinforced in one setting (e.g., the classroom) but not elsewhere (e.g., home), may initially perform the behavior in the extra-therapy or home setting, but responding probably will not be maintained since no contingencies are being provided. This discussion is followed by descriptions of how contingencies may be manipulated to facilitate the maintenance of responding over time.

The third section of the chapter examines the phenomenon of *behavioral contrast.* It is often noted anecdotally that when contingencies are applied to a target behavior in one setting, that target behavior actually deteriorates in another. For example, when a teacher reinforces compliance in the classroom, it is not uncommon for parents to report that compliance is decreasing at home. A discussion of how teachers can program to reduce and/or eliminate contrast effects concludes this section.

The final section of the chapter provides a summary of what the literature on generalization and maintenance of behavior change means for teachers. Stressed is the importance of incorporating into daily activities programs for ensuring the occurrence of both phenomena.

Variables Influencing Stimulus Generalization_____

Stimulus Control

When a stimulus specific to the treatment setting evokes a desired behavior, we say that the behavior has come under stimulus control. In this situation the student discriminates that the target behavior is reinforced in the presence of a particular stimulus (or stimuli) and consequently, only performs the desired behavior in situations in which the stimulus (or stimuli) is (are) present. Any stimulus or any stimuli in combination can serve as discriminative stimuli, including teachers, stimulus materials, classroom structure, and other various programmed and incidental cues.

Marholin, Siegel, and Phillips (1976) have suggested that when particular stimuli in the treatment setting set the occasion for a desired behavior, *generalization* will be limited to those extra-therapy settings which incorporate stimuli similar to those in the treatment environment. The effects of limited stimulus control on generalization of appropriate behavior and the generalized suppression of inappropriate behavior have been well documented. Stokes, Baer, and Jackson (1974), for example, designed a study to train four severely retarded subjects to perform a greeting response (hand wave) when encountering various individuals. Subjects were initially trained to perform the greeting response in the presence of one therapist, and after acquisition of the response, probes were conducted to evaluate performance across new therapists. The results demonstrated that training of the greeting response by one trainer was not sufficient for generalization of the response to adults who had not participated in the initial training. These findings are consistent with other investigations which have demonstrated how limited stimulus control (i.e., training with a specific therapist in a specific environment) may limit generalization (e.g., Marholin *et al.* 1975; Garcia 1974; Redd 1970; Redd and Birnbrauer 1969; Kale *et al.* 1968).

Lovaas and Simmons (1969) and Risley (1968) have provided evidence indicating that changes in *punished* behavior also appear to be specific to the setting in which the behavior is originally punished. Both investigations utilized response contingent electric shock with autistic children to suppress the occurrence of self-injurious behavior (Lovaas and Simmons) and dangerous climbing (Risley). The shock was administered in one environment and the effects on the target behavior were assessed both in therapy and extra-therapy (nonshock) settings. The results from both studies demonstrated that the target behavior was suppressed only in the original experimental setting when the therapist was present. The results of other investigations have also demonstrated how the generalized suppression of inappropriate behavior may be impeded when punishment is associated with a specific therapist and/or setting (e.g., Corte, Wolf, and Locke 1971; Birnbrauer 1968; Tate and Baroff 1966).

The implications of these two studies are important to classroom teachers, despite the fact that they will, in all probability, never employ contingent electric shock as a punishment technique. The studies suggest that teachers must be aware that when contingent punishment procedures *per se,* are employed in one setting, it is very likely that generalized suppression across nontreatment settings will not occur (Newsom, Favell, and Rincover in press).

The issue of limited stimulus control and its effects on generalizations is particularly relevant for autistic children. Numerous investigations have demonstrated that autistic children typically respond to only a very restricted part of their environment (see Chapter 6). Thus, if an autistic child's behavior comes under the control of a limited number of stimuli, it may limit the extent to which a behavior learned in a classroom (or any treatment setting) generalizes to other environments. This effect was clearly demonstrated by Rincover and Koegel (1975). In their study a teacher reinforced autistic children's imitation and instruction-following behaviors in a training setting. Immediately after each child had acquired the target response (e.g., "touch nose"), a second teacher requested the same response in a different setting in order to assess generalization. Four of the ten children did not perform the response in the new environment. The authors demonstrated that these children did not exhibit generalization in the new setting because they had initially learned the response on the basis of irrelevant cues. For example, one child's responding was controlled by incidental movements of the first teacher's hand and not the verbal instruction.

Koegel and Rincover (1974), in their investigation on teaching classroom behaviors to autistic children, also presented data demonstrating the effect of restricted stimulus control on generalization. Initially, eight autistic children were individually taught certain basic classroom behaviors (e.g., attending, imitation, etc.). Following acquisition of the behavior in a one-to-one situation, the children's performance of these same skills was assessed in groups of differing size (two-to-one and eight-to-one). The results demonstrated that the children rarely performed the responses nor acquired new behaviors when the student-teacher ratio was increased, even though they continued to respond consistently in one-to-one sessions. The authors suggested that restricted stimulus control may have been responsible for the limited generalization of one-to-one treatment gains to larger groups.

Taken together, the studies suggest that generalization may vary with the number of relevant cues that initially control the target behavior. In other words, the more restricted and idiosyncratic the stimuli that originally control the behavior, the less generalization there will be.

Programming Stimulus Generalization

A number of strategies for programming generalization have been reviewed in the literature (see Stokes and Baer 1977). Since problems of generalization appear to be a function of limited stimulus control, one method to achieve transfer beyond the treatment setting may be to ensure that sufficient stimuli are common to both settings.

Programming Common Stimuli   Stokes and Baer (1977) refer to this strategy as *programming common stimuli,* and noted that it has been employed in only a few investigations. The Rincover and Koegel (1975) study discussed previously exemplifies this approach. In that study, four of ten autistic children did not exhibit generalization to an extra-therapy setting. Cues present in the treatment environment were then systematically introduced into the extra-therapy setting. The stimuli that finally produced generalization were essentially irrelevant components of the treatment environment (e.g., hand prompts, presence of tables and chairs, etc.). These results emphasize the need for teachers and therapists to ensure that stimuli used in the therapy setting are identical to or approximate those found in the extra-therapy environments, and that relevant aspects of the stimuli used in treatment actually do control responding.

This strategy was also employed by Koegel and Rincover (1974) to program generalization of one-to-one treatment gains to a classroom-sized group. These authors faded in elements of the training setting into the generalization (classroom) environment. This transfer of stimulus control was extremely effective in producing increased responding in the classroom setting.

Stokes and Baer (1977) also suggested that the presence of peers may represent stimuli that are common to both therapy and extra-therapy settings. The use of *peers* as generalization agents was systematically examined by Stokes *et al.* (1978). In this study, two children were taught to discriminate different prepositional relationships, and each child served as the other's tutor on every other day. Generalization to an extra-therapy environment was measured in the absence (unfacilitated generalization) and presence of the peer (facilitated generalization). The results of the generalization probes demonstrated that neither child's performance generalized in the absence of the other child. Generalization only occurred when the peer was present, and the extent of generalization was a function of the amount of participation (i.e., salience) of the peer tutor in the generalization environment. These results partially replicated and extended findings by Stokes and Baer (1976) and Johnston and Johnston (1972). Stokes, *et al.* (1978) suggested that peers can be useful for promoting generalization because they are salient stimuli common to both therapy and extra-therapy settings. In addition, the authors noted that because peers are "naturally" present in extra-therapy settings, their use as agents of generalization requires very little restructuring of the extra-therapy environment. This may be a particularly useful strategy with autistic children since recent research has demonstrated that some autistic children can benefit from interactions with non-handicapped children (Egel, Richman, and Koegel in press and Chapter 13 this volume).

Training Sufficient Exemplars   A number of studies previously reviewed demonstrated how behavior can come under the control of a particular setting and/or person. Under such conditions, the child rarely responds in extra-therapy settings or in the presence of extra-therapy adults. Stokes and Baer (1977) suggested that one method for enhancing generalization may be to conduct treatment with a variety of teachers and/or therapists in a variety of settings. This should reduce the likelihood that irrelevant stimuli in the treatment environment would acquire control over responding.

This technique, entitled *training sufficient exemplars,* is, according to Stokes and Baer, one of the most frequently used procedures for promoting generalization. The strategy involves increasing the number of examples taught until generalization to novel stimuli, settings, or responses occurs. In the previously discussed Stokes *et al.* (1974) investigation, the authors employed this strategy in an effort to program greeting responses across therapists. The authors demonstrated that high levels of generalization did not occur until after a second therapist successfully taught and maintained the response. Whitman, Mercurio, and Caponigri (1970) used a similar strategy for programming the generalization of play skills in severely retarded children. The authors reported that generalization of appropriate play to novel age-mate peers was facilitated by employing a variety of peers in the initial training phase.

Multiple settings have also been used as a strategy for promoting generalization. Griffiths and Craighead (1972), for example, reinforced a retarded woman for correct articulation in a therapy setting and assessed generalization in an extra-therapy environment (cottage). Their results demonstrated that generalization to the extra-therapy environment did not occur until contingent reinforcement was provided in that setting. Training of these two exemplars, however, was sufficient to facilitate generalization to a third extra-therapy setting (classroom).

Handleman (1979) compared the effects of single versus multiple settings on school to home generalization of appropriate responses to common questions by autistic children. His results showed that very little generalization to the home was demonstrated when training occurred in a single setting. However, responding did generalize when training was conducted in a variety of locations in the classroom. The author suggested that training in multiple settings in the classroom may have more closely approximated the home environment, and thus facilitated generalization. These findings were replicated by Handleman and Harris (1980).

The effects of simultaneously varying several dimensions of the treatment setting on appropriate social behavior was assessed by Emshoff, Redd, and Davidson (1976). For one group of children in their study, each training session involved a change in therapists, setting, time of day, and activity, while these conditions were held constant for a second group. Generalization probes were conducted for both groups immediately following training. Overall, the results demonstrated that generalization of appropriate social behavior occurred only for the group that had received training under a variety of stimulus conditions.

All of the above findings are consistent with other investigators who have utilized the sufficient exemplar strategy to promote the generalization of appropriate behavior, as well as the generalized suppression of inappropriate behavior (e.g., Garcia 1974; Jackson and Wallace 1974; Allen 1973; Barrett and McCormack 1973; Corte, Wolf and Locke 1971; Lovaas and Simmons 1969). Stokes and Baer (1977) noted that the number of exemplars needed to produce generalization varies widely and is probably dependent on the target behavior, child, and stimulus conditions. Frequently, though, the training of a relatively small number of exemplars (two to five) is sufficient to facilitate generalization. Koegel and Rincover (1977) suggested that this strategy might be effective for promoting generalization with autistic children because training with multiple therapists, for example, might reduce the probability that a child's responding would be controlled by some idiosyncratic cue associated with a particular therapist.

Summary

The studies reviewed here demonstrate how stimulus control influences the generalization of behavior change. Generalization will be limited when stimuli that set the occasion for a response are present only in the treatment environment. The effects of restricted stimulus control on generalization appear to be particularly severe for autistic children since these children's behavior typically comes under the control of a very limited portion of the environment. Thus, if some idiosyncratic aspect of the classroom was discriminative for a response (rather than a teacher's instruction), generalization to another setting would not be expected unless both settings shared the initial discriminative stimulus.

Variables Influencing Maintenance____
Contingencies of Reinforcement

The extent to which treatment gains are maintained in settings outside of the original treatment environment often are a function of the presence or absence of reinforcement and/or punishment contingencies in extra-therapy settings (Marholin and Siegel 1978). Teachers, for example, who reinforce appropriate behavior in the classroom (e.g., quiet sitting) typically will find that, while improvements may initially generalize, they are frequently not maintained in other settings (home) where the contingencies are not in effect. The student, in this case, has learned when appropriate behavior will "pay off" and when it will not. In other words, a discrimination has been formed between reinforcing and non-reinforcing environments.

The dependence of behavior on the treatment contingencies present in a given environment has been demonstrated by a number of investigators. O'Leary, *et al.* (1969), for example, examined the disruptive behavior of pre-school children in morning and afternoon class periods. Following initial observations in both settings, a token economy was introduced in the afternoon period. O'Leary *et al.*'s data indicated that the initiation of the token economy in the afternoon class period resulted in a decreased frequency of disruptive behavior in both the afternoon and morning class periods. Subsequent assessments, however, demonstrated that the low frequency of disruptive behavior during the morning period was not maintained. In this investigation, it appeared that the children had formed a discrimination between the differential application of reinforcement contingencies. As a result, disruptive behavior in the morning (extra-therapy) class period returned to baseline levels of responding.

O'Leary *et al.*'s findings are similar to those presented by Herman and Tramontana (1971). These investigators measured rates of inappropriate behavior in a regular classroom setting following attempts to modify the behavior in an experimental environment. Initial observations revealed a high rate of inappropriate behavior in both the experimental and regular classrooms. The implementation of an instruction-reinforcement treatment program in the experimental classroom resulted in a decrease of inappropriate behavior. The data from the regular classroom indicates that, although there was an initial decrease in inappropriate behavior (possibly reflecting generalization), it was not maintained over the next few sessions. These data suggested that the students had learned to discriminate the setting in which appropriate behavior was reinforced (experimental classroom) from the regular classroom in which systematic reinforcement was not provided.

Koegel and Rincover (1977) provided the most comprehensive analysis of maintenance of treatment gains with autistic children. In their initial study (Rincover and Koegel 1975) they found that six of their ten children did generalize across settings without intervention. Rincover and Koegel suggested that when behavior does initially generalize (which may be the more common phenomenon), strategies for *maintaining* treatment gains should be emphasized. Koegel and Rincover (1977) extended their initial findings in a study designed to assess the difference between generalization and maintenance of extra-therapy responding. In this study, three autistic children were taught various receptive language tasks (e.g., clapping hands) in one setting and their behavior assessed in another (extra-therapy) environment. The results for two of the children demonstrated that, while responding did generalize to the extra-therapy setting, it was not maintained. Koegel and Rincover suggested that the lack of response maintenance in the extra-therapy setting may have been a function of the discriminability of one environment in which contingent reinforcers were provided, and one where few contingent reinforcers are given.

The studies reviewed above demonstrate that treatment gains are typically not maintained in extra-therapy environments in which systematic contingencies for the target behavior are not provided. As a result, the maintenance of behavior change continues to be of particular concern.

Programming Maintenance

Methods for programming the maintenance of behavior change have typically emphasized strategies for reducing the discriminability of contingencies in effect across environments. This appears to be a particularly good strategy since it is quite likely that limited maintenance of treatment gains is a function of the child's ability to discriminate between environments in which contingent reinforcement and/or punishment is provided, and settings where such contingencies are not systematically employed.

Training Significant Others   One method for reducing the discriminability of reinforcement contingencies (thus facilitating maintenance) is to employ the treatment environment contingencies in the nontreatment settings. This would make it difficult for a child to discriminate between reinforcing and nonreinforcing environments since the same contingencies would be applied in both settings (Marholin, Siegel, and Phillips 1976).

A number of investigators have programmed maintenance by training classroom *teachers* to employ contingencies similar to those used in experimental settings (see Chapter 11). Walker, Hops, and Johnson (1975), for example, encouraged regular classroom teachers to provide contingencies to maintain behaviors that students had learned in an experimental phase by offering course credit. Teachers were provided with instruction and feedback in the use of behavior modification, and student behavior was assessed in order to determine the effectiveness of the instructional feedback. The results demonstrated that student behavior learned in one environment was maintained in the regular classroom when the teacher systematically employed the contingencies used in the experimental settings.

Similar results were obtained by Russo and Koegel (1977), in a study designed to assess whether or not an autistic child could learn productively in a normal classroom. The authors found that child improvement in kindergarten was not maintained when the child graduated to first grade. Training of the first grade teacher in pertinent behavior modification techniques (i.e., those employed by the kindergarten teacher) resulted in the maintenance of appropriate responding over the following year.

Peers have often been used to modify various problems in children (Siegel and Steinman 1975; Solomon and Wahler 1973; Patterson and Anderson 1964). Given that peers can learn to modify behavior, it seems likely that peer training may be an effective strategy for maintaining behavior change outside of the treatment setting. This possibility was assessed by Walker and Buckley (1972), who trained members of a peer group to maintain a child's posttreatment, appropriate behavior in a regular classroom. Peers were taught to ignore inappropriate behaviors such as nonattending, while socially reinforcing appropriate social and academic behaviors. Their results demonstrated that peer training, when compared to three other maintenance programs, was the most effective strategy for maintaining gains in the regular classroom. Since peers are present in so many posttreatment environments, peer training represents one strategy for programming maintenance that could be utilized more often.

Parent training is another method frequently employed to introduce treatment contingencies into other environments and thus maintain a child's behavior change (see Chapter 14). Parents trained in the use of behavioral techniques and familiar with the contingencies employed in the classroom, would be able to apply those contingencies in a variety of environments, thus maintaining those gains made in the classroom or treatment environment. Wolf, Risley, and Mees (1964) found, for example, that gains made by an autistic child in a clinic setting were maintained by training the parents to continue their treatment program in the home. Similar findings were reported by O'Leary, O'Leary, and Becker (1967). The authors initially established cooperative behavior in an aggressive, hyperactive child, and then programmed maintenance in the home by training the mother how to employ the behavioral program used originally.

Further evidence of the importance of training parents to employ treatment contingencies in the home was presented by Lovaas *et al.* (1973). These investigators provided follow-up data on two groups of autistic children after each had participated in a one-year intensive behavior modification treatment program. One group of children were residents of a state hospital, while the children in the other group were seen in their homes. The parents of the children in this latter group were trained in behavior modification, and were an important component of the treatment program.

An analysis of pre- to posttreatment measures for both groups demonstrated that the behavior of all children improved as a function of treatment. Follow-up measures conducted one to four years later, however, showed significant between group differences in the maintenance of treatment gains. The institutional environment to which the one group of children were returned failed to provide systematic consequences for appropriate and inappropriate behavior, and as a result, treatment gains were not maintained. In marked contrast, the behavior of the second group was maintained and continued to improve when the parents were able to provide systematic reinforcement for appropriate behavior and to ignore inappropriate behavior.

Thus, it is clear that parent training may be an effective strategy for continuing the treatment or classroom contingencies in posttreatment settings, thus enhancing maintenance. The issue of how to train parents most effectively has been addressed by many investigators (Bernal and North 1978; Koegel, Glahn, and Nieminen 1978; Schreibman and Koegel 1975; Becker and Becker 1974; Kozloff 1973; Becker 1971; Hall 1971a, 1971b, 1971c) and is discussed in detail in Chapter 14.

The Use of Social Stimuli as Reinforcers   It is common in many behavioral programs to employ reinforcers (such as tokens or candy) that are typically not available or do not occur contingently in the natural environment. Consequently, the child may form a discrimination based on these artificial reinforcers, and as a result, responding in extra-therapy settings is not maintained. One solution to this problem may be to establish in the treatment environment those events which may serve as functional reinforcers in extra-therapy settings. This concept has led several investigators to recommend that social stimuli such as praise, smiles, and physical contact be substituted for the more artificial reinforcers typically employed.

While social stimuli have been established as reinforcers for other populations (Reisinger 1972; Hopkins 1968), they typically have not been effective with autistic children (Lovaas *et al.* 1966; Ferster 1961). Two studies have been conducted, however, which did establish social stimuli as reinforcers for autistic children. Lovaas, Shaeffer, and Simmons (1965) attempted to establish physical proximity to adults as reinforcing using a negative reinforcement paradigm in which an appropriate response to a therapists's instruction ("come here") was required to terminate an aversive stimulus. In the second study (Lovaas *et al.* 1966) verbal praise was established as a reinforcer by pairing it with food. Success was reported in both experiments; however, the social stimuli did not continue to serve as functional reinforcers outside of the original treatment environment.

Since the above reports were published, very little follow-up research has occurred. This is unfortunate, since the availability of social reinforcers in the natural environment would greatly increase the probability that target behaviors would be maintained outside of the treatment environment. It is possible that the use of physical contact (a sensory reinforcer — see Chapter 8) may provide some help in establishing social reinforcers in the future. Since the main problem cited in the above two studies was a lack of generalization, future research may be directed at combining the technology for programming generalization and maintenance with procedures for establishing social stimuli as reinforcers (cf., Rincover and Koegel 1977). Until then, teachers may be able to facilitate the development of social reinforcers by always pairing social approval with functional primary reinforcers.

Manipulating Schedules of Reinforcement   A second method for reducing the discriminability of contingencies involves employing *intermittent* schedules of reinforcement. The use of intermittent reinforcement schedules allows teachers to program contingencies in such a way as to prevent extinction of acquired responses, while employing a reinforcement schedule that makes it difficult for the student to discriminate reinforcing and nonreinforcing occasions. As a result of not knowing that reinforcement occurs only in one setting, the student may respond in other settings in the "hope" of obtaining reinforcement.

Most investigators have employed this strategy to program for maintenance of behavior change. Kazdin and Polster (1973), for example, examined the differential effects of intermittent and continuous schedules of reinforcement on the maintenance of social interaction by two retarded children. Initially, social interaction was established using continuous token reinforcement. Following an extinction period, social interaction was either reinforced on a continuous (Subject 1) or intermittent schedule (Subject 2). Assessment of social interaction during a second extinction phase showed that social interaction only was maintained by the subject who had received intermittent reinforcement.

The clearest example of using intermittent reinforcement schedules to program maintenance with autistic children was provided in the previously discussed investigation by Koegel and Rincover (1977). In the second part of their investigation on the distinction between generalization and maintenance in extra-therapy responding, Koegel and Rincover assessed the effects of various schedules of reinforcement on the durability of responding outside of the treatment environment. Each child, after acquiring a target behavior in the treatment setting, was given additional trials either on a continuous reinforcement schedule (CRF), a fixed-ratio 2 (FR2) in which reinforcement was delivered for every other response, or an FR5 where every fifth correct response was reinforced. Following this phase, responding was measured in a nontreatment setting. The results demonstrated that the responding of all four children initially generalized to the nontreatment setting. However, this responding extinguished within very few trials when a continuous schedule of reinforcement was used in the treatment environment. As the schedule of reinforcement was gradually thinned, responding in the nontreatment setting was maintained for longer periods of time.

Koegel and Rincover (1977) also demonstrated that presentations of non-contingent reinforcement (NCR) in extra-therapy settings can be effective in maintaining responding. The authors suggested that the presentation of NCR in the extra-therapy environment lessened the discriminability of therapy and extra-therapy settings, and thus responding in the extra-therapy setting was more durable. Furthermore, the results clearly demonstrated that a thin schedule of reinforcement in the treatment environment, coupled with the periodic use of NCR in the extra-therapy setting produced the most durable responding.

Summary

The ability to dramatically improve the behavior of an individual is clearly an important achievement. However, the significance of this change is questionable if the change in behavior is not maintained after the treatment contingencies are discontinued. The literature reviewed above indicates that maintenance of behavior change (with few exceptions) does not occur automatically; and, as a result, it must be systematically programmed.

Behavioral Contrast_____

All of the studies reviewed in the previous sections presented data demonstrating the lack of generalization and maintenance that occurs from limited stimulus control, and when contingencies are provided in one setting but not in others. However, there may be another aspect of behavior change that warrants examination. Teachers and parents frequently note that, while substantial progress is being made at school, behavior deteriorates when the child goes home. Similarly, it has often been noted that when two teachers work on the same behavior at different times of day, each may report that the other is having an adverse effect on the child. In situations such as these, the problem may be more than a lack of generalization or maintenance: the child's behavior is actually described as worsening in one environment, while improving in another setting.

This effect, termed *behavioral contrast,* was first noted and extensively discussed in operant research with animals (Reynolds 1961b). In this research, contrast was said to occur when an organism changed its responding during the presentation of one stimulus (e.g., a generalization environment such as the home) as a result of changing only the *contingencies* during the presentation of another stimulus (e.g., a treatment or classroom setting) (Brethower and Reynolds 1962; Reynolds 1961a, 1961c, 1961d; Hanson 1959). Other investigators (e.g., Forehand *et al.* 1979; Johnson, Bolstad, and Lobitz 1976; Waite and Osborne 1972; O'Brien 1968), who made note of similar effects with children, have suggested the need for more systematic research to better understand the variables that might contribute to "contrast-like" effects in the natural environment.

In a recent study Koegel, Egel, and Williams (1980) systematically assessed possible contrast effects in the treatment of autistic children. Specifically, the study sought to determine whether or not the presentation of highly discriminable contingencies in one environment would produce contrast-like trends in behavior change in another setting in which no systematic contingencies were provided. A second purpose was to see if the contrast effects could be reversed if the contingencies in the two environments were made less discriminable.

Eight children, each diagnosed as severely handicapped with major autistic characteristics, participated in this investigation. Target behaviors (e.g., compliance, visual orientation to a given stimulus) were initially measured in both therapy and extra-therapy settings. Following a different number of baseline trials for each child, treatment (e.g., reinforcement of compliance) was begun only in the therapy settings. While no systematic contingencies were applied in the extra-therapy settings, the target behavior was continuously measured to assess for any effects.

The results for three of the children are presented in Figure 15–2. The initial results showed that pretreatment responding in both the therapy and extra-therapy settings varied unsystematically about the mean pretreatment response level. When contingencies were provided in the treatment setting, however, a marked change in responding occurred in both therapy and extra-therapy environments. Specifically, when intervention was applied in the treatment environment, correct responding increased to and was maintained at very high levels. However, with the introduction of treatment in the therapy setting, re-

FIGURE 15–2.   Changes in behavior in both the therapy and extra-therapy settings. The solid vertical line represents the point at which treatment was begun in the therapy setting. (Reprinted from Koegel, R.L., Egel, A.L., and Williams, J.A. 1980. "Behavioral Contrast and Generalization across Settings in the Treatment of Autistic Children." *Journal of Experimental Child Psychology.* Copyright by Academic Press, Inc. Reprinted with permission.)

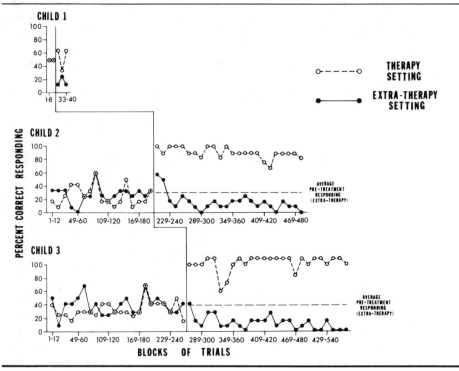

sponding in all the *extra-therapy* settings fell to well below the average pre-treatment levels. Additional assessments of other children demonstrated similar results. That is, the performance of all seven children in the first part of the investigation decreased in the extra-therapy settings after the implementation of highly discriminable reinforcement procedures in the therapy settings.

The second part of the Koegel *et al.* investigation was designed to examine the possibility of reversing contrast-like trends by making similar the (initially) different contingencies employed in the two (therapy and extra-therapy) settings. Two children (one from the first part of investigation) participated in this assessment. The target behavior for one child was aggression, while visual orientation to a given stimulus was the response selected for the second child. Each behavior was recorded in therapy and extra-therapy environments.

Initially, for one child, no contingencies were placed on her aggressive behavior in the extra-therapy setting. In the therapy setting, however, she was placed in time-out, contingent on any aggressive acts. Thus, each setting presented different contingencies for the target behavior. Following a predetermined number of baseline sessions, a time-out procedure similar to that employed in the therapy environment was introduced in the extra-therapy setting.

For the second child, the same contingencies were in effect as described in the first half of the investigation. The child was continuously reinforced for correct visual orientation in the therapy setting, while no systematic contingencies were provided in the extra-therapy environment. Conditions were then reversed such that the contingencies in each environment were made similar. Specifically, the therapists in both environments noncontingently reinforced the child on the first trial of each session. The reinforcement schedule in the therapy setting was then gradually thinned, and noncontingent reinforcement was delivered during (on the average) every seventh intertrial interval. In the extra-therapy setting, noncontingent rewards were provided during approximately every fifth intertrial interval, and following approximately every fifteenth correct response. These conditions were reversed in an ABAB fashion.

The results of the second part of the Koegel *et al.* study, presented in Figure 15–3, clearly demonstrate that both the introduction of treatment contingencies into the extra-therapy environment (first child) and the use of a "generalized

FIGURE 15–3. Changes in behavior in both the therapy and extra-therapy settings when different reinforcement procedures in the two settings were subsequently made similar. Since frequency data were recorded for Child 8, the sessions for that child are not broken down into blocks of trials. (Reprinted from Koegel, R.L., Egel, A.L., and Williams, J.A. 1980. "Behavioral Contrast and Generalization across Settings in the Treatment of Autistic Children." *Journal of Experimental Child Psychology.* Copyright by Academic Press, Inc. Reprinted with permission.)

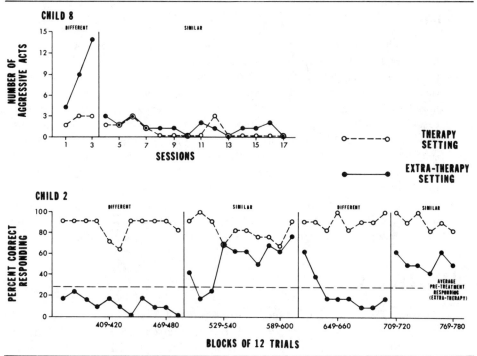

treatment" package consisting primarily of noncontingent reinforcement (child 2), reverse the contrast effects.

Koegel *et al.* and others (e.g., Johnson, Bolstad, and Lobitz 1976; Reynolds and Limpo 1968) have suggested that contrast effects may result from the discriminability of the different contingencies present in different settings. Working with normal children, Johnson, Bolstad and Lobitz (1976) for example, measured a variety of behavior problems in both school and home settings and then introduced treatment into one of the settings. Their results suggested that, for one group of children, behavior in the home setting appeared to be deteriorating (i.e., showing contrast) when treatment was introduced at school, and for a second group, the behavior at school seemed to be deteriorating when treatment was introduced in the home. The authors postulated that increases in inappropriate behavior in the nontreated setting may have been a function of the subjects forming a discrimination between the different reinforcement procedures that were in effect in each setting. Similar contrast effects may be observed in several other investigations (Forehand *et al.* 1979; Meichenbaum, Bowers and Ross 1968; Wahler 1969). Meichenbaum, Bowers, and Ross (1968) for instance, measured appropriate behavior in both a morning and afternoon classroom. Their results showed that contingent reinforcement for appropriate behavior in the afternoon class led to a decrease (from 54–36 percent) in appropriate behavior in the morning class. Since these results are consistent with those found by Koegel, Egel and Williams (1980) it seems plausible that they, too, may have been "contrast" results.

Summary

The results of the Koegel, Egel, and Williams (1980) investigation, together with the other literature discussed here, should alert teachers and clinicians that in some instances, contrast effects can occur, and that they are probably due to the discriminability of different contingencies used in different environments. It is interesting to note that the procedures used to reverse the contrast effects are essentially the same as those discussed earlier in the section on programming maintenance. Specifically, the procedures designed to reduce the discriminability of contingencies (and thus increase the probability of maintenance) can also be employed to prevent contrast effects. Overall, the data from Koegel *et al.* lend increased support to the importance of assessing the influence of therapy setting manipulation in extra-therapy environments so that treatment programs may be designed in the original therapy settings in a manner which has a high probability of producing generalization and maintenance beyond that setting.

Summary _____

Kazdin (1975) noted that the separation of generalization from maintenance is, in most situations, difficult to accomplish. But, as noted earlier (Koegel and Rincover 1977; Rincover and Koegel 1975), more recent experimental evidence illustrates that it may in fact be possible to separate these two phenomena. While Koegel and

Rincover have demonstrated that separation of generalization and maintenance is at least empirically possible, the *procedures* used to promote the two treatment goals are not mutually exclusive. Indeed, classroom teachers may use the procedures discussed in the preceding sections independently or together with one another.

For example, training significant others, such as parents, to systematically apply contingencies can influence both generalization and maintenance. Generalization from the original treatment environment is enhanced because the child will have received training from a variety of people (e.g., teachers and parents) and in a variety of settings (e.g., school, home, community settings, etc.). Maintenance of the response is ensured as a result of the contingencies being present in the extra-therapy setting (home), thus reducing the discriminability of reinforcing and nonreinforcing environments. Other procedures previously discussed can also be combined to simultaneously promote generalization and maintenance.

Teachers can also structure their classrooms and teaching procedures so that the probability of the target behavior both generalizing and maintaining is greatly enhanced. For example, a teacher might begin by employing stimuli that approximate those found in the extra-therapy environments, and ensuring that responding comes under the control of the relevant aspects of those stimuli (generalization programming). The teacher could then systematically thin the schedule of reinforcement and train parents or other individuals to administer contingencies in the nontreatment environment (thus ensuring maintenance).

Implications for Classroom Teachers

The preceding sections of this chapter presented a number of relevant concepts that teachers should be aware of when developing educational programs for autistic and other developmentally delayed children. Following are a number of practical points that classroom teachers (and other professionals) should be aware of as they program for the generalization and maintenance of newly acquired behavior.

Generalization and maintenance of behavior change (typically) does not occur automatically. It should be very clear from the literature reviewed in the previous sections that generalization and maintenance must, at the very least, be assessed, if not systematically programmed. The technology exists for assessing and programming these phenomena, and it must be utilized.

Classroom teachers should ensure that relevant aspects of discriminative stimuli control responding, and that the controlling stimuli have a high probability of occurring in environments other than the classroom. This point is especially important with autistic children, because of their tendency to selectively respond to irrelevant aspects of stimuli. Teachers must be careful to ensure that a behavior is not learned on the basis of stimuli that are highly idiosyncratic to a classroom environment. One approach would be to assess nonclassroom settings in order to determine which stimuli are relevant and functional in those environments, and then incorporate them into the classroom. If these stimuli can also be made functional in the classroom setting, it is likely that generalization will be enhanced.

Students should be taught in a number of settings and with a variety of persons. Varying the conditions of training is a good strategy for programming both generalization and maintenance of training. Teachers, by providing instruction in several situations and in the presence of various individuals, help to minimize the probability that responding will be controlled by an idiosyncratic cue in a particular setting or with a particular individual.

Significant others in the student's environment should be trained to provide contingencies in settings other than the classroom. Training significant others, such as parents, peers and/or siblings, to consistently apply appropriate consequences has been shown to help students maintain newly acquired skills. The literature provides numerous, data-based programs for training such individuals, and teachers and support staff can utilize them to teach other individuals the behavioral techniques necessary to maintain gains that occur in the classroom.

Teachers should attempt to establish social stimuli as functional reinforcers. This has proven to be very difficult with autistic children (see Chapter 8). Nevertheless, teachers should always attempt to pair social stimuli with other functional reinforcers (especially tactile reinforcers) so that the functional value of praise will be increased. This is very important, since outside of the classroom students are more likely to receive social approval for appropriate behavior, rather than tokens or candy. Thus, if social approval were functional as a reinforcer, it would greatly increase the probability of the behavior being maintained outside of the classroom.

Teachers should gradually reduce the amount of reinforcement once the student has acquired the target behavior. Behavior in the natural environment is not reinforced on a continual basis, as is often the case in the classroom setting. It is more likely that in the natural environment the student will experience more delayed and variable schedules of reinforcement. It thus helps to ensure maintenance of a response, if, *after* the child has acquired the behavior, teachers gradually move to an intermittent schedule of reinforcement. Under this condition, behavior is only reinforced after a certain number of responses have been emitted, or following a particular interval of time.

Conclusion _____

Too often, educators and clinicians have assumed that treatment gains occurring in the classroom will automatically generalize to and be maintained in other settings. As data were accumulated on these phenomena, it became clear that generalization and maintenance had to be systematically programmed: they were not "passive phenomena".

This chapter has emphasized the importance of stimulus control in programming generalization. Generalization will be limited when responding is controlled by stimuli that are only present in a particular setting and not others. Several techniques for reducing the likelihood of limited stimulus control and thus enhancing generalization have been discussed, including programming stimuli common to both treatment and generalization settings, ensuring that relevant features of the stimuli control responding, and providing treatment in a variety of settings and in the presence of several individuals.

It is clear that while these strategies may facilitate generalization, the behavior will extinguish unless systematic efforts are made to program maintenance. Procedures such as training significant others to provide appropriate contingencies outside of the treatment setting, the use of intermittent reinforcement within the treatment setting, and the establishment of social stimuli as functional reinforcers have been presented as strategies for programming maintenance of responding. Such procedures tend to reduce the student's ability to discriminate between reinforcing and nonreinforcing environments, and as a result, behavior is more likely to be maintained. Finally, it is important to realize that, in most areas, the procedures used to promote generalization and maintenance are not mutually exclusive, and in fact are often employed simultaneously. We have a technology for programming both phenomena that is continually being refined. It is now the responsibility of teachers and clinicians to apply the technology in their own programs.

Note _____

The author is grateful to Glen Dunlap, Richard Lee, and Nancy Neef for their helpful comments. The preparation of this chapter was supported by U.S. Office of Education Model Demonstration Grant #G008001720 from the Bureau of Education for the Handicapped.

References

Acker, L. 1966. *Errorless discrimination training in autistic and normal children*. Unpublished doctoral dissertation, University of California, Los Angeles.

Allen, G.T. 1973. Case Study: Implementational behavior modification techniques in summer camp setting. *Behavior Therapy* 4:570–75.

Anderson, L.T. and Herrmann, L. 1975. *Lesch-Nyhan Disease: A Specific Learning Disability*. Paper presented at the meeting of the Association for the Advancement of Behavior Therapy, San Francisco.

Anderson, N.A. and Rincover, A. 1980. The nature and generality of attentional deficits in autistic children. Unpublished Master's thesis. University of North Carolina at Greensboro.

Apolloni, T., Cooke, S.A., and Cooke, T.P. 1976. Establishing a normal peer as a behavioral model for developmentally delayed toddlers. *Perceptual and Motor Skills* 43:1155–65.

Applebaum, E., Egel, A.L., Koegel, R.L., and Imhoff, B. 1979. Measuring musical abilities of autistic children. *Journal of Autism and Developmental Disorders* 9:279–85.

Azrin, N.H., Gottlieb, L., Hughart, L., Wesolowski, M.D., and Rahn, T. 1975. Eliminating self-injurious behavior by educative procedures. *Behaviour Research and Therapy* 13:101–11.

Azrin, N.H., Hake, D.F., Holz, W.C., and Hutchinson, R.R. 1965. Motivational aspects of escape from punishment. *Journal of the Experimental Analysis of Behavior* 8:31–44.

Azrin, N.H., Hutchinson, R.R., and Hake, D.F. 1966. Extinction-induced aggression. *Journal of the Experimental Analysis of Behavior* 9:191–204.

Bachman, J.A. 1972. Self-injurious behavior: A behavioral analysis. *Journal of Abnormal Psychology* 80:211–24.

Baer, D.M. and Guess, D. 1971. Receptive training of adjectival inflections in mental retardates. *Journal of Applied Behavior Analysis* 4:129–39.

Baer, D.M. and Wolf, M. 1970. The entry into natural communities of reinforcement. In *Control of Human Behavior* vol. 1, eds. R. Ulrich, T. Stachnik, and J. Mabry (New York: Scott, Foresman and Company).

Baer, D.M., Wolf, M.M., and Risley, T. 1968. Some current dimensions of applied behavior analysis. *Journal of Applied Behavior Analysis* 1:91–7.

Bailey, J. and Meyerson, L. 1969. Vibration as a reinforcer with a profoundly retarded child. *Journal of Applied Behavior Analysis* 1:91–97.

Baker, B.L., Brightman, A.J., Heifetz, L.J., and Murphy, D.M. 1976. *Behavior Problems.* Champaign, Ill.: Research Press.

Baldwin, J., and Baldwin, J. 1976. The role of learning phenomena in the ontogeny of exploration and play. In *Bio-social development among primates,* eds. S. Chevalier-Skolnickoff, & F. Poirer. New York: Garland.

Ball, T.S., Seric, K., and Payne, C. 1971. Long term retention of self-help skill training in the profoundly retarded. *American Journal of Mental Deficiency* 76:378–82.

Bandura, A. 1976. Effecting change through participant modeling. In *Counseling methods,* eds. J.D. Krumboltz, and C.E. Thoreson (New York: Holt, Rinehart and Winston).

Bandura, A., Grusec, J.D., and Menlove, F.L. 1967. Vicarious extinction of avoidance behavior. *Journal of Personality and Social Psychology* 5:16–23.

Bandura, A. and Kupers, C.J. 1964. Transmission of patterns of self-reinforcement through modelling. *Journal of Abnormal and Social Psychology* 69:1–9.

Bandura, A. and Menlove, F.L. 1968. Factors determining vicarious extinction of avoidance behavior through symbolic modelling. *Journal of Personality and Social Psychology* 8:99–108.

Bandura, A., Ross, D., and Ross, S.A. 1963. Imitation of film-mediated aggressive models. *Journal of Abnormal and Social Psychology* 66:3–11.

Barkley, R.A. and Zupnick, S. 1976. Reduction of stereotypic body contortions using physical restraint and DRO. *Journal of Behavior Therapy and Experimental Psychiatry* 1:167–70.

Baroff, G.S. 1974. *Mental Retardation* (New York: Wiley).

Baroff, G.S. and Tate, B.G. 1968. The use of aversive stimulation in the treatment of chronic self-injurious behavior. *Journal of the American Academy of Child Psychiatry* 7:454–70.

Barrett, B.H. and McCormack, J.E. 1973. Varied teacher tutorials: A tactic for generating credible skills in severely retarded boys. *Mental Retardation* 11:14–19

Barry, N.J. and Overman, P.B. 1977. Comparison of the effectiveness of adult and peer models with EMR children. *American Journal of Mental Deficiency* 82:33–36.

Baumeister, A.A. and Forehand, R. 1973. Stereotyped acts. In *International Review of Research in Mental Retardation* vol. 6, eds. N.R. Ellis (New York: Academic Press, Inc.).

Beattie vs. State Board of Education 1919. 172 N.W. 153.

Becker, W.C. 1971. *Parents Are Teachers* (Champaign, Illinois: Research Press).

Becker, W.C. and Becker, J.W. 1974. *Successful Parenthood* (Chicago: Follett Publishing Company).

Benaroya, S., Wesley, S., Ogilvie, H., Klein, L.S., and Meany, M. 1977. Sign language and multisensory input training of children with communication and related developmental disorders. *Journal of Autism and Childhood Schizophrenia* 7:23–31.

Beres, D. 1952. Clinical notes on aggression in children. In *The Psychoanalytic Study of the Child* vol. 7, ed. R.S. Eissler (New York: International Universities Press).

Berger, S. 1972. A clinical program for developing multimedia responses with atypical deaf children. In *Language Intervention with the Retarded,* eds. J. McLean, D. Yoder, and R. Schiefelbusch (Baltimore: University Park Press).

Berkson, G. 1967. Abnormal stereotyped motor acts. In *Comparative Psychopathology – Animal and Human,* eds. J. Zubin and H.F. Hunt. (New York: Grune and Stratton.)

Berkson, G. and Davenport, R.K. 1962. Stereotyped movements in mental defectives: I. Initial survey. *American Journal of Mental Deficiency* 66:849–52.

Berkson, G. and Mason, W.A. 1964. Stereotyped movements of mental defectives: IV. The effects of toys and the character of the acts. *American Journal of Mental Deficiency* 68:511–24.

Berkson, G. and Mason, W.A. 1963. Stereotyped movements of mental defectives: III. Situation effects. *American Journal of Mental Deficiency* 68:409–12.

Berlyne, D.E. 1960. *Conflict, Arousal, and Curiosity* (New York: McGraw-Hill).

Berlyne, D.E. 1958. The influence of complexity and novelty in visual figures on orienting responses. *Journal of Experimental Psychology* 55:289–96.

Berlyne, D.E. 1955. The arousal and satiation of perceptual curiosity in the rat. *Journal of Comparative and Physiological Psychology* 48:238–46.

Berlyne, D.E. 1951. Attention to change. *British Journal of Psychology* 42:269–78.

Berlyne, D.E. 1950. Novelty and curiosity as determinants of exploratory behavior. *British Journal of Psychology* 41:68–80.

Berlyne, D.E. and Ditkofsky, J. 1976. Effects of novelty and oddity on visual selective attention. *British Journal of Psychology* 67:175–80.

Berlyne, D.E. and Slater, J. 1957. Perceptual curiosity, exploratory behavior and maze learning. *Journal of Comparative and Physiological Psychology* 50:228–32.

Bernal, M.E. and North, J.A. 1978. A survey of parent training manuals. *Journal of Applied Behavior Analysis* 4:533–44.

Bettelheim, B. 1967. *The Empty Fortress* (New York: The Free Press).

Bijou, S.W. 1978. *Behavioral Teaching of Young Handicapped Children: Problems of Application and Implementation*. Paper presented at the Fourth Annual Convention of the Association of Behavior Analysis, Chicago.

Bijou, S.W., Birnbrauer, J.S., Kidder, J.D., and Tague, C. 1966. Programmed instruction as an approach to teaching reading, writing, and arithmetic to retarded children. *Psychological Record.* 16:505–22.

Bilsky, L. and Heal, L.W. 1969. Cue novelty and training level in the discrimination shift performance of retardates. *Journal of Experimental Child Psychology* 8:503–11.

Birnbrauer, J.S. 1968. Generalization of punishment effects: A case study. *Journal of Applied Behavior Analysis* 1:201–11.

Birnbrauer, J.S., Kidder, J.D., and Tague, C. 1964. Programming reading from the teacher's point of view. *Programmed Instruction,* 3:1–2.

Birnbrauer, J.S., Peterson, C.P., and Solnick, J.V. 1974. The design and interpretation of studies of single subjects. *American Journal of Mental Deficiency* 79:191–203.

Blackstock, E. 1978. Cerebral asymmetry and the development of early infantile autism. *Journal of Autism and Childhood Schizophrenia* 8:339–53.

Blatt, B., Ozolins, A., and McNally, J. 1979. *The Family Papers: A Return to Purgatory* (New York and London: Longman).

Blough, P.M. 1971. The visual acuity of the pigeon for distant targets. *Journal of the Experimental Analysis of Behavior* 15:57–67.

Bogen, J. 1969. The other side of the brain II: An appositional mind. *Bulletin of the Los Angeles Neurological Societies* 34:135–62.

Bonvillian, J.D. and Nelson, K.E. 1976. Sign language acquisition in a mute autistic boy. *Journal of Speech and Hearing Disorders* 41:339–47.

Boucher, J. 1977a. Alternation and sequencing behavior, and response to novelty in autistic children. *Journal of Child Psychology and Psychiatry* 18:67–72

Boucher, J. 1977b. Hand preference in autistic children and their parents. *Journal of Autism and Childhood Schizophrenia* 7:177–87.

Bradley, B.H. 1970. Educational detours for the mentally retarded. *Journal of Special Education and Mental Retardation* 7:59–63.

Brethower, D.M. and Reynolds, G.S. 1962. A facilitative effect of punishment on unpunished behavior. *Journal of the Experimental Analysis of Behavior* 5:191–99.

Brooks, D. 1978. Evaluation of "hard to test" children and adults. In *Diagnostic Procedures in Hearing, Language and Speech,* eds. S. Singh and J. Lynch (Baltimore: University Park Press).

Brookshire, R.H. 1972. Effects of task difficulty on naming performance of aphasic subjects. *Journal of Speech and Hearing Research* 15:551–58.

Brown, J. 1972. *Aphasia, Apraxia and Agnosia* (Springfield: Charles C. Thomas).

Brown, L., Branston, M.B., Baumgart, D., Vincent, L., Falvey, M., and Schroeder, J. 1979. Utilizing the characteristics of a variety of current and subsequent least restrictive environments as factors in the development of curricular content for severely handicapped students. *AAESPH Review* 4:407–424.

Brown, L., Branston, M.B., Hamre-Nietupski, S., Pumpian, I., Certo, N., and Gruenwald, L. 1979. A strategy for developing chronological age appropriate and functional curricular content for severely handicapped adolescents and young adults. *Journal of Special Education* 13:81–90.

Brown, L., Certo. N., Belmore, K., and Crowner, T., eds. 1976. *Madison's Alternative for Zero Exclusion: Papers and Programs Related to Public School Services for Secondary and Severely Handicapped Students* vol. VI, part 1 (Madison: Madison Metropolitan School District).

Brown, L., Nietupski, I., and Hamre-Nietupski. S. 1976. The criterion of ultimate functioning and public school services for severely handicapped students in *Papers and programs related to public school services for secondary-age severely handicapped students,* eds. L. Brown, N. Certo, & T. Crowner. Madison, Wisconsin: Madison Metropolitan School District.

Brown, L. and Sontag, E., eds. 1972. *Toward the Development and Implementation of an Empirically-Based Public School Program for Trainable Mentally Retarded and Severely Emotionally Disturbed Children* vol. II (Madison: Madison Metropolitan School District).

Brown vs. Board of Education 1954. 347 U.S. 483.

Brown, L., Wilcox, B., Sontag, E., Vincent, L., Dodd, W., and Gruenwald, L. 1977. Toward the realization of the least restrictive educational environments for severely handicapped students. *AAESPH Review* 2:195–201.

Brunt, M. 1978. The staggered spondaic word test. In *Handbook of Clinical Audiology,* 1st edition, ed. J. Katz (Baltimore: Williams and Wilkins).

Brunt, M. 1972. The staggered spondaic word test. In *Handbook of Clinical Audiology,* 1st. edition, ed. J. Katz (Baltimore: Williams and Wilkins).

Bryson, Y., Sakati, N., Nyhan, W.L., and Fish, C.H. 1971. Self-mutilative behavior in the Cornelia de Lange syndrome. *American Journal of Mental Deficiency* 76:319–324.

Bucher, B. and Lovaas, O.I. 1968. Use of aversive stimulation in behavior modification. In *Miami Symposium on the Prediction of Behavior, 1967: Aversive Stimulation,* ed. M. Jones (Coral Gables: University of Miami Press).

Budoff, M. 1978. Implementing due process safeguards. In *Due Process: Developing Criteria for the Evaluation of Due Process Procedural Safeguards Provisions.* U.S. Office of Education, Bureau of Education for the Handicapped.

Buell, J., Stoddard, P., Harris, F., and Baer, D.M. 1968. Collateral social development accompanying reinforcement of outdoor play in a preschool child. *Journal of Applied Behavior Analysis* 1:167–73.

Burgess, E.W. and Cottrell, L., Jr. 1939. *Predicting Success or Failure in Marriage* (New York: Prentice Hall).

Burton, T.A. and Hirshoren, A. 1979. The education of severely and profoundly retarded children: Are we sacrificing the child to the concept? *Exceptional Children* 45:598–602.

Buter, R.A. and Woolpy, J.H. 1963. Visual attention in the rhesus monkey. *Journal of Comparative and Physiological Psychology* 56:324–28.

Butler, R.A. 1957. The effect of deprivation of visual incentives on visual exploration motivation in monkeys. *Journal of Comparative and Physiological Psychology* 50:177–79.

Butler, R.A. 1954. Incentive conditions which influence visual exploration. *Journal of Experimental Psychology* 48:19–23.

Butler, R.A. 1953. Discrimination learning by rhesus monkeys to visual exploration motivation. *Journal of Comparative and Physiological Psychology* 46:95–8.

Bychowski, G. 1954. Problems of infantile neurosis: A discussion. In *The Psychoanalytic Study of the Child* vol. 9, ed. R.S. Eissler (New York: International Universities Press).

Cain, A.C. 1961. The presuperego turning inward of aggression. *Psychoanalytic Quarterly* 30:171–208.

Caldwell, B.M. 1973. The importance of beginning early. In *Not All Little Wagons are Red. The Exceptional Child's Early Years,* eds. M.B. Karnes, J.B. Jordan, and R.F. Dailey (Reston: Council for Exceptional Children).

Cantor, J.H. and Cantor, G.N. 1964a. Children's observing behavior as related to amount and recency of stimulus familarization. *Journal of Experimental Child Psychology* 1:241–47.

Cantor, J.H. and Cantor, G.N. 1964b. Observing behavior in children as a function of stimulus novelty. *Child Development* 35:119–28.

Carpenter, M.B. 1976. *Human Neuroanatomy* (Baltimore: Williams and Wilkins).

Carr, E.G. 1981a. Generalization of treatment effects following educational intervention with autistic children and youth. In *Critical Issues in Educating Autistic Children and Youth,* eds. B. Wilcox and A. Thompson (Washington, D.C.: Publication of the Department of Education, Office of Special Education).

Carr, E.G. 1981b. Sign language. In *The Me Book: Teaching Manual for Parents and Teachers of Developmentally Disabled Children,* eds. O.I. Lovaas, A. Ackerman, D. Alexander, P. Firestone, M. Perkins, and D. Young (Baltimore: University Park Press).

Carr, E.G. 1981c. Some relationships between sign language acquisition and perceptual dysfunction in autistic children. In *Neuropsychology and Cognition,* vol. 2, eds. R.N. Malatesha and L.D. Hartlage (Alphen aan den Rijn, The Netherlands: Sijthoff and Noordhoff International Publishers).

Carr, E.G. 1979. Teaching autistic children to use sign language: Some research issues. *Journal of Autism and Developmental Disorders* 9:345–59.

Carr, E. 1977. The motivation of self-injurious behavior: A review of some hypotheses. *Psychological Bulletin* 84:800–16.

Carr, E.G., Binkoff, J.A., Kologinsky, E., and Eddy, E. 1978. Acquisition of sign language by autistic children. I. Expressive labelling. *Journal of Applied Behavior Analysis* 11:489–501.

Carr, E.G. and Dores, P. in press. Patterns of language acquisition following simultaneous communication with autistic children. *Analysis and Intervention in Developmental Disabilities.*

Carr, E.G. and Kologinsky, E. 1978. *Teaching Psychotic Children to use Sign Language: Development of Descriptive Generative Sentences.* Paper presented at the annual meeting of the Association for Advancement of Behavior Therapy, Chicago.

Carr, E.G. and Lovaas, O.I. in press. Contingent electric shock as a treatment for severe behavior problems. In *Punishment: Its Effects on Human Behavior,* eds. S. Axelrod and J. Apsche (Lawrence: H & H Enterprises, Inc.).

Carr, E., Newsom, C.D., and Binkoff, J.A. 1980. Escape as a factor in the aggressive behavior of two retarded children. *Journal of Applied Behavior Analysis* 13:101–17.

Carr, E.G., Newsom, C.D., and Binkoff, J.A. 1976. Stimulus control of self-destructive behavior in a psychotic child. *Journal of Abnormal Child Psychology* 4:139–53.

Carr, E.G. and Posner, D. *A Naturalistic Study of Spontaneous Sign Language Acquisition.* Unpublished manuscript, State University of New York at Stony Brook.

Carr, E.G. and Pridal, C. *Acquisition of Language by Autistic Children: Modality Preferences.* Unpublished manuscript, State University of New York at Stony Brook.

Carr, E.G., Schreibman, L., and Lovaas, O.I. 1975. Control of echolalic speech in psychotic children. *Journal of Abnormal Child Psychology* 3:331–51.

Carrier, J.K. 1974. Application of functional analysis and a nonspeech response made to teaching language. Developing systematic procedures for training children's language. Monograph 18. Washington, D.C., *American Speech and Hearing Association.*

Carroccia, D.F., Latham, S., and Carroccia, B.B. 1976. Rate contingent guitar rental to decelerate stereotyped head/face touching of an adult male psychiatric patient. *Behavior Therapy* 7:104–09.

Carrow, E. 1973. *Test for Auditory Comprehension of Language,* 5th edition (Austin: Learning Concepts).

Casey, L.O. 1978. Development of communicative behavior in autistic children: A parent program using manual signs. *Journal of Autism and Childhood Schizophrenia* 8:45–59.

Catania, A.C., ed. 1968. *Contemporary Research in Operant Behavior* (Glenview: Scott, Foresman and Company).

Cautela, J.R. and Baron, M.G. 1973. Multifaceted behavior therapy of self-injurious behavior. *Journal of Behavior Therapy and Experimental Psychiatry* 4:125–31.

Chan, K.S. and Keough, B.K. 1974. Interpretation of task interruption and feelings of responsibility for failure. *Journal of Special Education* 8:175–78.

Cheney, T. and Stein, N. 1974. Fading procedures and oddity learning in kindergarten children. *Journal of Experimental Child Psychology* 17:313–21.

Christoplos, F. 1973. Keeping exceptional children in regular classes. *Exceptional Children* 39:569–72.

Churchill, D.W. 1971. Effects of success and failure in psychotic children. *Archives of General Psychiatry* 25:208–14.

Churchill, D.W. Alpern, G.D., and DeMyer, M.K., eds. 1971. *Infantile Autism* (Springfield: Charles C. Thomas).

Clark, P. and Rutter, M. 1979. Task difficulty and task performance in autistic children. *Journal of Child Psychology and Psychiatry* 20:271–85.

Cleland, C.C. and Clark, C.M. 1966. Sensory deprivation and aberrant behavior among idiots. *American Journal of Mental Deficiency* 71:213–25.

Colby, K., and Parkinson, C. 1977. Handedness in autistic children. *Journal of Autism and Childhood Schizophrenia* 7:3–9.

Coleman, M. 1979. Studies of the autistic syndromes. In *Congenital and Acquired Cognitive Disorders,* ed. R. Katzman (New York: Raven Press).

Coleman, S.L. and Stedman, J.M. 1974. Use of a peer model in language training in an echolalic child. *Journal of Behavior Therapy and Experimental Psychiatry* 5:275–79.

Collins, D.T. 1965. Head banging: Its meaning and management in the severely retarded adult. *Bulletin of the Menninger Clinic* 4:205–11.

Cone, J.D., and Hawkins, R.P. 1977. *Behavioral Assessment* New York: Brunner/Mazel.

Cook, A.R. and Rincover, A. 1979. *Response Biases of Autistic and Normal Children: A Preliminary Assessment.* Paper presented at the 13th Annual Convention of the Association for the Advancement of Behavior Therapy, San Francisco.

Cook, A.R. and Rincover, A. 1978. *Evaluation and Remediation of Discrimination Learning Problems in Autistic Children.* Paper presented at the 12th Annual Convention of the Association for the Advancement of Behavior Therapy, Chicago.

Cornsweet, T.N. and Crane, H.D. 1973. Training the visual accommodative system. *Vision Research* 13:713–15.

Corte, H.E., Wolf, M.M., and Locke, B.J. 1971. A comparison of procedures for eliminating self-injurious behavior of retarded adolescents. *Journal of Applied Behavior Analysis* 4:201–13.

Council for Exceptional Children. 1977. *Implementing Procedural Safeguards* (Reston: Council for Exceptional Children).

Craighead, W.D., O'Leary, K.D., and Allen, J.S. 1973. Teaching and generalization of instruction following in an "autistic" child. *Journal of Behavior Therapy and Experimental Psychiatry* 4:171–76.

Creedon, M.P., ed. 1975. *Appropriate Behavior Through Communication* (Chicago: Michael Reese Medical Center, Dysfunctioning Child Center Publication).

Creedon, M.P. 1973. *Language Development in Nonverbal Autistic Children using a Simultaneous Communication System.* Paper presented at the biennial meeting of the Society for Research in Child Development, Philadelphia.

Cromwell, R.L. 1963. A social learning approach to mental retardation. In *Handbook of Mental Deficiency,* ed N.R. Ellis (New York: McGraw-Hill).

Cross, H.A. and Harlow, H.F. 1965. Prolonged and progressive effects of partial isolation on the behavior of Macaque monkeys. *Journal of Experimental Research in Personality* 1:39–49.

Cushing, P.J. and Rincover, A. 1978. *The Role of S + and S − in Discrimination Learning with Autistic and Retarded Children.* Unpublished manuscript. University of North Carolina at Greensboro.

◦ Cuvo, A.J., Veitch, U.D., Trace, M.W., and Konke, J.L. 1978. Teaching change computation to the mentally retarded. *Behavior Modification* 2:531–48.

Damasio, A. and Maurer, R. 1978. A neurological model for childhood autism. *Archives of Neurology* 35:777–86.

Davenport, R.K. and Berkson, G. 1963. Stereotyped movements of mental defectives: II. Effects of novel objects. *American Journal of Mental Deficiency* 67:879–82.

Debus, R.L. 1970. Effects of brief observation of model behavior on conceptual tempo of impulsive children. *Developmental Psychology* 2:22–32.

Deci, E.L. 1975. *Intrinsic Motivation* (New York: Plenum Press).

Deiker, T. and Bruno, R.D. 1976. Sensory reinforcement of eyeblink rate in a decorticate human. *American Journal of Mental Deficiency,* vol. 80, 6:665–67.

Deitz, S.M. and Repp, A.C. 1974. Differentially reinforcing low rates of misbehavior with normal elementary school children. *Journal of Applied Behavior Analysis* 7:622. (Abstract)

Deitz, S.M. and Repp, A.C. 1973. Decreasing classroom misbehavior through the use of DRO schedules of reinforcement. *Journal of Applied Behavior Analysis* 6:457–63.

de Lissovoy, V. 1964. Head banging in early childhood: Review of empirical studies. *Pediatric Digest* 6:49–55.

de Lissovoy, V. 1963. Head banging in early childhood: A suggested cause. *Journal of Genetic Psychology* 102:109–114

de Lissovoy, V. 1962. Head banging in early childhood. *Child Development* 33:43–56.

de Lissovoy, V. 1961. Head banging in early childhood. *Journal of Pediatrics* 58:803–05.

Dember, W.N. 1961. Alternation behavior. In *Functions of Varied Experience,* eds. D.W. Fiske and S.R. Maddi (Homewood: Dorsey Press).

DeMyer, M.K., Barton, S., DeMyer, W.E., Norton, J.A., Allen, J., and Steele, R. 1973. Prognosis in autism: A follow-up study. *Journal of Autism and Childhood Schizophrenia* 3:199–246.

Dennis, W. and Najarian, P. 1957. Infant development under environmental handicap. *Psychological Monographs* 7 (Whole No. 436).

Devany, J. and Rincover, A. 1979. *Assessment of the Effects of using Self-Stimulation as a Reinforcer.* Paper presented at the 13th Annual Convention, Association for the Advancement of Behavior Therapy, S.F.

Dizmang, L.H. and Cheatham, C.F. 1970. The Lesch-Nyhan syndrome. *American Journal of Psychiatry* 127:671–77.

Doke, L.A. and Epstein, L.H. 1975. Oral overcorrection: Side effects and extended applications. *Journal of Experimental Child Psychology* 20:496–511.

Dollard, J., Miller, N.E., Doob, L.W., Mowrer, O.H., and Sears, R.R. 1939. *Frustration and Aggression* (New Haven: Yale University Press).

Dorey, G.W. and Zeaman, D. 1973. The use of a fading technique in paired-associate teaching of a reading vocabulary with retardates. *Mental Retardation* 11:3–6.

Dorsey, M. 1979. The use of sensory extinction in the treatment of self-injurious behavior. Unpublished doctoral dissertation. Western Michigan University.

Duker, P. 1975. Behavior control of self-biting in a Lesch-Nyhan patient. *Journal of Mental Deficiency Research* 19:11–19.

Dunlap, G. and Koegel, R.L. 1980a. Programming the delivery of instructions for autistic children. In *Critical Issues in Educating Autistic Children and Youth,* eds. B. Wilcox and A. Thompson (Washington, D.C.: Publication of the Department of Education Office of Special Education).

Dunlap, G. and Koegel, R.L. 1980b. Motivating autistic children through stimulus variation. *Journal of Applied Behavior Analysis* 13:619–27.

Dunlap, G., Koegel, R.L. and Egel, A.L. 1979. Autistic children in school. *Exceptional Children* 45:552–58.

Dunn, L. 1959. *Peabody Picture Vocabulary Test* (Circle Pines: American Guidance Services).

Eason, L. and Rincover, A. 1980. *The "Tunnel Vision" Nature of Stimulus Overselectivity in Autistic Children.* Unpublished manuscript. University of North Carolina at Greensboro.

Egel, A.L. in press. Reinforcer variation: Implications for motivating developmentally delayed children. *Journal of Applied Behavior Analysis.*

Egel, A.L. 1980. The effects of constant versus varied reinforcer presentation on responding by autistic children. *Journal of Experimental Child Psychology* 30:455–463.

Egel, A.L., Koegel, R.L., and Schreibman, L. 1980. A review of educational-treatment procedures for autistic children. In *Fourth Review of Special Education,* eds. L. Mann and D. Sabatino (New York: Grune and Stratton).

Egel, A.L., Richman, G.S., and Koegel, R.L. 1981. Normal peer models and autistic children's learning. *Journal of Applied Behavior Analysis* 14:3–12.

Eisenberg, L. 1956. The autistic child in adolescence. *American Journal of Psychiatry* 112:607–12.

Eisenberg, L. and Kanner, L. 1956. Early infantile autism. *American Journal of Orthopsychiatry* 26:556–66.

Elgar, S. 1966. Teaching autistic children. In *Early Childhood Autism: Clinical, Educational and Social Aspects,* ed J.K. Wing (London: Pergamon Press, Inc. 205–37).

Elliot, R. and Vasta, R. 1970. The modeling of sharing: Effects associated with vicarious reinforcement, symbolization, age, and generalization. *Journal of Experimental Child Psychology* 10:8–15.

Emshoff, J.G., Redd, W.T., and Davidson, W.S. 1976. Generalization training and the transfer of treatment effects with delinquent adolescents. *Journal of Behavior Therapy and Experimental Psychiatry* 7:141–44.

Emsley, H.H. 1948. *Visual Optics* 4th ed. (London: Hatton Press).

Epstein, L.H., Doke, L.A., Sajwaj, T.E., Sorrell, S., and Rimmer, B. 1974. Generality and side-effects of overcorrection. *Journal of Applied Behavior Analysis* 7:385–90.

Fantino, E. 1973. Emotion. In *The Study of Behavior,* ed. J.A. Nevin (Glenview: Scott, Foresman and Company).

Fantz, R.L. 1964. Visual experience in infants: Decreased attention to familiar patterns relative to novel ones. *Science* 146:668–70.

Favell, J.E., McGimsey, J.S., and Jones, M.L. 1978. The use of physical restraint in the treatment of self-injury and as positive reinforcement. *Journal of Applied Behavior Analysis* 11:225–41.

Fellows, B.J. 1968. Chance stimulus sequences for discrimination tasks. *Psychological Bulletin* 67:87–92.

Ferster, C.B. 1974. Discussion. In *The Psychology of Depression: Contemporary Theory and Research,* eds. R.J. Freedman and M.M. Katz (Washington, D.C.: V.H. Winston).

Ferster, C.B. 1967. Arbitrary and natural reinforcement. *Psychological Record* 17:341–47.

Ferster, C.B. 1961. Positive reinforcement and behavioral deficits of autistic children. *Child Development* 32:437–56.

Ferster, C.B. and DeMyer, M.K. 1962. A method for the experimental analysis of the behavior of autistic children. *American Journal of Orthopsychiatry* 32:89–98.

Ferster, C.B. and DeMyer, M.K. 1961. The development of performances in an automatically controlled environment. *Journal of Chronic Diseases* 13:312–45.

Fields, L., Bruno, V., and Keller, K. 1976. The stages of acquisition in stimulus-fading. *Journal of the Experimental Analysis of Behavior* 26:295–300.

Fineman, K.R. 1968a. Visual color reinforcement in establishment of speech by an autistic child. *Perceptual and Motor Skills* 26:761–62.

Fineman, K.R. 1968b. Shaping and increasing verbalizations in an autistic child in response to visual color stimulation. *Perceptual and Motor Skills* 27:1071–74.

Fineman, K.R. and Ferjo, J. 1969. Establishing and increasing verbalizations in a deaf schizophrenic child through the use of contingent visual reinforcement. *Perceptual and Motor Skills* 29:647–52.

Forehand, R. and Baumeister, A.A. 1976. Deceleration of aberrant behavior among retarded individuals. In *Behavior Modification,* eds. M. Hersen, R.M. Eisler, and P.M. Miller (New York: Academic Press, Inc.).

Forehand, R., Sturgis, E.T., McMahon, R.J., Aguar, D., Green, K., Wells, K.C., and Breiner, J. 1979. Parent behavioral training to modify noncompliance: Treatment generalization across time and from school to home. *Behavior Modification* 3:3–25.

Fowler, H. 1971. The implications of sensory reinforcement. In *The Nature of Reinforcement,* ed. R. Glaser (New York: Academic Press, Inc.).

Fowler, H. 1967. Satiation and curiosity: Constructs for a drive and incentive-motivational theory of exploration. In *The Psychology of Learning and Motivation* vol. 1, eds. K.W. Spence and J.J. Spence (New York: Academic Press, Inc.).

Fowler, H. 1965. *Curiosity and Exploratory Behavior* (New York: MacMillan Company).

Foxx, R. and Azrin, N. 1973. The elimination of autistic self-stimulatory behavior by overcorrection. *Journal of Applied Behavior Analysis* 6:1–14.

Frankel, F. and Simmons, J.Q. 1976. Self-injurious behavior in schizophrenic and retarded children. *American Journal of Mental Deficiency* 80:512–22.

Frankl, L. 1963. Self-preservation and the development of accident proneness in children and adolescents. In *The Psychoanalytic Study of the Child* vol. 18, ed. R.S. Eissler (New York: International Universities Press).

Freeman, B.J. and Ritvo, E.R. 1976. Parents as paraprofessionals. In *Autism: Diagnosis, Current Research and Management,* ed. E.R. Ritvo (New York: Spectrum Publications).

Freud, A. and Burlingham, D.T. 1944. *Infants Without Families* (New York: International Universities Press).

Frisch, S.A. and Schumaker, J.B. 1974. Teaching generalized receptive prepositions in retarded children. *Journal of Applied Behavior Analysis* 7:611–21.

Fulwiler, R.L. and Fouts, R.S. 1976. Acquisition of American Sign Language by a noncommunicating autistic child. *Journal of Autism and Childhood Schizophrenia* 6:43–51.

Furman, W. 1980. Promoting social development: Developmental implications for treatment. In *Advances in Clinical Child Psychology* vol. 3, eds. B.B. Lahey and A.E. Kazdin (New York: Plenum Press).

Garcia, E. 1974. The training and generalization of a conversational speech form in nonverbal retardates. *Journal of Applied Behavior Analysis* 7:137–49.

Garcia, E., Guess, D., and Byrnes, J. 1973. Development of syntax in a retarded girl using imitation, reinforcement, and modelling. *Journal of Applied Behavior Analysis* 6:299–310.

Geschwind, N. 1974. The anatomical basis of hemispheric differences. In *Hemispheric Function in the Human Brain,* eds. S. Dimond and J. Beaumont (New York: Halstead Press).

Geschwind, N., Quadfasel, F., and Segarra, J. 1968. Isolation of the speech area. *Neuropsychologia* 6:327–40.

Gilhool, T. and Stutman, E. 1978. *Integration of Severely Handicapped students: Forward Criterion for Implementing and Enforcing the Integration Imperative of P.L., 94–142 and Section 504.* Paper presented at BEH National Conference on the Concept of the Least Restrictive Environment, Washington, D.C.

Glattke, T. 1973. Elements of auditory physiology. In *Normal Aspects of Speech, Hearing and Language,* eds. F. Minifie, T. Hixon and F. Williams (Englewood Cliffs: Prentice-Hall).

Gluck, J.P. and Sackett, G.P. 1974. Frustration and self-aggression in social isolate rhesus monkeys. *Journal of Abnormal Psychology* 83:331–34.

Goldfarb, W. 1958. Pain reactions in a group of institutionalized schizophrenic children. *American Journal of Orthopsychiatry* 28:777–85.

Goldstein, K. 1948. *Language and Language Disturbances* (New York: Grune and Stratton).

Goodenough, F. 1931. *Anger in Young Children* (Minneapolis: University of Minnesota Press).

Gottlieb, J. and Gottlieb, B.W. 1977. Stereotypic attitudes and behavioral intentions toward handicapped children. *American Journal of Mental Deficiency* 82:67–71.

Granzin, A.C. and Carnine, D.W. 1977. Child performance on discrimination tasks: Effects of amount of stimulus variation. *Journal of Experimental Child Psychology* 24:332–42.

Green, A.H. 1968. Self-destructive behavior in physically abused schizophrenic children. *Archives of General Psychiatry* 19:171–79.

Green, A.H. 1967. Self-mutilation in schizophrenic children. *Archives of General Psychiatry* 17:234–44.

Greenacre, P. 1954. Problems of infantile neurosis: A discussion. In *The Psychoanalytic Study of the Child* vol. 9, ed. R.S. Eissler (New York: International Universities Press).

Greenfeld, J. 1972. Who can reach Noah? In *West,* April 9, Los Angeles Times Magazine.

Greeno, J.G. 1964. Paired-associate learning with massed and distributed repetition of items. *Journal of Experimental Psychology* 67:286–95.

Griffiths, H. and Craighead, W.E. 1972. Generalization in operant speech therapy for misarticulation. *Journal of Speech and Hearing Disorders* 37:457–68.

Grossman, H.J., ed. 1973. *Manual on Terminology and Classification in Mental Retardation* [rev. ed.] (Washington, D.C.: American Association on Mental Deficiency).

Gruen, G.E., Ottinger, D.R., and Ollendick, T.H. 1974. Probability learning in retarded children with differing histories of success and failure in school. *American Journal of Mental Deficiency* 79:417–23.

Guess, D., Horner, R.D., Utley, B., Holvoet, J., Maxon, D., Tucker, D., and Warren, S. 1978. A functional curriculum sequencing model for teaching the severely handicapped. *AAESPH Review* 3:202–215.

Guess, D., Sailor, W., and Baer, D.M. 1976. *Functional Speech and Language Training for the Severely Handicapped,* parts 1–4 (Lawrence: H & H Enterprises, Inc.).

Guess, D., Sailor, W., Rutherford, G., and Baer, D.M. 1968. An experimental analysis of linguistic development: The productive use of the plural morpheme. *Journal of Applied Behavior Analysis* 1:297–306.

Gullickson, G.R. 1966. A note on children's selection of novel auditory stimuli. *Journal of Experimental Child Psychology* 4:158–62.

Gunderson, J.G., Autry, J.H., Mosher, L.R., and Buchsbaum, S. 1973. *Special Report: Schizophrenia Bulletin* 1(a):18–49.

Guralnick, M.J. 1976a. *Early Childhood Intervention: The Use of Nonhandicapped Peers as Educational and Therapeutic Resources.* Paper presented at the International Congress of the International Association for the Scientific Study of Mental Deficiency, Washington, D.C.

Guralnick, M.J. 1976b. The value of integrating handicapped and nonhandicapped preschool children. *American Journal of Orthopsychiatry* 46:236–45.

Hall, R.V. 1971a. *Behavior Modification: The Measurement of Behavior* (Lawrence: H & H Enterprises, Inc.).

Hall, R.V. 1971b. *Behavior Modification: Basic Principles* (Lawrence: H & H Enterprises, Inc.).

Hall, R.V. 1971c. *Behavior Modification: Applications in School and Home* (Lawrence: H & H Enterprises, Inc.).

Hall, S.M., and Talkington, L.W. 1970. Evaluation of a manual approach to programming for deaf retarded. *American Journal of Mental Deficiency* 75:378–80.

Halpern, W.I. 1970. Schooling of autistic children. *American Journal of Orthopsychiatry* 40:665–71.

Hamblin, R.L., Buckholdt, D., Ferritor, D.E., Kozloff, M.A., and Blackwell, L.J. 1971. *The Humanization Process* (New York: John Wiley and Sons).

Hamilton, J., Stephens, L., and Allen, P. 1967. Controlling aggressive and destructive behavior in severely retarded institutionalized residents. *American Journal of Mental Deficiency* 71:852–56.

Handelman, J.S. 1979. Generalization by autistic-type children of verbal responses across settings. *Journal of Applied Behavior Analysis* 12:273–82.

Handleman, J.S. and Harris, S.L. 1980. Generalization from school to home with autistic children. *Journal of Au-*

tism and Developmental Disorders 10:323–33.

Hanson, H. 1959. The effects of discrimination training on stimulus generalization. *Journal of Experimental Psychology* 58:321–35.

Harkness, J.E. and Wagner, J.E. 1975. Self-mutilation in mice associated with otitis media. *Laboratory Animal Science* 25:315–18.

Harlow, H.F. and Griffin, G. 1965. Induced mental and social deficits in rhesus monkeys. In *The Biosocial Basis of Mental Retardation,* eds. S.F. Osler and R.E. Cooke (Baltimore: Johns Hopkins Press).

Harlow, H.F. and Harlow, M.K. 1971. Psychopathology in monkeys. In *Experimental Psychopathology,* ed. H.D. Kimmel (New York: Academic Press, Inc.).

Harlow, H.F. and Harlow, M.K. 1962. Social deprivation in monkeys. *Scientific American* 207(5):136–46.

Harlow, H.F., Harlow, M.K., and Meyer, D.R. 1950. Learning motivated by a manipulation drive. *Journal of Experimental Child Psychology* 40:228–34.

Harris, S. and Romanczyk, R. 1976. A brief report on treating self-injurious behavior by overcorrection. *Behavior Therapy* 7:237.

Hart, B. and Risley, T.R. 1980. *In vivo* language intervention: Unanticipated general effects. *Journal of Applied Behavior Analysis* 13:407–32.

Hart, B.M. and Risley, T.R. 1978. Promoting productive language through incidental teaching. *Education and Urban Society* 10:407–29.

Hart, B.M. and Risley, T.R. 1976. Community-based language training. In *Intervention Strategies for High-Risk Infants and Young Children,* ed. T.D. Tjossem (Baltimore: University Park Press).

Hart, B.M. and Risley, T.R. 1975. Incidental teaching of language in preschool. *Journal of Applied Behavior Analysis* 8:411–20.

Hart, B.M. and Risley, T.R. 1974. Using preschool materials to modify the language of disadvantaged children. *Journal of Applied Behavior Analysis* 7:243–56.

Hart, B.M. and Risley, T.R. 1968. Establishing use of descriptive adjectives in the spontaneous speech of disadvantaged preschool children. *Journal of Applied Behavior Analysis* 1:109–20.

Hartmann, H., Kris, E., and Loewenstein, R.M. 1949. Notes on the theory of aggression. In *The Psychoanalytic Study of the Child* vols. 3 and 4, ed. R.S. Eissler (New York: International Universities Press).

Hartup, W.W. and Coates, B. 1967. Imitation of a peer as a function of reinforcement from the peer group and rewardingness of the model. *Child Development* 38:1003–16.

Hartup, W.W. and Lougee, M.D. 1975. Peers as models. *School of Psychology Digest* 4:11–21.

Hauser, S., DeLong, G., and Rosman, N. 1975. Pneumographic findings in the infantile autism syndrome. *Brain* 98:667–88.

Herbert, E.W., and Baer, E.M. 1972. Training parents as behavior modifiers: Self-recording of contingent attention. *Journal of Applied Behavior Analysis* 5:139–49.

Herman, S.H. and Tramontana, J. 1971. Instructions and group versus individual reinforcement in modifying disruptive group behavior. *Journal of Applied Behavior Analysis* 4:113–19.

Hermelin, B. and Frith, U. 1971. Psychological studies of childhood autism: Can autistic children make sense of what they see and hear? *Journal of Special Education* 5:107–17.

Hermelin, B. and O'Connor, N. 1970. *Psychological Experiments with Autistic Children* (London: Pergamon Press, Inc.).

Herrick, R.M. 1964. The successive differentiation of a lever displacement response. *Journal of the Experimental Analysis of Behavior* 7:211–15.

Herrnstein, R.J. 1977a. Doing what comes naturally: A reply to Professor Skinner. *American Psychologist* 32:1013–16.

Herrnstein, R.J. 1977b. The evolution of behaviorism. *American Psychologist* 32:593–603.

Hersen, M., and Barlow, D.H. 1976. *Single Case Experimental Designs: Strategies for Studying Behavior Change* (New York: Pergamon Press).

Hewett, F.M. 1966. The autistic child learns to read. *Slow Learning Child: The Australian Journal on the Education of Backward Children* 12:107–20.

Hewett, F.M. 1965. Teaching speech to autistic children through operant conditioning. *American Journal of Orthopsychiatry* 34:927–36.

Hewett, F.M. 1964. Teaching reading to an autistic boy through operant conditioning. *American Journal of Orthopsychiatry* 17:613–18.

Hicks, D.J. 1965. Imitation and retention of film-mediated aggressive peer and adult models. *Journal of Personality and Social Psychology* 2:97–100.

Hier, D., LeMay, M., and Rosenberber, P. 1979. Autism and unfavorable left-right asymmetries of the brain. *Journal of Autism and Developmental Disorders* 9:153–59.

Hineline, P.N. and Rachlin, H. 1969. Notes on fixed-ratio and fixed-interval escape responding in the pigeon. *Journal of the Experimental Analysis of Behavior* 12:397–401.

Hirsch, M.J. 1963. The refraction of children. In *Vision of Children,* ed. M.J. Hirch and R.E. Wick (Philadelphia: Chilton).

Hitzing, E.W. and Risley, T. *Elimination of Self-Destructive Behavior in a Retarded Girl by Noxious Stimulation.* Paper presented at the meeting of the Southwestern Psychological Association, Houston, April 1967.

Hobson, P.A. and Duncan, P. 1979. Sign learning and profoundly retarded people. *Mental Retardation* 17:33–37.

Hodgson, W. 1978. Testing infants and young children. In *Handbook of Clinical Audiology,* ed. J. Katz (Baltimore: Williams and Wilkins).

Hoefnagel, D. 1965. The syndrome of athetoid cerebral palsy, mental deficiency, self-mutilation, and hyperuricemia. *Journal of Mental Deficiency Research* 9:69–74.

Hoefnagel, D., Andrew, E.D., Mireault, N.G., and Berndt, W.O. 1965. Hereditary choreoathetosis, self-mutilation, and hyperuricemia in young males.

New England Journal of Medicine 273:130–35.

Hollien, H. 1975. Neural control of the speech mechanism. In *The Nervous System* vol. 3, ed. D. Tower (New York: Raven Press).

Hollis, J.H. 1965a. The effects of social and nonsocial stimuli on the behavior of profoundly retarded children: Part II. *American Journal of Mental Deficiency* 69:772–89.

Hollis, J.H. 1965b. The effects of social and nonsocial stimuli on the behavior of profoundly retarded children: Part I. *American Journal of Mental Deficiency* 69:775–71.

Holz, W.C. and Azrin, N.H. 1961. Discriminative properties of punishment. *Journal of the Experimental Analysis of Behavior* 4:225–32.

Hopkins, B.L. 1968. Effects of candy and social reinforcement, instructions, and reinforcement schedule learning on the modification and maintenance of smiling. *Journal of Applied Behavior Analysis* 1:121–29.

Horner, D.R. 1980. The effects of an environmental "enrichment" program on the behavior of institutionalized, profoundly retarded children. *Journal of Applied Behavior Analysis* 13:473–91.

Horowitz, F.D. 1965. *Developmental Studies of Simultaneous and Successive Discrimination Learning in Normal and Retarded Children.* Paper presented at the meeting of the Society for Research in Child Development, Minneapolis, March 1965. Cited in *Experimental Child Psychology,* eds. H.W. Reese, and L.P. Lipsett (New York: Academic Press, 1970, 184-85).

Hung, D.W. 1978. Using self-stimulation as reinforcement for autistic children. *Journal of Autism and Childhood Schizophrenia* 8:355–66.

Hunt, J.M. 1965. Traditional personality theory in the light of recent evidence. *American Scientist* 53:80–96.

Hutt, C. 1975. Degrees of novelty and their effects on children's attention and preference. *British Journal of Psychology* 66:487–92.

Hutt, C. 1967. Effects of stimulus novelty on manipulative exploration in an infant. *Journal of Child Psychology, Psychiatry and Allied Disciplines* 8:241–47.

Igelmo, C.I. 1976. The effects of peer model's age and sharing behavior on preschool boy's cooperation in a conflict situation. *Dissertation Abstracts International* 39(3–A):1438.

Ilg, F.L. and Ames, L.B. 1955 *Child Behavior* (New York: Harper and Row).

Jackson, D.A. and Wallace, R.F. 1974. The modification of voice loudness in a 15-year-old retarded girl. *Journal of Applied Behavior Analysis* 7:461–76.

Jakobson, R. 1968. *Child Language Aphasia and Phonological Universals* (Paris: The Hauge).

Jervis, G.A. and Stimson, C.W. 1963. De Lange syndrome. *Journal of Pediatrics* 63:634–45.

Johnson, G.O. 1962. Special education for the mentally handicapped — a paradox. *Exceptional Children* 29:62–9.

Johnson, S.M., Bolstad, D.D., and Lobitz, G.K. 1976. Generalization and contrast phenomena in behavior modification with children. In *Behavior Modification and Families,* eds. E.J. Mash, L.A. Hammerlynk, and L.C. Handy (New York: Brunner/Mazel).

Johnston, J.M. and Johnston, G.T. 1972. Modification of consonant speech-sound articulation in young children. *Journal of Applied Behavior Analysis* 5:233–46.

Jones, F.H., Simmons, J.Q., and Frankel, F. 1974. An extinction procedure for eliminating self-destructive behavior in a 9-year-old autistic girl. *Journal of Autism and Childhood Schizophrenia* 4:241–50.

Kale, R.J., Kaye, J.H., Whelan, P.A., and Hopkins, B.L. 1968. The effects of reinforcement on the modification, maintenance and generalization of social responses of mental patients. *Journal of Applied Behavior Analysis* 1:307–14.

Kanner, L. 1944. Early infantile autism. *Journal of Pediatrics* 25:211–17.

Kanner, L. 1943. Autistic disturbances of affective contact. *Nervous Child* 3:217–50.

Karnes, M.B. and Lee, R.C. 1979. Mainstreaming in the preschool. In *Current Topics in Early Childhood Education*, vol. 4, eds. L.G. Katz, M.Z. Glockner, G. Watkins and M.J. Spencer (Norwood: Amblex Publishing).

Karoly, P. and Rosenthal, M. 1977. Training parents in behavior modification: Effects on perceptions of family interaction and deviant child behavior. *Behavior Therapy* 8:406–10.

Katz, J. 1978. Clinical use of central auditory tests. In *Handbook of Clinical Audiology*, ed. J. Katz (Baltimore: Williams and Wilkins).

Katz, J. 1977a. The staggered spondaic word test. In *Central Auditory Dysfunction*, ed. R. Keith (New York: Grune and Stratton).

Katz, J. 1977b. *The SSW Test Manual* 2nd edition (St. Louis: Auditec).

Katz, J. 1976. *The Competing Environmental Sound Test Instructions* (St. Louis: Auditec).

Katz, J. 1968. The SSW test: An interim report. *Journal of Speech and Hearing Disorders* 33:132–46.

Katz, J., Harder, B., and Lohnes, P. 1977. *Lead/Lag Analysis of SSW Test Items*. Paper presented at the American Speech and Hearing Association Convention, Chicago.

Katz, J., and Illmer, R. 1972. Auditory perception in children with learning disabilities. In *Handbook of Clinical Audiology*, 1st edition, ed. J. Katz (Baltimore: Williams and Wilkins).

Kazdin, A.E. 1977. Assessing the clinical or applied importance of behavior change through social validation. *Behavior Modification* 1:427–50.

Kazdin, A.E. 1975. *Behavior Modification in Applied Settings* (Homewood: The Dorsey Press).

Kazdin, A.E. 1974. Covert modelling, model similarity, and reduction of avoidance behavior. *Behavior Therapy* 5:325–40.

Kazdin, A.E. and Bootzin, R.R. 1972. The token economy: An evaluative review. *Journal of Applied Behavior Analysis* 5:343–72.

Kazdin, A.E. and Moyer, W. 1976. Training teachers to use behavior modification. In *Teaching Behavior Modification*, eds. S. Yen and R. McIntire (Kalamazoo: Behaviordelia).

Kazdin, A. and Polster, R. 1973. Intermittent token reinforcement and response maintenance in extinction. *Behavior Therapy* 4:386–91.

Keith, S.J., Gunderson, J.G., Keifman, A., Buchsbaum, S., and Mosher, L.R. 1976. Special report: Schizophrenia. *Schizophrenia Bulletin* 2:509–65.

Keller, F.S. 1968. "Goodbye, teacher..." *Journal of Applied Behavior Analysis* 1:79-89.

Kerr, N., Meyerson, L., and Michael, J. 1965. A procedure for shaping verbalizations in a mute child. In *Case Studies in Behavior Modification*, eds. L.P. Ullman and L. Krasner (New York: Holt, Rinehart and Winston).

Kiernan, C. 1977. Alternatives to speech: A review of research on manual and other forms of communication with the mentally handicapped and other noncommunicating populations. *British Journal of Mental Subnormality* 23:6–28.

Kimura, D. 1973. The asymmetry of the human brain. *Scientific American* 228:70–78.

Kish, G.B. 1966. Studies of sensory reinforcement. In *Operant Behavior: Areas of Research and Application*, ed. W.K. Honig (New York: Appleton-Century-Crofts).

Kobasigawa, A. 1968. Inhibitory and disinhibitory effects of models on sex-inappropriate behavior in children. *Psychologia* 11:86–96.

Koegel, R.L. In Press. *How to Integrate Autistic and Other Severely Handicapped Children into a Classroom Group*. (Lawrence, Kansas: H&H Enterprises).

Koegel, R. and Covert, A. 1972. The relationship of self-stimulation to learning in autistic children. *Journal of Applied Behavior Analysis* 5:381–88.

Koegel, R.L., Dunlap, G., and Dyer, K. 1980. Intertrial interval duration and learning in autistic children. *Journal of Applied Behavior Analysis* 13:91-9.

Koegel, R.L., Dunlap, G., Richman, G., and Dyer, K. 1981. The use of specific orienting cues for teaching discrimination tasks. *Analysis and Intervention in Developmental Disabilities.*

Koegel, R.L. and Egel, A.L. 1979. Motivating autistic children. *Journal of Abnormal Psychology* 88:418–26.

Koegel, R.L., Egel, A.L., and Dunlap, G. 1980. Learning characteristics of autistic children. In *Methods of Instruction with Severely Handicapped Students,* eds. W.S. Sailor, B. Wilcox, and L.J. Brown (Baltimore: Brookes Publishers).

Koegel, R.L., Egel, A.L., and Williams, J.A. 1980. Behavioral contrast and transfer across settings in teaching autistic children. *Journal of Experimental Child Psychology* 30:422–37.

Koegel, R.L. and Felsenfeld, S. 1977. Sensory deprivation. In *Audiometry in Infancy,* ed. S. Gerber (New York: Grune and Stratton).

Koegel, R.L., Firestone, P.B., Kramme, K.W., and Dunlap, G. 1974. Increasing spontaneous play by suppressing self-stimulation in autistic children. *Journal of Applied Behavior Analysis* 7:521–28.

Koegel, R.L., Glahn, T.J., and Nieminen, G.S. 1978. Generalization of parent-training results. *Journal of Applied Behavior Analysis* 11:95–109.

Koegel, R.L. and Rincover, A. 1977. Some research on the difference between generalization and maintenance in extra-therapy settings. *Journal of Applied Behavior Analysis* 10:1–16.

Koegel, R.L. and Rincover, A. 1976. Some detrimental effects of using extra stimuli to guide learning in normal and autistic children. *Journal of Abnormal Child Psychology* 4:59–71.

Koegel, R.L. and Rincover, A. 1974. Treatment of psychotic children in a classroom environment. I. Learning in a large group. *Journal of Applied Behavior Analysis* 7:45–59.

Koegel, R.L., Russo, D.C., and Rincover, A. 1977. Assessing and training teachers in the generalized use of behavior modification with autistic children. *Journal of Applied Behavior Analysis* 10:197–205.

Koegel, R.L. and Schreibman, L. In Press. *How to Teach Autistic and Other Severely Handicapped Children.* (Lawrence, Kansas: H&H Enterprises).

Koegel, R.L. and Schreibman, L. 1977. Teaching autistic children to respond to simultaneous multiple cues. *Journal of Experimental Child Psychology* 24:299–311.

Koegel, R.L. and Schreibman, L. 1976. Identification of consistent responding to auditory stimuli by a functionally "deaf" autistic child. *Journal of Autism and Childhood Schizophrenia* 6:147–56.

Koegel, R.L., Schreibman, L., Britten, K., and Laitinen, R. 1979. The effect of schedule of reinforcement on stimulus overselectivity in autistic children. *Journal of Autism and Developmental Disorders* 9:383–97.

Koegel, R.L. and Wilhelm, H. 1973. Selective responding to the components of multiple visual cues by autistic children. *Journal of Experimental Child Psychology* 15:442–53.

Koegel, R.L., and Williams, J.A. 1980. Direct vs. indirect response reinforcer relationships in teaching autistic children. *Journal of Abnormal Child Psychology* 8:537–547.

Konstantareas, M.M., Oxman, J., and Webster, C.D. 1978. Iconicity: Effects on the acquisition of sign language by autistic and other severely dysfunctional children. In *Understanding Language through Sign Language Research,* ed. P. Siple (New York: Academic Press, Inc.).

Konstantareas, M.M., Oxman, J., and Webster, C.D. 1977. Simultaneous communication with autistic and other severely dysfunctional children. *Journal of Communicative Disorders* 10:267–82.

Konstantareas, M.M., Webster, C.D., and Oxman, J. 1979. Manual language acquisition and its influence on other areas of functioning in four autistic and autistic-like children. *Journal of Child Psychology and Psychiatry* 20:337–50.

Kopchick, G.A., Rombach, G.W., and Smilovitz, R. 1975. A total communication environment in an institution. *Mental Retardation* 13:22– 23.

Kornhaber, R.C. and Schroeder, H.E. 1975. Importance of model similarity on extinction of avoidance behavior in children. *Journal of Consulting and Clinical Psychology* 43:601– 07.

Kovatanna, P.M. and Kraemer, H.C. 1974. Response to multiple visual cues of color, size and form by autistic children. *Journal of Autism and Childhood Schizophrenia* 4:251– 61.

Kozloff, M.A. 1975. *Reaching the Autistic Child: A Parent-Training Program* (Champaign: Research Press).

Kozloff, M.A. 1974. *Educating Children with Learning and Behavior Problems* (New York: John Wiley and Sons).

Kozloff, M.A. 1973. *Reaching the Autistic Child* (Champaign: Research Press).

Krashen, S. 1976. Cerebral asymmetry. In *Studies in Neurolinguistics,* vol. 2, eds. H. Whitaker and H. Whitaker (New York: Academic Press, Inc.).

Kravitz, H., Rosenthal, V., Teplitz, Z., Murphy, J.B., and Lesser, R.E. 1960. A study of head banging in infants and children, *Diseases of the Nervous System* 21:203– 8.

Kulka, A., Fry, C., and Goldstein, F.J. 1960. Kinesthetic needs in infancy. *American Journal of Orthopsychiatry* 30:562– 71.

Larson, T. 1971. Communication for the nonverbal child. *Academic Therapy* 6:305– 12.

LeLaurin, K. and Risley, T. 1972. "Zone" *versus* "man-to-man" staff assignments. *Journal of Applied Behavior Analysis* 5:225–32.

Lesch, M. and Nyhan, W.L. 1964. A familial disorder of uric acid metabolism and central nervous system function. *American Journal of Medicine* 36:561– 70.

Levy, D.M. 1944. On the problem of movement restraint: Tics, stereotyped movements, and hyperactivity. *American Journal of Orthopsychiatry* 14:644– 71.

Lichstein, K.L. and Schreibman, L. 1976. Employing electric shock with autistic children: A review of the side ef-fects. *Journal of Autism and Childhood Schizophrenia* 6:163– 73.

Lipsett, L.P. 1961. Simultaneous and successive discrimination learning in children. *Child Development* 32:337– 47.

Locke, H.J. and Wallace, K.M. 1959. Short marital adjustment and prediction tests: Their reliability and validity. *Marriage and Family Living* 21:251– 55.

Lockyer, L. and Rutter, M. 1970. A 5 to 15-year follow-up study of infantile psychosis: IV. Patterns of cognitive ability. *British Journal of Social and Clinical Psychology* 9:152– 63.

Loess, H.B. and Duncan, C.P. 1952. Human discrimination learning with simultaneous and successive presentation of stimuli. *Journal of Experimental Psychology* 44:215– 21.

Lotter, V. 1974. Factors related to outcome in autistic children. *Journal of Autism and Childhood Schizophrenia* 4:263– 77.

Lourie, R.M. 1949. The role of rhythmic patterns in childhood. *American Journal of Psychiatry* 105:653– 60.

Lovaas, O.I. 1977a. *The Autistic Child: Language Development through Behavior Modification* (New York: Irvington).

Lovaas, O.I. 1977b. Parents as therapists. In *Autism,* eds. M. Rutter and E. Schopler (New York: Plenum Press).

Lovaas, O.I. 1969. *Behavior Modification: Teaching Language to Psychotic Children.* Instructional film (New York: Appleton-Century-Crofts).

Lovaas, O.I. 1968. A program for the establishment of speech in psychotic children. In *Operant Procedures in Remedial Speech and Language Training,* eds. H.N. Sloane and B.A. MacAulay (Boston: Houghton Mifflin).

Lovaas, O.I. 1966. A program for the establishment of speech in psychotic children. In *Early Childhood Autism,* ed. J.K. Wing (Oxford: Pergamon Press, Inc.).

Lovaas, O.I., Berberich, J.P., Perloff, B.F., and Schaeffer, B. 1966. Acquisition of imitative speech in schizophrenic children. *Science* 151:705– 7.

Lovaas, O.I., Freitag, G., Gold, U.J., and Kassorla, I.C. 1965. Experimental studies in childhood schizophrenia: Analysis of self-destructive behavior. *Journal of Experimental Child Psychology* 2:76–84.

Lovaas, O.I., Freitag, G., Kinder, M.I., Rubenstein, D.D., Schaeffer, B., and Simmons, J.Q. 1966. Establishment of social reinforcers in two schizophrenic children on the basis of food. *Journal of Experimental Child Psychology.* 4:109–25.

Lovaas, O.I., Freitas, L., Nelson, K., and Whalen, C. 1967. The establishment of imitation and its use for the establishment of complex behavior in schizophrenic children. *Behaviour Research and Therapy* 5:171–81.

Lovaas, O.I., Glahn, T.J., Russo, D.C., Chock, P.N., Kohls, S., and Mills, D. in press. Teaching homes for autistic and retarded persons: I. Basic rationale. *Journal of Autism and Developmental Disorders.*

Lovaas, O.I. and Koegel, R.L. 1973. *Behavior Modification in Education, NSSE Yearbook* (Chicago: University of Chicago Press).

Lovaas, O.I., Koegel, R.L., and Schreibman, L. 1979. Stimulus overselectivity in autism: A review of research. *Psychological Bulletin* 86:1236–54.

Lovaas, O.I., Koegel, R.L., Simmons, J.Q., and Long, J.S. 1973. Some generalization and follow-up measures on autistic children in behavior therapy. *Journal of Applied Behavior Analysis* 6:131–66.

Lovaas, O.I., Litrownik, A., and Mann, R. 1971. Response latencies to auditory stimuli in children engaged in self-stimulatory behavior. *Behaviour Research and Therapy* 934–49.

Lovaas, O.I. and Newsom, C.D. 1976. Behavior modification with psychotic children. In *Handbook of Behavior Modification and Behavior Therapy,* ed. H. Leitenberg (Englewood Cliffs: Prentice-Hall).

Lovaas, O.I., Schaeffer, B., and Simmons, J.O. 1965. Experimental studies in childhood schizophrenia: Building social behaviors by use of electric shock. *Journal of Experimental Research in Personality* 1:99–109.

Lovaas, O.I., Schreibman, L., and Koegel, R.L. 1974. A behavior modification approach to the treatment of autistic children. *Journal of Autism and Childhood Schizophrenia* 4:111–29.

Lovaas, O.I. and Schreibman, L. 1971. Stimulus overselectivity of autistic children in a two-stimulus situation. *Behaviour Research and Therapy* 9:305–10.

Lovaas, O.I., Schreibman, L., Koegel, R.L., and Rehm, R. 1971. Selective responding by autistic children to multiple sensory input. *Journal of Abnormal Psychology* 77:211–22.

Lovaas, O.I. and Simmons, J.Q. 1969. Manipulation of self-destruction in three retarded children. *Journal of Applied Behavior Analysis* 2:143–57.

Lowell, M. 1976. Audiological assessment. In *Autism: Diagnosis, Current Research and Management,* ed. E. Ritvo (New York: Spectrum Publications).

Luria, A. 1980. *Higher Cortical Functions in Man* (New York: Basic Books).

Luria, A. 1973. *The Working Brain* (New York: Basic Books).

Lutzker, J.R. and Sherman, J.A. 1974. Producing generative sentence usage by imitation and reinforcement procedures. *Journal of Applied Behavior Analysis* 7:447–60.

MacAulay, B.A. 1968. A program for teaching speech and beginning reading to nonverbal retardates. In *Operant Procedures in Remedial Speech and Language Training,* eds. H.N. Sloane and B.A. MacAulay (Boston: Houghton Mifflin).

Macht, J. 1971. Operant measurement of subjective visual acuity in nonverbal children. *Journal of Applied Behavior Analysis* 4:23–36.

Macht, J.E. 1970. Examination and reevaluation of prosthetic lenses employing an operant procedure for measuring subjective visual acuity in a retarded child. *Journal of Experimental Child Psychology* 10:139–45.

Mack, J.E., Webster, C.D., and Gokcen, I. 1980. Where are they now and how are they faring? Follow-up of 51 severely handicapped, speech-deficient children, four years after an operant-based program. In *Autism: New Directions in Research and Education* eds. C.D. Webster, M.M. Konstantareas, J. Oxman, and J.E. Mack (New York: Pergamon Press, Inc.).

MacMillan, D.L. 1975. Effect of experimental success and failure on the situational expectancy of EMR and non-retarded children. *American Journal of Mental Deficiency* 80:90–95.

MacMillan, D.L. 1971. The problem of motivation in the education of the mentally retarded. *Exceptional Children* 37:579–86.

Maddi, S.R. 1961. Exploratory behavior and variation-seeking in man. In *Functions of Varied Experience,* eds. D.W. Fiske and S.R. Maddi (Homewood: Dorsey Press).

Madsen, C.H., Jr. and Madsen, C.K. 1970. *Teaching/Discipline* (Boston: Allyn and Bacon).

Maloney, D.M., Harper, T.M., Braukmann, C.J., Fixsen, D.L., Phillips, E.L., and Wolf, M.M. 1976. Teaching conversation-related skills to predelinquent girls. *Journal of Applied Behavior Analysis* 9:371.

Manley, S. and Miller, F.D. 1968. Factors affecting children's alternation and choice behaviors. *Psychonomic Science* 13:65–66.

Marholin, II, D. and Siegel, L.J. 1978. Beyond the law of effect: Programming for the maintenance of behavioral change. In *Child Behavior Therapy,* ed. D. Marholin, II (New York: Gardner Press, Inc.).

Marholin, II, D., Siegel, L.J., and Phillips, D. 1976. Transfer and treatment: A search for empirical procedures. In *Progress in Behavior Modification* vol. 3, eds, M. Hersen, R.M. Eisler and P.M. Miller (New York: Academic Press, Inc.).

Marholin, II, D., Steinman, W.M., McInnis, E.T., and Heads, T.B. 1975. The effect of a teacher's presence on the classroom behavior of conduct-problem children. *Journal of Abnormal Child Psychology* 3:11–25.

Marks, J.F., Baum, J., Keele, D.K., Kay, J.L., and MacFarlen, A. 1968. Lesch-Nyhan syndrome treated from the early neonatal period. *Pediatrics* 42:357–59.

Marshall, G.R. 1966. Toilet training of an autistic 8-year-old through operant conditioning therapy: A case report. *Behaviour Research and Therapy* 4:242–45.

Marshall, N.R. and Hegrenes, J.R. 1970. Programmed communication therapy for autistic mentally retarded children. *Journal of Speech and Hearing Disorders* 35:70–83.

Martin, F. 1978. *Pediatric Audiology* (Englewood Cliffs: Prentice-Hall).

Martin, G.L., England, G., Kaprowy, E., Kilgour, K., and Pilek, V. 1968. Operant conditioning of kindergarten class behavior in autistic children. *Behaviour Research and Therapy* 6:281–94.

Mayhew, G.L. and Harris, F.C. 1978. Some negative side-effects of a punishment procedure for stereotyped behavior. *Journal of Behavior Therapy and Experimental Psychiatry* 9:245–51.

McAdoo, G.W. and DeMyer, M.K. 1978. Personality characteristics of parents. In *Autism: A Reappraisal of Concepts and Treatment* (New York: Plenum Press).

McClannahan, L.E. and Krantz, P.J. 1979. *Developing Group Homes for Autistic and Severe Behavior Problem Children.* Paper presented at the Fifth Annual Convention of the Association for Behavior Analysis, Dearborn.

McHale, S.M. and Simeonsson, R.J. 1980. Effects of interaction on nonhandicapped children's attitudes toward autistic children. *American Journal of Mental Deficiency* 85:18–24.

McLean, L.P. and McLean, J.E. 1974. A language-training program for nonverbal autistic children. *Journal of Speech and Hearing Disorders* 39:186–94.

Meichenbaum, D.M., Bowers, K., and Ross, R.R. 1968. Modification of classroom behavior of institutionalized female adolescent offenders. *Behaviour Research and Therapy* 6:343–53.

Metz, J.R. 1965. Conditioning generalized imitation in autistic children. *Journal of Experimental Child Psychology* 2:389–99.

Miller, A. and Miller, E.E. 1973. Cognitive-developmental training with elevated boards and sign language. *Journal of Autism and Childhood Schizophrenia* 3:65–85.

Miller, W.R. and Seligman, M.E.P. 1975. Depression and learned helplessness in man. *Journal of Abnormal Psychology* 84:228–238.

Mills vs. Board of Education of the District of Columbia 1972. 348 F. Supp. 866 (O.D.C.)

Minkin, N., Braukmann, C.J., Minkin, B.L., Timbers, G.D., Timbers, B.J., Fixsen, D.L., Phillips, E.L., and Wolf, M.M. 1976. The social validation and training of conversational skills. *Journal of Applied Behavior Analysis* 9:127–39.

Miran, M.D. 1975. The effects of school experiences, maturation, and peer models on boys' sex role behavior. *Dissertation Abstracts International* 36(5–B):2479–80.

Mizuno, T. and Yugari, Y. 1975. Prophylactic effect of L-5-hydroxytryptophan on self-mutilation in the Lesch-Nyhan syndrome. *Neuropaediatrie* 6:13–23.

Montgomery, K.C. 1952. Exploratory behavior and its relation to spontaneous alternation in a series of maze exposures. *Journal of Comparative and Physiological Psychology* 45:50-7

Montgomery, K.C. 1951. The relationship between exploratory behavior and spontaneous alternation in the white rat. *Journal of Comparative and Physiological Psychology* 44:582-89.

Moos, R.H., Insel, P.M., and Humphrey, B. 1974. *Combined Preliminary Manual for the Family, Work, and Group Environment Scales* (Palo Alto: Consulting Psychologists Press, Inc.).

Moscovitch, M. 1977. The development of lateralization of language functions and some theoretical speculations. In *Language Development and Neurological Theory,* eds. S. Segalowitz and F. Gruber (New York: Academic Press, Inc.).

Mosher, L.R., Gunderson, J.G., and Buchsbaum, S. 1973. Special report on schizophrenia: 1972. *Schizophrenia Bulletin* 1(7):13–45.

Mulligan, M., Guess, D., Holvoet, J., and Brown, F. 1980. *The Individualized Curriculum Sequencing Model (I): Implications from Research on Massed, Distributed, or Spaced Trial Training.* Unpublished manuscript, University of Kansas.

Myers, J.J. and Deibert, A.N. 1971. Reduction of self-abusive behavior in a blind child by using a feeding response. *Journal of Behavior Therapy and Experimental Psychiatry* 2:141–44.

Myerson, L., Kerr, N., and Michael, J.L. 1967. Behavior modification in rehabilitation. In *Child Development: Readings in Experimental Analysis,* eds. S.W. Bijou and D.M. Baer (New York: Appleton-Century-Crofts).

National Society for Autistic Children 1978. Definition of the syndrome of autism. *Journal of Autism and Childhood Schizophrenia* 8:162–67.

National Society for the Prevention of Blindness 1971. *Vision Screening of Children* (New York: Author).

Nedelman, D. and Sulzbacher, S.I. 1972. Dicky at 13 years of age: A long term success following early application of operant conditioning procedures. In *Behavior Analysis and Education,* ed. G. Semb (Lawrence: University of Kansas Press).

Neef, N.A., Iwata, B.A., and Page, T.J. 1978. Public transportation: *In vivo* versus classroom instruction. *Journal of Applied Behavior Analysis* 11:331–44.

Nelson, R.O. and Evans, I.M. 1968. The combination of learning principles and speech techniques in the treatment of noncommunicative children. *Journal of Child Psychology and Psychiatry* 9:111–24.

Nelson, R.O., and Hayes, S.C. 1979. The nature of behavior assessment: A commentary. *Journal of Applied Behavior Analysis* 12:491–500.

Nemoy, E.M. and Davis, S.F. 1972. *Correction of Defective Consonant Sounds* (Boston: Expression Co.).

Newsom, C.D., Carr, E., and Lovaas, O.I. 1977. Experimental analysis and modification of autistic behavior. In *Experimental Analysis of Clinical Phenomena,* ed. R.S. Davidson (New York: Gardner Press).

Newsom, C.D., Favell, J.E., and Rincover, A. in press. The side effects of punishment. In *Punishment: Its effects on Human Behavior,* eds. S. Axelrod and J. Apsche (Lawrence: H & H Enterprises, Inc.).

Newsom, C.D. and Rincover, A. 1979. Behavioral assessment of autistic children. In *Behavioral Assessment of Childhood Disorders,* eds. E.J. Mash and L.G. Terdal. (New York: Guilford Press).

Nirje, B. 1980. The normalization principle. In *Normalization, Social Integration, and Community Services,* eds. R.J. Flynn and K.E. Nitsch. (Baltimore: University Park Press).

Noback, C.R. and Demarest, R.J. 1977. *The Nervous System: Introduction and Review* (New York: McGraw-Hill).

Nordquist, V.M. and Wahler, R.G. 1973. Naturalistic treatment of an autistic child. *Journal of Applied Behavior Analysis* 6:79–87.

Norris, M.S. 1978. *Utilization of Peer Tutors with Autistic Children: An Analysis of Training and Academic Outcomes.* Paper presented at the Midwestern Association of Behavior Analysis, Chicago.

Notterman, J.M. and Mintz, D.E. 1962. Exteroceptive cueing of response force. *Science* 135:1070–71.

Nye, F.I. and MacDougall, E. 1959. The dependent variable in marital research. *Pacific Sociological Review* 2:67–70.

Nyhan, W.L. 1968. Lesch-Nyhan syndrome: Summary of clinical features. *Federation Proceedings* 27:1034–41.

Nyhan, W.L. 1976. Behavior in the Lesch-Nyhan syndrome. *Journal of Autism and Childhood Schizophrenia* 6:235–52.

Nyhan, W.L., Oliver, W.J., and Lesch, M. 1965. A familial disorder of uric acid metabolism and central nervous system function: II. *Journal of Pediatrics* 67:257–63.

Nyhan, W.L., Pesek, J., Sweetman, L., Carpenter, D.G., and Carter, C.H. 1967. Genetics of an X-linked disorder of uric acid metabolism and cerebral function. *Pediatric Research* 1:5–13.

O'Brien, F. 1968. Sequential contrast effects with human subjects. *Journal of the Experimental Analysis of Behavior* 11:537–42.

O'Connor, N. and Hermelin, B. 1967. The selective visual attention of psychotic children. *Journal of Child Psychology and Psychiatry.* 8:167-79.

Odom, R.D., Liebert, R.M., and Fernandez, L. 1969. Effects of symbolic modelling on the syntactical productions of retardates. *Psychonomic Science* 17:104–5.

O'Gorman, G. 1967. *The Nature of Childhood Autism* (New York: Appleton-Century-Crofts).

Oldfield, R. 1971. The assessment and analysis of handedness: The Edinburgh inventory. *Neuropsychologia* 9:97–113.

O'Leary, K.D. 1972. Behavior modification in the classroom: A rejoinder to Winett and Winkler. *Journal of Applied Behavior Analysis* 5:505–11.

O'Leary, K.D., Becker, W.C., Evans, M.B., and Saudargas, S.A. 1969. A token reinforcement program in a public school: A replication and systematic analysis. *Journal of Applied Behavior Analysis* 2:3–13.

O'Leary, K.D. and Drabman, R. 1971. Token reinforcement programs in the classroom: A review. *Psychological Bulletin* 75:379–98.

O'Leary, K.D., O'Leary, S., and Becker, W.C. 1967. Modification of a deviant sibling interaction pattern in the home. *Behaviour Research and Therapy* 5:113–20.

Ollendick, T.H., Balla, D., and Zigler, E. 1971. Expectancy of success and the probability learning performance of retarded children. *Journal of Abnormal Psychology* 77:275–81.

Orden, S. and Bradburn, N. 1968. Dimensions of marriage happiness. *American Journal of Sociology* 23:715–31.

Ornitz, E. 1974. The modulation of sensory input and motor output in autistic children. *Journal of Autism and Childhood Schizophrenia* 4:197–215.

Ornitz, E. 1973. Childhood autism: A review of the clinical and experimental literature. *California Medicine* 118:21–47.

Oswald, I. 1964. Physiology of sleep accompanying dreaming. In *The Scientific Basis of Medicine: Annual Reviews,* eds. J.P. Ross. (London: Athlone Press).

Overmier, O.B. and Seligman, M.E.P. 1967. Effects of inescapable shock upon subsequent escape and avoidance learning. *Journal of Comparative and Physiological Psychology* 63:28–33.

Page, T.J., Iwata, B.A., and Neef, N.A. 1976. Teaching pedestrian skills to retarded persons: Generalization from the classroom to the natural environment. *Journal of Applied Behavior Analysis* 9:433–44.

Panyan, M.D. and Hall, R.V. 1978. Effects of serial versus concurrent task sequencing on acquisition, maintenance and generalization. *Journal of Applied Behavior Analysis* 11:67–74.

Parsonson, B.S., Baer, A.M., and Baer, D.M. 1974. The application of generalized correct social contingencies: An evaluation of a training program. *Journal of Applied Behavior Analysis* 7:427–37.

Patterson, G.R. and Anderson, D. 1964. Peers as social reinforcers. *Child Development* 35:951–60.

Peck, C.H., Apolloni, T., Cooke, T.P., and Raver, S.A. 1978. Teaching retarded preschoolers to imitate the free-play behavior of nonretarded classmates: Training and generalized effects. *Journal of Special Education* 12:195–207.

Penfield, W. and Roberts, L. 1966. *Speech and Brain Mechanisms* (New York: Atheneum).

Pennsylvania Association of Retarded Children vs. Commonwealth of Pennsylvania, 343 Supp. 279 (E.D. Pa., 1972) Consent Agreement.

Peterson, R.F. and Peterson, L.R. 1968. The use of positive reinforcement in the control of self-destructive behavior in a retarded boy. *Journal of Experimental Child Psychology* 6:351–60.

Phillips, E.L., Phillips, E.A., Wolf, M.M., and Fixsen, D.L. 1973. Achievement Place: Development of the elected manager system. *Journal of Applied Behavior Analysis* 6:541–61.

Phillips, R.H. and Alkan, M. 1961. Some aspects of self-mutilation in the general population of a large psychiatric hospital. *Psychiatric Quarterly* 35:421–23.

Plummer, S., Baer, D.M., and LeBlanc, J.M. 1977. Functional consideration in the use of procedural time-out and an effective alternative. *Journal of Applied Behavior Analysis* 10:689–705.

Premack, D. 1970. A functional analysis of language. *Journal of the Experimental Analysis of Behavior* 14:107–25.

Premack, D. 1959. Toward empirical behavior laws: I. Positive reinforcement. *Psychological Review* 66:219–33.

Pridal, C. and Carr, E.G. *Teaching Sign Language to Low Functioning Autistic Children.* Unpublished manuscript, State University at Stony Brook.

Prior, M.R. 1977. Conditional matching learning set performance in autistic children. *Journal of Child Psychology and Psychiatry* 18:183–89.

Pronovost, W., Wakstein, M.P., and Wakstein, D.J. 1966. A longitudinal study of the speech behavior and language comprehension of 14 children diagnosed as atypical or autistic. *Exceptional Children* 33:19–26.

Province, R.R. and Enoch, J.M. 1975. On voluntary ocular accommodation. *Perception and Psychophysics* 17:209–12.

Quay, H.C. 1968. The facets of educational exceptionality: A conceptual framework for assessment, grouping, and instruction. *Exceptional Children* 35:25–32.

Rabb, E. and Hewett, F.M. 1967. Development of appropriate classroom behaviors in a severely disturbed group of institutionalized children with a behavior modification model. *American Journal of Orthopsychiatry* 37:313–14.

Ragland, E.U., Kerr, M.M., and Strain, P.S. 1978. Effects of peer social initiation on the behavior of withdrawn autistic children. *Behavior Modification* 2:565–78.

Raver, S.A., Cooke, T.P., and Apolloni, T. 1978. Developing nonretarded toddlers as verbal models for retarded classmates. *Child Study Journal* 8:1–8.

Ray, B.A. and Sidman, M. 1970. Reinforcement schedules and stimulus control. In *The Theory of Reinforcement Schedules,* ed. W.N. Schoenfeld (New York: Appleton-Century-Crofts).

Redd, W.H. 1970. Generalization of adult's stimulus control of children's behavior. *Journal of Experimental Child Psychology* 9:286–96.

Redd, W.H. and Birnbrauer, J.S. 1969. Adults as discriminative stimuli for differential reinforcement contingencies with retarded children. *Journal of Experimental Child Psychology* 17:61–78.

Reisinger, J.J. 1972. The treatment of "anxiety-depression" via positive reinforcement and response cost. *Journal of Applied Behavior Analysis* 5:125–30.

Repp, A.C., Deitz, S.M., and Deitz, D.E.D. 1976. Reducing inappropriate behaviors in classrooms and in individual sessions through DRO schedules of reinforcement. *Mental Retardation* 14:11–15.

Reynolds, B.S., Newsom, C.D., and Lovaas, O.I. 1974. Auditory overselectivity in autistic children. *Journal of Abnormal Child Psychology* 2:253–63.

Reynolds, G.S. 1961a. Behavioral contrast. *Journal of the Experimental Analysis of Behavior* 4:57–71.

Reynolds, G.S. 1961b. An analysis of interaction in a multiple schedule. *Journal of the Experimental Analysis of Behavior* 4:107–77.

Reynolds, G.S. 1961c. Contrast, generalization, and the process of discrimination. *Journal of the Experimental Analysis of Behavior* 4:289–94.

Reynolds, G.S. 1961d. Relativity of response and reinforcement in a multiple schedule. *Journal of the Experimental Analysis of Behavior* 4:179–84.

Reynolds, G.S. and Limpo, A.J. 1968. On some causes of behavioral contrast. *Journal of the Experimental Analysis of Behavior* 11:543–48.

Ridberg, E.H., Parke, R.D., and Hetherington, E.M. 1971. Modification of impulsive and reflective cognitive styles through observation of film-mediated models. *Developmental Psychology* 5:369–77.

Riggs, L.A. 1971. Vision. In *Woodworth and Schlosberg's Experimental Psychology,* 3rd edition, ed. J.W. Kling and L.A. Riggs (New York: Holt, Rinehart and Winston), pp. 273–314.

Rimland, B. 1978. Inside the mind of an autistic savant. *Psychology Today* 12:68–80.

Rimland, B. 1971. The differentiation of childhood psychoses: An analysis of checklists for 2,218 psychotic children. *Journal of Autism and Childhood Schizophrenia* 1:161–174.

Rimland, B. 1964. *Infantile Autism* (New York: Appleton-Century-Crofts).

Rincover, A. 1978. Sensory extinction: A procedure for eliminating self-stimulatory behavior in psychotic children. *Journal of Abnormal Child Psychology* 6:299–310.

Rincover, A. 1978. Variables affecting stimulus fading and discriminative responding in psychotic children. *Journal of Abnormal Psychology* 8:235–46.

Rincover, A. Cook, R., Peoples, A., and Packard, D. 1979. Using sensory extinction and sensory reinforcement principles for programming multiple adaptive behavior change. *Journal of Applied Behavior Analysis* 12:221–33.

Rincover, A. and Devany, J.M. in press. Comparing the motivational properties of edible and sensory reinforcers. *Analysis and Intervention in Developmental Disabilities.*

Rincover, A. and Devany, J.M. in press. Treating self-injury with sensory extinction. *Analysis and Intervention in Developmental Disabilities.*

Rincover, A. and Devany, J.M. 1979. *The Nature and Role of Side Effects in Research on Ethics.* Paper presented at the Association for Behavior Analysis Annual Meeting, Dearborn, Michigan.

Rincover, A. and Devany, J.M. 1978. *Experimental Analysis of Ethical issues: I. Using Self-Stimulation as a Reinforcer in the Treatment of Developmentally Delayed Children.* Paper presented at the 12th Annual Meeting, Association for the Advancement of Behavior Therapy, Chicago.

Rincover, A. and Koegel, R.L. 1977a. Classroom treatment of autistic children: II. Individualized instruction in a group. *Journal of Abnormal Child Psychology* 5:113–26.

Rincover, A. and Koegel, R.L. 1977b. Research on the education of autistic children: Recent advances and future directions. In *Advances in Clinical Child Psychology,* vol. 1, eds, B.B.

Lahey and A.E. Kazdin (New York: Plenum Press).

Rincover, A. and Koegel, R.L. 1975. Setting generality and stimulus control in autistic children. *Journal of Applied Behavior Analysis* 8:235–46.

Rincover, A., Koegel, R.L., and Russo, D.C. 1978. Some recent behavioral research on the education of autistic children. *Education and Treatment of Children* 1:31–45.

Rincover, A., Newson, C.D. and Carr, E.G. 1979. Using sensory extinction procedures in the treatment of compulsivelike behavior of developmentally disabled children. *Journal of Consulting and Clinical Psychology* 47:695–701.

Rincover, A., Newson, C.D., Lovaas, O.I., and Koegel, R.L. 1977. Some motivational properties of sensory stimulation in psychotic children. *Journal of Experimental Child Psychology* 24:312–23.

Risley, T.R. 1968. The effects and side effects of punishing the autistic behaviors of a deviant child. *Journal of Applied Behavior Analysis* 1:21–35.

Risley, T.R. and Hart, B. 1968. Developing correspondence between the non-verbal and behavior of preschool children. *Journal of Applied Behavior Analysis* 1:267–81.

Risley, T.R. and Wolf, M.M. 1967. Establishing functional speech in echolalic children. *Behaviour Research and Therapy* 5:73–88.

Ritvo, E.R. and Freeman, B.J. 1978. National Society for Autistic Children definition of the syndrome of autism. *Journal of Autism and Childhood Schizophrenia* 8:162–67.

Rodda, M. 1977. Language and language-disordered children. *Bulletin of the British Psychological Society* 30:139–42.

Romanczyk, R.G. and Goren, E.R. 1975. Severe self-injurious behavior: The problem of clinical control. *Journal of Consulting and Clinical Psychology* 43:730–39.

Romanczyk, R. and Kistner, J. in press. Self-stimulatory and self-injurious behavior: Etiology and treatment. In *Advances in Child Behavior Analysis and Therapy,* eds. P. Karoly and J. Steffen.

Rosenbaum, M.S. and Breiling, J. 1976. The development and functional control of reading-comprehension behavior. *Journal of Applied Behavior Analysis* 9:323–34.

Rosenberger, P.B. 1970. Response-adjusting stimulus intensity. In *Animal Psychophysics,* ed. W.C. Stebbins (New York: Plenum Press), pp. 161–84.

Rosenkrans, M.A. 1967. Imitation in children as a function of perceived similarity to a social model and vicarious reinforcement. *Journal of Personality and Social Psychology* 7:307–15.

Rosenzweig, M.R. 1976. Effects of environment on brain and behavior in animals. In *Psychopathology and Child Development: Research and Treatment,* eds. E. Schopler and R. Reichler (New York: Plenum Press).

Ross, A.O. 1976. *Psychological Aspects of Learning Disabilities and Reading Disorders* (New York: McGraw-Hill)

Ross, R.R., Meichenbaum, D.H., and Humphrey, C. 1971. Treatment of nocturnal head banging by behavior modification techniques: A case report. *Behaviour Research and Therapy* 9:151–54.

Russo, D.C. and Koegel, R.L. 1977. A method for integrating an autistic child into a normal public school classroom. *Journal of Applied Behavior Analysis* 10:579–90.

Rutter, M. 1978. Diagnosis and definition of childhood autism. *Journal of Autism and Childhood Schizophrenia* 8:139–161.

Rutter, M. 1970. Autism: Educational issues. *Special Education* 59:6–10.

Rutter, M. 1968a. Concepts of autism: A review of research. *Journal of Child Psychology and Psychiatry* 9:1–25.

Rutter, M. 1966a. Behavioral and cognitive characteristics of a series of psychotic children. In *Early Childhood Autism,* ed. J.D. Wing (London: Pergamon Press, Inc.).

Rutter, M. 1966b. Prognosis: Psychotic children in adolescence and early adult life. In *Early Childhood Autism,* ed. J.D. Wing (London: Pergamon Press, Inc.).

Rutter, M., Greenfield, D., and Lockyer, L. 1967. A 5 to 15-year follow-up study of infantile psychosis. II. Social and behavioral outcome. *British Journal of Psychology* 113:1183–99.

Sailor, W. and Horner, R.D. 1976. Educational and assessment strategies for the severely handicapped. In *Teaching the Severely Handicapped,* vol. 1, eds. G. Haring and J. Brown (New York: Grune and Stratton).

Sailor, W. and Taman, T. 1972. Stimulus factors in the training of prepositional usage in three autistic children. *Journal of Applied Behavior Analysis* 5:183–92.

Sailor, W., Wilcox, B., and Brown, L. 1980. *Methods of Instruction for Severely Handicapped Students* (Baltimore: Paul H. Brookes).

Sajway, T., Libbet, J., and Agras, S. 1974. Lemon juice therapy: The control of life-threatening rumination in a 6-month-old infant. *Journal of Applied Behavior Analysis* 7:557–63.

Sajwaj, T., Twardosz, S., and Burke, M. 1972. Side effects of extinction procedures in a remedial preschool. *Journal of Applied Behavior Analysis* 5:163–76.

Salvin, A., Routh, D.K., Foster, R.E., and Lovejoy, K.M. 1977. Acquisition of modified American sign language by a mute autistic child. *Journal of Autism and Childhood Schizophrenia* 7:359–71.

Saposnek, D.T. and Watson, L.S. 1974. The elimination of the self-destructive behavior of a psychotic child: A case study. *Behavior Therapy* 5:79–89.

Schaefer, H.H. 1970. Self-injurious behavior: Shaping head banging in monkeys. *Journal of Applied Behavior Analysis* 3:111–16.

Schaeffer, B., Kollinzas, G., Musil, A., and McDowell, P. 1977. Spontaneous verbal language for autistic children through signed speech. *Sign Language Studies* 17:287–328.

Schell, R.E., Stark, J., and Giddan, J.J. 1969. Development of language behavior in an autistic child. *Journal of Speech and Hearing Disorders* 34:3–19.

Schopler, E. and Reichler, R.J. 1971. Parents as co-therapists in the treatment of psychotic children. *Journal of Autism and Childhood Schizophrenia* 1:87–102.

Schover, L.R. and Newsom, C.D. 1976. Overselectivity, developmental level, and overtraining in autistic and normal children. *Journal of Abnormal Child Psychology* 4:289–98.

Schreibman, L. 1975. Effects of within-stimulus and extra-stimulus prompting on discrimination learning in autistic children. *Journal of Applied Behavior Analysis* 8:91–112.

Schreibman, L., Charlop, M.H., and Koegel, R.L. in press. Teaching autistic children to use extra-stimulus prompts. *Journal of Experimental Child Psychology.*

Schreibman, L. and Koegel, R.L. in press. Multiple-cue responding in autistic children. In *Advances in Child Behavior Analysis and Therapy,* eds. P. Karoly and J.J. Steffen (New York: John Wiley and Sons).

Schreibman, L. and Koegel, R.L. 1981. A guideline for planning behavior modification programs for autistic children. In *Handbook of Clinical Behavior Therapy,* eds. S.M. Turner, K.S. Calhoun and H.E. Adams (New York: John Wiley and Sons).

Schreibman, L. and Koegel, R.L. 1975. Autism: A defeatable horror. *Psychology Today* 8:61–7.

Schreibman, L., Koegel, R.L., Charlop, M., and Egel, A.L. in press. Autism. In *International Handbook of Behavior Modification and Therapy,* ed. A. Bellack (New York: Plenum Press).

Schreibman, L., Koegel, R.L., and Craig, M.S. 1977. Reducing stimulus overselectivity in autistic children. *Journal of Abnormal Child Psychology* 5:425–36.

Schreibman, L., Koegel, R.L., Mills, J.I., and Burke, J.C. in press. Social validation of behavior therapy with autistic children. *Behavior Therapy.*

Schreibman, L. and Lovaas, O.I. 1973. Overselectivity responding to social stimuli by autistic children. *Journal of Abnormal Child Psychology* 1:152–68.

Schreibman, L. and Mills, J.I. in press. Infantile autism. In *Handbook of Child*

Psychopathology, eds. T.H. Ollendick and M. Hersen (New York: Plenum Press).

Schroeder, G.L. and Baer, D.M. 1972. Effects of concurrent and serial learning on generalized vocal imitation in retarded children. *Developmental Psychology* 6:293–301.

Schusterman, R.J. 1967. Attention shift and errorless reversal learning by the California sea lion. *Science* 156:833–35.

Scott, W.E. 1975. The effects of extrinsic rewards on "Intrinsic Motivation": A critique. *Organizational Behavior and Human Performance* 15:117–29.

Searleman, A. 1977. A review of right hemisphere linguistic capabilities. *Psychological Bulletin* 84:503–28.

Seegmiller, J.E. 1976. Inherited deficiency of hypoxanthineguanine phosphoribosyltransferase in X-linked uric aciduria (the Lesch-Nyhan syndrome and its variants). In *Advances in Human Genetics,* vol. 6, eds. H. Harris and K. Hirschhorn (New York: Plenum Press).

Seegmiller, J.E. 1972. Lesch-Nyhan syndrome and the X-linked uric acidurias. *Hospital Practice* 7:79–90.

Seegmiller, J.E. 1969. Diseases of purine and pyrimidine metabolism. In *Duncan's Diseases of Metabolism,* 6th ed., ed. P.K. Bondy (Philadelphia: Saunders).

Seegmiller, J.E., Rosenbloom, F.M., and Kelley, W.N. 1967. Enzyme defect associated with a sex-linked human neurological disorder and excessive purine synthesis. *Science* 155:1682–84.

Seligman, M.E.P., Klein, D.C., and Miller, W.R. 1976. Depression. In *Handbook of Behavior Modification,* ed. H. Leitenberg (New York: Appleton-Century-Crofts).

Seligman, M.E.P. and Maier, S.F. 1967. Failure to escape traumatic shock. *Journal of Experimental Psychology* 74:1–9.

Shear, C.S., Nyhan, W.L., Kirman, B.H., and Stern, J. 1971. Self-mutilative behavior as a feature of the deLange syndrome. *Journal of Pediatrics* 78:506–09.

Shilton, P. and Fuqua, W. 1979. Access to self-stimulatory objects as a reinforcer for "academic" behaviors. Unpublished manuscript.

Shintoub, S.A. and Soulairac, A. 1961. L'enfant automutilateur. *Psychiatrie de l'Enfant* 3:111–45.

Sidman, M. and Stoddard, L.T. 1967. The effectiveness of fading in programming a simultaneous form discrimination for retarded children. *Journal of the Experimental Analysis of Behavior* 10:3–15.

Sidman, M. and Stoddard, L.T. 1966. Programming perception and learning for retarded children. In *International Review of Research in Mental Retardation,* vol. II, ed. N.R. Ellis. (New York: Academic Press, Inc.).

Siegel, L.J. and Steinman, M.W. 1975. The modification of a peer-observer's classroom behavior as a function of his serving as a reinforcing agent. In *Behavior Analysis: Areas of Research and Application,* eds. E. Ramp and G. Semb (Englewood Cliffs: Prentice-Hall, Inc.).

Silberstein, R.M., Blackman, S., and Mandell, W. 1966. Autoerotic head banging. *Journal of the American Academy of Child Psychiatry* 5:235–42.

Siperstein, G.N. and Gottlieb, J. 1977. Physical stigma and academic performance as factors affecting children's first impressions of handicapped peers. *American Journal of Mental Deficiency* 81:455–62.

Siqueland, E. and Delucia, C.A. 1969. Visual reinforcement of non-nutritive sucking in human infants. *Science* 165:1144–46.

Skinner, B.F. 1938. *The Behavior of Organisms* (New York: Appleton-Century-Crofts).

Skinner, B.F. and Ferster, C.B. 1957. *Schedules of Reinforcement* (New York: Appleton-Century-Crofts).

Sloane, H.N., Jr., Johnston, M.K., and Harris, F.R. 1968. Remedial procedures for teaching verbal behavior to speech deficient or defective young children. In *Operant Procedures in Remedial Speech and Language Training,* eds. H.N. Sloane and B.A. MacAulay (Boston: Houghton Mifflin).

Smeets, P.M. 1978. Establishing generative performance and cross modal generalization of the manual plural sign in a severely retarded deaf girl. *British Journal of Disorders of Communication* 13:49–57.

Smith, C.H. 1975. Total communication using the simultaneous method. In *Appropriate Behavior through Communication,* ed. M.P. Creedon (Chicago: Michael Reese Medical Center, Dysfunctioning Child Center Publication), pp. 45–74.

Smith, N.V. 1973. *The Acquisition of Phonology: A Case Study* (London: Cambridge University Press).

Smolev, S.R. 1971. Use of operant techniques for the modification of self-injurious behavior. *American Journal of Mental Deficiency* 76:295–305.

Snyder, L., Apolloni, T., and Cooke, T.P. 1977. Integrated settings at the early childhood level: The role of nonretarded peers. *Exceptional Children* 43:262–66.

Solnick, J.V., Rincover, A., and Peterson, C. 1977. Some determinants of the reinforcing and punishing effects of time-out. *Journal of Applied Behavior Analysis* 10:415–24.

Solomon, R.W. and Wahler, R.G. 1973. Peer reinforcement control of classroom problem behavior. *Journal of Applied Behavior Analysis* 6:49–56.

Sontag, E., Burke, P.J., and York, R. 1973. Considerations for serving the severely handicapped in the public schools. *Education and Training of the Mentally Retarded* 8:20–6.

Sontag, E., Certo, N., Button, J. 1979. On a distinction between the education of the severely and profoundly handicapped and a doctrine of limitation. *Exceptional Children* 45:604–16.

Sontag, E., Smith, J., and Certo, N. eds. 1977. *Educational Programming for the Severely and Profoundly Handicapped* (Reston: Council for Exceptional Children).

Spanier, G.B. 1976. Measuring dyadic adjustment: New scales for assessing the quality of marriage and similar dyads. *Journal on Marriage and Family* 38:15–30.

Stebbins, W.C., ed. 1970. *Animal Psychophysics* (New York: Plenum Press).

Stevens-Long, J. and Rasmussen, M. 1974. The acquisition of simple and compound sentence structure in an autistic child. *Journal of Applied Behavior Analysis* 7:473–79.

Stevenson, H.W. and Odom, R.O. 1964. Visual reinforcement with children. *Journal of Experimental Child Psychology* 1:248–55.

Stokes, T.F. and Baer, D.M. 1977. An implicit technology of generalization. *Journal of Applied Behavior Analysis* 10:349–68.

Stokes, T.F. and Baer, D.M. 1976. Preschool peers as mutual generalization-facilitating agents. *Behavior Therapy* 7:549–56.

Stokes, T.F., Baer, D.M., and Jackson, R.L. 1974. Programming the generalization of greeting responses in four retarded children. *Journal of Applied Behavior Analysis* 7:599–610.

Stokes, T.F., Doud, C.C., Rowbury, T.G., and Baer, D.M. 1978. Peer facilitation of generalization in a preschool setting. *Journal of Abnormal Child Psychology* 6:203–9.

Storm, R.H. and Robinson, P.W. 1973. Application of a graded choice procedure to obtain errorless learning in children. *Journal of Applied Behavior Analysis* 20:405–10.

Strain, P.S., Kerr, M.M., and Ragland, E.U. 1979. Effects of peer mediated social initiation and promoting/reinforcement procedures on the social behavior of autistic children. *Journal of Autism and Developmental Disorders* 9:41–54.

Student, M. and Sohmer, H. 1978. Evidence from auditory nerve and brainstem evoked responses for an organic brain lesion in children with autistic traits. *Journal of Autism and Childhood Schizophrenia* 8:13–20.

Sulzer, B., and Mayer, G.R. 1972. *Behavior modification procedures for school personnel.* Hinsdale: The Dryden Press.

Sutherland, N.S. and MacKintosh, N.J. 1971. *Mechanisms of animal discrimination learning* (New York: Academic Press).

Taber, J.I. and Glaser, R. 1962. An exploratory evaluation of a discriminative transfer program using literal prompts. *Journal of Educational Research* 55:508– 12.

Talkington, L.W., Hall, S.M., and Altman, R. 1973. Use of a peer modelling procedure with severely retarded subjects on a basic communication response skill. *Training School Bulletin* 69:145– 49.

Tanguay, P. 1976. Clinical and electrophysiological research. In *Autism: Diagnosis, Current Research and Management,* ed. E. Ritvo (New York: Spectrum Publications).

Tanner, B. and Zeiler, M. 1975. Punishment of self-injurious behavior using aromatic ammonia as the aversive stimuli. *Journal of Applied Behavior Analysis* 8:53– 7.

Tate, B.G. 1972. Case study: Control of chronic self-injurious behavior by conditioning procedures. *Behavior Therapy* 3:72– 83.

Tate, B.G. and Baroff, G.S. 1966. Aversive control of self-injurious behavior in a psychotic boy. *Behaviour Research and Therapy* 4:281– 87.

Teitelbaum, P. 1966. The use of operant methods in the assessment and control of motivational states. In *Operant Behavior: Areas of Research and Application,* ed. W.K. Honig (Englewood Cliffs: Prentice-Hall).

Terrace, H.S. 1963. Errorless transfer of a discrimination across two continua. *Journal of the Experimental Analysis of Behavior* 6:223– 46.

Topper, S. 1975. Gesture language for a nonverbal severely retarded male. *Mental Retardation* 13:30– 1.

Touchette, P.E. 1971. Transfer of stimulus control: Measuring the moment of transfer. *Journal of the Experimental Analysis of Behavior* 15:347– 54.

Touchette, P.E. 1969. Tilted lines as complex stimuli. *Journal of the Experimental Analysis of Behavior* 12:211– 14.

Touchette, P.E. 1968. The effects of graduated stimulus change on the acquisition of a simple discrimination in severely retarded children. *Journal of the Experimental Analysis of Behavior* 11:39– 48.

Twardosz, S. and Baer, D.M. 1973. Training two severely retarded adolescents to ask questions. *Journal of Applied Behavior Analysis* 6:655– 61.

United States Education Department/ Office of Special Education 1980. *Second Annual Report to Congress on the Implementation of Public Law 94 – 142: The Education for All Handicapped Children Act* (draft). Washington, D.C.

United States Office of Education/Bureau of Education for the Handicapped 1980. *Response by the Board of Education for the Handicapped to the Task Force on Deinstitutionalization of the Mentally Disabled* (draft). Washington, D.C.

United States Office of Education/Bureau of Education for the Handicapped 1979. *First Annual Report to Congress on the Implementation of Public Law 94 – 142: The Education for All Handicapped Children Act.* Washington, D.C.

Van den Pol, R.A., Iwata, B.A., Ivancic, M.T., Page, T.J., Neef, N.A., and Whitely, F.P. in press. Teaching the handicapped to eat in public places: Acquisition, generalization, and maintenance of restauranting skills. *Journal of Applied Behavior Analysis*

Varni, J.W., Lovaas, O.I., Koegel, R.L., and Everett, N.L. 1979. An analysis of observational learning in autistic and normal children. *Journal of Abnormal Child Psychology* 7:31– 43.

Wahler, R.G. 1969. Setting generality: Some specific and general effects of child behavior therapy. *Journal of Applied Behavior Analysis* 2:239– 46.

Wahler, R.G., Sperling, F.A., Thomas, M.R., Teeter, N.C., and Loper, H.L. 1970. The modification of childhood stuttering. Some response-response relationships. *Journal of Experimental Child Psychology* 9:411– 28.

Waite, W.W. and Osborne, J.G. 1972. Sustained behavioral contrast in children. *Journal of the Experimental Analysis of Behavior* 18:113– 17.

Walker, H.M. and Buckley, N.K. 1972. Programming generalization and maintenance of treatment effects across time and across settings. *Journal of Applied Behavior Analysis* 5:209–24.

Walker, H.M., Hops, H., and Johnson, S.M. 1975. Generalization and maintenance of classroom treatment effects. *Behavior Therapy* 6:128–200.

Watson, L.S. 1973. *Child Behavior Modification: A Manual for Teachers, Nurses, and Parents* (New York: Pergamon Press, Inc.).

Webster, C.D., McPherson, H., Sloman, L., Evans, M.A., and Kuchar, E. 1973. Communicating with an autistic boy by gestures. *Journal of Autism and Childhood Schizophrenia* 3:337–46.

Weiher, R.G. and Harman, R.E. 1975. The use of omission training to reduce self-injurious behavior in a retarded child. *Behavior Therapy* 6:261–68.

Welker, W.I. 1956. Some determinants of play and exploration in chimpanzees. *Journal of Comparative and Physiological Psychology* 49:181–85.

Wetherby, A., and Gaines, B. in press. Cognition and language development in autism. *Journal of Speech and Hearing Disorders.*

Wetherby, A., Koegel, R.L., and Mendel, M. in press. Central auditory nervous system dysfunction in echolalic autistic individuals. *Journal of Speech and Hearing Research*

Weymouth, F.W. 1963. Visual acuity of children. In *Vision of Children,* eds. M.J. Hirsch and R.E. Wick (Philadelphia: Chilton), pp. 119–43.

White, E. 1977. Children's performance on the SSW test and Willeford battery: Interim clinical data. In *Central Auditory Dysfunction,* ed. R. Keith (New York: Grune and Stratton).

White, O.R. 1980. Adaptive performance objectives: Form vs. function. In *Methods of Instruction for Severely Handicapped Students,* eds. W. Sailor, B. Wilcox, and L. Brown (Baltimore: Brookes Publishers).

White, S.M. 1966. Age differences in reaction to stimulus variation. In *Experience, Structure and Adaptability,* ed. O.J. Harvey (New York: Springer Publishing Co.).

White, S.M. 1965. Discrimination learning with ever-changing positive and negative cues. *Journal of Experimental Child Psychology* 2:154–62.

Whitman, T., Mercurio, J., and Caponigri, V. 1970. Development of social responses in two severely retarded children. *Journal of Applied Behavior Analysis* 3:133–38.

Wilhelm, H. and Lovaas, O.I. 1976. Stimulus overselectivity: A common feature in autism and mental retardation. *American Journal of Mental Deficiency* 81:227–41.

Willeford, J. and Billger, J. 1978. Auditory perception in children with learning disabilities. In *Handbook of Clinical Audiology,* ed. J. Katz (Baltimore: Williams and Wilkins).

Williams, J.A., Koegel, R.L., and Egel, A.L. 1981. Response-reinforcer relationships and improved learning in autistic children. *Journal of Applied Behavior Analysis* 14:53–60.

Wilson, M.M. 1974. Novelty as a reinforcer for position learning in children. *Journal of Experimental Child Psychology* 18:51–61.

Wilson, P.S. 1974. *Sign Language as a Means of Communication for the Mentally Retarded.* Paper presented at the annual meeting of the Eastern Psychological Association, Philadelphia.

Wing, L. 1972. *Autistic Children: A Guide for Parents and Professionals* (New York: Brunner/Mazel).

Wolf, M.M. 1978. Social validity: The case for subjective measurement, or how applied behavior analysis is finding its heart. *Journal of Applied Behavior Analysis* 11:203–14.

Wolf, M.M., Risley, T., Johnston, M., Harris, F., and Allen, E. 1967. Application of operant conditioning procedures to the behavior problems of an autistic child: A follow-up and extension. *Behaviour Research and Therapy* 5:103–11.

Wolf, M.M., Risley, T., and Mees, H. 1964. Application of operant conditioning procedures to the behavior problems of an autistic child. *Behaviour Research and Therapy* 1:305–12.

Wolfensberger, W.A. 1980. A brief overview of the principle of normalization. In *Normalization, Social Integration and Community Services,* eds. R.J. Flynn and K.E. Nitsch (Baltimore: University Park Press).

Yates, A.J. 1970. *Behavior Therapy* (New York: John Wiley and Sons).

Young, S. 1969. Visual attention in autistic and normal children: Effects of stimulus novelty, human attributes, and complexity. Unpublished doctoral dissertation, University of California, Los Angeles.

Yost, W.A. and Nielsen, D.W. 1977. *Fundamentals of Hearing: An Introduction* (New York: Holt, Rinehart and Winston).

Zeaman, D., and House, B.J. 1963. The role of attention in retardate discrimination learning. In *Handbook of Mental Deficiency,* ed. N.R. Ellis (New York: McGraw-Hill).

Zeaman, D., House, B.J., and Orlando, R. 1968. Use of special training conditions in visual discrimination learning with imbeciles. *American Journal of Mental Deficiency* 63:453–59.

Zemlin, W.R. 1968. *Speech and Hearing Science: Anatomy and Physiology* (Englewood Cliffs: Prentice-Hall).

Zigler, E. 1966. Motivational determinants in the performance of retarded children. *American Journal of Orthopsychiatry* 36:848–56.

Zigler, E. and Butterfield, E.C. 1968. Motivational aspects of changes in IQ test performance of culturally-deprived nursery school children. *Child Development* 39:1–14.

Zubek, J.P. 1969. *Sensory Deprivation: Fifteen Years of Research* (New York: Appleton-Century-Crofts).

Subject Index

330

Author Index